CW00971957

Charles Cavendish
Fulke Greville

The Greville Memoirs
A Journal of the Reigns of
King George IV
and
King William IV

Volume 1

Elibron Classics
www.elibron.com

Elibron Classics series.

© 2006 Adamant Media Corporation.

ISBN 1-4021-7612-0 (paperback)
ISBN 1-4212-8586-X (hardcover)

This Elibron Classics Replica Edition is an unabridged facsimile
of the edition published in 1875 by Longmans, Green, and Co.,
London.

THE

GREVILLE MEMOIRS

VOLUME I.

LONDON : PRINTED BY
SPOTTISWOODE AND CO., NEW-STREET SQUARE
AND PARLIAMENT STREET

THE GREVILLE MEMOIRS

A JOURNAL OF THE REIGNS

OF

KING GEORGE IV.

AND

KING WILLIAM IV.

BY THE LATE

CHARLES C. F. GREVILLE, Esq.

CLERK OF THE COUNCIL TO THOSE SOVEREIGNS

EDITED BY

HENRY REEVE

REGISTRAR OF THE PRIVY COUNCIL

IN THREE VOLUMES

VOL. I.

FIFTH EDITION

LONDON

LONGMANS, GREEN, AND CO.

1875

'IT IS OF THE ESSENCE OF THESE MEMOIRS NOT TO SOFTEN OR TONE DOWN JUDGMENTS BY THE LIGHT OF ALTERED CONVICTIONS, BUT TO LEAVE THEM STANDING AS CONTEMPORARY EVIDENCE OF WHAT WAS THOUGHT AT THE TIME THEY WERE WRITTEN.'

Note by the Author

PREFACE

BY THE EDITOR.

THE AUTHOR of these Journals requested me, in January 1865, a few days before his death, to take charge of them with a view to publication at some future time. He left that time to my discretion, merely remarking · that Memoirs of this kind ought not, in his opinion, to be locked up until they had lost their principal interest by the death of all those who had taken any part in the events they describe. He placed several of the earlier volumes at once in my hands, and he intimated to his surviving brother and executor, Mr. Henry Greville, his desire that the remainder should be given me for this purpose. The injunction was at once complied with after Mr. Charles Greville's death, and this interesting deposit has now remained for nearly ten years in my possession. In my opinion this period of time is long enough to remove every reasonable objection to the publication of a contemporary record of events already separated from us by a much longer interval, for the transactions related in these volumes commence in 1818 and end in 1837. I therefore commit to the press that portion of these Memoirs which embraces the Reigns of King George IV. and King William IV., ending with the Accession of her present Majesty.

In accepting the trust and deposit which Mr. Greville thought fit to place in my hands, I felt, and still feel, that I undertook a task and a duty of considerable responsibility; but from the time and the manner in which it was offered me I could not decline it. I had lived for more than five-and-twenty years in the daily intercourse of official life and private friendship with Mr. Greville. Sir George Cornewall Lewis, to whom he had previously intended to leave these Journals, died before him. After that event, deeply to be regretted on so many accounts, Mr. Greville did me the honour to select me for the performance of this duty, which was unexpected by myself; and my strong attachment and gratitude to him for numberless acts of kindness and marks of confidence bound me by every consideration to obey and execute the wishes of my late friend.

In the discharge of this trust I have been guided by no other motive than the desire to present these Memorials to the world in a manner which their Author would not have disapproved, and in strict conformity with his own wishes and injunctions. He himself, it should be said, had frequently revised them with great care. He had studiously omitted and erased passages relating to private persons or affairs, which could only serve to gratify the love of idle gossip and scandal. The Journals contain absolutely nothing relating to his own family, and but little relating to his private life. In a passage (not now

published) of his own writings, the Author remarks :—
' A journal to be good, true, and interesting, should be
' written without the slightest reference to publication,
' but without any fear of it : it should be the transcript
' of a mind that can bear transcribing. I always contem-
' plate the possibility that hereafter my journal will be
' read, and I regard with alarm and dislike the notion of
' its containing matters about myself which nobody will
' care to know ' (*January 2nd*, 1838).

These notes were designed chiefly to preserve a record
of the less known causes and details of public events which
came under the Author's observation, and they are inter-
spersed with the conversations of many of the eminent men
with whom he associated. But it must be borne in mind
that they are essentially what they profess to be—a *contemporary* record of facts and opinions, not altered or made
up to square with subsequent experience. Hence some
facts may be inaccurately stated, because they are given in
the shape they assumed at the time they were recorded,
and some opinions and judgments on men and things are
at variance (as he himself acknowledges and points out)
with those at which the writer afterwards arrived on the
same persons and subjects. Our impressions of what is
passing around us vary so rapidly and so continually, that
a contemporary record of opinion, honestly preserved,
differs very widely from the final and mature judgment of
history : yet the judgment of history must be based upon
contemporary evidence. It was remarked by an acute
observer to Mr. Greville himself, that the *nuances* in
political society are so delicate and numerous, the

details so nice and varying, that unless caught at the moment they escape, and it is impossible to collect them again. That is the charm and the merit of genuine contemporary records.

The two leading qualities in the mind of Mr. Greville were the love of truth and the love of justice. His natural curiosity, which led him to track out and analyse the causes of events with great eagerness, was stimulated by the desire to arrive at their real origin, and to award to everyone, with judicial impartiality, what appeared to him to be a just share of responsibility. Without the passions or the motives of a party politician, he ardently sympathised with the cause of Liberal progress and Conservative improvement, or, as he himself expresses it, with Conservative principles on a Liberal basis. He was equally opposed to the prejudices of the old Tory aristocracy, amongst whom he had been brought up, and to the impetuous desire of change which achieved in his time so many vast and various triumphs. His own position, partly from the nature of the permanent office he held in the Privy Council, and partly from his personal intimacies with men of very opposite opinions, was a neutral one ; but he used that neutral position with consummate judgment and address to remove obstacles, to allay irritations, to compose differences, and to promote, as far as lay in his power, the public welfare. Contented with his own social position, he was alike free from ambition and from vanity. No man was more entirely disinterested in his judgments on public affairs, for he had long made up his mind that he had nothing to gain or to lose by them, and in the opinions he formed, and on occasion energetically maintained, he cared for nothing but their justice and their truth. I trust that I do not deceive myself in the belief that the impressions of such a man, faithfully rendered at the time, on the events happening around him, will be thought to possess a permanent value and interest. But I am aware that opinions governed by no party standard will appear to a certain extent to be fluctuating and even inconsistent. I have not thought it consistent with my duty as the Editor of these papers to suppress or modify any of the statements or opinions of their Author on public men or public events ; nor do I hold myself in any way responsible for the tenor of them. Some of these judgments of the writer may be thought harsh and severe, and some of them were subsequently mitigated by himself. But those who enter public life submit their conduct and their lives to the judgment of their contemporaries and of posterity, and this is especially true of those who fill the most exalted station in society. Every act, almost every thought, which is brought home to them leaves its mark, and those who come after them cannot complain that this mark is as indelible as their fame. The only omissions I have thought it right to make are a few passages and expressions relating to occurrences in private life, as to which I have sought to publish nothing which could give pain or annoyance to persons still alive, and two or three more anecdotes which appeared to sin against this rule have been obliterated in this edition.

It will be observed that these Journals begin in the
year 1818, when Mr. Greville was barely twenty-four
years of age, and indeed I possess some notes of an earlier
period, which it was not thought desirable to include
in this publication. At that age Mr. Greville had
but a short experience of life, without the opportunities of information which he subsequently enjoyed ; consequently the first two or three chapters of the first
volume are of secondary interest, and the political value of
the work begins with the retirement of Lord Liverpool.
But it is by his own express desire that these chapters are
retained to complete the series, and the particulars relating
to the Duke of York and to the Queen's trial are not
without interest. As the Author advanced in life his
narrative increases in value both in substance and in
style, and the most important portion of it is that which
must at present be reserved for future publication.

Of the Author of these Journals it may suffice to say
that Charles Cavendish Fulke Greville was the eldest of
the three sons of Charles Greville (who was grandson of
the fifth Lord Warwick), by Lady Charlotte Cavendish
Bentinck, eldest daughter of William Henry, third Duke
of Portland, K.G., who filled many great offices of State.
He was born on the 2nd of April, 1794. Much of his
childhood was spent at his grandfather's house at Bulstrode.
He was educated at Eton and at Christ Church, Oxford;
but he left the University early, having been appointed
private secretary to Earl Bathurst before he was twenty.

The influence of the Duke of Portland obtained for
him early in life the sinecure appointment of the Secre-

taryship of Jamaica, the duties of that office being performed by deputy, and likewise the reversion of the Clerkship of the Council. He entered in 1821 upon the duties of Clerk of the Council in Ordinary, which he discharged for nearly forty years. During the last twenty years of his life Mr. Greville occupied a suite of rooms in the house of Earl Granville in Bruton Street, and there, on the 18th of January, 1865, he expired. I was with him on the previous evening until he retired to rest; from that sleep he never woke.

No additions whatever have been made to the text of these Journals. The passages occasionally interposed in a parenthesis, at a later date, to correct or comment upon a previous statement, are all by the hand of the Author. So likewise are the notes distinguished by no mark. For the notes included in brackets [ ] the Editor is responsible. I am much indebted to the critics, whether friendly or hostile, who have enabled me by their investigations to correct the inaccuracies which had crept into the earlier editions of this work, and I have gladly availed myself of their suggestions to render it more accurate. Some additional notes have also been inserted containing information which has been recently obtained. I may therefore venture to hope that this edition (the fourth) is more correct than those which have preceded it, and more worthy of the favour with which these journals have been received by the public.

HENRY REEVE.

CONTENTS

OF

THE FIRST VOLUME.

———◦◦◦———

CHAPTER I.

CHAPTER II.

CHAPTER III.

CHAPTER IV.

CHAPTER V.

CHAPTER VI.

CHAPTER VII.

CHAPTER VIII.

CHAPTER IX.

CHAPTER X.

A JOURNAL

OF THE

REIGN OF KING GEORGE THE FOURTH.

CHAPTER I.

Queen Charlotte—Duchesses of Cumberland and Cambridge—Westminster Election—Contest between Sir Francis Burdett and Sir Murray Maxwell —London Election—Oatlands—The Duke of York—Duchess of York— Ampthill—Tixall—Mr. Luttrell—Lady Granville—Teddesley—Macao— Burleigh—Middleton—Lady Jersey—The New Parliament—Tierney and Pitt—Princess Lieven—Madame de Staël on the French Revolution— Westminster Election—Hobhouse Defeated—Scarlett's Maiden Speech— Influence of Party—Play—The Persian Ambassador at Court—Prince Leopold—Woburn—Anecdote of the Allies—Death of George III.— Illness of George IV.—Queen Caroline—Fleury de Chabaulon—The Cato Street Conspiracy—George IV. at Ascot—Marchioness of Conyngham —Queen Caroline in London—Message to Parliament—Debates—Insubordination in the Guards—Wilberforce's Motion—Proceedings against the Queen—'Les Liaisons dangereuses'—The Queen's Trial—The Duke of Wellington on the Battle of Waterloo and the Occupation of Paris.

1818.

I BEGAN to keep a Journal some time ago, and, after continuing it irregularly, dropped it entirely. I have since felt tempted to resume it, because, having frequent opportunities of mixing in the society of celebrated men, some particulars about them might be interesting hereafter.

June 7th.—The dissolution of Parliament is deferred on account of the mistakes which have been made in passing the Alien Bill. On Friday night the exultation of the Opposition was very great at what they deemed a victory over the Ministers. It is said that there will be 100 contests, and that Government will lose twenty or thirty members. The Queen was so ill on Friday evening that they expected she would die. She had a severe spasm. [1]

The Duchess of Cambridge [2] has been received in a most flattering manner here, and it is said that the Duchess of Cumberland is severely mortified at the contrast between her reception and that of her sister-in-law. On the Sunday after her arrival the Duke took her to walk in the Park, when she was so terrified by the pressure of the mob about her that she nearly fainted away.

The Regent drives in the Park every day in a tilbury, with his groom sitting by his side; grave men are shocked at this undignified practice.

June 21st.—I dined at Holland House last Thursday. The party consisted of Lord Lansdowne, Mr. Frere, and Mrs. Tierney and her son. After dinner Mr. Frere repeated to us a great deal of that part of ' Whistlecraft ' which is not yet published. [3] I laughed whenever I could, but as I have never read the first part, and did not understand the second, I was not so much amused as the rest of the company.

On Friday I went to the Stud-house, where a great party was assembled to see the stock and buy them. After visiting the paddocks, Bloomfield [4] gave a magnificent dinner to

---

[1] [Queen Charlotte, consort of George III., died on the 17th of November of this year, 1818.]

[2] [Prince Adolphus Frederick, Duke of Cambridge, seventh son of George III., married on the 7th of May, 1818, Augusta Wilhelmina Louisa, Princess of Hesse, youngest daughter of the Landgrave of Hesse-Cassel. Ernest, Duke of Cumberland, the King's fourth son, married on the 29th of August, 1815, at Strelitz, the Princess Frederica, third daughter of the Duke of Mecklenburg-Strelitz. This lady had been twice married before, first to Prince Frederic Louis Charles of Prussia, and secondly to the Prince of Salms-Braunfels. As the Duchess of Cumberland had been divorced from her last husband, the Queen received her with great coldness; and the position in which she was placed contrasted strongly with that of the Duchess of Cambridge on her marriage.]

[3] [The whole poem of ' Whistlecraft ' has since been republished in the collected works of the Right Hon. Hookham Frere.]

[4] [Sir Benjamin Bloomfield filled the offices of Marshal and Chief Equerry to the Regent, and in 1817 he became Receiver-General of the

the company in a tent near the house; it was the finest
feast I ever saw, but the badness of the weather spoilt the
entertainment.

The Queen's illness was occasioned by information which
she received of the Duchesses of Cumberland and Cambridge
having met and embraced. This meeting took place as if
by accident, but really by appointment, in Kew Gardens;
and the Duke of Cambridge himself informed the Queen of
it. She was in such a rage that the spasm was brought on,
and she was very near dying.

June 24*th.*—The elections are carried on with great
violence, and every day we hear of fresh contests being in
agitation. The disgraceful scenes which have taken place
in Westminster excite universal shame and indignation.
The mob seem to have shaken off the feelings and the usual
character of Englishmen, and in the brutal attacks which
they have made on Captain Maxwell have displayed the
savage ferocity which marked the mobs of Paris in the worst
times. He has been so much hurt that his life is now in
danger. Sir F. Burdett told me this morning that as soon
as he was at the head of the poll he thought he should
appear upon the hustings and thank the people for having
raised him thus high. It is supposed that Burdett has laid
out 10,000*l.* on this election, though his friends do not
acknowledge that he has spent anything. It is clear that
the open houses, cockades, and bands of music we have seen
these three days were not procured for nothing.

Lord Castlereagh went to the hustings, and voted for
Sir Murray Maxwell; he was hooted, pelted, and got off
with some difficulty. His Lordship's judgment was not very
conspicuous on this occasion; both Sir Murray's friends and
enemies are of opinion that Lord Castlereagh's vote did him
a great deal of harm and turned many men against him.
The severest contests will be in Wiltshire, Herefordshire,
Devonshire, and Lincolnshire. The elections are going

Duchy of Cornwall and Keeper of the Privy Purse to the Prince. The
Stud-house of Hampton Court had been given him as a residence. He was
raised to the peerage in 1825.]

against Government generally; in London particularly, as the
Ministers lose one seat in the Borough and two in the City.
This last election is the most unexpected of all.   Curtis
has been member for twenty-eight years, and has been used
to come in very high on the poll.   On this occasion the contest between him and Alderman Thorpe was severe, but
Curtis would have carried it had not Wood and Waithman
coalesced with Thorpe the last day, and thrown their spare
votes over to him; this determined the election in his favour.[1]

June 30th.—There was an affray yesterday afternoon in
Covent Garden.   Sir Murray Maxwell's people paraded about
a large boat drawn by six horses.   Burdett's mob attacked and
demolished the boat, and this action having raised their spirits,
the contest continued.   The consequence was that a large
party of Horse Guards were marched into Covent Garden, and
paraded there during the rest of the night.   The people expressed their discontent by cries of 'This is what they call
freedom of election!' 'Burdett for ever!' &c.[2]

August 4th.—I went to Oatlands[3] on Saturday.   There was
a very large party—Mr. and Mrs. Burrell, Lord Alvanley,
Berkeley Craven, Cooke, Arthur Upton, Armstrong, Foley,
Lord Lauderdale, Lake, Page, Lord Yarmouth.   We played
at whist till four in the morning.   On Sunday we amused
ourselves with eating fruit in the garden, and shooting at a
mark with pistols, and playing with the monkeys.   I bathed
in the cold bath in the grotto, which is as clear as crystal and
as cold as ice.   Oatlands is the worst managed establishment
in England; there are a great many servants, and nobody
waits on you; a vast number of horses, and none to ride or
drive.

August 15th.—The parties at Oatlands take place every

[1] [Sir William Curtis was the Ministerial candidate in the City of
London: he was thrown out, and Messrs. Wood, Waithman, Wilson, and
Thorpe were returned.]

[2] [The Westminster election terminated as follows:—Sir Samuel
Romilly, 5,339; Sir Francis Burdett, 5,238; Sir Murray Maxwell, 4,808;
Henry Hunt, 84.]

[3] [Oatlands Park, Weybridge, at that time the residence of the Duke of
York.]

Saturday, and the guests go away on Monday morning. These
parties begin as soon as the Duchess leaves London, and last
till the October meetings. During the Egham races there is
a large party which remains there from the Saturday before
the races till the Monday se'nnight following ; this is called
the Duchess's party, and she invites the guests. The Duke is
only there himself from Saturday to Monday. There are
almost always the same people, sometimes more, sometimes
less. We dine at eight, and sit at table till eleven. In about
a quarter of an hour after we leave the dining-room the Duke
sits down to play at whist, and never stirs from the table as
long as anybody will play with him. When anybody gives
any hint of being tired he will leave off, but if he sees no
signs of weariness in others he will never stop himself. He
is equally well amused whether the play is high or low, but
the stake he prefers is fives and ponies.[1] The Duchess generally plays also at half-crown whist. The Duke always gets
up very early, whatever time he may go to bed. On Sunday
morning he goes to church, returns to a breakfast of tea and
cold meat, and afterwards rides or walks till the evening.
On Monday morning he always sets off to London at nine
o'clock. He sleeps equally well in a bed or in a carriage.
The Duchess seldom goes to bed, or, if she does, only for an
hour or two ; she sleeps dressed upon a couch, sometimes in
one room, sometimes in another. She frequently walks out
very late at night, or rather early in the morning, and she
always sleeps with open windows. She dresses and breakfasts at three o'clock, afterwards walks out with all her dogs,
and seldom appears before dinner-time. At night, when she
cannot sleep, she has women to read to her. The Duchess
of York [2] is clever and well-informed; she likes society and
dislikes all form and ceremony, but in the midst of the most
familiar intercourse she always preserves a certain dignity
of manner. Those who are in the habit of going to Oatlands
are perfectly at their ease with her, and talk with as much

---

[1] [Five-pound points and twenty-five pounds on the rubber.]

[2] [The Duchess of York was born Princess Royal of Prussia; she married
the Duke of York in 1791, and died on the 6th of August, 1820.]

freedom as they would to any other woman, but always with great respect. Her mind is not perhaps the most delicate; she shows no dislike to coarseness of sentiment or language, and I have seen her very much amused with jokes, stories, and allusions which would shock a very nice person. But her own conversation is never polluted with anything the least indelicate or unbecoming. She is very sensible to little attentions, and is annoyed if anybody appears to keep aloof from her or to shun conversing with her. Her dogs are her greatest interest and amusement, and she has at least forty of various kinds. She is delighted when anybody gives her a dog, or a monkey, or a parrot, of all of which she has a vast number; it is impossible to offend her or annoy her more than by ill-using any of her dogs, and if she were to see anybody beat or kick any one of them she would never forgive it. She has always lived on good terms with the Royal Family, but is intimate with none of them, and goes as little as possible to Court. The Regent dislikes her, and she him. With the Princess Charlotte she was latterly very intimate, spent a great deal of time at Claremont, and felt her death very severely. The Duchess has no taste for splendour or magnificence, and likes to live the life of a private individual as much as possible.

The Duke of York is not clever, but he has a justness of understanding, which enables him to avoid the errors into which most of his brothers have fallen, and which have made them so contemptible and unpopular. Although his talents are not rated high, and in public life he has never been honourably distinguished, the Duke of York is loved and respected. He is the only one of the Princes who has the feelings of an English gentleman; his amiable disposition and excellent temper have conciliated for him the esteem and regard of men of all parties, and he has endeared himself to his friends by the warmth and steadiness of his attachments, and from the implicit confidence they all have in his truth, straightforwardness, and sincerity. He delights in the society of men of the world and in a life of gaiety and pleasure. He is very easily amused, and particularly with

jokes full of coarseness and indelicacy; the men with whom
he lives most are *très-polissons,* and *la polissonnerie* is the *ton* of
his society. But his aides-de-camp and friends, while they do
not scruple to say everything before and to him, always treat
him with attention and respect. The Duke and the Duchess
live upon the best terms; their manner to one another is
cordial, and while full of mutual respect and attention, they
follow separately their own occupations and amusements
without interfering with one another. Their friends are
common to both, and those who are most attached to the
Duke are equally so to the Duchess. One of her few foibles is
an extreme tenaciousness of her authority at Oatlands; one
way in which this is shown is in the stable, where, although
there are always eight or ten carriage horses which seldom do
any work, it is impossible ever to procure a horse to ride or
drive, because the Duchess appropriates them all to herself.
The other day one of the aides-de-camp (Cooke) wanted to
drive Burrell (who was there) to Hampton Court; he spoke
of this at breakfast, and the Duke hearing it, desired he
would take the curricle and two Spanish horses which had
been given to him. The Duchess, however, chose to call
these horses hers, and to consider them as her own. The
curricle came to the door, and just as they were going to
mount it a servant came from the Duchess (who had heard
of it) and told the coachman that her Royal Highness knew
nothing of it, had not ordered it, and that the curricle must
go home, which it accordingly did.

September 3rd.—I went to Oatlands for the Egham races.
The party lasted more than a week; there was a great
number of people, and it was very agreeable. Erskine was
extremely mad; he read me some of his verses, and we had
a dispute upon religious subjects one morning, which he
finished by declaring his entire disbelief in the Mosaic
history. We played at whist every night that the Duke was
there, and I always won. The Duchess was unwell most of
the time. We showed her a *galanterie* which pleased her
very much. She produced a picture of herself one evening,
which she said she was going to send to the Duchess of

Orleans; we all cried out, said it was bad, and asked her why she did not let Lawrence paint her picture, and send a miniature copied from that. She declared she could not afford it; we then said, if she would sit, we would pay for the picture, which she consented to do, when all the men present signed a paper, desiring that a picture should be painted and a print taken from it of her Royal Highness. Lawrence is to be invited to Oatlands at Christmas to paint the picture. The men who subscribe are Culling Smith, Alvanley, B. Craven, Worcester, Armstrong, A. Upton, Rogers, Luttrell, and myself, who were present. The Duchess desired that Greenwood and Taylor might be added. From Oatlands I went to Cirencester, where I stayed a week and then returned to Oatlands, expecting to find the Queen dead and the house empty, but I found the party still there.

Ampthill,[1] *September 9th.*—I rode down here to-day, Alvanley and Montrond came in a chaise and four, and were only three hours and three-quarters coming from town. Luttrell and Rogers are here. The dinner very bad, because the cook is out of humour. The evening passed off heavily.

Ampthill, September 11th.—The Duke and Duchess of San Carlos came yesterday with their two daughters, one of whom is fourteen and the other twelve or thirteen years old. The eldest is betrothed to the Count Altimira, a boy of seventeen years old, son of one of the richest Spanish grandees. He has 70,000*l.* a year. The Duke of Medina-Cœli before the French invasion had 215,000*l.* a year.

Lord Holland was talking to Mr. Fox the day after the debate on the war (after the Peace of Amiens) about public speakers, and mentioned Sheridan's speech on the Begums. Fox said, 'You may rest assured that that speech was the finest that ever was made in Parliament.' Lord Holland said, 'It is very well of you to say so, but I think your speech last night was a pretty good one.' Fox said, 'And that was a devilish fine speech too.'

---

[1] [Ampthill Park, at that time the seat of Lord and Lady Holland, who had inherited it from the Earl of Upper Ossory. On the death of Lady Holland Ampthill was purchased by the Duke of Bedford, and has since been inhabited by Lord and Lady Wensleydale.]

Teddesley, November 30th.—I went to Tixall[1] on Tuesday, the 10th of November. There were Luttrell, Nugent, Montagu, Granville Somerset (who went away the next day), and afterwards Granville Vernon, Wilmot, and Mr. Donald. I never remember so agreeable a party—'le bon goût, les ris, l'aimable liberté.' Everybody was pleased because each did what he pleased, and the tone of the society was gay, simple, and clever.

It is hardly possible to live with a more agreeable man than Luttrell. He is difficult to please, but when pleased and in good spirits, full of vivacity. He has a lively imagination, a great deal of instruction, and a very retentive memory, a memory particularly happy for social purposes, for he recollects a thousand anecdotes, fine allusions, odd expressions, or happy remarks, applicable to the generality of topics which fall under discussion. He is extremely sensitive, easily disconcerted, and resents want of tact in others, because he is so liable to suffer from any breach of it. A sceptic in religion, and by no means austere in morals, he views with indulgence all faults except those which are committed against society, but he looks upon a bore with unconcealed aversion. He is attached to a few persons whose talents he respects and whose society he covets, but towards the world in general he is rather misanthropical, and prides himself upon being free from the prejudices which he ridicules and despises more or less in everybody else. Detesting the importance and the superiority which are assumed by those who have only riches or rank to boast of, he delights in London, where such men find their proper level, and where genius and ability always maintain an ascendancy over pomp, vanity, and the adventitious circumstances of birth or position. Born in mystery,[2] he has always shrouded himself in a secresy which none of his acquaintance have ever endeavoured to penetrate. He has

[1] [Tixall, the seat of Sir Clifford Constable in Staffordshire, was let at this time to Lord and Lady Granville.]

[2] [Mr. Luttrell was believed to be a natural son of Lord Carhampton. He had sat in the last Irish Parliament before the Union, and died about 1855 at a very advanced age.]

connections, but they are unknown or only guessed at.   He
has occupations, amusements, and interests unconnected
with the society in which he publicly moves.   Of these he
never speaks, and no one ever ventures to ask him any
questions.   Ostensibly he has no friend.   Standing thus
alone in the world, he derives but little of his happiness from
others; and he seems to delight in the independence of his
feelings as well as of his situation.   He is very witty and
says excellent things, brilliant in general society and pleasant
in *téte-à-téte*.   Many men infinitely less clever *converse* more
agreeably than he does, because he is too epigrammatic, and
has accustomed himself so much to make brilliant observa-
tions that he cannot easily descend to quiet, unlaboured talk.
This only applies to him when in general society; when alone
with another person he talks as agreeably as possible.

Nugent is clever, and in many respects a more amiable
companion than Luttrell, though very inferior to him in
ability.   He is well-informed, gentlemanlike, sensible, with
good manners, good taste, and has a talent for music; he is
always in good humour, and discriminating without being
difficult.

Lady Granville [1] has a great deal of genial humour,
strong feelings, enthusiasm, delicacy, refinement, good taste,
naïveté which just misses being affectation, and a *bonhomie*
which extends to all around her.

Nothing could exceed the agreeableness of the life we led
at Tixall.   We breakfasted about twelve or later, dined at
seven, played at whist and macao the whole evening, and
went to bed at different hours between two and four.   'Nous
faisions la bonne chère, ce qui ajoute beaucoup à l'agrément
de la société.   Je ne dis pas ceci par rapport à mes propres
goûts; mais parce que je l'ai observé, et que les philosophes
n'y sont pas plus indifférents que les bons vivants.'

When the party at Tixall was over we all removed to

---

[1] [Henrietta Elizabeth, daughter of William, fifth Duke of Devon-
shire, married in 1809 to Lord Granville Leveson Gower, created Viscount
Granville in 1815, and Earl Granville in 1833, during his embassy at the
Court of France.]

Teddesley. Littleton[1] is good-natured, liberal, hospitable,
and anxious to oblige, but he wants tact, and his table is
more copious than refined. The house is ugly and in an
ugly situation; the rooms are small, but not ill furnished.
The dinners were not good, and Luttrell and Nugent were
both very angry at the badness of the fare. We had a
brilliant *chasse*. Luttrell left Teddesley on Monday, the
Granvilles on Sunday, and Nugent and I on Tuesday; we
travelled together to Oxford. He is very agreeable, full of
information, and has a great facility in expressing himself.
We parted at Oxford. I went to Redrice and came to town
on Sunday.

Tixall was the most agreeable party I ever was at. We
were all pleased and satisfied; we played at whist, and afterwards at macao. Littleton was the greatest winner and
Lord Granville the loser. I wrote a description of the macao
in verse :—

MACAO.

The solemn chime from out the ancient tower[2]
Invites to Macao at th' accustomed hour.
The welcome summons heard, around the board
Each takes his seat and counts his iv'ry hoard.
'Tis strange to see how in the early rounds
The cautious punters risk their single pounds,
Till, fired with generous rage, they double stake
And offer more than prudent dealers take.
My Lady[3] through her glass with keen delight
Observes the brisk beginnings of the fight;
To some propitious, but to me unkind,
With candour owns the bias of her mind,
And asks of Fortune the severe decree
T' enrich the happy Skew,[4] to ruin me.
The fickle Goddess heard one-half the prayer,
The rest was melted into empty air;
For while she smiled complacent on the Skew,[5]
On me she shed some trifling favours too.

---

[1] [Edward Littleton, Esq., at that time M.P. for the county of Stafford;
raised to the Privy Council in 1833, when he became Chief Secretary for
Ireland, and to the peerage under the title of Baron Hatherton in 1835.]
[2] A clock tower.   [3] Lady Granville.
[4] E. Montagu.   [5] We gave him this nickname.

Sure Granville's luck exceeds all other men's
Led through a sad variety of tens;[1]
The rest have sometimes eights and nines, but he
Is always followed by 'the jolly three;'[2]
But the great Skew some guardian sylph protects,
His judgment governs, and his hand directs
When to refrain, when boldly to put in
And catch with happy nine the wayward pin.[3]

The next morning Luttrell came down with a whole
paper full of epigrams (I had been winning at macao, and
had turned up five nines in my deal) :—

Why should we wonder if in Greville's verses
Each thought so brilliant and each line so terse is?
For surely he in poetry must shine
Who is, we know, so favoured by the nine.[4]

THE JOLLY TENS.

Quoth Greville, ' The commandments are divine;
    But as they're ten, I lay them on the shelf:
O could they change their number and be nine,
    I'd keep them all, and keep them to myself!'

Thus we trifled life away.

1819.

January 17th.—I went to Burleigh on the 23rd of December; there was no one there but Irby. The house disappointed me very much, but it is a very fine showplace. I went away on the 27th to Middleton; there were the Culling Smiths, Worcesters, Sir James Mackintosh, Ossulstons, Nugent, &c.; it was very agreeable, and the house extremely comfortable. Lady Jersey [5] is an extraordinary woman, and has many good qualities; surrounded as she

---

[1] Tens, ruinous at macao.   [2] Tens.
[3] The middle pin, a large gain.
[4] *Nines* are the grand desiderata at macao.
[5] [Sarah Sophia, eldest daughter of John, tenth Earl of Westmoreland, and heiress of Robert Child, Esq. of Osterley Park, her maternal grandfather.]

is by flatterers and admirers, she is neither proud nor con-
ceited. She is full of vivacity, spirit, and good nature, but
the wide range of her sympathies and affections proves that
she has more general benevolence than particular sensibility in her character. She performs all the ordinary duties
of life with great correctness, because her heart is naturally
good ; and she is, perhaps, from her temperament exposed to
fewer temptations than the generality of her sex. She is
deficient in passion and in softness (which constitute the
greatest charm in women), so that she excites more of
admiration than of interest ; in conversation she is lively and
pleasant, without being very remarkable, for she has neither
wit, nor imagination, nor humour; her understanding is
active rather than strong, and her judgment is too often
warped by prejudice to be sound. She has a retentive
memory and a restless mind, together with a sort of intellec-
tual arrangement, with which she appears rather to have
been gifted by nature than to have derived it from the cultivation of her reasoning faculties.

I went from Middleton to Oatlands. The Duke was not
there. We had the Smiths, Worcesters, Alvanley, Stanhope,
Rogers, Luttrell, George Dawson, Lord Lauderdale, &c.
Lord Erskine was ill, and Lord Lauderdale was taking care
of him. The house was very uncomfortable, and the room I
was in small, noisy, and inconvenient.

I came to London on Friday last. Parliament having
met on the Thursday, it is very full, and is filling more and
more every day. The Opposition expect to divide 180 on the
Bank question ; they talk of re-establishing the dinners
which they used to have in Fox's time.

Rogers is in a nervous state about his poem, and trembles
at the reviewers.[1]

January 28*th*.—I went to Gorhambury on the 24th to
shoot. The Duke of York was there. We should have had
a brilliant *chasse*, but it rained. We went out at three and
killed 105 pheasants.

[1] [Rogers' poem entitled ' Human Life ' was on the eve of publication.
The reviewers treated it more tenderly than it deserved, as appears below.]

There has been some skirmishing in the House of Commons, particularly the night before last, on Dr. Halloran's petition, when the Opposition (Bennet *duce*) got completely beaten. Many of the new members have spoken, but Mr. Lawson, a *soi-disant* wit, and Sir R. Wilson have failed lamentably. It is odd enough that Wilson made a reply to an attack which Cobbett had inserted in one of his papers upon him. Cobbett said that he would make a silly speech in Parliament and destroy himself, and it is just what he did. The Opposition were very angry with Sir J. Coffin, who, with the candour of a novice, had made himself informed of the facts of the petition, and finding they were against his friends, said so in the House.

Arbuthnot told me some particulars about Tierney. He began by being a friend of Mr. Pitt, and in one of his speeches on the Southwark or Colchester election he praised him in opposition to Mr. Fox. This latter never liked him, and the Regent assured Arbuthnot he had letters of Tierney in his possession thanking him for having endeavoured to remove Mr. Fox's antipathy to him. When Addington came in, Pitt advised him to get Tierney, as nobody would be so useful to him. He did accordingly, and so Tierney became a member of the Administration.[1] When Pitt came again into office a negotiation was opened with him through the medium of Charles Long. He was offered the Chief Secretaryship in Ireland, which he wished to have, but he made it a condition that he should not be in Parliament. To this Mr. Pitt would not agree, as he said that he must commit himself with them entirely or not join them at all; he refused, not choosing to commit himself, and the negotiations broke off.

January 31st.—I dined with Lady Bathurst yesterday. We talked of the approaching contests in Parliament, and she said that she felt more apprehensive now than ever she had done for the safety of the Government, that it was impos-

---

[1] [Right Hon. George Tierney, Treasurer of the Navy and P.C. in 1803, President of the Board of Control in October, 1806, Member of the Mint in 1827.]

sible for Ministers to stay in if they were defeated, as they
had occasionally been in the last Parliament, and that if they
were defeated she should attribute it all to Vansittart, who
is a millstone about their necks. I asked why they did not
• get rid of him, and she said that it was from good-nature;
they had scruples about telling him he was inefficient and
must resign. She said that Canning's conduct had been
so good towards them, they were very anxious to put him in
some more considerable office.

February 3rd.—I went with Bouverie to Newmarket on
Monday to look at the horses. On Wednesday I came to
town and went on to Oatlands. Madame de Lieven was there.
This woman is excessively clever, and when she chooses brilliantly agreeable. She is beyond all people fastidious. She
is equally conscious of her own superiority and the inferiority
of other people, and the contempt she has for the understand-
ings of the generality of her acquaintance has made her
indifferent to please and incapable of taking any delight in
general society. Her manners are very dignified and graceful, and she is extremely accomplished. She sometimes
endeavours to assume popular and gracious manners, but
she does this languidly and awkwardly, because it is done
with an effort. She carries *ennui* to such a pitch that even
in the society of her most intimate friends she frequently owns
that she is bored to death. She writes memoirs, or rather a
journal, of all that falls under her observation. She is so
clever, has so much imagination and penetration, that they
must be very entertaining. She writes as well as talks with
extraordinary ease and gracefulness, and both her letters and
her conversation are full of point; yet she is not liked, and
has made hardly any friends. Her manners are stately and
reserved, and so little *bonhomie* penetrates through her
dignity that few feel sufficiently attracted to induce them to
try and thaw the ice in which she always seems bound.[1]

[1] [A very imperfect character of Princess Lieven, with whom Mr.
Greville was at this time but slightly acquainted. But in after years he
became one of her most intimate and confidential friends, and she frequently
reappears in the course of these memoirs.]

February 5th.—I have finished Madame de Staël's 'Considérations sur la Révolution Française.' It is the best of her works, extremely eloquent, containing the soundest political opinions conveyed in a bold and eloquent style. It is perhaps too philosophical and not sufficiently relieved by anecdotes and historical illustrations. Her defence of her father is written with much enthusiasm and great plausibility, but the judgment of the world concerning Necker is formed, and it is too late to alter it. The effect of her eloquence is rather weakened by the recollection of her conduct to him, for she lived with him as little as possible, because she could not bear the *ennui* of Coppet.[1]

February 9th.—The Opposition are in a state of the highest exultation on account of the division in the House of Commons last night on Brougham's being added to the Bank Committee. The numbers were 173 to 135. They triumph particularly in this strong minority because the attack upon Brougham in the 'Quarterly Review' was deemed so successful by the Ministerial party that they thought he would not be able to lift up his head again. The review is extremely well done, as all allow. It is supposed to be written by Dr. Ireland [it was by Dr. Monk[2]], and that Canning supplied the jokes, but Arbuthnot assured me he had no hand in it.

February 10th.—Wilberforce made a speech last night which reminded one of the better days of the House of

[1] [In the latter years of Madame de Staël's life Coppet became one of the most brilliant social resorts in Europe, for she attracted there the Schlegels, B. Constant, Bonstetten, Sismondi, Byron, and a host of other celebrities. Towards her father Madame de Staël expressed the most passionate regard.]

[2] [Dr. Monk, not Dr. Ireland, was the author of the article. Monk became Bishop of Gloucester in 1830. This passage relates to the celebrated article on the Report of Mr. Brougham's Committee on the Education of the People which appeared in the 'Quarterly Review' of December 1818. The article was a violent one, but it is amusing to see the effects attributed to it at the time. Some controversy has since taken place as to the share Canning had in it. I have myself seen the letters from Gifford (editor of the 'Review') to Dr. Monk, in which he speaks of the additions which have been made to the article; and there is the strongest internal evidence that these *purpurei panni* were added by Canning. The subject is discussed in the 'Edinburgh Review' for July 1858.]

Commons.   He presented a petition from the Quakers against the Criminal Code, and introduced a compliment to Romilly.   Castlereagh was in a minority in the Committee concerning the equerries of the Windsor establishment; he wished to keep two more than Tierney proposed; the latter had eight to six in the Committee.[1]

February 14*th*.—George Lamb has been proposed in opposition to Hobhouse.[2]   The latter drew this opposition upon himself by his speech, and still more by the reports of his Committee, in which they abused the Whigs in unmeasured terms.   Lambton went to Hobhouse and asked him if he would disavow the abuse of Lord Grey, which his Committee had inserted in the document they printed; he refused, on which the opposition was determined upon and begun.   McDonald proposed Lamb, but they would not hear him; Evans seconded him.   G. Jones made a very good speech in proposing Cartwright.   Burdett and Kinnaird both spoke with moderation in proposing Hobhouse.   It is generally supposed that Lamb will win.

Rogers' poem is disliked; the cry is all against it; some of the lines are pretty, but it is not perspicuous enough, and is deficient in novelty and force.

February 18*th*.—Yesterday Lamb was only seven behind Hobhouse on the poll; everybody thinks he is sure to win, even if Burdett should come forward with money.   The day before there was great uproar and much abuse on the hustings.   Burdett made a shameful speech full of blasphemy and Jacobinism, but he seems to have lost his popularity in a great measure even with the blackguards of Westminster. Hobhouse yesterday was long and dull; he did not speak

---

[1] [In consequence of the death of Queen Charlotte in the preceding month of November, the Government visited the Windsor establishment. The Duke of York was appointed *custos personæ* of the King, and received in that capacity 10,000*l.* a year, which had previously been allowed to the Queen.   A debate took place on this subject on the 25th of February, which is referred to by Mr. Greville under that date.]

[2] [The death of Sir Samuel Romilly in November 1818 caused a vacancy in the representation of Westminster, and another election took place upon the meeting of Parliament.   The numbers were: Hon. George Lamb, 4,465; John Cam Hobhouse, 3,861; Major Cartwright, 38.]

like a clever man, and if the people would have heard Lamb, and he has any dexterity in reply, he must have crushed him—it was so answerable a speech.

I went to the Berrys [1] in the evening, where the blues and the wits were assembled; as Sydney Smith said, 'the conversation raged,' but there was nothing remarkably entertaining.

February 25th.—The debate on the 10,000*l.* to the Duke of York on Monday produced four very good speeches—Peel and the Solicitor-General on one part, and Tierney and Scarlett [2] on the other. This latter spoke for the first time, and in reply to the two former. The Opposition came to Brooks's full of admiration of his speech, which is said to be the best *first speech* that ever was made in the House of Commons. I, who hear all parties and care for none, have been amused with the different accounts of the debate; one man says Peel's speech was the best of the night and the finest that has been made in the House for a length of time; another prefers the Solicitor-General's; then on the other side it is said that Tierney was excellent, Mr. Scarlett beyond all praise. The friends of Government allow great merit to the two latter speakers, but declare that Peel was unanswerable, besides having been beautifully eloquent, and that Scarlett's speech was a fallacy from beginning to end. Again I am told Peel was not good; his was a speech for effect, evidently prepared, showy, but not argumentative; Scarlett triumphantly refuted all his reasoning. Thus it is that a fair judgment is never formed upon any question; the spirit of party influences every man's opinions. It is not extraordinary that each individual of a party connected by general similarity of opinion should adhere to the great body, even in cases where he may not happen to agree with them, and excellent reasons may be adduced for his sacrificing his own

---

[1] [Miss Berry's well-known *salon*, No. 8 Curzon Street, which was for more than a half century the resort of the best company in London.]

[2] [Sir James Scarlett, afterwards Lord Abinger and Lord Chief Baron. It is remarkable that his first speech in the House of Commons was delivered on the Whig side of the House. He afterwards became a decided Tory.]

view for the great object of unanimity; but it is very improbable that on a particular question, unconnected with any general system, where arguments are adduced from opposite sides, and submitted to the enlightened judgment of an assembly, the same arguments which are looked upon as satisfactory and unanswerable by one set of men should be deemed without exception utterly fallacious by another. If any proof were requisite of the mighty influence of party spirit, it would be found in a still stronger light in the State trials in the House of Lords. I have in my mind the trial of Lord Melville; when each Peer had to deliver his judicial opinion upon the evidence adduced in a matter so solemn, and in the discharge of a duty so sacred, it might be imagined that all party feelings would be laid aside, and that a mature judgment and an enlightened conscience would alone have regulated the conduct of every individual. Yet either by an extraordinary accident or by the influence of party spirit we beheld all the Peers on the Ministerial side of the House declaring Lord Melville innocent, and all those of the Opposition pronouncing him guilty.

March 5th.—George Lamb was to have been chaired on the day he was elected, but the mob was outrageous and would not suffer it. They broke into his committee room, and he and McDonald were forced to creep out of a two pair of stairs window into the churchyard. His partisans, who assembled on horseback, were attacked and pelted, and forced to retreat after receiving many hard knocks. In the evening the mob paraded the town, and broke the windows of Lord Castlereagh's and Lord Sefton's houses.

The other night Sir James Mackintosh [1] made a splendid speech on the Criminal Laws; it was temperate and eloquent, and excited universal admiration. The Ministerial party spoke as highly of it as the Opposition themselves. Last night Canning moved the thanks to Lord Hastings, and they say it was the finest speech he ever made, in the best

---

[1] [Sir James Mackintosh's motion for the appointment of a Committee on Capital Punishments was carried against the Government on the 2nd of March by 148 to 128.]

taste, the clearest narrative, and the most beautiful language.

June 12th.—I have been at Oatlands for the Ascot party. On the course I did nothing. Ever since the Derby ill fortune has pursued me, and I cannot win anywhere. Play is a detestable occupation; it absorbs all our thoughts and renders us unfit for everything else in life. It is hurtful to the mind and destroys the better feelings; it incapacitates us for study and application of every sort; it makes us thoughtful and nervous; and our cheerfulness depends upon the uncertain event of our nightly occupation. How anyone can play who is not in want of money I cannot comprehend; surely his mind must be strangely framed who requires the stimulus of gambling to heighten his pleasures. Some indeed may have become attached to gaming from habit, and may not wish to throw off the habit from the difficulty of finding fresh employment for the mind at an advanced period of life. Some may be unfitted by nature or taste for society, and for such gaming may have a powerful attraction. The mind is excited; at the gaming-table all men are equal; no superiority of birth, accomplishments, or ability avail here; great noblemen, merchants, orators, jockeys, statesmen, and idlers are thrown together in levelling confusion; the only pre-eminence is that of success, the only superiority that of temper. But why does a man play who is blessed with fortune, endowed with understanding, and adorned with accomplishments which might ensure his success in any pursuit which taste or fancy might incite him to follow? It is contrary to reason, but we see such instances every day. The passion of play is not artificial; it must have existed in certain minds from the beginning; at least some must have been so constituted that they yield at once to the attraction, and enter with avidity into a pursuit in which other men can never take the least interest.

June 14th.—The other night in the House of Commons on the Foreign Enlistment Bill Sir James Mackintosh made a brilliant speech; all parties agree in commending it. Canning answered him, but not successfully. The Duke of Wellington told me on Friday that there was a good debate in the House of Lords the night before on the Catholic question, but he thought his side had the worst of it; he acknowledged that Lord Grey's speech had done much to shake his opinion, and that he had not conceived that his propositions would have been framed in so unobjectionable a manner.[1]

June 25th.—The Persian Ambassador has had a quarrel with the Court. He wanted to have precedence over all other Ambassadors, and because this was not allowed he was affronted and would not go to Court. This mark of disrespect was resented, and it was signified to him that his presence would be dispensed with at Carlton House, and that the Ministers could no longer receive him at their houses. On Sunday last the Regent went to Lady Salisbury's, where he met the Persian, who, finding he had given offence, had made a sort of apology, and said that illness had prevented him from going to Court. The Regent came up to him and said, 'Well, my good friend, how are you? I hope you are better?' He said, 'Oh, sir, I am very well, but I am very sorry I offended your Royal Highness by not going to Court. Now, sir, my Sovereign he tell me to go first, and your Congress, about which I know nothing, say I must go last; now this very bad for me (pointing to his head) when I go back to Persia.' The Regent said, 'Well, my good friend, never mind it now; it does not signify.' He answered, 'Oh yes, sir; but your Royal Highness still angry with me, and you have not asked me to your party to-morrow night.' The Regent laughed and said, 'I was only going to have a few children to dance, but if you like to come I shall be very happy to see you.' Accordingly he went to Carlton House, and they are very good friends again.

August 11th.—The Vice-Chancellor was going to Italy, but his journey is stopped, as he says, because the Prince

[1] [On the 10th of June Earl Grey submitted to the House of Lords a Bill to relieve Roman Catholics from taking the declaratory oaths against Transubstantiation and the Invocation of Saints, but it was thrown out by 141 to 92.]

Regent has desired him to stay in England in consequence of the approaching return of the Princess of Wales.

August 30th.—I am just returned from Oatlands; we had an immense party, the most numerous ever known there. The Duchess wished it to have been prolonged, but there were no funds. The distress they are in is inconceivable. When the Duchess came down there was no water in the house. She asked the reason, and was informed that the water came by pipes from St. George's Hill, which were stopped up with sand; and as the workmen were never paid, they would not clear them out. She ordered the pipes to be cleared and the bills brought to her, which was done. On Thursday there was a great distress, as the steward had no money to pay the tradespeople, and the Duke was prevailed on with great difficulty to produce a small sum for the purpose. The house is nearly in ruins.

December 24th.—The Duke of Kent gave the name of Alexandrina to his daughter [1] in compliment to the Emperor of Russia. She was to have had the name of Georgiana, but the Duke insisted upon Alexandrina being her first name. The Regent sent for Lieven and made him a great many compliments (*en le persiflant*) on the Emperor's being godfather, but informed him that the name of Georgiana could be second to no other in this country, and therefore she could not bear it at all.

The frost is intense. The town is empty. I returned from Whersted last Wednesday se'nnight, and went to Oatlands on Thursday; there was nearly the same party. Prince Leopold came and dined there on Saturday. He is very dull and heavy in his manner, and seems overcome with the weight of his dignity.. This Prince will not succeed here; everybody is civil to him from the interest he excited at the time of the Princess's death—an interest which has not yet subsided. There seems to be no harm in him, but everybody contrasts his manners with those of the Duke of York, and the comparison is not to his ad-

---

[1] [The Princess, afterwards Queen, Victoria, born 24th of May, 1819.]

vantage. The Duchess likes the society of men of wit and
letters ; more, I think, from the vanity of having them around
her than from any pleasure she takes in their conversation.
Lord Alvanley is the man in whom she takes the greatest
delight.

1820.

London, January 20th.—I went last Sunday se'nnight
to Woburn. The Duke of York, Duke of Wellington,
Lievens, Jerseys, Worcesters, Tavistocks, Mr. Russell, Lady
Sandwich, Alvanley, C. Smith, Huntleys, Frederick Ponsonby,
Lauderdale, and others were there. The house, place,
establishment, and manner of living are magnificent. The
chasse was brilliant ; in five days we killed 835 pheasants,
645 hares, 59 rabbits, 10 partridges, and 5 woodcocks. The
Duchess was very civil and the party very gay. I won at
whist, and liked it very much.

January 22nd.—Just before the advance of the allied
army on Paris a council of war was held, when it was
unanimously resolved to retreat. The Emperor of Russia
entered the room, and said he had reasons for advancing,
and ordered the advance ; the generals remonstrated, but
the Emperor was determined. Woronzoff told Sydenham
that that day a courier arrived at his outposts with a letter
for the Emperor in the handwriting of Talleyrand. This
was told me by Frederick Ponsonby.

February 4th.—I returned to Woburn on Sunday. We
shot the whole week and killed an immense quantity of
game ; the last two days we killed 245 and 296 pheasants,
322 and 431 head. On Sunday last arrived the news of the
King's death.[1] The new King has been desperately ill. He
had a bad cold at Brighton, for which he lost eighty ounces
of blood ; yet he afterwards had a severe oppression, amounting almost to suffocation, on his chest. Halford was gone
to Windsor, and left orders with Knighton not to bleed him
again till his return. Knighton was afraid to bleed him.

---

[1] [King George III. died on the 29th of January, 1820.]

Bloomfield sent for Tierney,[1] who took upon himself to take fifty ounces from him. This gave him relief; he continued, however, dangerously ill, and on Wednesday he lost twenty ounces more. Yesterday afternoon he was materially better for the first time. Tierney certainly saved his life, for he must have died if he had not been blooded. Brougham sent a courier to the Queen immediately after the late King's death, and gave notice at Carlton House that he had applied for a passport for a courier to her Majesty the Queen.

The King has given to Lady Bloomfield the Ranger-ship of Hampton Court Park. He wished to give it to both of them with the survivorship, but Lord Liverpool submitted to him that the House of Commons had pro-nounced so strongly their dislike to reversionary grants that it would be unadvisable, and it was accordingly given to Lady B. only.

February 14*th.*—The Cabinet sat till past two o'clock this morning. The King refused several times to order the Queen to be prayed for in the alteration which was made in the Liturgy. The Ministers wished him to suffer it to be done, but he peremptorily refused, and said nothing should induce him to consent, whoever might ask him. Lord Harrowby told me this last night.

I think Fleury's book [2] almost the most interesting memoir I ever read; it is excessively well written, and his partiality to Bonaparte has not blinded him to the errors he committed. This book was wanted to bring under the same view the immediate causes of his return to France and the situation in which he found himself when seated on the throne. This was essentially different from that in which he had been before his abdication; so much so that I do not believe, if he had concluded a peace with the Allies, he could have remained upon the throne. Not only his civil power was

---

[1] [Sir Matthew Tierney, one of His Majesty's physicians.]

[2] [M. Fleury de Chabaulon was a young *auditeur* at the Conseil d'État who had joined Napoleon at Elba, and afterwards returned with him to France, when he was attached to the Imperial Cabinet during the Hundred Days. His memoir of that period is here referred to.]

reduced within very narrow limits, but his military authority was no longer the same; men seemed to have lost that reverential submissiveness which caused all his orders to be so blindly and implicitly obeyed.   During the height of his power none of his generals would have dared to neglect or oppose his orders as Ney did at the battles of the 16th of June.   It is impossible now to determine what might have been the political result in France of the success of Bonaparte's arms had he gained the battle of Waterloo.   He would probably have made peace with the Allies.   Had he returned to Paris triumphant, he might have dissolved the Chambers and re-established the old Imperial Government. In such a measure he must have depended upon his army for success.   But a spirit of liberty had sprung up in France during his absence, which seemed to be the more vigorous from having been so long repressed.   The nation, and even the army, appear to have imbibed the principles of freedom ; and if upon this occasion Bonaparte was placed on the throne by the force of opinion, he could not have restored the ancient despotism without exciting universal dissatisfaction.   Men seem formerly to have been awed by a conviction of his infallibility, and did not suffer themselves to reason upon the principles of action of a man who dazzled their imaginations by the magnificence of his exploits and the grandeur of his system.

February 20th.—The Ministers had resigned last week because the King would not hear reason on the subject of the Princess.   It is said that he treated Lord Liverpool very coarsely, and ordered him out of the room.   The King, they say, asked him ' if he knew to whom he was speaking.'   He replied, ' Sir, I know that I am speaking to my Sovereign, and I believe I am addressing him as it becomes a loyal subject to do.'   To the Chancellor he said, ' My Lord, I know your conscience always interferes except where your interest is concerned.'   The King afterwards sent for Lord Liverpool, who refused at first to go ; but afterwards, on the message being reiterated, he went, and the King said, ' We have both been too hasty.' This is probably all false, but it is very true that they offered to resign.

February 24th.—The plot[1] which has been detected had for its object the destruction of the Cabinet Ministers, and the chief actor in the conspiracy was Arthur Thistlewood. I was at Lady Harrowby's last night, and about half-past one o'clock Lord Harrowby came in and told us the following particulars:—A plot has been in agitation for some time past, of the existence of which, the names and numbers of the men concerned, and of all particulars concerning their plans, Government has been perfectly well informed. The conspirators had intended to execute their design about last Christmas at a Cabinet dinner at Lord Westmoreland's, but for some reason they were unable to do so and deferred it. At length Government received information that they were to assemble to the number of from twenty to thirty at a house in Cato Street, Edgware Road, and that they had resolved to execute their purpose last night, when the Cabinet would be at dinner at Lord Harrowby's. Dinner was ordered as usual. Men had been observed watching the house, both in front and rear, during the whole afternoon. It was believed that nine o'clock was the hour fixed upon for the assault to be made. The Ministers who were expected at dinner remained at Fife House, and at eight o'clock Mr. Birnie with twelve constables was despatched to Cato Street to apprehend the conspirators. Thirty-five foot guards were ordered to support the police force. The constables arrived upon the spot a few moments before the soldiers, and suspecting that the conspirators had received intimation of the discovery of their plot, and were in consequence preparing to escape, they did not wait for the soldiers, but went immediately to the house. A man armed with a musket was standing sentry, whom they secured. They then ascended a narrow staircase which led to the room in which the gang were assembled, and burst the door open. The first man who entered was shot in the head, but

[1] [The Cato Street Conspiracy.]

was only wounded ; he who followed was stabbed by Thistlewood and killed. The conspirators then with their swords
put out the lights and attempted to escape. By this time
the soldiers had arrived. Nine men were taken prisoners;
Thistlewood and the rest escaped.

March 1st.—Thistlewood was taken the morning after the
affair in Cato Street. It was the intention of these men to
have fired a rocket from Lord Harrowby's house as soon as
they had completed their work of destruction ; this was to
have been the signal for the rising of their friends. An oil
shop was to have been set on fire to increase the confusion
and collect a mob ; then the Bank was to have been attacked
and the gates of Newgate thrown open. The heads of the
Ministers were to have been cut off and put in a sack which
was prepared for that purpose. These are great projects,
but it does not appear they were ever in force sufficient to
put them in execution, and the mob (even if the mob had
espoused their cause, which seems doubtful), though very
dangerous in creating confusion and making havoc, are quite
inefficient for a regular operation.

June 4th.—I went to Oatlands on Tuesday. The Duchess
continues very ill; she is not expected to recover. The King
was at Ascot every day ; he generally rode on the course,
and the ladies came in carriages. One day they all rode.
He was always cheered by the mob as he went away. One
day only a man in the crowd called out, 'Where's the
Queen ? ' The Duke of Dorset was at the Cottage, and says
it was exceedingly agreeable. They kept very early hours.
The King always breakfasted with them, and Lady Conyngham looked remarkably well in the morning, her complexion
being so fine. On Friday she said she was bored with the
races and should not go ; he accordingly would not go either,
and sent word to say he should not be there. They stay
there till to-morrow. In the meantime the Queen is coming
to England, and Brougham is gone to meet her. Nobody
knows what advice he intends to give her, but everybody
believes that it is his intention she should come. It was
supposed that Lady Conyngham's family (her son and

brother) had set their faces against her connection with the King; but Lord Mount Charles was at the Cottage, and Denison was at the levee and very well received.

June 7th.—The Queen arrived in London yesterday at seven o'clock. I rode as far as Greenwich to meet her. The road was thronged with an immense multitude the whole way from Westminster Bridge to Greenwich. Carriages, carts, and horsemen followed, preceded, and surrounded her coach the whole way. She was everywhere received with the greatest enthusiasm. Women waved pocket handkerchiefs, and men shouted wherever she passed. She travelled in an open landau, Alderman Wood sitting by her side and Lady Ann Hamilton and another woman opposite. Everybody was disgusted at the vulgarity of Wood in sitting in the place of honour, while the Duke of Hamilton's sister was sitting backwards in the carriage. The Queen looked exactly as she did before she left England, and seemed neither dispirited nor dismayed. As she passed by White's she bowed and smiled to the men who were in the window. The crowd was not great in the streets through which she passed. Probably people had ceased to expect her, as it was so much later than the hour designated for her arrival. It is impossible to conceive the sensation created by this event. Nobody either blames or approves of her sudden return, but all ask, 'What will be done next? How is it to end?' In the House of Commons there was little said; but the few words which fell from Creevy, Bennett, or Denman seem to threaten most stormy debates whenever the subject is discussed. The King in the meantime is in excellent spirits, and the Ministers affect the greatest unconcern and talk of the time it will take to pass the Bills to 'settle her business.' 'Her business,' as they call it, will in all probability raise such a tempest as they will find it beyond their powers to appease; and for all his Majesty's unconcern the day of her arrival in England may be such an anniversary to him as he will have no cause to celebrate with much rejoicing.[1]

[1] [On the day that the Queen landed at Dover a royal message was sent down to Parliament, by which the King commended to the Lords an enquiry

June 9th.—Brougham's speech on Wednesday is said by his friends to have been one of the best that was ever made, and I think all agree that it was good and effective. The House of Commons is evidently anxious to get rid of the question if possible, for the moment Wilberforce expressed a wish to adjourn the county members rose one after another and so strongly concurred in that wish that Castlereagh was obliged to consent. The mob have been breaking windows in all parts of the town and pelting those who would not take off their hats as they passed Wood's door. Last night Lord Exmouth's house was assaulted and his windows broken, when he rushed out armed with sword and pistol and drove away the mob. Frederick Ponsonby saw him. Great sums of money have been won and lost on the Queen's return, for there was much betting at the clubs. The alderman showed a specimen of his taste as he came into London; when the Queen's coach passed Carlton House he stood up and gave three cheers.

It is odd enough Lady Hertford's windows have been broken to pieces and the frames driven in, while no assault has been made on Lady Conyngham's. Somebody asked Lady Hertford 'if she had been aware of the King's admiration for Lady Conyngham,' and 'whether he had ever talked to her about Lady C.' She replied that 'intimately as she had known the King, and openly as he had always talked to her upon every subject, he had never ventured to speak to her upon that of his mistresses.'

June 16th.—The speech which Canning made on the occasion of the King's message has been violently attacked by all parties, and is said to have given as great dissatisfaction to the Queen as to the King. It is not easy to discover what the Queen could have objected to in the speech, for it was highly favourable and flattering to her. It was gene-

into the conduct of the Queen. In the House of Commons there was some vehement speaking; and on the following day, before Lord Castlereagh moved the address in answer to the message, Mr. Brougham read to the House a message from the Queen, declaring that her return to England was occasioned by the necessity her enemies had laid upon her of defending her character.]

rally supposed last Sunday that he would resign in the
course of the week, and bets were laid that he would not be
in office next Sunday. On Wednesday he had an audience
of the King at the levee, which lasted fifty-two minutes by
Yarmouth's watch; nobody knows what passed between
them. Lord Fitzwilliam and Lord Sefton have refused to
act as negotiators for the Queen.

There was some indiscipline manifested in a battalion of
the 3rd Guards the day before yesterday; they were dissatisfied
at the severity of their duty and at some allowances that
had been taken from them, and on coming off guard they
refused to give up their ball cartridges. They were ordered
off to Plymouth, and marched at four yesterday morning.
Many people went from the ball at Devonshire House to see
them march away. Plymouth was afterwards changed for
Portsmouth in consequence of their good behaviour on the
route. Worcester [1] met many of them drunk at Brentford,
crying out, ' God save Queen Caroline !' There was some
disturbance last night in consequence of the mob assembling
round the King's mews, where the rest of the battalion that
had marched to Portsmouth still remained.

June 23rd.—I never remember to have seen the public
curiosity so excited as on Wilberforce's motion last night.[2]
Nearly 520 members voted in the House, and some went
away; as many people as could gain admission attended to
hear the debate. The speaking on the Opposition side was
excellent, but as everybody differs in opinion with regard to
the comparative merit of the speakers, it is impossible for
one who was not present to form a correct judgment on the
subject. The best speeches were Brougham's, Denman's,
Burdett's, and Canning's. Denman's speech was admirable
and, all agree, most judicious and effective for his client.
Burdett's was extremely clever, particularly the first part of

---

[1] [The Marquis of Worcester, afterwards seventh Duke of Beaufort.]

[2] [Mr. Wilberforce moved an address to the Queen to stop the investigation, by entreating her Majesty, under the assurance of the protection of
her honour by the Commons, to yield the point of the insertion of her name
in the Liturgy. This proposal the Queen courteously declined.]

it. In the meantime it is doubtful whether anything is gained by the resolution carried last night. Public opinion seems very equally divided as to the probability of the Queen agreeing to the expressed or implied wish of the House of Commons, and even if she refuses to consent to the omission of her name in the Liturgy it seems doubtful whether the green bag will ever be opened, so strong is the repugnance of the House of Commons to enter upon such an investigation. It is this feeling in the House which emboldens the Queen to hold out with the firmness and constancy she has hitherto displayed. The House of Lords cuts a most ridiculous figure, having precipitately agreed to go into the Committee. They have since been obliged to put off the investigation by repeated adjournments, in order to see what steps the House of Commons will take. Lord Grey made an indignant speech last night on this very subject; they say Lord Liverpool spoke remarkably well in reply.

June 25th.—The Queen's refusal to comply with the desire of the House of Commons keeps conjecture afloat and divides opinions as to the opening of the bag. The Opposition call her answer a very good one; those of the other party I have seen think it too long, and not neatly and clearly worded. Brougham declined advising her as to her answer; he told her she must be guided by her own feelings, and was herself the only person capable of judging what she had best do. The discussion of the Queen's business is now become an intolerable nuisance in society; no other subject is ever talked of. It is an incessant matter of argument and dispute what will be done and what ought to be done. All people express themselves tired of the subject, yet none talk or think of any other. It is a great evil when a single subject of interest takes possession of society; conversation loses all its lightness and variety, and every drawing-room is converted into an arena of political disputation. People even go to talk about it from habit long after the interest it excited has ceased.

June 27th.—The mob was very abusive to the member who

carried up the resolution to the Queen, and called Wilberforce 'Dr. Cantwell.' The Queen demanded to be heard by
counsel at the bar of the House of Lords. Contrary to order
and contrary to expectation, the counsel were admitted, when
Brougham made a very powerful speech. Denman began exceedingly well; Lord Holland said his first three or four sen-
tences were the best thing he ever heard; *si sic omnia*, he
would have made the finest speech possible; but on the whole
he was inferior to Brougham. If the House had refused to
hear her counsel, it is said that she would have gone down
to-day to the House of Lords and have demanded to be
heard in person. As usual Brougham's speech is said by
many of his political adversaries to have been weak in argument. Many, however, do him the justice to acknowledge
that it was a very powerful appeal for his client.

June 28th.—The debate last night in the House of Lords
was excellent. Lord Grey made a powerful speech, very much
against the Queen, a speech for office. The manager announced at Drury Lane that the Queen would go to the play
to-night. Brougham knew nothing of this; she never told
him. Mrs. Brougham told me so last night, and that he was
quite worn out with the business.[1]

July 6th.—Since the report of the Secret Committee
public opinion is entirely changed as to the result of the
proceedings against the Queen. Everybody thinks the
charges will be proved and that the King will be divorced.
It is impossible to discover what effect the report may have
in the country; it is certain hitherto that all ranks of men
have been decidedly favourable to the Queen, and disbelieve
the charges against her. The military in London have shown
alarming symptoms of dissatisfaction, so much so that it
seems doubtful how far the Guards can be counted upon in
case of any disturbance arising out of this subject. Luttrell
says that 'the extinguisher is taking fire.'

[1] [The report of the Secret Committee of the Lords was made on the 4th
of July. It declared that the evidence against the Queen was such as to
demand a solemn enquiry. The trial, or rather investigation, began on
the 17th of August. The defence was opened on the 3rd of October, and
the Bill was abandoned on the 6th of November.]

July 8th.—I was in the House of Lords the night before last to hear Brougham and Denman speak at the bar. Brougham's speech was uncommonly clever, very insolent, and parts of it very eloquent. A very amusing episode was furnished by the Bishop of Exeter, who moved that the counsel should withdraw, and then asked the House whether they were not out of order. Lord Holland cut him up in the most beautiful style, and excited universal laughter. Nobody came to the assistance of the Bishop, and the counsel were called in again and resumed. Brougham's speech is reported in the 'Morning Chronicle' of yesterday word for word.

July 14th.—I have been at Newmarket, where I had the first fortunate turn this year. The conversation about the Queen begins to subside; everybody seems to agree that it is a great injustice not to allow her lists of the witnesses; the excuse that it is not usual is bad, for the proceedings are anomalous altogether, and it is absurd to attempt to adhere to precedent; here there are no precedents and no analogies to guide to a decision. London is drawing to a close, but in August it will be very full, as all the Peers must be here. They say the trial will last six months.

Luttrell's poem[1] has succeeded. The approbation it receives is general but qualified; in fact, it was difficult to make such a sketch of life and manners sufficiently piquant without the infusion of a little satire, and his fear of giving offence has induced him to be so good-natured that he is occasionally rather insipid. ' Il y a des tracasseries de société.' I cannot record them, though perhaps years hence, when I may look over what I now write, I might be amused with stories of long-forgotten jealousies and various interests extinguished by the lapse of time, or perhaps silenced in the grave; still it would be melancholy to retrace the days of my youth and to bring before my imagination the blooming faces and the gaiety and brilliancy of those who once shone the meteors of society, but who would then be so changed in

---

[1] [Mr. Luttrell's 'Advice to Julia,' published in 1820.]

form and mind, and with myself rapidly descending to our last home.

Read 'Les Liaisons dangereuses.' Much has been said about the dangerous tendency of certain books, and probably this would be considered as one pregnant with mischief. I consider this a mere jargon, and although I would never recommend this book (because it is so grossly indecent) I should never apprehend the smallest danger to the most inexperienced mind or the warmest passions from its immoral tendency. The principle upon which books of this description are considered pernicious is the notion that they represent vice in such glowing and attractive colours as to make us lose sight of its deformity and fill our imagination with the idea of its pleasures. No one who has any feeling or a spark of generosity or humanity in his breast can read this book without being moved with compassion for Madame de Tourval and with horror and disgust towards Valmont and Madame de Merteuil. It raised in my mind a detestation of such cold-blooded, inhuman profligacy, and I felt that I would rather every pleasure that can flow from the intercourse of women were debarred me than run such a course. The moral effect upon my mind was stronger than any which ever resulted from the most didactic work, and if anyone wants to excite remorse in the most vicious mind I would recommend him to make use of 'Les Liaisons dangereuses' for the purpose.

The Duchess of York died on Sunday morning of water on her chest. She was insensible the last two days. She is deeply regretted by her husband, her friends, and her servants. Probably no person in such a situation was ever more really liked. She has left 12,000l. to her servants and some children whom she had caused to be educated. She had arranged all her affairs with the greatest exactitude, and left nothing undone.

The Queen's letter was brought to the King whilst he was at dinner (at the Cottage). He said, 'Tell the Queen's messenger that the King can receive no communication from her except through the hands of his Ministers.' Esterhazy was present, and said he did this with extraordinary dignity.

Newmarket, October 2nd.—I left town in the middle of August with George Fox. We went down with extraordinary rapidity. I never was happier than to escape from London and to find myself in Yorkshire. It was a new world, and the change was most refreshing. The refinement of London was not there, but there was a good humour, gaiety, and hospitality which amused and delighted me.

London, October 8th.—I came to town with Payne on Friday, having won a little at Newmarket. He told me a good story by the way. A certain bishop in the House of Lords rose to speak, and announced that he should divide what he had to say into twelve parts, when the Duke of Wharton interrupted him, and begged he might be indulged for a few minutes, as he had a story to tell which he could only introduce at that moment. A drunken fellow was passing by St. Paul's at night, and heard the clock slowly chiming twelve. He counted the strokes, and when it had finished looked towards the clock and said, 'Damn you! why couldn't you give us all that at once?' There was an end of the bishop's story.

The town is still in an uproar about the trial, and nobody has any doubt that it will finish by the Bill being thrown out and the Ministers turned out. Brougham's speech was the most magnificent display of argument and oratory that has been heard for years, and they say that the impression it made upon the House was immense; even his most violent opponents (including Lord Lonsdale) were struck with admiration and astonishment.

October 15th.—Since I came to town I have been to the trial every day. I have occupied a place close to Brougham, which, besides the advantage it affords of enabling me to hear extremely well everything that passes, gives me the pleasure of talking to him and the other counsel, and puts me behind the scenes so far that I cannot help hearing all their conversation, their remarks, and learning what witnesses they are

going to examine, and many other things which are interesting and amusing. Since I have been in the world I
never remember any question which so exclusively occupied
everybody's attention, and so completely absorbed men's
thoughts and engrossed conversation. In the same degree
is the violence displayed. It is taken up as a party question
entirely, and the consequence is that everybody is gone
mad about it. Very few people admit of any medium between
pronouncing the Queen quite innocent and judging her
guilty and passing the Bill. Until the evidence of Lieut.
Hownam it was generally thought that proofs of her guilt
were wanting, but since his admission that Bergami slept
under the tent with her all unprejudiced men seem to think
the adultery sufficiently proved. The strenuous opposers of
the Bill, however, by no means allow this, and make a mighty
difference between sleeping dressed under a tent and being
shut up at night in a room together, which the supporters of
the Bill contend would have been quite or nearly the same
thing. The Duke of Portland, who is perfectly impartial,
and who has always been violently against the Bill, was so
satisfied by Hownam's evidence that he told me that after
that admission by him he thought all further proceedings
useless, and that it was ridiculous to listen to any more
evidence, as the fact was proved; that he should attend no
longer to any evidence upon the subject. This view of the
case will not, however, induce him to vote for the Bill,
because he thinks that upon grounds of expediency it ought
not to pass. The Ministers were elated in an extraordinary
manner by this evidence of Hownam's. The Duke of
Wellington told Madame de Lieven that he was very tired;
'mais les grands succès fatiguent autant que les grands
revers.' They look upon the progress of this trial in the
light of a campaign, and upon each day's proceedings as a
sort of battle, and by the impression made by the evidence
they consider that they have gained a victory or sustained a
defeat. Their anxiety that this Bill should pass is quite
inconceivable, for it cannot be their interest that it should
be carried; and as for the King, they have no feeling what-

ever for him. The Duke of Portland told me that he conversed with the Duke of Wellington upon the subject, and
urged as one of the reasons why this Bill should not pass the
House of Lords the disgrace that it would entail upon the
King by the recrimination that would ensue in the House of
Commons. His answer was ' that the King was degraded as
low as he could be already.' The vehemence with which
they pursue this object produces a corresponding violence in
their language and sentiments. Lady Harrowby, who is
usually very indifferent upon political subjects, has taken this
up with unusual eagerness. In an argument which I had
with her the day before yesterday, she said that if the House
of Lords was to suffer itself to be influenced by the opinions
and wishes of the people, it would be the most mean and
pusillanimous conduct, and that after all what did it signify
what the people thought or what they expressed if the army
was to be depended upon? I answered that I never had
expected that the day would come when I should be told that
we were to disregard the feelings and wishes of the people
of this country, and to look to our army for support. In
proportion as the Ministers were elated by what came out in
Hownam's cross-examination so were they depressed by the
unlucky affair of Rastelli,[1] which has given such an important advantage to their adversaries. Mr. Powell's explanation
was extremely unsatisfactory, and in his examination yesterday they elicited from him what is tantamount to a contradiction of what he had said the day before. It is not
possible to doubt what is the real state of the case. Rastelli
is an active, useful agent, and they had occasion for his
services; consequently they sent him off, and trusted that he
would be back here before he could possibly be called for, if
ever he should be called for again. It was a rash speculation,

---

[1] [Rastelli was a witness for the Bill—not a very important one. After
his examination was over he was allowed to leave the country. Brougham
found this out, and instantly demanded that he should be recalled for
further cross-examination, well knowing this could not at the moment be
done. This answered his purpose, and he then turned with incredible
vehemence on the other side, and accused them of spiriting away the
witness.]

which failed. The last two days have been more amusing
and interesting than the preceding ones. The debates in
the House, a good deal of violence, and some personalities
have given spirit to the proceedings, which were getting
very dull. Lord Holland made a violent speech, and Lord
Carnarvon a clever one, which was violent enough too, on
Rastelli's affair. Lord Holland made one or two little
speeches which were very comical. Lord Lauderdale made
a violent speech the other day, and paid himself in it a great
many compliments. It must be acknowledged that the zeal
of many of the Peers is very embarrassing, displayed as it is
not in the elucidation of the truth, but in furtherance of that
cause of which they desire the success. There is no one more
violent than Lord Lauderdale,[1] and neither the Attorney-
General nor the Solicitor-General can act with greater zeal
than he does in support of the Bill. Lord Liverpool is
a model of fairness, impartiality, and candour. The Chancellor is equally impartial, and as he decides personally
all disputes on legal points which are referred to the
House, his fairness has been conspicuous in having generally decided in favour of the Queen's counsel. Yesterday
morning some discussion arose about a question which
Brougham put to Powell. He asked him who was his
principal, as he was an agent. The question was objected
to, and he began to defend it in an uncommonly clever
speech, but was stopped before he had spoken long. He
introduced a very ingenious quotation which was suggested to him by Spencer Perceval, who was standing near
him. Talking of the airy, unsubstantial being who was the

[1] [In the course of the trial, in order to show that the Queen had associated in Italy with ladies of good character, it was stated that a Countess
T—— frequented her society at Florence. On cross-examination it came out
that the Countess spoke a provincial dialect, anything but the purest Tuscan,
whence it was implied that she was a vulgar person, and Lord Lauderdale
especially pointed out this inference, speaking himself in very broad Scotch.
Upon which Lord Auckland, a member of the Opposition, said to the witness,
'Have the goodness to state whether Countess T—— spoke Italian with as
broad an accent as the noble Earl who has just sat down speaks with in his
native tongue.'• The late Sir Henry Holland was present when this
occurred, and used to relate the anecdote.]

principal, and one of the parties in this cause, he said he
wished to meet

> This shape—
> If shape it could be called—that shape had none,
> Distinguishable in member, joint, or limb;
> Or substance might be called that shadow seemed,
> For each seemed either . . .
> What seemed its head
> The likeness of a kingly crown had on.
>
> *Paradise Lost*, ii. 666.

Whersted, December 10*th.*—I left Woburn on Thursday
night last, and got here on Friday morning. The Lievens,
Worcesters, Duke of Wellington, Neumann, and Montagu
were here. The Duke went away yesterday. We acted
charades, which were very well done. Yesterday we went
to shoot at Sir Philip Brookes'. As we went in the
carriage, the Duke talked a great deal about the battle of
Waterloo and different things relating to that campaign.
He said that he had 50,000 men at Waterloo. He began
the campaign with 85,000 men, lost 5,000 on the 16th, and
had a corps of 20,000 at Hal under Prince Frederick. He
said that it was remarkable that nobody who had ever spoken
of these operations had ever made mention of that corps,[1]
and Bonaparte was certainly ignorant of it. In this corps
were the best of the Dutch troops; it had been placed there
because the Duke expected the attack to be made on that
side. He said that the French army was the best army
that was ever seen, and that in the previous operations
Bonaparte's march upon Belgium was the finest thing that
ever was done—so rapid and so well combined. His object
was to beat the armies in detail, and this object succeeded in so far as that he attacked them separately; but
from the extraordinary celerity with which the allied armies

---

[1] [The Duke of Wellington has frequently been criticised for leaving so
important a body of troops at Hal, so far upon his right that they were of
no use in the battle. He always defended this disposition, and maintained
that the greater probability was that Napoleon would attack his extreme
right and advance by Hal. On this occasion (in 1820) he himself drew
attention to it, as is explained in the text.]

were got together he was not able to realise the advantages he had promised himself. The Duke says that they certainly were not prepared for this attack, as the French had previously broken up the roads by which their army advanced; but as it was in summer this did not render them impassable. He says that Bonaparte beat the Prussians in a most extraordinary way, as the battle[1] was gained in less than four hours; but that it would probably have been more complete if he had brought a greater number of troops into action, and not detached so large a body against the British corps. There were 40,000 men opposed to the Duke on the 16th, but he says that the attack was not so powerful as it ought to have been with such a force. The French had made a long march the day before the battle, and had driven in the Prussian posts in the evening. I asked him if he thought Bonaparte had committed any fault. He said he thought he had committed a fault in attacking him in the position of Waterloo; that his object ought to have been to remove him as far as possible from the Prussian army, and that he ought consequently to have moved upon Hal, and to have attempted to penetrate by the same road by which the Duke had himself advanced. He had always calculated upon Bonaparte's doing this, and for this purpose he had posted 20,000 men under Prince Frederick at Hal. He said that the position at Waterloo was uncommonly strong, but that the strength of it consisted alone in the two farms of Hougoumont and La Haye Sainte, both of which were admirably situated and adapted for defence. In Hougoumont there were never more than from 300 to 500 men, who were reinforced as it was necessary; and although the French repeatedly attacked this point, and sometimes with not less than 20,000 men, they never could even approach it. Had they obtained possession of it, they could not have maintained it, as it was open on one side to the whole fire of the English lines, whilst it was sheltered on the side towards the French. The Duke said the farm of La Haye

---

[1] [The battle of Ligny, 16th of June, 1815.]

Sainte was still better than that of Hougoumont, and that it never would have been taken if the officer who was commanding there had not neglected to make an aperture through which ammunition could be conveyed to his garrison.

When we arrived at Sir Philip Brookes' it rained, and we were obliged to sit in the house, when the Duke talked a great deal about Paris and different things. He told us that Blücher was determined to destroy the Bridge of Jena. The Duke spoke to Müffling, the Governor of Paris, and desired him to persuade Blücher to abandon this design. However, Blücher was quite determined. He said the French had destroyed the pillar at Rossbach and other things, and that they merited this retaliation. He also said that the English had burnt Washington, and he did not see why he was not to destroy this bridge. Müffling, however, concerted with the Duke that English sentinels should be placed on the bridge, and if any Prussian soldiers should approach to injure it, these sentinels were not to retire. This they conceived would gain time, as they thought that previous to making any attempt on the bridge Blücher would apply to the Duke to withdraw the English sentinels. This was of no avail. The Prussians arrived, mined the arches, and attempted to blow up the bridge, sentinels and all. Their design, however, was frustrated, and the bridge received no injury. At length Müffling came to the Duke, and said that he was come to propose to him a compromise, which was that the bridge should be spared and the column in the Place Vendôme should be destroyed instead. ' I saw,' said the Duke, ' that I had got out of the frying-pan into the fire. Fortunately at this moment the King of Prussia arrived, and he ordered that no injury should be done to either.' On another occasion Blücher announced his intention of levying a contribution of 100 millions on the city of Paris. To this the Duke objected, and said that the raising such enormous contributions could only be done by common consent, and must be a matter of general arrangement. Blücher said,

'Oh! I do not mean to be the only party who is to levy anything; you may levy as much for yourselves, and, depend upon it, if you do it will all be paid; there will be no difficulty whatever.' The Duke says that the two invasions cost the French 100 millions sterling. The Allies had 1,200,000 men clothed at their expense; the allowance for this was 60 francs a man. The army of occupation was entirely maintained; there were the contributions, the claims amounting to ten millions sterling. Besides this there were towns and villages destroyed and country laid waste.

CHAPTER II.

1821.

London, February 7th.—The King went to the play last
night (Drury Lane) for the first time, the Dukes of York
and Clarence and a great suite with him. He was received
with immense acclamations, the whole pit standing up,
hurrahing and waving their hats. The boxes were very
empty at first, for the mob occupied the avenues to the
theatre, and those who had engaged boxes could not get to
them. The crowd on the outside was very great. Lord
Hertford dropped one of the candles as he was lighting the
King in, and made a great confusion in the box. The King
sat in Lady Bessborough's box, which was fitted up for him.
He goes to Covent Garden to-night. A few people called
' The Queen,' but very few. A man in the gallery called out,
' Where's your wife, Georgy ? '

February 11*th.*—I came to town from Euston the end of last month. The debates were expected to be very stormy and the minorities very large, not that anybody expected Ministers to go out. It has all ended as such anticipations usually do, in everything going off very quietly and the Government obtaining large majorities. Their Parliamentary successes and the King's reception have greatly elated them, and they think (and with reason probably) that they are likely to enjoy their places for the term of their natural lives, not that they care about the King's popularity except in as much as it may add strength to their Administration. They do not conceal their contempt or dislike of him, and it is one of the phenomena of the present times that the King should have Ministers whom he abuses and hates, and who entertain corresponding sentiments of aversion to him; yet they defend all his errors and follies, and he affords them constant countenance and protection. However, the King was delighted by his reception at the theatres, and told Lady Bessborough, as he came downstairs, he never was more gratified.

February 23*rd.*—Yesterday the Duke of York proposed to me to take the management of his horses, which I accepted. Nothing could be more kind than the manner in which he proposed it.[1]

March 5*th.*—I have experienced a great proof of the vanity of human wishes. In the course of three weeks I have attained the three things which I have most desired in the world for years past, and upon the whole I do not feel that my happiness is at all increased; perhaps if it were not for one cause it might be, but until that ceases to exist it is in vain that I acquire every other advantage or possess the means of amusement.[2]

March 22*nd.*—I was sworn in the day before yesterday,

[1] [Mr. Greville continued to manage the racing establishment of the Duke of York from this time till the death of his Royal Highness.]

[2] [One of these things was Mr. Greville's appointment as Clerk of the Council; the second was his connection with the Duke of York in his racing establishment; I am ignorant of the third.]

and kissed hands at a Council at Carlton House yesterday morning as Clerk of the Council.

March 25th.—Lord Fife has been dismissed from his place of Lord of the Bedchamber for voting against the Malt Tax, and Lord Lovaine has been appointed instead.

April 19th.—The night before last Hobhouse made his furious attack upon Canning. Last night everybody expected that Canning would speak, and was extremely anxious to hear what notice he would take of Hobhouse. The army estimates came on first in the evening, and almost all the members went away, intending to return to the Reform debate, but when Reform came on there were only 100 members in the House. 'Le combat finit faute de combattans,' and when everybody came crowding down at nine o'clock the House had been up half an hour, having divided 53 to 41.[1]

May 2nd.—When the Canonry of Windsor became vacant Lady Conyngham asked the King to give it to Mr. Sumner,[2] who had been Mount Charles's tutor. The King agreed: the man was sent for, and kissed hands at Brighton. A letter was written to Lord Liverpool to announce the

[1] [On the 17th of April Mr. Lambton (afterwards Earl of Durham) moved for a Committee of the whole House to consider the state of the representation of the people in Parliament. It was owing to the misapprehension described in the text that the division was so small.]

[2] [Afterwards Bishop of Winchester. This was the beginning of the fortune of that amiable prelate, of whom it must be said that if he owed his early advancement to a questionable influence, no man has filled the episcopal office with more unaffected piety, dignity, and goodness. The difference between George IV. and Lord Liverpool on this occasion was a very serious one. The Duke of Wellington referred to it in a confidential letter to Lord Liverpool, written on the 26th of October, 1821, in the following terms:—' As I told you at Windsor, the King has never forgiven your opposition to his wishes in the case of Mr. Sumner. This feeling has influenced every action of his life in relation to his Government from that moment; and I believe to more than one of us he avowed that his objection to Mr. Canning was that his accession to the Government was peculiarly desirable to you. Nothing can be more unjust or more unfair than this feeling; and as there is not one of your colleagues who did not highly approve of what you did respecting Mr. Sumner, so there is not one of them who would not suffer with you all the consequences of that act.' ('Correspondence of the Duke of Wellington,' Second Series, vol. i. p. 195; published in 1867.)]

appointment. In the meantime Lord Liverpool had sent a list of persons, one of whom he should recommend to succeed to the vacancy, and the letters crossed. As soon as Lord Liverpool received the letter from Brighton he got into his carriage and went down to the King, to state that unless he was allowed to have the distribution of this patronage without any interference, he could not carry on the Government, and would resign his office if Sumner was appointed. The man was only a curate, and had never held a living at all. The King 'chanta palinodie,' and a sort of compromise was made, by which Lady Conyngham's friend was withdrawn, and the King begged it might be given to Dr. Clarke, to which appointment Lord Liverpool consented, although he did not approve of him; he did not, however, wish to appear too difficult.

Lady Conyngham lives in one of the houses in Marlborough Row. All the members of her family are continually there, and are supplied with horses, carriages, &c., from the King's stables. She rides out with her daughter, but never with the King, who always rides with one of his gentlemen. They never appear in public together. She dines there every day. Before the King comes into the room she and Lady Elizabeth join him in another room, and he always walks in with one on each arm. She comports herself entirely as mistress of the house, but never suffers her daughter to leave her. She has received magnificent presents, and Lady Elizabeth the same; particularly the mother has strings of pearls of enormous value. Madame de Lieven said she had seen the pearls of the Grand Duchesses and the Prussian Princesses, but had never seen any nearly so fine as Lady Conyngham's. The other night Lady Bath was coming to the Pavilion. After dinner Lady Conyngham called to Sir William Keppel and said, 'Sir William, do desire them to light up the saloon' (this saloon is lit by hundreds of candles). When the King came in she said to him, 'Sir, I told them to light up the saloon, as Lady Bath is coming this evening.' The King seized her arm and said with the greatest tenderness, 'Thank you, thank you,

my dear; you always do what is right; you cannot please
me so much as by doing everything you please, everything
to show that you are mistress here.'

May 12th.—I have suffered the severest pain I ever had
in my life by the death of Lady Worcester.[1] I loved her
like a sister, and I have lost one of the few persons in the
world who cared for me, and whose affection and friendship
serve to make life valuable to me. She has been cut off in
the prime of her life and in the bloom of her beauty, and so
suddenly too. Seven days ago she was at a ball at Court,
and she is now no more. She died like a heroine, full of
cheerfulness and courage to the last. She has been snatched
from life at a time when she was becoming every day more
fit to live, for her mind, her temper, and her understanding
were gradually and rapidly improving; she had faults, but
her mind was not vicious, and her defects may be ascribed
to her education and to the actual state of the society in
which she lived. Her virtues were inherent in her character; ·
every day developed them more and more, and they were
such as to make the happiness of all who lived with her and
to captivate the affection of all who really knew her. I have
never lost anyone I loved before, and though I know the
grief I now feel will soon subside (for so the laws of nature
have ordained), long, long will it be before I forget her, or
before my mind loses the lively impression of her virtues
and of our mutual friendship.

This is one of those melancholy events in life to which
the mind cannot for a long time reconcile or accustom itself.
I saw her so short a time ago 'glittering like the morning
star, full of life and splendour and joy;' the accents of her
voice still so vibrate in my ear that I cannot believe I shall
never see her again. What a subject for contemplation and
for moralising! What reflections crowd into the mind!

Dr. Hume told me once he had witnessed many death-

[1] [Georgiana Frederica, Marchioness of Worcester, daughter of the Hon.
Charles Fitzroy, married to Henry, afterwards seventh Duke of Beaufort, in
1814, died 11th of May, 1821. This lamented lady left two daughters, afterwards Lady Augusta Neumann and Lady Georgiana Codrington.]

beds, but he had never seen anything like the fortitude and
resignation displayed by her.   She died in his arms, and
without pain.   As life ebbed away her countenance changed,
and when at length she ceased to breathe, a beautiful and
tranquil smile settled upon her face.

> Call round her tomb each object of desire,
> Each purer frame informed by purer fire;
> Let her be all that cheers or softens life,
> The tender sister, daughter, friend, and wife:
> Bid her be all that makes mankind adore,
> Then view this marble, and be vain no more.

June 24th.—The King dined at Devonshire House last
Thursday se'nnight.   Lady Conyngham had on her head a
sapphire which belonged to the Stuarts, and was given by
Cardinal York to the King.   He gave it to the Princess
Charlotte, and when she died he desired to have it back,
Leopold being informed it was a crown jewel.   This crown
jewel sparkled in the headdress of the Marchioness at the
ball.   I ascertained the Duke of York's sentiments upon this
subject the other day.   He was not particularly anxious to
discuss it, but he said enough to show that he has no good
opinion of her.   The other day, as we were going to the
races from Oatlands, he gave me the history of the Duke
of Wellington's life.   His prejudice against him is excessively strong, and I think if ever he becomes King the
other will not be Commander-in-Chief.   He does not deny
his military talents, but he thinks that he is false and
ungrateful, that he never gave sufficient credit to his officers,
and that he was unwilling to put forward men of talent who
might be in a situation to claim some share of credit, the
whole of which he was desirous of engrossing himself.
He says that at Waterloo he got into a scrape and allowed
himself to be surprised, and he attributes in great measure
the success of that day to Lord Anglesea, who, he says,
was hardly mentioned, and that in the coldest terms, in
the Duke's despatch.[1]

[1] [The unjust and unfavourable opinion expressed of the Duke of Wellington by the Duke of York dated from the appointment of Sir Arthur

December 18*th.*—I have not written anything for months. ' Quante cose mi sono accadute!' My progress was as follows, not very interesting :—To Newmarket, Whersted, Riddlesworth, Sprotborough, Euston, Elveden, Welbeck, Caversham, Nun Appleton, Welbeck, Burghley, and London. Nothing worth mentioning occurred at any of these places. Sprotborough was agreeable enough. The Grevilles, Montagu, Wilmot, and the Wortleys were there. I came to town, went to Brighton yesterday se'nnight for a Council. I was lodged in the Pavilion and dined with the King. The gaudy splendour of the place amused me for a little and then bored me. The dinner was cold and the evening dull beyond all dulness. They say the King is anxious that form and ceremony should be banished, and if so it only proves how impossible it is that form and ceremony should not always inhabit a palace. The rooms are not furnished for society, and, in fact, society cannot flourish without ease; and who can feel at ease who is under the eternal constraint which etiquette and respect impose? The King was in good looks and good spirits, and after dinner cut his jokes with all the coarse merriment which is his characteristic. Lord Wellesley did not seem to like it, but of course he bowed and smiled like the rest. I saw nothing very particular in the King's manner to Lady Conyngham. He sat by her on the couch almost the whole evening, playing at patience, and he took her in to dinner; but Madame de Lieven and Lady Cowper were there, and he seemed equally civil to all of them. I was curious to see the Pavilion and the life they lead there, and I now only hope I may never go there again, for the novelty is past, and I should be exposed to the whole weight of the bore of it without the stimulus of curiosity.

December 19*th.*—I dined with Lord Gwydir yesterday, and sat next to Prince Lieven. He told me that Bloomfield

Wellesley to a high command, and afterwards to the chief command of the army in Portugal. The Duke of York had at one moment entertained hopes of commanding that army, but when he was made to understand that this was impossible he erroneously attributed this disappointment to the intrigues of those who were preferred before him. This matter is explained with further particulars *sub* 24th of December, 1822.

is no longer in favour, that he has been supplanted by Lord Francis Conyngham,[1] who now performs almost all the functions which formerly appertained to Bloomfield. He is quite aware of his decline, and submits himself to it in a manly way. He is no longer so necessary to the King as he was, for a short time ago he could not bear that Bloomfield should be absent, and *now* his absence is unfelt. Francis goes to the King every morning, usually breakfasts with him, and receives all his orders. He was invited to go to Panshanger for two days, and was very anxious to go, but he could not obtain leave from the King to absent himself. Bloomfield does not put himself forward; ' même il se retire,' he said, and it is understood that he has made up his mind to resign his situation and leave the Court. The King is still perfectly civil and good-humoured to him, but has withdrawn his confidence from him, and Bloomfield is no longer his first servant.

I asked Lieven whether Francis Conyngham, in performing the other duties which had been hitherto allotted to Bloomfield, also exercised the functions of Private Secretary, because this involved a much more serious question. He said that he did not know; all he knew was that whilst he was at Brighton Bloomfield was absent for five days, and that during that time the other had ostensibly occupied the place which Bloomfield used to hold about the King's person. The commencement of this revolution in the King's sentiments is to be dated from the journey to Hanover. Now Bloomfield sits amongst the guests at dinner at the Pavilion; the honours are done by the father on one side and the son on the other.

1822.

July 16*th*.—Since I wrote last I have been continually in town. I have won on the Derby, my sister is married,[2] and

---

[1] [Lord Francis Conyngham, second son of the first Marquis of Conyngham (who was raised to the British peerage in June 1821), afterwards himself Marquis of Conyngham.]

[2] [Miss Greville married Lord Francis Leveson Gower, afterwards Earl of Ellesmere, in 1822.]

I have done nothing worth recording. How habit and practice change our feelings, our opinions; and what an influence they have upon our thoughts and actions! Objects which I used to contemplate at an immeasurable distance, and to attain which I thought would be the summit of felicity, I have found worth very little in comparison to the value my imagination used to set upon them. . . . London is nearly over, has been tolerably agreeable; but I have been very often bored to death by the necessity of paying some attention to keep up an interest.

July 30*th*.—Madame de Lieven is ill with the King, and is miserable in consequence. Lady Cowper is her *confidante*, and the Duke of Wellington; but this latter pretends to know nothing of it, and asked me the other day what it was, I am sure in order to discover what people say. When the Duke was at Brighton in the winter, he and the King had a dispute about the army. It began (it was at dinner) by the King's saying that the Russians or the Prussians (I forget which) were the best infantry in the world. The Duke said, 'Except your Majesty's.' The King then said the English cavalry were the best, which the Duke denied; then that an inferior number of French regiments would always beat a superior number of English, and, in short, that they were not half so effective. The King was very angry; the dispute waxed warm, and ended by his Majesty rising from table and saying, 'Well, it is not for me to dispute on such a subject with your Grace.' The King does not like the Duke, nor does the Duke of York. This I know from himself.

August 13*th*.—I went to Cirencester on Friday and came back yesterday. At Hounslow I heard of the death of Lord Londonderry.[1] When I got to town I met several people who had all assumed an air of melancholy, a *visage de circonstance*, which provoked me inexpressibly, because it was certain that they did not care; indeed, if they felt at

---

[1] [Lord Castlereagh, far better known by that name, succeeded as second Marquis of Londonderry on the 11th of April, 1821—only sixteen months before his death.]

all, it was probably rather satisfaction at an event happening than sorrow for the death of the person. It seems Lord Londonderry had been unwell for some time, but not seriously, and a few days before this catastrophe he became much worse, and was very much dejected. He told Lord Granville some time ago that he was worn out with fatigue, and he told Count Münster the other day that he was very ill indeed. The Duke of Wellington saw him on Friday, and was so struck by the appearance of illness about him that he sent Bankhead to him. He was cupped on Saturday in London, got better, and went to Foot's Cray. On Sunday he was worse, and the state of dejection in which he appeared induced his attendants to take certain precautions, which unfortunately, however, proved fruitless. They removed his pistols and his razors, but he got hold of a penknife which was in the room next his, and on Sunday night or early on Monday morning he cut his throat with it. There is not a Minister in town but Lord Liverpool, Vansittart, and the Chancellor. Lord Bathurst is at Cirencester, the Duke of Wellington in Holland, Lord Sidmouth in Yorkshire, Peel and Lord Melville in Scotland with the King. No event ever gave rise to more speculation with the few people there are left to speculate, and the general opinion seems to be that Canning will not go to India,[1] but will be appointed in his room. It certainly opens a door to his ambition as well as to that of Peel, who, unless Canning comes into office, must of necessity lead the House of Commons. Another speculation is that Lord Liverpool will take this opportunity of resigning, and that the King will form a Whig Ministry. I do not believe Lord Liverpool wishes to resign, and my opinion is that Canning will come into office.

I had hardly any acquaintance with Lord Londonderry, and therefore am not in the slightest degree affected by his death. As a Minister he is a great loss to his party, and still greater to his friends and dependents, to whom he was the best of patrons; to the country I think he is none.

---

[1] [Mr. Canning had just accepted the office of Governor-General of India, and was about to go out to that country.]

Nobody can deny that his talents were great, and perhaps he owed his influence and authority as much to his character as to his abilities.   His appearance was dignified and imposing; he was affable in his manners and agreeable in society.   The great feature of his character was a cool and determined courage, which gave an appearance of resolution and confidence to all his actions, and inspired his friends with admiration and excessive devotion to him, and caused him to be respected by his most violent opponents.   As a speaker he was prolix, monotonous, and never eloquent, except, perhaps, for a few minutes when provoked into a passion by something which had fallen out in debate.   But, notwithstanding these defects, and still more the ridicule which his extraordinary phraseology had drawn upon him, he was always heard with attention.   He never spoke ill; his speeches were continually replete with good sense and strong argument, and though they seldom offered much to admire, they generally contained a great deal to be answered.   I believe he was considered one of the best managers of the House of Commons who ever sat in it, and he was eminently possessed of the good taste, good humour, and agreeable manners which are more requisite to make a good leader than eloquence, however brilliant.   With these qualities, it may be asked why he was not a better Minister, and who can answer that question?   or who can aver that he did not pursue the policy which he conscientiously believed to be most advantageous to his country?   Nay, more, who can say but from surmise and upon speculation that it was not the best?   I believe that he was seduced by his vanity, that his head was turned by emperors, kings, and congresses, and that he was resolved that the country which he represented should play as conspicuous a part as any other in the political dramas which were acted on the Continent.   The result of his policy is this, that we are mixed up in the affairs of the Continent in a manner we have never been before, which entails upon us endless negotiations and enormous expenses.   We have associated ourselves with the members of the Holy Alliance, and countenanced the acts of

ambition and despotism in such a manner as to have drawn
upon us the detestation of the nations of the Continent; and
our conduct towards them at the close of the war has brought
a stain upon our character for bad faith and desertion which
no time will wipe away, and the recollection of which will
never be effaced from their minds.

August 19*th.*—I went to Brighton on Saturday to see the
Duke [of York]; returned to-day. The Pavilion is finished.
The King has had a subterranean passage made from the
house to the stables, which is said to have cost 3,000*l.* or
5,000*l.*; I forget which. There is also a bath in his apartment, with pipes to conduct water from the sea; these pipes
cost 600*l.* The King has not taken a sea bath for sixteen
years.

The Marquis of Londonderry is to be buried to-morrow
in Westminster Abbey. It is thought injudicious to have
anything like an ostentatious funeral, considering the circumstances under which he died, but it is the particular
wish of his widow. She seems to consider the respect
which is paid to his remains as a sort of testimony to his
character, and nothing will pacify her feelings or satisfy her
affection but seeing him interred with all imaginable honours.
It seems that he gave several indications of a perturbed
mind a short time previous to his death. For some time
past he had been dejected, and his mind was haunted with
various apprehensions, particularly with a notion that he
was in great personal danger. On the day (the 3rd of
August) he gave a great dinner at Cray to his political
friends, some of them finding the wine very good, wished to
compliment him upon it, and Arbuthnot called out, ' Lord
Londonderry!' He instantly jumped up with great vivacity,
and stood as if in expectation of something serious that was
to follow. When he was told that it was about the wine
they wished to speak to him, he sat down; but his manner
was so extraordinary that Huskisson remarked it to Wilmot
as they came home. In the last interview which the Duke of
Wellington had with him he said he never heard him converse upon affairs with more clearness and strength of mind

than that day. In the middle of the conversation, however, he said, 'To prove to you what danger I am in, my own servants think so, and that I ought to go off directly, that I have no time to lose, and they keep my horses saddled that I may get away quickly; they think that I should not have time to go away in a carriage.' Then ringing the bell violently, he said to the servant, 'Tell me, sir, instantly who ordered my horses here; who sent them up to town?' The man answered that the horses were at Cray, and had never been in town. The Duke desired the man to go, and in consequence of this strange behaviour wrote the letter to Bankhead which has been since published.

August 20*th*.—Knighton went with the King to Scotland, and slept in one of his Majesty's own cabins, that next to him. He is supposed to have been appointed Privy Purse. Bloomfield has got the mission to Stockholm. When Bloomfield was dismissed a disposition was shown to treat him in a very unceremonious manner; but he would not stand this, and displayed a spirit which he was probably enabled to assume in consequence of what he knows. When they found he was not to be bullied they treated with him, and gave him every honour and emolument he could desire.

September 22*nd*.—I saw Lady Bathurst on the 13th. Canning had not then sent his answer, and greatly surprised were the Ministers at the delay. Lord Liverpool's proposal to him was simple and unclogged with conditions—the Foreign Office and the lead in the House of Commons. The King's repugnance to his coming into office was extreme, and it required all the efforts of his Ministers to surmount it. The Duke of Wellington and Peel have all the credit of having persuaded the King to consent, but Lord Bathurst's arguments influenced him as much as those of any person, and he told Lady Conyngham that he was more satisfied by what Lord Bathurst had said to him on the subject than by any of the Ministers. I know that amongst the Canning party Lord Bathurst is supposed to have joined with the Chancellor in opposing his appointment. The danger in which the Duke of Wellington was sensibly affected the King, because

at this moment the Duke is in high favour with him; and
when he heard he was so ill he sent Knighton to him to
comfort him with a promise that he would reconsider the
proposal of receiving Canning, and the next day he signified
his consent.   I saw a note from Lady Conyngham to Lady
Bathurst, in which she gave an account of the uneasiness
and agitation in which the King had been in consequence of
the Duke's illness, saying how much she had suffered in
consequence, and how great had been *their* relief, when
Knighton brought word that he was better.   The ' dear
King,' she said, was more composed.   She added that she
(Lady B.) would hear that evening what would give her
pleasure, and this was that the King had agreed to take
Canning.   In a conversation also Lady C. said that she
did hope, now the King had yielded his own inclination
to the wishes and advice of his Ministers, that they would
behave to him better than they had done.   Canning was
sworn in on Monday.   His friends say that he was very well
received.   The King told Madame de Lieven that having
consented to receive him, he had behaved to him, *as he
always did,* in the most gentlemanlike manner he could, and
that on delivering to him the seals, he said to him that he
had been advised by his Ministers that his abilities and
eloquence rendered him the only fit man to succeed to the
vacancy which Lord Londonderry's death had made, and
that, in appointing him to the situation, he had only to
desire that he would follow the steps of his predecessor.
This Madame de Lieven told to Lady Jersey, and she to me.
It seems that the King was so struck with Lord Londonderry's manner (for he said to the King nearly what he said
to the Duke of Wellington), and so persuaded that some
fatal catastrophe would take place, that when Peel came to
inform him of what had happened, he said to him before he
spoke, 'I know you are come to tell me that Londonderry
is dead.'   Peel had just left him, and upon receiving the
despatches immediately returned; and when Lady Conyngham was told by Lord Mount Charles that there was a report
that he was dead, she said, 'Good God! then he has de-

stroyed himself.   She knew what had passed with the King,
and was the only person to whom he had told it.

September 23rd.—George Bentinck, who thinks there
never existed such a man as Canning, and who probably has
heard from him some circumstances connected with his
resignation at the time of the Queen's trial, told —— that
it was in consequence of a dispute between the King and
his Ministers concerning the payment of the expenses of the
Milan Commission.   The Ministers wished the King to pay
the expenses himself, and he wished them to be defrayed by
Government.   Lord Londonderry promised the King (without the concurrence of the other Ministers) that the expenses
should be paid by Government, but with money ostensibly
appropriated to other purposes.   This Canning could not
endure, and resigned.   Such is his story, which probably is
partly true and partly false.

November 5th.—I have been to Newmarket, Euston,
Riddlesworth, Rendlesham, Whersted, besides going to town
several times and to Brighton.   Since I left London for the
Doncaster races I have travelled near 1,200 miles.   At
Riddlesworth the Duke of York told me a great deal about the
Queen and Brougham, but he was so unintelligible that part
I could not make out and part I do not remember.   What
I can recollect amounts to this, that the Emperor of Austria
was the first person who informed the King of the Queen's conduct in Italy, that after the enquiry was set on foot a negotiation was entered into with the Queen, the basis of which was
that she should abdicate the title of Queen, and that to this
she had consented.   He said that Brougham had acted a
double part, for that he had acquiesced in the propriety of
her acceding to those terms, and had promised that he
would go over to her and confirm her in her resolution to
agree to them; that he had not only not gone, but that
whilst he was making these promises to Government he had
written to the Queen desiring her to come over.   The Duke
told me that a man (whose name he did not mention) came
to him and said, ' So the Queen comes over? '   He said, ' No,
she does not.'   The man said, ' I know she does, **for**

Brougham has written to her to come; I saw the letter.'
If Lord Liverpool and Lord Londonderry had thought
proper to publish what had been done on the part of
Brougham, he would have been covered with infamy; but
they would not do it, and he thinks they were wrong. The
rest I cannot remember.[1]

Welbeck, November 16th.—I have had a great deal of
conversation with Titchfield,[2] particularly about Canning,
and he told me this curious fact about his coming into
office :—When the King had consented to receive him he
wrote a letter nearly in these words to Lord Liverpool:
' The King thinks that the brightest jewel in the crown is
to extend his forgiveness [I am not sure that this was the
word[3]] to a subject who has offended him, and he therefore informs Lord L. that he consents to Mr. Canning
forming a part of the Cabinet.' This letter was communicated by Lord Liverpool to Canning, and upon reading it he
was indignant, as were his wife and his daughter. The

[1] [This is an erroneous and imperfect account of this important transaction, the particulars of which are related by Lord Brougham in his 'Memoirs,'
cap. xvi. vol. ii. p. 352, and still more fully by Mr. Yonge in his 'Life of
Lord Liverpool,' vol. iii. p. 52. Mr. Brougham had sent his brother James
to the Queen at Geneva to dissuade her from setting out for England, but,
as he himself observes, ' I was quite convinced that if she once set out she
never would stop short.' He met her himself at St. Omer, being the bearer
of a memorandum dated the 15th of April, 1820, which contained the terms
proposed by the King's Government. He went to St. Omer in company
with Lord Hutchinson, but Mr. Brougham, and not Lord Hutchinson, was
the bearer of these propositions. Lord Hutchinson had no copy of the document. The extraordinary part of Mr. Brougham's conduct was that he never
at all submitted or made known to the Queen the memorandum of the 15th
of April; and she knew nothing of it till she had reached London, when all
negotiation was broken off. This fact Lord Brougham does not explain in
his 'Memoirs;' but Lord Hutchinson declared in his report to Lord Liverpool that in truth Brougham ' did not appear to possess the smallest
degree of power, weight, or authority over the mind of the Queen' when at
St. Omer.]
[2] [The Marquis of Titchfield, eldest son of the fourth Duke of Portland,
Mr. Greville's first cousin, died in the twenty-eighth year of his age.]
[3] [The exact words in the King's letter to Lord Liverpool are ' extend
his grace and favour to a subject who may have incurred his displeasure.'
This letter, Lord Liverpool's letter transmitting it to Mr. Canning, and
Mr. Canning's answer to Lord Liverpool, are now all published in Mr.
Yonge's 'Life and Administration of Lord Liverpool,' vol. iii. p. 200.]

consequence was that he wrote a most violent and indignant reply, addressed to the same person to whom the other
letter had been addressed, and which was intended in like
manner to be shown to the King, as the King's letter was
to him.   Upon hearing what had passed, however, down
came Lord Granville and Mr. Ellis in a great hurry, and
used every argument to dissuade him from sending the
letter, urging that he had entirely misunderstood the pur-
port of the letter which had offended him; that it was
intended as an invitation to reconciliation, and contained
nothing which could have been meant as offensive; that the
country would be so dissatisfied (which ardently desired and
expected that he should come into office) if he rejected this
overture that he would not be justified in refusing his
services to the public, who so anxiously wished for them.
These arguments, vehemently urged and put in every
possible shape, prevailed, and the angry reply was put in
the fire, and another written full of gratitude, duty, and
acquiescence.

   London, November 24th.—The morning I left Welbeck I
had a long conversation with Titchfield upon various matters
connected with politics and his family, particularly relating
to Lord William's correspondence with Lord Liverpool about
the Government of India.   He showed me this correspondence, in which, as I anticipated, Lord William had the
worst of it.   Lord Liverpool's answer was unanswerable.
He showed me also a very long letter which he had received
from Lord William, together with the copies of the correspondence, which was written the evening before he went
abroad.   In this letter (which I only read once, and which
was so long that I cannot recollect it) he gave a detailed
account of his sentiments upon the Indian matter, with the
reasons for his having acted as he did, also his feelings with
regard to the manner in which Canning had behaved upon
the occasion and a conversation which he had with Mrs.
Canning.[1]   This latter I think exceedingly curious, because

   [1] [Mrs. Canning was the younger sister of Henrietta, wife of the fourth
Duke of Portland, both of them being the daughters and coheiresses of

it serves to show what the object and the pretensions of
Canning are in taking office, and exhibit that ambition the
whole extent of which he dares not show.   It seems that
the Directors were anxious that Lord William should be
appointed Governor-General, and this he knew through
friends of his in the Court.   Government, however, having
signified their dissent to his nomination, Lord Amherst was
nominated by the Court and accepted.   Lord William's
displeasure with Canning arises from an idea that Canning
was backward in supporting his interests in this matter, and
that he kept aloof from Lord William, and acquiesced in
his rejection without ever communicating with him on the
subject.   Had Canning stated to him the difficulties under
which he laboured, from his anxiety to serve him on the
one hand and his obligation of coinciding with his colleagues on the other, Lord William would not have hesitated to *desire* him to abandon his interests rather than
involve himself in any embarrassment on his account.   He
wrote to Lord Liverpool to complain that the Court of
Directors being inclined to nominate him, Lord L. had interposed his influence to prevent that nomination; that he
did not ask Lord L. to consent to his appointment, but
he did ask him not to interpose his influence to prevent
his nomination, because that nomination was essential to
his character, as proving that the Court of Directors were
satisfied of the injustice with which he had been treated in
the affair of the Vellore mutiny.   Lord Liverpool's answer
was short and civil, assuring him that he had neither
directly nor indirectly exerted any influence at all, main-
taining his right to give his opinion to the Directors in
case it had been asked, and stating that Lord Amherst had
been proposed by the Court and accepted by Government.[1]

Major-General John Scott of Balcomie. Lord William Bentinck, the Duke's
brother, was therefore a near connection, and Lord George Bentinck and
Lord John Bentinck, the Duke's sons, were by their mother's side Mrs.
Canning's nephews. Lady Charlotte Greville, Mr. Charles Greville's mother,
was of course connected with Mrs. Canning in the same degree as her brother
Lord William Bentinck.]

[1] [Lord Liverpool's letter to the King on this appointment has been published by Mr. Yonge in his Life of that statesman. He stated strongly to

Whilst this matter was still pending, and before Lord Amherst's appointment had been made known, Lord William went to Gloucester Lodge. He saw Mrs. Canning, and being anxious to acquire information concerning the Indian appointment, he told her that she had an opportunity of obliging him by telling him anything she knew concerning it. She answered very quickly and in a very bad humour, 'Oh, it is all settled; Lord Amherst is appointed.' She then put into his hand a letter which Canning had received that morning from the Duke of Portland, declining his offer of the Private Secretaryship for John and George, alleging as a reason the hostile politics of Lord William and Titchfield. Mrs. Canning said that she had no idea that they would not have supported Canning, that she was aware they differed on some matters of minor importance, but that she had imagined their general opinions to be similar; that she had conceived Lord William's opposition to have been directed against Lord Londonderry, and that it would have ceased with his death; that 'the present must be considered as a new Administration, and that Canning must be virtually Minister of the country.' Lord William replied that he could not view it in that light, that he thought it likely the introduction of Canning into the Cabinet might effect a beneficial influence on the measures of Government, and more particularly that a system of foreign policy might be adopted more congenial to his sentiments upon that subject; that it would give him the greatest pleasure to see such a change of measures as would enable him to give his support to a Government of which Canning was so conspicuous a member, but that he could not think that to be a new Administration which was composed (with the sole exception of

George IV. his opinion that although Lord William Bentinck was supported by a powerful party in the Court of Directors, he thought it would be 'humiliating to the Government and productive of the very worst effects to appoint to such a station a man who had taken so strong a part in Parliamentary Opposition. George IV. replied that he thought it 'highly unadvisable that Lord William Bentinck should be the successor of the Marquis of Hastings.' (Yonge's 'Life of Lord Liverpool,' vol. iii. p. 204.) Lord William Bentinck had previously been Governor of Madras at the time of the mutiny at Vellore.]

Canning) of precisely the same persons of which it consisted before he joined them.

George,[1] after having refused the Private Secretaryship, was talked over by Canning and accepted it. He tried to gain over John, but he refused to share it.

Canning wished that Manners Sutton should be appointed Governor-General, in order that Wynn might be made Speaker, and room made for Huskisson in the Cabinet; but Wynn would not have given up his situation, and it is very much suspected that if he had, the strength of Government would have been insufficient to procure his election as Speaker, so unpopular is he in the House.

December 24*th*.—The other day I went to Bushy with the Duke [of York], and as we passed over Wimbledon Common he showed me the spot where he fought his duel with the Duke of Richmond. He then told me the whole story and all the circumstances which led to it, most of which are in print. That which I had never heard before was that at a masquerade three masks insulted the Prince of Wales, when the Duke interfered, desired the one who was most prominent to address himself to him, and added that he suspected him to be an officer in his regiment (meaning Colonel Lennox), and if he was he was a coward and a disgrace to his profession; if he was not the person he took him for, he desired him to unmask, and he would beg his pardon. The three masks were supposed to be Colonel Lennox, the Duke of Gordon, and Lady Charlotte. This did not lead to any immediate consequences, but perhaps indirectly contributed to what followed. The Duke never found out whether the masks were the people he suspected.

The last time I was with him he told me a variety of particulars about the Duke of Wellington's conduct at the siege of Seringapatam, of Lord Harris's reluctance to entrust the command of a storming party to him, of his not arriving at the place of rendezvous the first night, of Lord Harris's

---

[1] [Lord George Bentinck, third son of the fourth Duke of Portland; born 1802, died 1848; distinguished in 1846 as the leader of the Protectionist party.]

anger and the difficulty with which he was brought to consent to his being employed the second night, when he distinguished himself so signally. Amongst various other matters, of which it was impossible to bring away a perfect recollection, from his confused manner of narrating, and particularly his inaccuracy as to dates, he told me (with many recommendations to secrecy) that which immediately explained to me the dislike which he certainly bears to the Duke and (which I did not know before) to Lord Londonderry. He said that after the retreat of our army under Sir J. Moore from Spain (he was not quite certain himself as to the exact period, though a reference to the history of that period will probably elucidate the matter) Lord L. sent for him, and communicated to him that it was the intention of Government to send out an expedition to Portugal, and to confer the command of it upon him. He replied that if called upon he should consider it his duty to serve, but he should never solicit any command. Nothing more passed at that time, but the newspapers by some means immediately got hold of this project and violently attacked the Government for thinking of sending him out. He does not appear to have known what intermediate deliberation led to a change in the determination of the Ministers in regard to himself. He says that Lord Chatham, who was much attached to him, and was then a Cabinet Minister, came to him one day and told him he was betrayed, and that he was sacrificed to make way for Sir A. Wellesley; that soon after this Lord L. sent for him, and said that he was extremely sorry that public opinion was so strongly against his appointment to the command of the army that it was impossible for Government to confer it upon him. Soon after this the expedition was formed, and Sir A. Wellesley was appointed to the command. This was the Duke's own version of the transaction.

1823.

Some particulars concerning the late King's will were told me by the Duke of York as we were going to Oatlands to shoot on Wednesday, the 8th of January, 1823. The King was empowered by Act of Parliament to make a will about the year 1766. In 1770 he made a will, by which he left all he had to the Queen for her life, Buckingham House to the Duke of Clarence, some property to the Duke of Kent, and to the Duke of York his second best George and some other trifling remembrance. He considered the Duke of York provided for by the Bishopric of Osnaburgh. Of this will three copies were made; one was deposited in the German *chancellerie* in England, one in Hanover, and the other it was believed the King kept himself. He afterwards resolved to cancel this will, and two of the copies of it were destroyed, the third still existing (I could not make out by what means—if he told me I have forgotten—or which copy it was that survived). In 1810 the King made another will, but for various reasons he always put off signing it, once or twice because he wished to make alterations in it; at length he appointed a day to sign it, but when the Chancellor brought it one of the witnesses was absent, and the signature was again postponed. Other days were afterwards fixed for this purpose, but before the signature was affixed the King was taken ill, and consequently the will never was signed. After the death of the King the only good will, therefore, was his original will of 1770, which was produced and read in the presence of the King, the Chancellor, Vice-Chancellor, Lord Liverpool, the Duke of York, Adair, the King's solicitor (Spyer his name), and one or two others whom he mentioned. Buckingham House, which had been left to the Duke of Clarence, had been twice sold; the Queen and the Duke of Kent were dead ; the only legatee, therefore, was the Duke of York. Now arose a difficulty—whether the property of the late King demised to the King or to the Crown. The Chancellor said that the only person who had anything to say to the will was the Duke of York; but the Duke and the King differed with regard to the right of inheritance, and the Duke, wishing to avoid any dispute or discussion on the subject, begged to wash his hands of the whole matter. The King conceives that the whole of the late King's property devolves upon him personally, and not upon the Crown, and he has consequently appropriated to himself the whole of the money and jewels. The money did not amount to more than 120,000*l.* So touchy is he about pecuniary matters that his Ministers have never dared to remonstrate with him, nor to tell him that he has no right so to act. The consequence is that he has spent the money, and has taken to himself the jewels as his own private property. The Duke thinks that he has no right thus to appropriate their father's property, but that it belongs to the Crown. The King has acted in a like manner with regard to the Queen's [Charlotte's] jewels. She possessed a great quantity, some of which had been given her by the late King on her marriage, and the rest she had received in presents at different times. Those which the late King had given her she conceived to belong to the Crown, and left them back to the present King; the rest she left to her daughters. The King has also appropriated the Queen's [Caroline's] jewels to himself, and conceives that they are his undoubted private property. The Duke thinks that the Ministers ought to have taken the opportunity of the coronation, when a new crown was to be provided, to state to him the truth with regard to the jewels, and to suggest that they should be converted to that purpose. This, however, they dared not do, and so the matter remains. The King had even a design of selling the library collected by the late King, but this he was obliged to abandon, for the Ministers and the Royal Family must have interfered to oppose so scandalous a transaction. It was therefore presented to the British Museum.

January 25*th.*—I came from Gorhambury with the Duke of Wellington last Wednesday, and he was very communicative. He gave me a detailed history of the late Congress,

VOL. I.   F

and told me many other things which I should be glad to recollect.

After the two treaties of Paris and Vienna the Allied Powers agreed to meet in Congress from time to time to arrange together any matters of general interest which might arise, and to settle and discuss any differences which might occur between any two Powers, a rule being laid down that the affairs of no Power should be discussed without that Power being invited to the deliberation. The affairs of Naples were the first that attracted their attention. Austria complained that the ramifications of the secret political societies which had sprung up at Naples tended to disturb and revolutionise the Italian possessions, and demanded the consent of the Allied Powers that she should abate the nuisance. The cause was deemed sufficient to justify her interference, and the events followed which are known. The Congress at Verona was assembled for the purpose of taking into consideration the affairs of Italy, and for discussing the propriety of relieving Naples from the burden of that military force which had been maintained there for the purpose of extinguishing the revolutionary spirit. At this Congress France came forward and complained that the revolution which had taken place in Spain menaced her internal tranquillity, and demanded the advice of Congress as to the measures she should adopt. In this it will be observed that the rule of every Power being called upon to attend a deliberation in which its affairs were to be discussed was dispensed with. Austria, Russia, and Prussia immediately replied that if she considered the Spanish revolution to be dangerous to her repose, she would be justified in stifling that revolution by force of arms, and offered to-coperate with her in the attempt. England refused to give any answer to the demands of France, and demanded in return what was her case against Spain. To this no answer was given. The part then taken by the Duke was to deprecate hostilities, both publicly as Plenipotentiary of England and privately in the various conversations which he had with the Emperor of Russia, who seems to have been the strongest advocate for making war with Spain. The imprudence of the Spaniards has afforded some colour to the right assumed by their enemies of interfering with their affairs, for they have upon several occasions attempted to foment the troubles which either existed or threatened to appear both in Naples and Piedmont; and the Emperor of Russia told the Duke that he had detected the Spanish Minister at St. Petersburg in an attempt to corrupt his soldiers at the time of the mutiny of the Guards, and that he had consequently sent him out of the country. The Duke replied that if the Emperor of Russia had reasonable grounds of complaint against Spain, he would be fully justified in declaring war against her, and that he would advise him to do so if he could march 150,000 men into Spain; but in suffering three years to elapse without making any complaint he had virtually renounced his right to complain, and that it was unfair to rake up a forgotten grievance against Spain at a time when she was menaced by another Power upon other grounds. The Duke said that the Emperor of Russia once talked to him of the practicability of marching an army into Spain, and seemed to think he might do so. The Duke said that the French Government would never allow it, when he said he could send them by sea. The Duke told him it would take 2,000 ships. One of the arguments of the Emperor of Russia was this : that constituted as their Governments were (military Governments) it was impossible for them to tolerate consistently with their own security any revolution which originated in military insubordination.

After the Congress the Duke returned to Paris, and found that not only Monsieur de Villèle was averse to war, but that the King, Monsieur, and the Duke and Duchess of Angoulême were equally disinclined to commence hostilities. His endeavours have been incessantly directed to confirm their pacific dispositions, and to induce the Spanish Government to display moderation in their language and conduct. I asked him if such were the sentiments of the ruling powers in France upon what the question now turned, and why all idea of war was not abandoned, since both parties

were pacifically inclined.   He said[1] that France had been
led into a dilemma by a series of erroneous measures, that
hers was a false position, that having made the demands she
had done to the Allied Powers, having held such lofty
language, and having made such a show of military preparation, her difficulty was how to retract and retrace her steps
with honour and credit to herself; that she was a nation
whose character depended in great measure upon her
military renown, and that it would reflect disgrace upon her
to have made such mighty preparations and assumed so
peremptory a tone without performing any action commen-
surate with the expectations she had raised.   He said that
appearances certainly became more warlike, but that he still
hoped peace would be maintained; that if war ensued it
would be entered into contrary to the interests and inclinations of all the parties concerned, and that it would have
been brought about by a succession of circumstances over
which they had no control; that it was impossible for two
armies to remain for a length of time so near each other
without mutual incursions being made, insults and injuries
exchanged, which must inevitably end in a state of warfare
and hostility; that the recall of the French Minister from
Madrid would contribute to this result, for both in the

---

[1] All this reasoning appears to me exceedingly false, and I do not understand a Government being compelled to adopt measures adverse to her
inclinations and injurious to her interests by circumstances which she could
not control.   A wise and vigorous statesman would break through such a
web as that in which the French politics are entangled, and I cannot comprehend how the honour of a nation is to be supported by an obstinate adherence to measures which she had been led incautiously to adopt, and which
were afterwards found to militate with her true interests.   If the councils of
France were directed by a Minister of a vigorous and independent character
—if such a Minister were to come forward and state frankly to Spain, and
announce to all Europe, that he would not invade the liberty and the rights
of Spain, and instantly put a stop to all hostile preparations, finding arguments for an act of magnanimity, moderation, and justice, which are never
wanting when some deed of lawless ambition and violent aggression is to be
perpetrated, would not such a man acquire a more solid reputation than he
who sacrifices to some punctilio the interests of his own country and the
happiness and repose of millions, how great soever might be the success
with which his efforts should be crowned?—[C. C. G.]

Cortes and the Andalusian Junta expressions would be
uttered offensive to the French Government, and misrepresentations would be made which would have the effect of
exasperating the parties and of widening the breach; and
that there being no agent of France at Madrid to furnish
explanations and destroy the effect of the misrepresentations,
there would be a constant correspondence between Madrid
and Paris, in which vent would be given to all the angry
feelings that ever existed.[1] The Duke advised that no
answer should be given to the notes of the three Powers, nor
to that of the French Minister. Had the Spanish Government declined to take notice of the notes, they would have
imposed upon them the difficulty of taking the next steps.
However, he admitted that the answer to the French note
was very moderate. There is no statesman in Spain. There
are some eloquent men in the Cortes, particularly Torreno
and Arguelles. Torreno is the ablest man, but he has
injured his character by peculation. The state of Spain is
such that the most violent and turbulent possess the greatest
share of influence. Portugal is in a state of greater intel-
lectual improvement, and amongst the Portuguese there are
some men of ability—Palmella, and another whose name I
have forgotten. But Spain is not only deficient in men of
education and talent to direct her councils, but she has no
army, and not one officer of capacity. Not one was formed
by the late war, for such were their vanity and ignorance
that they would learn nothing from the English.

Upon one occasion only the Spaniards gained a victory
the day on which St. Sebastian was stormed. Soult attacked
a Spanish corps commanded by General Freyre. When the
Duke was informed of the attack he hastened to the scene of
action and placed two British divisions in reserve, to support
the Spaniards, but did not allow them to come into action.
He found the Spaniards running away as fast as they could.

---

[1] These notes were addressed by the respective Courts to their own
Ministers at Madrid. The Spanish Minister for Foreign Affairs need not
have taken any notice of them whatever according to the forms of diplomatic
communication.—[C. C. G.]

He asked them where they were going. They said they were taking off the wounded. He immediately sent and ordered the gates of Irun, to which they were flying, to be shut against them, and sent to Freyre to desire he would rally his men. This was done, and they sustained the attack of the French; but General Freyre sent to the Duke to beg he would let his divisions support him, as he could not maintain himself much longer. The Duke said to Freyre's aide-de-camp, 'If I let a single man fire, the English will swear they gained the victory, and he had much better do it all himself; besides, look through my glass, and you will see the French are retreating.' This was the case, for a violent storm of rain had occurred, and the French, who had crossed a river, finding that it began to swell, and that their bridges were in danger of being carried away, had begun to retreat. The Spaniards maintained their position, but the Duke said he believed they owed it to the storm more than to their own resolution.

The Duke wrote to Alava some time ago (three years, I think) and desired him to advise the King from him, now that he had accepted the Constitution, to throw himself upon his Ministers. He has not written to Alava, nor Alava to him, for three years, because he knows that all letters are opened and read. He says the King of Spain is not clever, but cunning; his manners are good. He is in correspondence with the Allied Sovereigns, and is playing false. He has the means of corresponding, because, although his household is composed of men friendly to the revolution, there is no restraint upon his person, and he sees whomsoever he pleases. In case of war the French would obtain complete success. He conceives their object would be to obtain possession of the person of the King, to overthrow the Constitution, establish the King upon the throne with a Constitution perhaps similar to the French Charte, and to establish an army of occupation to maintain such an order of things till he should be able to form an army of his own.

The Duke saw the King of France twice while he was in Paris. He was much broken, but talked of living twelve or

fourteen years. The second time he was in better health and
spirits than the first time. Madame du Cayla sent to the Duke
to ask him to call upon her; he went twice and she was not at
home. At his levee the King said, ' Il y a une personne qui
regrette beaucoup de n'avoir pas eu le plaisir de vous voir.'
The courtiers told him the King meant Madame du C.
He went the same evening and saw her. She is a fine
woman, about forty, and agreeable. She sees the King every
Wednesday; he writes notes and verses to her, and he has
given her a great deal of money. He has built a house for
her, and given her a *terre* near St. Denis which is valued at
1,500,000 francs. The King likes M. de Villèle [1] exceedingly.
He has occasionally talked to the Duke of Bonaparte. One
day, when they were standing together at the window which
looks upon the garden of the Tuileries, he said, ' One day
Bonaparte was standing here with ——, and he said, pointing
to the Chamber of Deputies, " Vous voyez ce bâtiment-là: si
je les démuselais, je serais détrôné." " I," said the King,
" have given them freedom of debate, and I think I go on
very well with it." '

The Duke said he had been struck down by a musket
shot whilst reconnoitring the enemy as they were retreating
in the Pyrenees. The people round him thought he was
killed, but he got up directly. Alava was wounded a few
minutes before him, and Major Brooke nearly at the same
time. He is of opinion that Massena was the best French
general to whom he was ever opposed.

He said that Bonaparte had not the patience requisite
for defensive operations. His last campaign (before the
capture of Paris) was very brilliant, probably the ablest of

---

[1] Villèle was a lieutenant in the navy, and afterwards went to the
Isle of France, where he was a member of the council (or whatever the
legislation was called). At the revolution he returned to France and
lived with his family near Toulouse, became a member of the departmental
body, and subsequently Mayor of Toulouse; he was afterwards elected a
Member of the Chamber, when he distinguished himself by his talents for
debate, and became one of the chiefs of the Ultra party. He was a member
of the Duc de Richelieu's Government, which he soon quitted, and was one
of the principal instruments in overturning it. He anticipates a long administration.—[C. C. G.]

all his performances. The Duke is of opinion that if he had possessed greater patience he would have succeeded in compelling the Allies to retreat; but they had adopted so judicious a system of defence that he was foiled in the impetuous attacks he made upon them, and after a partial failure which he met with, when he attacked Blücher at Laon and Craon, he got tired of pursuing a course which afforded no great results, and leaving a strong body under Marmont to watch Blücher, he threw himself into the rear of the Grand Army. The march upon Paris entirely disconcerted him and finished the war. The Allies could not have maintained themselves much longer, and had he continued to keep his force concentrated, and to carry it as occasion required against one or other of the two armies, the Duke thinks he must eventually have forced them to retreat, and that their retreat would have been a difficult operation. The British army could not have reached the scene of operations for two months. The Allies did not dare attack Napoleon; if he had himself come up he should certainly have attacked him, for his army was the best that ever existed.

The Duke added that he traced back the present politics of France to their chagrin at the dissolution of the Family Compact. At the general pacification the Duke, on the part of the English Government, insisted upon that treaty not being renewed, and made a journey to Madrid for the purpose of determining the Spanish Government. Talleyrand and the King of France made great efforts to induce the Duke to desist from his opposition to the renewal of the treaty, and both were exceedingly mortified at being unable to shake the determination of our Government on this point.

The Duke of Wellington told me that Knighton[1] managed the King's affairs very well, that he was getting him out of debt very quickly, and that the Ministers were

---

[1] [Sir William Knighton, who was originally the King's physician, had been appointed Keeper of the King's Privy Seal and Receiver of the Duchies of Lancaster and Cornwall; but in fact he acted as the King's Private Secretary, and it was to the duties of that delicate office that the Duke's advice applied.]

well satisfied with him.   When he was appointed to the
situation he now holds, he called at Apsley House to announce it to the Duke, and expressed his hopes that the appointment would not displease him.   The Duke said that he
could have no objection, but he would give him a piece of
advice he trusted he would take in good part : this was,
that he would confine himself to the discharge of the functions
belonging to his own situation, and that he would not in
any way interfere with the Government; that as long as he
should so conduct himself he would go on very well, but that
if ever he should meddle with the concerns of the Ministers
he would give them such offence that they would not suffer
him to remain in a situation which he should thus abuse.
Knighton thanked him very much for his advice, and
promised to conform himself to it.   It seems that he told
this to the King, for the next time the Duke saw him the
King said he had heard the advice which he had given to
' a person,' and that he might depend upon that person's
following it entirely.

November 29th.—In the various conversations which I
have with the Duke of York he continually tells me a variety
of facts more or less curious, sometimes relating to politics,
but more frequently concerning the affairs of the Royal
Family, that I have neglected to note down at the time, and
I generally forget them afterwards.   I must acknowledge,
however, that they do not interest me so much as they
would many other people.   I have not much taste for Court
gossip.   Another reason, too, is the difficulty of making a
clear narrative out of his confused communications.   The
principal anecdotes he has told me have been, as well as I
recollect, relative to the Duchess of Gloucester's marriage,
to the Duke of Cumberland's marriage and all the dissensions to which that event gave rise in the Royal Family, the
differences between the King and Prince Leopold, and other
trifling matters which I have forgotten.   In all of these
histories the King acted a part, in which his bad temper,
bad judgment, falseness, and duplicity were equally conspicuous.   I think it is not possible for any man to have

a worse opinion of another than the Duke has of the King.
From various instances of eccentricities I am persuaded
that the King is subject to occasional impressions which
produce effects like insanity; that if they continue to
increase he will end by being decidedly mad. The last
thing which I have heard was at Euston the other day. I
went into the Duke's room, and found him writing; he got
up and told me that he was thrown into a great dilemma by
the conduct of the King, who had behaved extremely ill to
him. The matter which I could collect was this :—Upon the
disturbances breaking out in the West Indies it became
necessary to send off some troops as quickly as possible. In
order to make the necessary arrangements without delay,
the Duke made various dispositions, a part of which consisted in the removal of the regiment on guard at Windsor
and the substitution of another in its place. Orders were
expedited to carry this arrangement into effect, and at the
same time he communicated to the King what he had done
and desired his sanction to the arrangement. The Duke's
orders were already in operation, when he received a letter
from the King to say that he liked the regiment which
was at Windsor, and that it should not move; and in consequence of this fancy the whole business was at a stand-
still. Thus he thought proper to trifle with the interests of
the country to gratify his own childish caprice. He gave,
too, great offence to the Duke, in hindering his dispositions
from being carried into effect, at the same time.

The Duke told me another thing which he thought was indirectly connected with the first. It seems one of the people
about the Court had ordered some furniture to be removed
from Cumberland Lodge to Windsor (something for the Chapel).
Stephenson, as head of the Board of Works, on being informed this was done, wrote to the man to know by what orders
he had done it. The man showed the letter to the King, who
was exceedingly incensed, and wrote to Lord Liverpool to say
that Stephenson's letter was insulting to him, and desired he
might be turned out. After some correspondence on the
subject Lord Liverpool persuaded the King to reinstate

him; but he was obliged to make all sorts of apologies and
excuses for having done what it was his duty to do.
Stephenson is a friend and servant of the Duke's, and in his
ill-humour he tried to revenge himself upon the Duke as
well as on Stephenson, and he thwarted the Duke in his
military arrangements. What made his conduct the less
excusable was that it was important that these things should
be done quickly, and as the Duke was out of town a correspondence became necessary, by which great delay would be
caused.

1824.

March 6th.—Poor Titchfield [1] died last night at eight
o'clock, having lingered for some days in a state which
gave to his family alternate hopes and fears. He was
better till yesterday afternoon, when he was removed into
another room; soon after this he grew weaker, and at eight
o'clock he expired. He is a great loss to his family, of
which he was by much the cleverest member, and he was
well calculated to fill the situation in which fortune had
placed him. His talents were certainly of a superior description, but their efficacy was counteracted by the eccen-
tricity of his habits, the indolence of his mind, and his
vacillating and uncertain disposition. He was, however,
occasionally capable of intense application, and competent
to make himself master of any subject he thought fit to
grapple with; his mind was reflecting, combining, and
argumentative, but he had no imagination, and to passion,
'the sanguine credulity of youth, and the fervent glow of
enthusiasm' he was an entire stranger. He never had any
taste for society, and attached himself early to politics. He
started in life with an enthusiastic admiration for Mr.
Canning, but after two or three years, being thrown into the
society of many of his political opponents, he began to
entertain opinions very different from those of Mr. Canning.
He never, however, enlisted under any political banner, and

---

[1] [William Henry, Marquis of Titchfield, eldest son of the fourth Duke
of Portland.]

his great object seemed to be to prove to the world that he belonged to no party. After Mr. Canning came into office he took the earliest opportunity of informing his constituents that he was unfettered by any political connection with him. Titchfield was never at a public school, but was educated at home. Such an education—the most injudicious which can be given to a young man destined to fill a great situation— was not without its effect upon his mind. The superior indulgences and the early habits of authority and power in which he was brought up, without receiving correction from any of those levelling circumstances which are incidental to public schools, threw a shade of selfishness and reserve over his character, which time, the commerce of the world, and a naturally kind disposition had latterly done much to correct. The subject to which he had principally devoted his attention was political economy, and in the discussions in the House of Commons upon currency he had particularly distinguished himself. Whatever he attempted he had done so well that great expectations were entertained of his future success, and the indications he had given of talent will ensure to his memory a lasting reputation. He has died at a moment the most fortunate, perhaps, for his fame as a public man ; but his loss to his family is very great, and by them will be long felt and deeply lamented.

[An interval of two years occurs in the Journal, during which Mr. Greville wrote nothing.]

CHAPTER III.

The Panic of 1825—Death of Emperor Alexander—The Duke of Wellington's Embassy to St. Petersburg—Robinson Chancellor of the Exchequer—Small Notes Bill—Death of Arthur de Ros—George III. and Lord Bute —Illness and Death of the Duke of York—His Funeral—Lord Liverpool struck with Paralysis—Rundell's Fortune and Will—Copley and Philpots—The Cottage—Formation of Mr. Canning's Administration—Secession of the Tories—The Whigs join him—Dinner at the Royal Lodge—Difficulties of Canning's Government—Duke of Wellington visits the King—Canning's Death—Anecdotes of Mr. Canning—Recognition of South American States—His Industry—The Duke of Wellington on Canning—Lord Goderich's Administration formed—The Difficulty about Herries—Position of the Whigs—The King's letter to Herries—Peel and George IV.—Interview of Lord Lansdowne with the King—Weakness of the Government—First Resignation of Lord Goderich—Lord Harrowby declines the Premiership—Lord Goderich returns—Brougham and Rogers—Conversation and Character of Brougham—Lord Goderich's Ministry dissolved—Cause of its Dissolution—Hostility of Herries—Position of Huskisson and his Friends—Herries and Huskisson both join the New Cabinet.

1826.

February 12*th.*—The last three months have been remarkable for the panic in the money market, which lasted for a week or ten days—that is, was at its height for that time. The causes of it had been brewing for some months before, and he must be a sanguine and sagacious politician who shall predict the termination of its effects. There is now no panic, but the greatest alarm, and every prospect of great distress, and long continuation of it. The state of the City, and the terror of all the bankers and merchants, as well as of all owners of property, is not to be conceived but by those who witnessed it. This critical period drew forth many examples of great and confiding liberality, as well as some of a very opposite character. Men of great wealth and parsimonious habits came and placed their whole fortunes at the disposal of their bankers in order to support their credit. For many days the evil continued to augment so rapidly, and the demands upon the Bank were so great and increasing, that a Bank restriction was expected by everyone. So determined, however, were Ministers against this measure, that rather than yield to it they suffered the Bank to run the greatest risk of stopping; for on the evening of the day on which the alarm was at its worst there were only 8,000 sovereigns left in the till.[1] The next day gold was poured in, and from that time things got better.

In the midst of all this the Emperor Alexander died, and after a short period of doubt concerning his successor it was found that Nicholas was to mount the throne. The first act of the Russian Government was to communicate to ours their resolution no longer to delay a recognition of the independence of Greece, and their determination to support that measure if necessary by force of arms. They invited us to co-operate in this object, but intimated that if we were not disposed to join them they should undertake it alone. The Duke of Wellington is gone to Russia, ostensibly to compliment the new Emperor, but really to concert measures with the Russian Ministry for carrying this measure into effect; and it is remarkable that the Duke, upon taking leave of his friends and family to set out on this journey,

---

[1] [Mr. Baring (Lord Ashburton) stated in his pamphlet on this crisis, 'The gold of the Bank was drained to within a very few thousand pounds, for although the public returns showed a result rather less scandalous, a certain Saturday night closed with nothing worth mentioning. It was then that the Bank applied to Lord Liverpool for an Order in Council to suspend cash payment. A conference took place between Lord Liverpool, Mr. Huskisson, the governor of the Bank, and Mr. Baring. The suspension of cash payments was happily averted, chiefly as it was said by the accidental discovery of a box of one-pound Bank of England notes, to the amount of a million and a half, which had never been issued, and which the public were content to receive.' Mr. Tooke, however, states in his 'History of Prices' (Continuation, vol. iv. p. 342) that the lowest amount of the banking treasure was on the 24th of December, 1825: Coin 426,000*l.*; bullion, 601,000*l.*: in all, 1,027,000*l.*]

was deeply affected, as if he had some presentiment that he should never return. Alava told me that he had frequently taken leave of him, when both expected that they should never meet again, yet neither upon that occasion nor upon any other in the course of the seventeen years that he has known him did he ever see him so moved. Lady Burghersh said that when he took leave of her the tears ran down his cheeks; he was also deeply affected when he parted from his mother.

In the discussion which took place on Friday night in the House of Commons, when the Chancellor of the Exchequer [1] opened his financial plan, he is deemed to have made a very bad speech, and Huskisson a very good one. Robinson is probably unequal to the present difficult conjuncture; a fair and candid man, and an excellent Minister in days of calm and sunshine, but not endowed with either capacity or experience for these stormy times, besides being disqualified for vigorous measures by the remissness and timidity of his character. However, though it is the peculiar province of the Finance Minister to find a remedy for these disorders, he may well be excused for not doing that which the united wisdom of the country seems unequal to accomplish. All men agree as to the existence of the evil, and all differ as to the causes of it and the measures which will effect its removal; not one man seems to see his way clearly through the difficulty; however, 'time and the hour runs through the roughest day,' and probably the country will what is called right itself, and then great credit will be given to somebody or other who deserves none.

February 20th.—The Small Notes Bill,[2] as it is called, lowered the funds and increased the alarm among the

---

[1] [Right Hon. Frederick John Robinson, Chancellor of the Exchequer from January 1823 to April 1827; afterwards Viscount Goderich and Earl of Ripon.]

[2] [On the 10th of February the Chancellor of the Exchequer moved in Committee 'That all promissory notes payable on demand issued by licensed bankers in England or by the Bank of England for less than 5*l*. shall not be issued or circulated beyond the 5th of April next.' Mr. Huskisson made an able speech in support of the proposal, showing that the inflation pro-

monied men. Numerous were the complaints of the inefficacy of the measure for present relief, numerous the
predictions of the ultimate impossibility of carrying it into
effect. In the City, however, on Thursday afternoon, things
began to improve; there was more confidence and cheerfulness. On Friday evening the Chancellor of the Exchequer comes down to the House and surprises everyone
by abandoning one part of his plan, and authorising the
Bank to issue one pound notes till October. The immediate
cause of this alteration was a communication which Hudson
Gurney made to the Chancellor, that if he persisted in his
Bill he should send up 500,000l. which he had in Bank of
England notes and change them for sovereigns, and that all
country bankers would follow his example. From this he
found that it would be impossible to persist in his original
plan. The great evil now is a want of circulating medium,
and as the immediate effect of the measure would be another
run upon the Bank, and that probably all the gold drawn
from it would disappear—for men now are anxious to hoard
gold—this evil would be increased tenfold. The whole
country is in distress from the absence of circulating medium for the common purposes of life; no country banker
will issue notes, for they are instantly returned upon his
hands and exchanged for gold.· The circulation of country
notes being generally confined within a very limited extent,
the holders of them can easily present them for payment.
The circulation of a quantity of Bank of England paper will
relieve the immediate distress arising from this necessity,
and the difficulty of exchanging them for gold will ensure
the continuance of their circulation. When men find that
they must take notes, and that gold is not to be had without
so much pain and trouble, they will be contented to take
the notes to which they have been accustomed, and will

duced by the small note paper currency had greatly contributed to cause
and aggravate the panic ('Huskisson's Speeches,' vol. ii. p. 444). Mr.
Baring, afterwards Lord Ashburton, opposed the restriction of small notes,
but with small success. The period allowed for the contraction of their
circulation was, however, extended to the 10th of October.]

think the paper of their own bankers as good as that of the Bank of England, besides the advantage of being less exposed to the losses arising from forgery. This is the argument of the opponents of Robinson's Bill. It is generally thought that the Ministers have disgraced themselves by their precipitation and by the crudeness of their measures. Hitherto they have done nothing towards removing the present distress, or satisfying the minds of men, but the contrary. Robinson is obviously unequal to the present crisis. His mind is not sufficiently enlarged, nor does he seem to have any distinct ideas upon the subject; he is fighting in the dark.

Everybody knows that Huskisson is the real author of the finance measures of Government, and there can be no greater anomaly than that of a Chancellor of the Exchequer who is obliged to propose and defend measures of which another Minister is the real though not the apparent author. The funds rose nearly two per cent. upon this alteration in the Bill before the House, on account of the prospect of an abundance of money. Still it is thought that nothing will be sufficient to relieve the present distress but an issue of Exchequer bills. So great and absorbing is the interest which the present discussions excite that all men are become political economists and financiers, and everybody is obliged to have an opinion.

February 24th.—I have been since yesterday the spectator of a melancholy scene and engaged in a sad office. Arthur de Ros,[1] who was taken ill a fortnight ago, became worse on Monday night. After this time he was scarcely ever sensible, and yesterday, at a quarter-past two, he expired. After they had given up all hopes they were induced again to suffer them to revive from the disappearance of the most unfavourable symptoms; but this was only the weakness which preceded dissolution, and a few moments after his brother Henry had told me that he did not despair he came and said that all was over, and a little while after Rose

[1] [Colonel the Hon. Arthur John Hill de Ros, born 1793, died February 1826. He was aide-de-camp to his Royal Highness the Duke of York.]

announced that he had ceased to breathe. He died tranquilly, and did not suffer at all. I never saw such a distress. His father, mother, sisters, William, and his wife went immediately to Boyle Farm. Henry would have followed them, but I persuaded him to go home. He went first to Mrs. ——, to whom Arthur had been attached for ten years, and after a painful interview with her he came to his own house; he has since been too ill to move. I have never seen grief so strong and concentrated as his; it has exhausted his body and overwhelmed his mind, and though I knew him to have been much attached to his brother, I did not believe him capable of feelings so acute as those which he has evinced. William is much more calm and resigned, a strange, unaccountable thing considering the characters of the two men —the one so indifferent, and with feelings so apparently deadened to the affections of this world, and the other with a sensibility so morbid, and such acute susceptibility and strong feelings, that the least thing affects him more deeply than very serious concerns do other men.

Arthur was an excellent creature, and will be regretted by the Duke and deeply lamented by all who knew him intimately. His talents were not brilliant, but he had good sound sense, and was besides modest, diligent, honest, and trustworthy in a high degree. There breathed not a more honourable man, and as his ambition did not extend beyond the sphere in which fortune had placed him and he was contented with his destiny, but for this illness his career might have been long and prosperous. I went last night to sleep at the house, that it might not appear to have been entirely abandoned to the care of servants. The only wish he expressed was that Francis Russell should succeed him, which I have no doubt he will do.

February 25th.—Received a letter from the Duke of York (to whom I had written to announce poor Arthur's death) expressive of the greatest regret for his loss.

March 2nd.—I am just come from poor Arthur's funeral. There were present William de Ros, the two Hills, Craufurd, Torrens, Taylor, Francis Russell, Campbell, and B. Paget. The Duke appointed Francis his aide-de-camp directly.

July 2nd.—Four months since I have written anything. The Duke of York has been dangerously ill, and it is still doubtful whether he will recover. I was with him at Frogmore before Ascot; we went with the King to see Windsor Castle. His Majesty has since been very much annoyed about the Duke, cried a great deal when he heard how bad he was, and has been twice to see him.

The elections have been particularly violent and the contests very numerous. A batch of Peers has been made; everybody cries out against Charles Ellis's peerage[1] (Lord Seaford); he has no property, and is of no family, and his son is already a Peer. The King, when these other Peers were created, asked Canning to name somebody. He said he had nobody about whom he was interested but Charles Ellis, and the King consenting to his elevation, it was all arranged without his knowledge. However, it is thought very ridiculous, and that he would have done much better to have declined it. Clanricarde, too, being made a Marquis and an English Peer is thought an indirect exertion of Canning's influence.

London, December 14th.—The Duke of York very ill; has been at the point of death several times from his legs mortifying. Canning's speech the night before last was most brilliant; much more cheered by the Opposition than by his own friends. He is thought to have been imprudent, and he gave offence to his colleagues by the concluding sentence of his reply, when he said, '*I* called into existence the new world to redress the balance of the old.' The *I* was not relished. Brougham's compliment to Canning was magnificent, and he was loudly cheered by Peel; altogether it was a fine display.

Yesterday the Duke [of York] told me that the late King

---

[1] [Charles Rose Ellis, created Baron Seaford in 1826. Lord Seaford was the father of Charles Augustus Ellis, who succeeded to the title of Lord Howard de Walden through his mother, Elizabeth Catherine Caroline Hervey, granddaughter of the fourth Earl of Bristol, who was the last Baron Howard de Walden, as heir general of Thomas, first Baron. The son of Lord Seaford had married a daughter of the fifth Duke of Portland, and was consequently a connection of Mr. Canning.]

[George III.] was walking with him one day at Kew, and his Majesty said, 'The world tells many lies, and here is one instance. I am said to have held frequent communication with Lord Bute, and the last time I ever saw or spoke to him was in that pavilion in the year 1764.' The King went over to breakfast with his mother, the Princess Dowager, and she took him aside and said, ' There is somebody here who wishes very much to speak to you.' ' Who is it ?' ' Lord Bute.' ' Good God, mamma! how could you bring him here? It is impossible for me to hold any communication with Lord Bute in this manner.' However, he did see him, when Lord Bute made a violent attack upon him for having abandoned and neglected him. The King replied that he could not, in justice to his Ministers, hold any communication with him unknown to them, when Lord Bute said that he would never see the King again. The King became angry in his turn, and said, ' Then, my Lord, be it so, and remember from henceforth we never meet again.' And from that day he never beheld Lord Bute or had any communication with him.

1827.

Friday night, January 5th, half-past one.—I am just come from taking my last look at the poor Duke.[1] He expired at twenty minutes after nine. Since eleven o'clock last night the physicians never left his room. He never moved, and they repeatedly thought that life was extinct, but it was not till that hour that they found it was all over. The Duke of Sussex and Stephenson were in the next room; Taylor, Torrens and Dighton, Armstrong and I were upstairs. Armstrong and I had been there about half an hour when they came and whispered something to Dighton and called out Taylor. Dighton told Torrens and they went out; immediately after Taylor came up, and told us it was all over and begged we would go downstairs. We went directly into the room. The Duke was sitting exactly as at the

---

[1] [His Royal Highness the Duke of York, second son of King George III., died on the 5th of January, 1827.]

moment he died, in his great arm-chair, dressed in his grey dressing-gown, his head inclined against the side of the chair, his hands lying before him, and looking as if he were in a deep and quiet sleep. Not a vestige of pain was perceptible on his countenance, which, except being thinner, was exactly such as I have seen it a hundred times during his life. In fact, he had not suffered at all, and had expired with all the ease and tranquillity which the serenity of his countenance betokened. Nothing about or around him had the semblance of death; it was all like quiet repose, and it was not without a melancholy satisfaction we saw such evident signs of the tranquillity of his last moments.

In about a quarter of an hour Taylor and Halford set off to Windsor to inform the King; the Duke of Sussex went to the Princess Sophia; letters were written to all the Cabinet Ministers, to the Archbishop of Canterbury, the Bishop of London, and the Speaker of the House of Commons. Orders were given that the great bell of St. Paul's should toll. The servants were then admitted to see the Duke as he lay. Worley [1] was very much affected at the sight, and one woman, the wife of Kendal, cried bitterly, and I saw her stoop down and kiss his hand. The room was then cleared and surrendered to the Lord Chamberlain's people. Thus did I take my last leave of the poor Duke. I have been the minister and associate of his pleasures and amusements for some years, I have lived in his intimacy and experienced his kindness, and am glad that I was present at this last sad occasion to pay my poor tribute of respect and attachment to his remains.

After the October meetings of 1825 the Duke came to town, not in good health. At the end of November the Duchess of Rutland died, which was a great blow to him, and probably made him worse. A short time after her funeral he went to Belvoir, when the Duke of Rutland took him down into the vault, where he stayed an hour and returned excessively chilled. From that moment he grew

---

[1] [Worley was the Duke's stud-groom.]

worse till the time of the Ascot races. We went to Frogmore two days before the party began, and for those two
days he led a quiet life. When the party was assembled he
lived as he had been used to do, going to the races, sitting at
table, and playing for hours at whist. He slept wretchedly
and seldom went to bed, but passed the greater part of the
night walking about the room or dozing in his chair. I
used to go into his room, which was next to mine, the
moment I was out of bed, and generally found him in his
dressing-gown, looking harassed and ill. He showed me his
legs, which were always swelled. Still he went on till the
last day of the party, and when we got to town he was so
ill that M'Gregor, who came to him that night, thought
him in danger. From that moment the illness was established which has ended in his death. They began by
putting him through several courses of mercury, and they
sent him to the Greenwoods' villa at Brompton. Here he
continued to receive everybody who called on him, and went
out in his carriage every day. They always said that he was
getting better. In August he went to Brighton, and soon
after his arrival his legs mortified. It was then that Taylor
went down to him and told him that he was in great and
immediate danger. He received the information with perfect composure. The gangrene, however, was stopped, and he
came to town to the Duke of Rutland's house. The dropsy
continued to make rapid progress, and some time in September he was tapped; twenty-two pints of water were drawn
from him. This operation was kept secret, for the Duke
did not like that his situation should be known. He recovered from the operation and regained his strength; no
more water formed in his body, but there was still water in
his system, and a constant discharge from his legs, which
occasioned him great pain and made wounds which were
always open and extending. These wounds again produced
gangrene, but they always contrived to stop its progress,
and put the legs in a healing condition. As often, however,
as the legs began to heal the water began to rise, and the
medicines that were given to expel the water drove it again

to the legs, through which it made its way, making fresh
sores and entailing fresh mortification. In this way he
went on, the strength of his constitution still supporting
him, till towards the end of December, when the constitution could resist no longer; his appetite totally failed, and
with loss of appetite came entire prostration of strength,
and in short a complete break-up. From that moment it
was obvious that his recovery was impossible, but he continued to struggle till the 5th of January, although he had
tasted no solid food whatever for above a fortnight. At all
the different periods at which his state was critical it was
always made known to him, and he received the intimation
with invariable firmness and composure. He said that he
enjoyed life but was not afraid to die. But though perfectly
acquainted with his own danger he never could bear that
other people should be informed of it, and so far from
acknowledging it, he always told his friends that he was
better, and his language was invariably that of a man who
did not doubt of his recovery. He was particularly anxious
that nobody should know he had been tapped, and it was
not till many weeks after that operation that he talked of it
one day to me. Up to the last moment that I saw him (the
day week before he died) he told me he was better, and he
desired me to tell Montrond, who had called upon him, that
he would see him as soon as he was well enough. He held
the same language to everybody until the day previous to
his death, when he sent for Taylor and Stephenson into his
room. He could then hardly speak, but he took hold of
Stephenson's hand, and looking at Taylor, said, ' I am now
dying.' He tried to articulate something else, but he was
unintelligible. About a fortnight before his death, soon
after his appetite began to fail, Taylor had to announce to
him his danger. He received the intelligence with the
same coolness he had before shown, but it was not without
difficulty that he admitted the conviction. A few days after
he received the Sacrament, which was administered by the
Bishop of London, in the presence of Sir H. Halford, Taylor,
and the Princess Sophia. He was then very weak, but calm

and collected during the ceremony. When it was over he shook hands with the men and kissed the Princess. The King saw him the next day, but he was in a lethargic state nearly the whole time that he was there. For many days before his death the physicians thought that every day must close the scene, but such was the natural strength of his constitution that he evinced a tenacity of life and maintained a struggle which astonished them all, and of which they unanimously declared that their practice had never furnished them with a similar instance. It seems that three years ago, when he was very unwell, M'Gregor told him that unless he was more prudent he would certainly be afflicted with dropsy. He had been subject to spasms, and in consequence of them was averse to lie down in bed, and to this pernicious habit and that of sitting for many hours together at table, or at cards, they attribute the origin of the complaint which has terminated so fatally. Had he been a more docile patient, from the amazing vigour of his constitution he might have looked forward to a very long life. His sufferings in the course of his illness have been very great, and almost without cessation. Nothing could exceed the patience and courage with which he endured them ; his serenity and good humour were never disturbed, and he never uttered a word or complaint, except occasionally at the length of his confinement. He not only saw all the visitors who chose to call upon him, even those with whom he was not in habits of intimacy, but he transacted the whole of his public business every day, and every paper was laid before him and every detail gone through as if he had been in perfect health. This he continued to within a few days of his death, till his strength was so entirely exhausted that he lay in a state of almost complete insensibility. It is remarkable that from the beginning to the end of his illness I never saw him that he did not tell me that he was a great deal better, and he never wrote to me without assuring me that he was going on as well as possible.

February 12th.—The Duke of York was no sooner dead than the public press began to attack him, and while those

private virtues were not denied him for which he had
always been conspicuous, they enlarged in a strain of severe
invective against his careless and expensive habits, his
addiction to gambling; and above all they raked up the old
story of Mrs. Clark and the investigation of 1809, and published many of his letters and all the disgusting details of
that unfortunate affair, and that in a manner calculated to
throw discredit on his character. The newspapers, however,
soon found they had made a mistake, that this course was
not congenial to public feeling, and from that moment their
columns have been filled with panegyrics upon his public
services and his private virtues. The King ordered that the
funeral should be public and magnificent; all the details of
the ceremonial were arranged by himself. He showed great
feeling about his brother and exceeding kindness in pro-
viding for his servants, whom the Duke was himself unable
to provide for. He gave 6,000l. to pay immediate expenses
and took many of the old servants into his own service.
There appeared a few days after the Duke's death an
infamous forgery, purporting to be a letter or declaration
written by him a short time before his death (principally
upon the subject of the Catholic question), which, however, was
disavowed by Taylor, but not till after many thousand copies
had been sold. I dare say many people believe still that he
was the author of this pamphlet. All his effects either have
been or will be sold by auction. The funeral took place a
fortnight after his death.   Nothing could be managed
worse than it was, and except the appearance of the soldiers
in the chapel, which was extremely fine, the spectacle was
by no means imposing; the cold was intense, and it is only
marvellous that more persons did not suffer from it. As it
is the Bishop of Lincoln has died of the effects of it;
Canning has been dangerously ill, and is still very unwell;
and the Dukes of Wellington and Montrose were both very
seriously unwell for some days after. The King was very
angry when he heard how miserably the ceremony had been
performed. I have been this evening to hear Peel move the
address of condolence to the King, which Canning would

have done if he had been here; and it is a pity he was not, for Peel did it very ill: it was poor and jejune, and undistinguished by eloquence or the appearance of deep feeling. I was greatly disappointed, for I expected to hear a worthier tribute to his merits. Canning was very anxious to have been here to have performed this duty himself. The letters which he wrote to the Royal Family abroad announcing the event of his death were admirable and gave great satisfaction to the King.

February 21st.—Three days ago Lord Liverpool was seized with an apoplectic or paralytic attack. The moment it was known every sort of speculation was afloat as to the probable changes this event would make in the Ministry. It was remarked how little anybody appeared to care about the *man;* whether this indifference reflects most upon the world or upon him, I do not pretend to say. A report was generally circulated that the Duke of Cumberland was dead, which was believed, but turns out to be untrue.

Old Rundell (of the house of Rundell and Bridge, the great silversmiths and jewellers) died last week, and appointed Robarts one of his executors. Robarts called on me this morning, and told me he had been yesterday to Doctors' Commons to prove the will. Rundell was eighty years old, and died worth between 1,400,000*l.* and 1,500,000*l.*, the greater part of which is vested in the funds. He has left the bulk of his property to his great-nephew, a man of the name of Neal, who is residuary legatee and will inherit 900,000*l.*—this Mr. Neal had taken care of him for the last fourteen years—to a woman who had lived with him many years, and in whose house he died, and to two natural sons by her he only left 5,000*l.* apiece. The old man began the world without a guinea, became in the course of time partner in that house during its most flourishing period, and by steady gains and continual parsimony amassed this enormous wealth. He never spent anything and lived wretchedly. During the panic he came to Robarts, who was his banker, and offered to place at his disposal any sum he might require. When the executors went to prove the will, they were told at Doctors' Commons that it was the largest sum that ever had been registered there.

March 13*th.*—Since the debate on the Catholic question there has been a great expectation that Canning would resign. Many of his friends think he made an imprudent speech that night, and if he had not lashed the Master of the Rolls so severely that he would have got more votes.[1] The truth is he was mightily nettled by Dr. Philpots' pamphlet and at Copley making a speech taken entirely from it. The Master protested that he had no idea of offending Canning, and until he got up had no notion that Canning had taken offence at his speech. The question was lost by accident; several pro-Catholics were suddenly taken ill or arrived too late for the division, and the election petitions went all against them.

March 16*th.*—On Wednesday at the Council at St. James's the King desired I would go down to Windsor, that he might speak to me. I went down on Thursday to the Cottage, and, after waiting two hours and a half, was ushered into his bedroom. I found him sitting at a round table near his bed, in a *douillette*, and in pretty good health and spirits. He talked about his horses and told some old stories, lamented the death of the Duke of York, which he said was a loss to him such as no one could conceive, and that he felt it every instant. He kept me about an hour, was very civil, and then dismissed me.

Canning made an apology to the Master of the Rolls for his severity in the debate on the Catholic question.

March 25*th.*—When the King heard of Lord Liverpool's illness he was in great agitation. He sent for Peel in the night, and told him he must see the Duke of Wellington. Peel endeavoured to dissuade him, but in vain. The Duke was sent for, but he refused to go. He sent the King word that he had nothing to say to him, and that it would not be

---

[1] [Sir John Copley was then Master of the Rolls, but this occurrence did not prevent Canning from making him Lord Chancellor on the 2nd of May following, when he was raised to the peerage with the title of Baron Lyndhurst.]

fair to his colleagues that he should see the King at such a moment. Consequently he saw none of his Ministers till he saw Canning, who was taken to the Pavilion in a chair one day. There have been a variety of reports about Lord Liverpool's successor and a new Administration, as always happens on such occasions.

The King is in very good health and excellent spirits. He had a large party at the Lodge last week, and Canning, the Granvilles, Carlisles, Lievens, are going there next week. Mount Charles told me yesterday that next week he thinks something must be decided, and he told me what I did not know, that the King's opinions on the Catholic question are just the same as those of the Duke of York, and equally strong. This is the great difficulty which Canning has to get over with him. He does not much like Canning, though C. does everything he can to gratify and please him. Mount Charles told me that his mother (Lady Conyngham) has strong opinions in favour of the Catholics, but that she never talks to the King on the subject, nor indeed upon politics at all.

April 13th.—The King came to town a week ago. From the moment of his arrival every hour produced a fresh report about the Administration; every day the new appointment was expected to be declared, and the Ministers Peel, Lord Bathurst, Duke of Wellington, and Canning were successively designated as the persons chosen to form a Government. He had no sooner arrived than he saw his Ministers *seriatim,* but nothing could induce him to come to any determination. He wavered and doubted, and to his confidants, with whom he could bluster and talk big, he expressed in no measured terms his detestation of Liberal principles, and especially of Catholic Emancipation. He begged his Ministers to stand by him, and day after day elapsed, and nothing was settled. In the meantime London was alive with reports; and the *on dit* of the day, repeated with every variety of circumstance and with the usual positiveness of entire ignorance, would fill a volume. Time trept on, and Parliament was to adjourn on the 13th (this day). On the 9th Canning went to the King, and, after a long audience, he came away without anything being settled. On the 10th he went again, and told his Majesty that longer delay was impossible, and that he must come to some determination. On the evening of the 10th we received a note from Lord Bathurst, saying that the King had desired Canning to form an Administration on the principles of that of which Lord Liverpool had been at the head. This was not generally known that evening. Last night it was said that the Duke of Wellington would not remain in the new Cabinet, and we heard that Peel had resigned. To-day everything will probably be known. Canning and his friends say that the King has behaved admirably in this business, and they affect to consider his appointment unconditional and unfettered ; but this is by no means the view which the others take of it. The King, however, has acted in such a way that all his Ministers (except those whose interest it now is to laud him to the skies) are disgusted with his doubting, wavering, uncertain conduct, so weak in action and so intemperate in language. It is now supposed that he has been influenced by Knighton in coming to this determination, in which he certainly has acted in a manner quite at variance with his professions and the whole tenor of his language. It must be owned, if this is so, that although Canning has gained his point—has got the power into his hands and is nominally Prime Minister—no man ever took office under more humiliating circumstances or was placed in a more difficult and uncertain situation ; indeed, a greater anomaly cannot be imagined. Canning, disliked by the King, opposed by the aristocracy and the nation, and unsupported by the Parliament, is appointed Prime Minister. The King, irresolute and uncertain, is induced to nominate a man whose principles and opinions he fears and dislikes by the advice and influence of his physician. The measure which is of paramount importance Canning cannot carry as he desires and believes to be necessary ; he must form a Cabinet full of disunion,

and he is doubtful what support he can expect from the old
adherents of Government, by whom he is abhorred.

The writ was moved for Canning yesterday by Wynne,
'he having accepted the office of First Commissioner of
the Treasury.' This morning the Chancellor, Peel, Lord
Westmoreland, and the Duke of Wellington resigned.
Lord Bathurst immediately wrote to Canning, saying that,
finding they had resigned, he could not avoid sending in
his resignation also; that it was unnecessary to enter
into explanations, which could only tend to widen the
breach such a separation must make. Afterwards Lord
Melville resigned, although well with Canning and a
friend to the Catholics; he said he could not desert the
men with whom he had acted for so many years. The
Whigs seem greatly elated at the breaking up of this Administration. The Tories evidently think Canning is in a
scrape, that he will not be able to form a Government, and
that the power will return into their hands. How Canning
and his friends feel is not yet known, nor what the King
feels at being deserted by half his Cabinet. The opinion
prevalent with the Opposition is that Canning has been
deserted by his colleagues, who induced him to accept the
Government by promising their support and adherence, and
that when he had taken the final step they left him to make
the arrangements and fill up their places as he could. This,
however, is not the case. I saw George Dawson [1] this evening,
and he assured me that Canning had received ample notice
from all these Ministers that they would not hold office
under him, and that if he was appointed Prime Minister
they should resign. Peel told him this three weeks ago:
'that he could not, with a due regard to his own character,
continue in office under a man whose opinions are so dia-
metrically opposite to his own upon the most important
question; that he had no views of personal ambition, but

[1] [The Right Hon. George Robert Dawson was Secretary of the Treasury
from 1828 to 1830, and was made a Privy Councillor on resigning that office.
He married in 1816 Mary, the eldest daughter of the first Sir Robert Peel
and was consequently the brother-in-law of Mr. Peel, the Minister.]

that as the administration of Ireland was his peculiar province it was impossible they should not come into constant
collision upon that subject.' They had no objection to act
with Canning, always considering him as one of the most
influential members of the Cabinet, but they could not hold
offices *under* him. He said that he could not imagine how
Canning with his knowledge could take such a step, and it is
evident that he has no idea of his being able to carry on the
Government at all.

April 30th.—From the period of Canning's acceptance
of office up to Thursday night there have been continual
negotiations between Canning and the Whigs, and it is not
possible to imagine greater curiosity and more intense anxiety
than have been exhibited during the interval.   The violence
and confusion of parties have been extreme—the new Ministers
furious with their old colleagues, the ex-Ministers equally
indignant with those they left behind them.

May 12th.—It is necessary to go back to the first formation of the Government.[1]   As soon as Canning had got
the King's commission he began to negotiate, and the
Whigs readily enough entered into negotiation.   The friends
of Ministers resigned one after another, and for some time it
seemed very doubtful whether Canning would be able to form
a Government at all.   His first measure was, however, very

[1] [The Administration formed by Mr. Canning was thus constituted :—
Mr. Canning, First Lord of the Treasury and Chancellor of the Exchequer.
Lord Lyndhurst, Lord High Chancellor.
Earl of Harrowby, Lord President of the Council.
Duke of Portland, Lord Privy Seal, and afterwards the Earl of Carlisle.
Lord Dudley, Secretary of State for Foreign Affairs.
Lord Goderich, Secretary of State for Colonial Affairs and War.
Mr. Sturges Bourne, Secretary of State for the Home Department
(this office was shortly afterwards transferred to the Marquis of Lansdowne.)
Mr. Huskisson, President of the Board of Trade.
Mr. Wynn, President of the Board of Control.
Lord Bexley, Chancellor of the Duchy of Lancaster.
Viscount Palmerston, Secretary at War.
Mr. Tierney, Master of the Mint.
The Duke of Clarence was named Lord High Admiral.
The office of Commander-in-Chief remained vacant during the Adminis-
tration of Mr. Canning. This Administration lasted one hundred and twenty
days, until the death of Mr. Canning.]

judicious—that of appointing the Duke of Clarence Lord
High Admiral—nothing served so much to disconcert his
opponents.   The negotiations went on (through the Duke
of Devonshire) up to the end of the Easter recess, when
Lord Lansdowne came to town, and after much delay it was
announced that the Whigs would support the new Government, but that none of them would take office immediately.
The places were all filled up, but the appointments were
understood to be only provisional, and the Duke of Portland,
Lord Dudley, and Sturges Bourne were considered to hold
their offices until Lord Lansdowne, Lord Carlisle, and Tierney
should join the Cabinet.   With this arrangement Parliament
met, and the rage which had been accumulating in the
minds of the seceders soon burst forth in a furious attack on
this provisional arrangement.   The Whigs have nearly in a
body joined Government, with the exception of Lord Grey in
the House of Lords, who in a speech full of eloquence
attacked Canning's political life and character, and announced his intention of remaining neuter.   In the meantime it was understood that there was a reason for Lord
Lansdowne not joining Government immediately, which was
not to be made public till that event took place, and this
secret was only imparted to a very few people; it was even
concealed from Brougham and the leaders of the party.
The secret, however, turns out to be this: Lord Lansdowne
insisted upon modelling the Irish Government as he pleased—
that is, in putting a Lord-Lieutenant, a Chancellor, and a
Secretary there favourable to the Catholic claims, to which
the King would not consent.   Canning entreated Lord Lansdowne to have patience, to allow time to elapse, during
which the King's scruples might be removed, and promised
that every endeavour should be made to reconcile the King
to the arrangement Lord Lansdowne desired.   After much
discussion it was resolved that Lord Lansdowne should
support Government, but that he should not take office
until this point was settled; and so the matter has remained.

June 3rd.—Soon after writing this Lord Lansdowne came

into the Cabinet, together with Tierney and Lord Carlisle,
M'Donald and Abercromby also taking places. They found so
many objections to the unsettled state of the Cabinet, and
the provisional arrangements had brought so much odium
and ridicule upon the Government, that it was thought necessary to settle this matter without loss of time, but Lord
Lansdowne would not consent to take the Home Office except
upon the conditions on which he had before insisted. He
therefore came into the Cabinet without a place. But it is
quite evident that the present state of affairs is far from
satisfactory; the Government is not established on a firm or
secure basis, and the members of it are not altogether satisfied with each other or themselves. Lord Lansdowne particularly does not feel comfortable where he is, and does not
think that he has been well treated by his own friends. It
seems that when first overtures were made to him by
Canning he called a meeting of his friends at Lansdowne
House, at which he declared his own sentiments and the
conditions on which he would join the Government. The
persons there assembled unanimously agreed with him, but
a few days after a meeting was called at Brooks's which
was more numerously attended, and there certain resolutions
were agreed upon which were not in conformity with the
opinions expressed in Lansdowne House, and these resolutions
were communicated to Canning as the sentiments of the
great body of the Whigs, but without the same being imparted to Lord Lansdowne, who was then at Bowood (this
fact I had last night from Duncannon[1] and Hobhouse[2]).
Matters, however, went on quietly enough till the other
night, when the Government was beat in the House of
Lords upon the clause in the Corn Bill, and this defeat it
is obvious has enraged and embarrassed them to the greatest

---

[1] [John William, Viscount Duncannon, afterwards fourth Earl of Bessborough.]

[2] [Mr. John Cam Hobhouse, M.P. for Westminster, afterwards Sir John
C. Hobhouse, Bart., raised to the peerage in 1851 by the title of Baron
Broughton de Giffard.]

degree.[1] Duncannon, who is entirely in the confidence of
the moderate Whig party, says that it is impossible the
thing can go on in this way; three Lords in the King's
household (Errol, Macclesfield, and Delawarr) voted against
the Bill, and if they are not dismissed it will be such a
proof of the feebleness of Government as will disgust
all the Whigs and make their support very lukewarm.[2]
Burdett, who was more active and zealous than anybody
in bringing about the Coalition, is very much disgusted
already, and there appears altogether such a want of confidence and unanimity among them as must lead to the
dissolution of the Government unless Canning can by some
vigorous measures establish his credit and convince the
world of his strength. In Ireland the Chancellor[3] has refused to put the Great Seal to the appointment of Doherty
as Solicitor-General. It is supposed that he will take this
occasion to resign, and it will then be seen what part the
King will take in the nomination of his successor. The
King sees numbers of people, talks incessantly, and does
nothing. Canning was with him yesterday evening, and the
result of his audience will be very interesting, because it will
appear whether he has insisted upon, and the King consented
to, the dismissal of the refractory Lords, as well as what he
will do about the Irish Chancellor. Government are indignant with the Duke of Wellington and the other ex-Ministers
for opposing the Corn Bill, which they had been themselves
(when in office) instrumental in framing, as well as for the
use which the Duke made of Huskisson's letter.

June 17th.—I was at the Royal Lodge for one night last

[1] [It was with reference to this defeat that Canning said soon afterwards
in the House of Commons that 'the Duke of Wellington had been made the
instrument of others for their own particular views,' and he pledged himself
to bring in another Corn Bill in the following session. But these were
almost the last words uttered by Canning in Parliament.]

[2] [Lord Delawarr resigned of his own accord, Lord Errol was obliged to
resign, and Lord Macclesfield came over and voted with Government on the
second reading of the Corn Bill.]

[3] [Lord Manners was still Lord Chancellor of Ireland, as he had been
since 1807. Mr. Doherty was made Solicitor-General for Ireland on the
18th of June.]

c

Wednesday; about thirty people sat down to dinner, and the company was changed nearly every day. It is a delightful place to live in, but the rooms are too low and too small for very large parties. Nothing can exceed the luxury of the internal arrangements; the King was very well and in excellent spirits, but very weak in his knees and could not walk without difficulty. The evening passed off tolerably, owing to the Tyrolese, whom Esterhazy brought down to amuse the King, and he was so pleased with them that he made them sing and dance before him the whole evening; the women kissed his face and the men his hand, and he talked to them in German. Though this evening went off well enough, it is clear that nothing would be more insupportable than to live at this Court; the dulness must be excessive, and the people who compose his habitual society are the most insipid and uninteresting that can be found. As for Lady Conyngham, she looks bored to death, and she never speaks, never appears to have one word to say to the King, who, however, talks himself without ceasing. Canning came the day I went away, and was very well received by his Majesty; he looked dreadfully ill. The only thing which interested me was the account I heard from Francis Conyngham about Knighton. He is seldom there, and when he comes scarcely stays above a night or two. But he governs everything about the house, and cannot endure anybody who is likely to dispute his empire. The King certainly does not like him, is always happier when he is away, and never presses him to stay or to return. When he is there he has constant access to the King at all times and whenever he pleases. He is on bad terms with Mount Charles, he bullies Lord Conyngham, and he is barely civil to Lady C.; he knows that Mount Charles is independent of him, and that the King likes him and admits him continually and familiarly to his presence, and of this it seems that he is jealous. I was more struck with one word which dropped from him than with all he told me of Sir W. Knighton. While the Tyrolese were dancing and singing, and there was a sort of gay uproar going on, with which the King was greatly delighted, he said, ' I would

give ten guineas to see Knighton walk into the room now,'
as if it were some master who was absent, and who should
suddenly return and find his family and servants merry-
making in his absence; it indicates a strange sort of power
possessed by him.

The King was very civil to the Duke of Dorset, and
repeatedly told him that what had passed would make no
difference in their private friendship. In the meantime the
Corn Bill has been thrown out, and I think political animosities are full as strong as ever, though they have taken rather
a sulky than a violent tone. I had a long conversation with
Duncannon yesterday, who is fully possessed of the sentiments of all the Whigs, and by what he says it is clear that
they are extremely dissatisfied; they want Canning to display
his power by some signal act of authority, and to show that
he is really supported cordially by the King. The opposite
party are persuaded that the King is secretly inclined to them
and averse to his present Government, and this opinion
obtains more or less with the public in consequence of the
impunity with which Canning has been braved by the Chancellor in Ireland. The appointment of Doherty as Solicitor-
General has never yet passed the Great Seal, and Lord
Manners refuses to sanction it; he has likewise refused to
put Sir Patrick Bellew (a Catholic) in the Commission of the
Peace, though he is a respectable man and he has been
strongly pressed to do it even by Protestants. This refusal
so disgusted Duncannon that he was very near withdrawing
his name from the Commission, and if he had his example
would have been followed by many others, but Lord Spencer
dissuaded him from doing so. Lord Grey is in such a state
of irritation that he will hardly speak to any of his old
friends, and he declares that he will never set his foot in
Brooks's again. All this is the more extraordinary, and the
vivacity of his temper the more unaccountable, because he
has constantly declined taking an active part in politics when
invited to do so for a long time past; and whenever Duncannon has asked his advice or consulted his opinions or
wishes, he has invariably referred him to Lord Lansdowne as

the person whom his friends were to look upon as their
leader, asserting that he had withdrawn himself from public
life and would have no more concern with politics. More
than this, when first overtures were made by Canning to the
Whigs, it was the unanimous opinion of all those who have
since joined the Government that Lord Lansdowne and his
friends could not join an Administration of which Peel was
to be a member (for at that time the resignation of Peel was
not contemplated as a probable event), and this opinion was
warmly combated by Lord Grey, who contended that there
was no reason why they should not coalesce with Canning
and Peel. What induced him to alter his opinion so decidedly and to become so bitter an enemy to the present
arrangements does not appear, unless it is to be attributed
to a feeling of pique and resentment at not having been
more consulted, or that overtures were not made to himself.
The pretext he took for declaring himself was the appointment of Copley to be Chancellor, when he said that it was
impossible to support a Government which had made such
an appointment.

   July 5th.—The session is over, and has been short but
violent enough. There is apparently a majority against the
Ministry in the House of Lords, though they seem safe in the
House of Commons. All depends upon Canning's prudence
and firmness during the recess. As to the King, he seems
desirous of living a quiet life and disposing of all patronage ;
public measures and public men are equally indifferent to
him. The Duke of Wellington, who knows him well, says
he does not care a farthing about the Catholic question, but
he does not like to depart from the example of his father
and the Duke of York, to which they owed so much of their
popularity. His conduct is entirely influenced by selfish
considerations, and he neither knows nor cares what measures
the exigencies of the country demand. The present state of
parties is so extraordinary that it cannot last, and it remains
to be seen whether Lord Grey and the other Whigs will
reunite themselves to the main body and support Canning's
Government, or whether they will join with the Tories in

their efforts to overturn it. Lord Grey's temper, irritated by the attacks which have been made on him, seems likely to urge him to the latter alternative.

July 25th.—Canning is gone to Chiswick, where he has had the lumbago, and could not go to the Council last week. He is very unwell, and in a very precarious state, I think. I was at the Council last Monday week; it was held for the appointment of Lords Lansdowne and Carlisle, Lord Lansdowne having consented to take the Home Office, and Lord Carlisle the Privy Seal; the only Cabinet Ministers present were the four who changed places. It was the first time the King had given Lord Lansdowne an audience, but I believe he was very civil to him. The King gave him an account of the Duke of Buckingham's visit to him (from Dropmore), the result of which was that he sent his proxy to Lord Goderich, but not with a good grace.

The Duke of Wellington has been to the Lodge, and great is the speculation thereupon.[1] It is fiercely debated whether he went by invitation or not, and how long he stayed. He was only with the King twenty minutes, for so Prince Leopold, who was there, told Lambton, who told me. I don't know if he was invited or no. The King has taken from Prince Leopold the plate that was given, or, as they now say, lent to him, on his marriage. The Chamberlain sent to Sir R. Gardiner for it in the Prince's absence, and he refused to give it up without his Royal Highness's orders, but the Prince, as soon as he heard of it, ordered it to be sent to the Chamberlain.

The Irish Chancellor has given way about Doherty's appointment, and put the Great Seal to it before his own resignation. He did it with a good grace, Lord Lansdowne told me.

We went all over the Castle the other day; his Majesty will not let anybody see it now. I don't think enough is effected for the enormous sums expended, though it is a fine

[1] [The causes and consequences of this visit, which was by invitation from the King, are related in the Duke of Wellington's 'Correspondence,' New Series, vol. iv. p. 63 *et seq.*]

and will be a good house; still, how far (as a palace) from
Versailles, St. Cloud, and the other palaces in France ! The
external terrace has spoilt the old one, and is altogether a
frightful excrescence, and should never have been made.

August 9th.—Canning died yesterday morning at four
o'clock. His danger was only announced on Sunday night,
though it had existed from the preceding Wednesday.
When he saw the King on Monday his Majesty told him he
looked very ill, and he replied that 'he did not know what
was the matter with him, but that he was ill all over.'
Nothing could exceed the consternation caused by the announcement of his danger and the despair of his colleagues.
From the first there was no hope. He was aware of his
danger and said, 'It is hard upon the King to have to fight
the battle over again.' The Cabinet met on Monday, and
great unanimity prevailed among them. They all agreed to
stand by each other in the event of his death. As soon as
it happened Lord Lansdowne went down to Windsor and
saw the King. His Majesty spoke with great affection of
Canning, and said something of the difficulties in which he
was again involved. Lord L. replied that he had come
down, as it was his official duty to do, to announce to him
the event; that nothing could be further from his wish or
intention than to elicit from him any opinion as to the
future, and he begged his Majesty would not say one word
upon that subject. The King said that the first thing he
should do would be to show every mark of respect to the
memory and attachment to the person of Canning, and that
he should therefore send for those of his Ministers who had
been the most closely connected with him in public and
private life. He sent immediately for Lord Goderich and
Sturges Bourne, who went down to him when Lord Lansdowne returned.

Yesterday I saw some letters from Mr. Arbuthnot [1] (Gosh)

---

[1] [Right Hon. Charles Arbuthnot, the most confidential friend of the
Duke of Wellington, with whom he lived. He was known in society by
the nickname of 'Gosh,' by which he is frequently described in these
Journals.]

giving an account of the break-up of the old Government, and of the reasons by which they had been influenced in resigning. They were three in number, very violent and indignant, defending the Duke and attacking Canning, but they contained little more than has since appeared and been made public. The only fact that appeared to me of consequence was this: that Peel, though he had resigned on different grounds, was indignant at the way in which the Duke had been treated, and was resolved never to take office till full reparation had been made to him; that Lord Bathurst had begged Gosh (Mr. Arbuthnot) not to mention this, as it might do harm. The next letter was a long tirade with a great deal of wrath and indignation, such as might be expected. He says that they knew Canning was negotiating with the Whigs while he was pretending that he wished the old Government to go on; and that in the course of the negotiation with his old colleagues he offered Peel, if he would stay with him, to recall the pro-Catholic Lord-Lieutenant and send a Protestant. Peel wanted the Duke to give up the army and take the Treasury, which he would not hear of. He was miserable at the idea, and opposed it so strongly that they could not press it upon him. However, the Peers—meaning all the Lords who had made such a stir —applied to the Duke to put himself at the head of the Government, but he hardly sent an answer to their application—he would not hear of it.

I may here introduce some anecdotes of Canning told me by Lord George Bentinck, his private secretary:—

Some time after they had been in office (after Lord Londonderry's death) they found in a drawer, which apparently had been forgotten or overlooked, some papers, which were despatches and copies of correspondence between Lord Castlereagh and Lord Stewart. These despatches were very curious, and more particularly so after his attack last year on Canning for misappropriating the secret service money, for they gave an account of his own employment of the secret service money in getting Italian witnesses for the Queen's trial. There was likewise an account of the discovery

Stewart had made of the treachery of an office messenger, who had for a long time carried all his despatches to Metternich before he took them to England, and Lord Stewart says, 'I tremble when I think of the risk which my despatches have incurred of coming before the House of Commons, as there were letters of Lord Londonderry's written expressly "to throw dust in the eyes of the Parliament."' These were his own expressions, and he said, 'You will understand this and know what to say to Metternich.' In fact, while Lord Castlereagh was obliged to pretend to disapprove of the Continental system of the Holy Alliance he secretly gave Metternich every assurance of his private concurrence, and it was not till long after Mr. Canning's accession that Metternich could be persuaded of his sincerity in opposing their views, always fancying that he was obliged to act a part as his predecessor had done to keep the House of Commons quiet.

From the moment Mr. Canning came into the Cabinet he laboured to accomplish the recognition of the South American Republics, but all the Cabinet were against him except Lord Liverpool, and the King would not hear of it. The King was supported in his opposition by the Duke of Wellington and by Lieven and Esterhazy, whom he used to have with him; and to them he inveighed against Canning for pressing this measure. The Duke of Wellington and those Ambassadors persuaded his Majesty that if he consented it would produce a quarrel between him and his allies, and involve him in inextricable difficulties. Canning, who knew all this, wrote to Mrs. Canning in terms of great bitterness, and said if the King did not take care he would not let him see these Ambassadors except in his presence, and added, 'I can tell his Majesty that his father would never have acted in such a manner.' At length after a long contest, in the course of which Peel came round to him, he resolved to carry the measure or resign. After a battle in the Cabinet which lasted three hours, and from which he came heated, exhausted, and indignant, he prepared a memorial to the King, and Lord Liverpool another, in which they tendered their resig-

nations, alleging at length their reasons, and this they submitted to the Cabinet the following day.   When their
colleagues found they were in earnest they unanimously
surrendered, and agreed upon a declaration to the King that
they would all resign unless the measure was adopted.   This
communication was made to his Majesty by the Duke of
Wellington, who told him that he found Canning was in
earnest, and that the Government could not go on without
him, and he must give way.   The King accordingly gave
way, but with a very ill grace.[1]   When he saw Canning he
received him very ill, and in a letter to him signifying his
assent to the measure he said that it must be his business to
have it carried into effect in the best way it would admit of.
Canning took fire at the ungracious tone of the letter, and
wrote for answer that he feared he was not honoured with
that confidence which it was necessary that the King should
have in his Ministers, and that his Majesty had better dismiss
him at once.   The King sent no answer, but a gracious message, assuring him he had mistaken his letter, and desiring
he would come to the Cottage, when he received him very
well.   From that time he grew in favour, for when the King
found that none of the evils predicted of this measure had
come to pass, and how it raised the reputation of his
Minister, he liked it very well, and Canning dexterously gave
him all the praise of it, so that he soon fancied it had
originated with himself, and became equally satisfied with
himself and with Canning.

Canning concealed nothing from Mrs. Canning, nor from
Charles Ellis.   When absent from Mrs. C. he wrote everything to her in the greatest detail.   Canning's industry was
such that he never left a moment unemployed, and such was
the clearness of his head that he could address himself
almost at the same time to several different subjects with
perfect precision and without the least embarrassment.   He
wrote very fast, but not fast enough for his mind, composing

---

[1] [The memorial of Mr. Canning on this subject, the counter-opinions of
the Duke of Wellington, and the King's minute upon them have been published in the second volume of the New Series of the ' Duke of Wellington's
Correspondence,' pp. 354, 364, and 402.]

much quicker than he could commit his ideas to paper. He could not bear to dictate, because nobody could write fast enough for him; but on one occasion, when he had the gout in his hand and could not write, he stood by the fire and dictated at the same time a despatch on Greek affairs to George Bentinck and one on South American politics to Howard de Walden, each writing as fast as he could, while he turned from one to the other without hesitation or embarrassment.

August 10*th*.—The Cabinet sat yesterday morning and again at night. It is generally believed that Lord Goderich will succeed Canning at the Treasury, and Lord Lansdowne has no objection to serve under him. The Tories were full of hope and joy at first, but in proportion as they were elated at first so were they dejected yesterday, when they found that the King sent for Lord Goderich and not for the Duke of Wellington. He never seems to have thought of the Duke at all. It will all be out to-day or to-morrow. The Tories may now give the King up. They have taken leave of office, except Peel, who will come in some day or other.

[They remained out of office five months. What a prophecy!—*January* 28*th*, 1828.]

The Duke of Wellington talked of Canning the other day a great deal at my mother's. He said his talents were astonishing, his compositions admirable, that he possessed the art of saying exactly what was necessary and passing over those topics on which it was not advisable to touch, his fertility and resources inexhaustible. He thought him the finest speaker he had ever heard; though he prided himself extremely upon his compositions, he would patiently endure any criticisms upon such papers as he submitted for the consideration of the Cabinet, and would allow them to be altered in any way that was suggested; he (the Duke) particularly had often 'cut and hacked' his papers, and Canning never made the least objection, but was always ready to adopt the suggestions of his colleagues. It was not so, however, in conversation and discussion. Any difference of opinion or dissent from his views threw him into ungovernable rage, and on such occasions he flew out with a violence which, the Duke said, had often compelled him to be silent that he might not be involved in bitter personal altercation. He said that Canning was usually very silent in the Cabinet, seldom spoke at all, but when he did he maintained his opinions with extraordinary tenacity. He said that he was one of the idlest of men. This I do not believe, for I have always heard that he saw everything and did everything himself. Not a despatch was received that he did not read, nor one written that he did not dictate or correct.

August 20*th.*—There was a Council at Windsor Castle on Friday last, which was a very curious scene. What I saw puzzled me very much till matters have since been explained to me.

On Tuesday morning Drummond, Lord Goderich's private secretary, came to me at my office and told me the Council would be held on Friday, and that Herries was to be appointed Chancellor of the Exchequer, and was going down that day with Lord Goderich to Windsor. Accordingly when I arrived at the Castle I found Herries in the room, and I asked him if he was to take an oath as Chancellor of the Exchequer, because there was none in the oath-book for Chancellor, but one for the Treasurer of the Exchequer, and whether he was to take that. He said he did not know, upon which I asked Wynn if he knew. He did not; when we all agreed to wait till Lord Bexley came,[1] and enquire of him what he had done. When Lord Bexley arrived we asked him, and he said that Herries would only be sworn then as a Privy Councillor, and must take the oath of Chancellor of Exchequer in the Court of Exchequer. Shortly after we walked round the Castle, and some conversation occurring about the elevation of the Round Tower, which Wyattville was anxious to accomplish, Herries said to him, 'But it is my business now to ask you what you will do it for, how much it will cost. Will you do it for 10,000*l.* ?'

---

[1] [Lord Bexley as Mr. Vansittart had been Chancellor of the Exchequer from 1812 to 1823.]

Wyattville said, ' You must give me 15,000*l.*,' so that I
could have no doubt that Herries was Chancellor of the Exchequer. In the meantime all the Ministers arrived, the
whole Cabinet being present except the Chancellor and Lord
Anglesey, who arrived afterwards. As soon as Lord Goderich
and Lord Lansdowne were come they retired into the next
room and had a long conference. Shortly afterwards the
King came, when Lord Goderich went into his room. He
stayed some time, when the Duke of Portland went in, then
Herries. When Lord Goderich came out he had another
conference with Lord Lansdowne, at the end of which he
went again to the King. He came out, and at the end of
three-quarters of an hour went a third time, and after him
Herries a second time, and with him Lord Bexley. Another
very animated conversation took place between Lord Lansdowne and Lord Goderich, when the latter went to the King
a fourth time, and after him Lord Lansdowne, Goderich
whispering something to him as he went in. Previous to
this I remarked a conference between Lord Lansdowne,
Goderich, and Carlisle, after which Carlisle took Tierney into
the next room, evidently communicating what had passed.
Something was clearly going on, but I could not make out
what. I fancied that Lord Lansdowne insisted upon Lord
Holland's being in the Cabinet. Yesterday, however, I discovered that it was all about Herries and his appointment.
The appointment was the King's, with whom Herries had
ingratiated himself by transacting some of his pecuniary
business, and getting odds and ends for him out of *droits*,
&c. The King then named him, and Goderich made no objection. Herries came to Windsor, not doubting but that he
was to receive the seals, which in fact Goderich brought down
with him on purpose. Lord Lansdowne, however, declared
that he would not consent to the appointment, and hence
arose all the conferences and audiences for which I could not
account at the time. The Whigs dislike Herries' politics,
and still more do they object to the King taking upon himself to nominate the members of the Government without
consulting his Ministers. They are determined to resist this

nomination, and the consequence of Lord Lansdowne's re-
monstrance was the suspension at least of the appointment.
Such is the state of affairs, and not a very agreeable state
certainly.

The Whigs are satisfied of the candour, fairness, and
plain dealing of Goderich, but dissatisfied with his facility
and want of firmness. The King is grasping at power and
patronage, and wants to take advantage of the weakness of
the Government and their apparent dependence upon him to
exercise all the authority which ought to belong to the
Ministers. The Whigs are not easy in their places. They
feel that they are not treated with the consideration to which
they are entitled. But they have got too far to recede, and
they evidently are alarmed lest, if they exasperate the King,
he should accept their resignation and form a Government
by a junta of the old Tories with the rest of his Administration, by which their exclusion would be made certain and
perpetual. I find that the Duke of Portland was likewise
named by the King himself. They do not object to the
Duke, on the contrary, but they object greatly to his being
so appointed. All this I have from Tierney, who added, if
the Duke had been proposed to the King by Lord Goderich,
not a member of the Cabinet would have objected, but they
don't like his being named by the King. At the end of the
Council, on Friday, Lord Anglesey arrived, having travelled
day and night, and brought with him the Duke of Wellington's acceptance of the command of the army. Altogether
it was a day of unusual interest, and unlike the dulness of
ordinary Councils.

September 1st.—Since the Council on the 17th the affair
of Herries has still been going on. It appears that when
Goderich went in to the King (at the Council) to announce
to him the objection that had been raised, his Majesty was
very angry, angry at having been so committed and at
being obliged to give up a nomination he liked. Herries
naturally felt himself very ill treated and nettled by the
attacks upon him in the newspapers. He has ever since
insisted upon being admitted to the Cabinet as the only

thing which could afford due reparation to his honour, and prove that he had not been rejected for the reasons which had been assigned. This the Ministers opposed, and it was at length determined that this matter should rest till Huskisson's return. Huskisson agreed with his colleagues about Herries, went to the King, and spoke to him openly and firmly on the subject. The King consented that another arrangement should be made; the one proposed was, that Sturges Bourne should be Chancellor of the Exchequer, and Herries take the Woods and Forests without a seat in the Cabinet. Herries, who had constantly refused to accede to any arrangement by which he was to be excluded from the Cabinet, said he would consider of it; but in the meantime Sturges took fright, and refused to take the Exchequer. In vain Huskisson offered to take all the trouble on himself, and they all tried to persuade Sturges. He would not do it, and so this arrangement fell to the ground. They went again to the King yesterday to report progress and state to him what had occurred. When they came back (Goderich, Huskisson, Sturges, Herries, and the Chancellor) Goderich wrote a long letter to Lord Lansdowne, and he is to go to the King again this evening.

I had a long conversation with Tierney yesterday, and I find that the Whig Ministers are sick to death of their situation and anxious to resign. They think they are not treated with the consideration which is due to them whether as individuals or as the representatives of a great party who are supporting the Government. Then they think Goderich has behaved so ill in this affair that they can have no confidence in him. They believe so much in the integrity of his character that they do not suspect him of any duplicity in what has passed, but his conduct has been marked by such deplorable weakness as shows how unfit he is for the situation he occupies. He has acted equally ill to the King, to his colleagues, and to Herries himself. The history of the transaction is this :—While Goderich was Chancellor of the Exchequer Herries was the man upon whose assistance he relied to carry on the business of his office, and who in fact

did it all for him. As soon as he was at the head of the
Treasury he felt that Herries would be equally necessary to
him, and he accordingly pressed him to take the office of
Chancellor of the Exchequer, which Herries declined. After
repeated solicitations, Herries told him that he had no
objection to belong to his Government, and that he would
take the office of Vice-President of the Board of Trade, and
do all his Treasury business for him (this is the account of
Herries' friends, which seems to me somewhat doubtful),
though he did not wish to be in the Cabinet. At last,
however, Goderich prevailed on Herries to let him propose
him to the King, which was done. The appointment was
particularly agreeable to the King, who wrote a letter with
his own hand to Herries, desiring him to take the place.
When Goderich returned to town, with this letter in his
pocket, he went (before he delivered it) to the Cabinet, and
then mentioning Herries, without saying what had passed,
he found that the Cabinet would not approve of the appointment, on which he went to Herries, and said that he found
that it would not do, and begged him to allow his appointment to be cancelled. Herries told him that he had never
desired it, and was quite ready to give it up. As soon as
Herries had agreed to give it up Goderich pulls out of his
pocket the King's letter, and says, 'By-the-by, here is a
letter which I ought to have given you before.' When
Herries had read this letter he said, 'This puts me quite in
another situation, and though I am still ready to give up
being Chancellor of the Exchequer, I must have my conduct
explained to the King, and you must take me down to
Windsor to-morrow for that purpose.' This Goderich refused to do, when Herries said he should go down by himself.
He did so, and then passed all which I have described above
in the account of the Council on the 19th. I ought to have
mentioned, as not the least curious circumstance of the
Council, that in the middle of it the King sent for Sir
William Knighton, who was closeted with him for an
hour. I see this account is not altogether the same as
the preceding, a proof of the inaccuracy of anecdotes

and historical facts whenever they differ. This is the true one.

Henry de Ros told me that he saw George Dawson, Peel's brother-in-law, at Brighton, who told him that he believed there was nobody the King was more exasperated against than Peel, and for this reason :—When the late Government (Canning's) was forming, Peel went to the King, and in reply to his desire that he should form a part of it told him he could not continue in any Government the head of which was a supporter of Catholic Emancipation. The King proposed to him to remain, with a secret pledge and promise from him that the question should not be carried. This of course Peel refused, and the King, who construed his rejection of the disgraceful proposal as conveying a doubt of his word, dismissed him with much resentment.

September 15th.—Taking up the account from where I left off, Goderich went to the King, and it was settled Herries was to be Chancellor of the Exchequer. He returned and wrote to Lord Lansdowne entreating him to acquiesce. Lord Lansdowne went to the King, and the result of his interview was that he retained office together with his friends. He wrote a letter to one of them, which he intended might be communicated to others, giving an account of his conduct and motives. I saw this letter. He said the King received him very well and spared no entreaties to him to keep office. The King said that he was most anxious the present Government should continue on every account, but more particularly on account of what was now passing on the Continent; that Lord Lansdowne's holding office was indispensable for this object, and he asked him in his own name and for the sake of the country not to resign; that what had occurred had arisen out of a series of blunders which, ' let me say,' he added, ' were neither yours nor mine.' Lord Lansdowne said it was put to him in such a way that he could not do otherwise; that he had insisted with Goderich that Stanley and Mackintosh[1] should be employed. This

---

[1] [Mr. Stanley, afterwards Earl of Derby, did not take office under Mr. Canning, as was stated in former editions of this book, when the Government

was the pith of his letter. I have been with Huskisson for
a week in the country; he is in good health and excellent
spirits. Capo d'Istria was there, going to Greece. Huskisson told me he wanted money. He owned to me that he
considered Greece as a great humbug. I discovered from
what he said that they only interfered that they might keep
the Russians quiet and prevent a war between Russia and
Turkey. The Sultan had announced his intention of sending
any Minister to the Seven Towers who should communicate
the treaty to him.[1]   Everything is now quiet for the
moment, and will probably continue so till the meeting of
Parliament.

December 13th.—Three months have passed since the
above was written. I went to Doncaster and Chatsworth,
then to Newmarket, and returned to town the middle of last
month.   The battle of Navarino has been fought, and
after three weeks' expectation we know very little about
the matter. The strong part of the Cabinet, with Huskisson
at the head, are for letting things take their course, and for
suffering Russia to go to war with Turkey, and leaving it to
her to enforce the articles of the Treaty of London. The
plan is that Russia should occupy Moldavia and Wallachia;
that the terms should then be offered to the Sultan, and
that on his yielding the Greek independence these provinces
should be evacuated by the Russians; this is what they
propose that our mediation shall effect. In the meantime
the Ministers are uneasy about the approaching meeting of
Parliament.   They anticipate a violent opposition in the
House of Lords; they are by no means sure of a majority
in that House, and there is not one among them who has
spirit and character enough to face it. Lord Dudley is terri-

was formed in April 1827, but he did accept the office of Under-Secretary
of State for the Colonies in the month of September, after Mr. Canning's
death. Lord Lansdowne was wont to express his satisfaction at having
introduced so eminent a man to office.]

    [1] [The Treaty of London for the Settlement of the Affairs of Greece was
signed by England, France, and Russia on the 7th of July, 1827. It was
of course received with indignation by the Porte, and led three months
afterwards to the battle of Navarino, which was fought on the 20th of
October.]

fied to the greatest degree at the notion of being attacked
by Lord Grey. Then, though they are not disunited, they
derive no strength from mutual co-operation and support,
and the tone which the King has assumed, and the peremptory manner in which he has claimed the disposal of every
sort of patronage, is both a proof of the weakness of Government, a source of discord among themselves, and the cause
of distrust mixed with contempt on the part of many of
their friends. The King and the Duke of Clarence made
the promotions and dispensed the honours after the battle
of Navarino without consulting the Ministers. The King
gave Sumner the Bishopric of Winchester in the same way,[1]
and there is a very general opinion that the Cabinet is
weak, that they do not act together with cordiality, that
they have neither energy nor authority, and are not likely
to keep their places. It has been currently reported that
they would willingly have censured Codrington, and have
thrown the responsibility of the battle from their own
shoulders upon his, if they had dared, but that they were
prevented by the precipitate approbation expressed by the
King. These things are greatly exaggerated, but are not
without foundation.

December 15th.—The Ministry is at an end. Goderich
resigned either by letter to the King yesterday or at the
Council on Thursday. They have been going on ill together for some time. Goderich has no energy, and his
colleagues are disgusted at his inefficiency, and at the
assumption by the King of all power in disposing of
patronage. Huskisson is away, and wishes to be out. They
are embarrassed with the Greek question, and have to meet
Parliament with an immense deficiency in the revenue.
This state of things and mutual irritation and dissatisfaction have at length produced Goderich's resignation.

---

[1] [*Vide supra*, p. 45, when Lord Liverpool caused the nomination of
Mr. Sumner to a canonry of Windsor to be cancelled, because he had not
been consulted. The King took the earliest opportunity of appointing
him to the See of Llandaff, whence he was soon afterwards translated to that
of Winchester. He died in 1874.]

Yesterday the Chancellor, Dudley, and Huskisson were backwards and forwards to the King all day, and when he went to Windsor at half-past five they were still in the Palace, and he left them there in consultation. He is gone, but Knighton remains behind to negotiate and communicate. In the meantime I find that the King is quite mad upon the Catholic question, and that his real desire is to get rid of the Whigs, take back the Duke of Wellington, and make an anti-Catholic Government. This seems to be quite impossible in the present state of affairs, but a few days will probably produce some decisive change.

1828.

January 2nd.—As soon as Lord Goderich had resigned they sent to Lord Harrowby and offered him the Premiership. He came to town directly, and went to the King, but refused the place. His refusal was immediately known, and of course there were a variety of conjectures and opinions afloat as to the man who would be chosen. A few days, however, put an end to these, for it was announced, to the astonishment of everybody, that Goderich had returned to town, and that he would not resign. Here ended this matter, which made a great noise for a few days; but the effects of what passed are yet to be seen when Parliament meets. The injury which Goderich's conduct has done to the Government is incalculable, for it has brought them into such low estimation that it is the general opinion they will not be able to retain their places, and there are a great variety of persons in both Houses of Parliament who are disposed to withdraw from them the support which they did give to Canning's Government, and which they were previously inclined to give to this. As matters now stand they do not themselves know upon whom they can count, nor who are their friends and who their foes. They are, however, to have Lord Holland in the Cabinet, to help them on in the House of Lords, but it is very doubtful whether his appointment will not lead to the resignation of some of the Tory members of the Government and the secession of some of its Tory supporters. Nothing can exceed the alarm which they feel at the prospect of the approaching contest in Parliament, and thus, full of fears and weakness, neither inspiring nor feeling confidence, there seems a bad chance of their getting through the session.

I have heard no more of the King and of his intentions, except that he said he did not see why he was to be the only gentleman in his dominions who was not to eat his Christmas dinner in quiet, and he was determined he would. Don Miguel has been with him at the Cottage these two days. He has been received with great magnificence; they say he behaves well enough, but is very shy. He went out stag-hunting in red coat and full hunting costume, and rode over the fences like anybody else.

M'Gregor told me the other day that not one of the physicians and surgeons who attended the Duke of York through his long and painful illness had ever received the smallest remuneration, although their names and services had been laid before the King. He told me in addition that during sixteen years that he attended the Duke and his whole family he never received one guinea by way of fee or any payment whatever.

About three weeks ago I passed a few days at Panshanger, where I met Brougham; he came from Saturday till Monday morning, and from the hour of his arrival to that of his departure he never ceased talking. The party was agreeable enough—Luttrell, Rogers, &c.—but it was comical to see how the latter was provoked at Brougham's engrossing all the talk, though he could not help listening with pleasure. Brougham is certainly one of the most remarkable men I ever met; to say nothing of what he is in the world, his almost childish gaiety and animal spirits, his humour mixed with sarcasm, but not ill-natured, his wonderful information, and the facility with which he handles every subject, from the most grave and severe to the most trifling, displaying a mind full of varied and extensive information and a memory which has suffered nothing to escape it, I never saw any man whose conversation impressed me with such

an idea of his superiority over all others. As Rogers said
the morning of his departure, ' this morning Solon, Lycurgus,
Demosthenes, Archimedes, Sir Isaac Newton, Lord Chesterfield, and a great many more went away in one post chaise.'
He told us a great many details relating to the Queen's trial,
and amongst other things (which I do not believe) his conviction that the Queen had never had any intrigue with
Bergami. He told us the whole story of his finding out the
departure of Rastelli, which happened from a friend of his
accidentally seeing Rastelli in the street, recognising him, and
telling Brougham.[1] Brougham told none of his colleagues,
and at first did not believe the story, but by putting artful
questions, and watching their effect, he found it was so, and
then out he came with it. There was a grand discussion
whether they should not throw up their briefs and stop there,
and he was all for it, but was overruled and gave way. The
person who was most anxious they should go on was Lord
Grey, for he had got a notion that they could not any of them
speak to evidence, and he wanted to make such a speech, which
he fancied he could do very well. Brougham said that as
leading counsel for the Queen he always reserved to himself
the power of acting as he thought fit, whatever the opinions
of his colleagues might be, though they always consulted
together and gave their sentiments upon every debated
point *seriatim*. He and Denman invariably thought alike.
The Queen never could bear him, and was seldom civil to
him. When she had to answer the address of the House of
Commons she appealed to her counsel for their advice,
which they declined to give, and she was furious, for she
wanted to make them advise her to accept the propositions
of the House, which would have been very unpopular, and
then throw the odium of doing so on them.[2] He spoke very

---

[1] [For the use made by Mr. Brougham of the accidental departure of
Rastelli during the Queen's trial *vide supra*, p. 37.]

[2] [This was the address moved by Mr. Wilberforce on the 22nd of June,
1820 (*vide supra*, p. 30). Lord Brougham states in his 'Memoirs' that the
Queen resolved to reject the advice of Parliament without consulting her
lawyers. In one of Lord Brougham's letters written at the time he calls

highly of Alderman Wood, who behaved very well, never annoyed or interfered with them, and seems to have been altogether a *brave homme*.

If it had been possible to recollect all that Brougham said on this and a hundred other subjects, it would be well worth writing down, but such talk is much too evanescent, and I remember no more.

After all Brougham is only a living and very remarkable instance of the inefficacy of the most splendid talents, unless they are accompanied with other qualities, which scarcely admit of definition, but which must serve the same purpose that ballast does for a ship. Brougham has prospered to a certain degree ; he has a great reputation and he makes a considerable income at the bar ; but as an advocate he is left behind by men of far inferior capacity, whose names are hardly known beyond the precincts of their courts or the boundaries of their circuits. As a statesman he is not considered eligible for the highest offices, and however he may be admired or feared as an orator or debater, he neither commands respect by his character nor inspires confidence by his genius, and in this contrast between his pretensions and his situation more humble abilities may find room for consolation and cease to contemplate with envy his immense superiority. To suppose that his ambition can be satisfied in the possession of natural and acquired powers far greater than the majority of mankind would be contrary to all experience. Such men consider their acquirements as means for the attainment of greater ends, and the disappointments which they frequently meet with in the pursuit of their objects of ambition more than counteract all the feelings of pride and satisfaction which conscious superiority is calculated to inspire. The life of a politician is probably one of deep mortification, for the race is not always to the swift nor the battle to the strong, and few things can be more galling than to see men far inferior to ourselves enabled by fortune and circumstances to attain what we

Wood 'the ass and alderman called *Thistle*-wood,' and attributed to him the intrigue which brought the Queen to England.]

toil after in vain, and to learn from our own experience how many things there are in this life of greater practical utility than splendid abilities and unwearied industry.

London, January 19th.—The Ministry is at last settled, and now for its history. Early in last week Goderich went down to the King and told him there was such a quarrel in the Cabinet between Huskisson and Herries about the Finance Committee that both could not remain, and that Huskisson would resign if he had not his own way. The King was furious at this new disturbance, and said he could not understand it; if Huskisson resigned, the Government was at an end. 'Go,' he ended, 'and send the Chancellor to me.' The Chancellor [Lord Lyndhurst] went, and was desired to bring the Duke of Wellington. The Government was dissolved and the King desired the Duke to form a new one. All this was immediately known, and first it was asked, 'What is the quarrel between Huskisson and Herries which broke up the old Cabinet?' The friends of each put about a story, one of which appeared in the 'Times,' the other in the 'Morning Chronicle.' The question was Lord Althorp's appointment as chairman of the Finance Committee. Huskisson's story is this:—In November Tierney went to Goderich and proposed Althorp as a good man to be in the chair of that Committee. Goderich assented, and said, 'But you had better speak to Huskisson about it, as it is a House of Commons matter.' He did so, and Huskisson approved of it. A few days after Tierney called on Huskisson and found Herries with him, when they discussed the matter generally, as well as the particular appointment of Althorp, and Herries made no objection, and, as they thought, agreed with them; but shortly after Herries went to Goderich, complained that this matter had been settled without his knowledge and concurrence, that it was a slight put upon him, and said he would not agree to Althorp's nomination, nor stay in office if it were persisted in.

This is one story, told me by Sefton, who had it (I am sure) from Brougham, and *verbatim* the same by Robarts, who had it (he told me himself) from Tierney. Herries'

story only differs in this : it omits the interview between
the three Ministers, and declares the matter was never
mentioned to him at all till they had decided on it, when it
was shown him as a plan which was not to be discussed,
but which he was at once to assent to.   It appears difficult
to know which to believe, and at first my impression was
that they had probably not treated Herries with as much
consideration as he was entitled to as Finance Minister, and
that he had been prone to take offence and touchy from
old recollections, which were probably not effaced.   But a
circumstance I heard afterwards convinced me that Herries
has been all along full of ill-will towards his colleagues,
and not a little desirous of breaking up the Ministry. When
he found, too, with what difficulties they would have to
contend in Parliament and the weakness of Goderich, he
probably thought they would never be able to go on, and
was not sorry to find an opportunity of accelerating their
dissolution.   The circumstance is this :—In the old business
of his appointment to the Chancellorship of the Exchequer,
when he thought he was *not* to be appointed, he wrote to
Arbuthnot telling him how ill he had been treated, and
promising to send him all the correspondence on the subject.
Subsequently he *was* appointed, when he wrote again to
A., saying that as it was settled and he was appointed, he
did not think it would be right to send him the correspondence, which he was sure he would understand ; that
there he was, and he should do his best to act cordially with
his new colleagues ; but he finished, ' I shall hail the day
which brings all of you back again.'   Such an expression
to a man who was the bitterest enemy of the Government
of which he was a member did not evince much cordiality
towards his colleagues.

The first thing to be done by the Duke was to negotiate
with Huskisson.   He sent forthwith for his own friends,
Peel, Lord Bathurst, and Melville, and for many days the
great question was whether Huskisson would join or not,
the Whigs of course most anxious he should refuse, the new
Government ready to make great concessions to tempt him to

join them.   He has acceded, however, but much to the disgust
of many of his friends, some of whom think he has behaved
shabbily in abandoning the Whigs, who supported him, and
who had supported Canning at his utmost need.   Some
think he was pledged never to act with the men who they
consider to have behaved so ill to Canning, and some think
he has compromised his dignity and independence by not
insisting on higher terms, particularly the lead in the House
of Commons.   At present the exact terms of his bargain are
not known, and without being acquainted with all that has
passed *de part et d'autre* it is impossible to form a judgment
as to the wisdom or the fairness of his conduct.   Those
who think he would have acted a wiser part and have
made himself of greater importance by heading a third
party in the House of Commons and keeping aloof, judge
too hastily.   He would have been followed by all those who
call themselves Canning's personal friends, and probably by
a considerable body of neutrals, who would not have been
disposed to support a Tory Government, and still less to join
a Whig Opposition.   But however weak the Ministry (without Huskisson) might have appeared at first sight in the
House of Commons, it would very possibly have proved
stronger than was imagined.   Strength and weakness are
relative terms, and it remained to be seen what sort of
power would have been brought against it, and to what
attacks the Government would have exposed itself.   The
old Tory Ministry, which was voted out for incapacity by
the House of Commons, was the strongest and longest that
we have seen for many years, though opposed by all the
talent and power of an Opposition more formidable than this
can be.   To be sure it must always be remembered that they
floated through their difficulties on the tide of the Duke of
Wellington's victories.   Of all the party who would have
ranged themselves under Huskisson, only Canning's friends,
a select few, would have considered themselves bound to
him, and the rest, if they found the Government strong and
likely to last, would probably have dropped off and gradually
joined it.   In that case Huskisson would never have been

able to treat as an independent power, and though they might have been glad to take him into the Administration, he could not have made his own terms. I do not think he ever could have looked to overturning the Tory Government and coming in with the whole body of the Whigs, for he has no natural partiality (any more than Canning had) for that party, and he is fully aware how odious they are to the King and how unpopular in the country, which is always more inclined to the Tories than to them. If the Tories have agreed to those measures (except the Catholic question, for that is to remain on its old footing) which he deems necessary, and of which he is the author—that is, of Free Trade, &c.—he would probably rather act with them than with the Whigs; and in joining Government he is liable to no reproach but that of having shaken off his Whig colleagues too easily. But it remains to be proved whether they could have gone on, and at all events Lords Lansdowne and Carlisle might have remained in office if they pleased, though certainly it was not probable that they would do so. The part of the transaction which will appear extraordinary is, that the Government having been broken up by a quarrel between Huskisson and Herries, the opposite party come in and both these Ministers remain with them. In private life the transaction would look very like a fraud, and be open to great suspicion. It would appear as if they had got up a sham quarrel in order to get out their colleagues and stay in themselves with the Tories. This, however, I believe not to have been the case, at least as far as Huskisson is concerned, though perhaps Herries may not be altogether so clear.

CHAPTER IV.

The Duke of Wellington's Administration—Huskisson's Speech—Irritation of Mr. Canning's Friends—Tom Duncombe's Maiden Speech—Mr. Huskisson resigns and the Canningites quit the Government—Princess Lieven hostile to the Duke—The Catholic Question—Jockey Club Dinner at St. James's—Lord Lyndhurst—Sir Robert Adair—Fox and Burke—Fox and Pitt—The Lord High Admiral dismissed by the King—Dawson's Speech on Catholic Emancipation—The King's Health—His Pages—State of Ireland—Marquis of Anglesey—O'Connell—His Influence in Ireland—Lord Belmore Governor of Jamaica—The Duke's Letter to Dr. Curtis—Recall of Lord Anglesey from Ireland—Causes of this Event—Excitement of the King on the Catholic Question—His Aversion to Sir William Knighton—Character of George IV.—Denman's Silk Gown—Pension to Lady Westmeath—Duke of Wellington on Russia—The Reis-Effendi—Duke of Northumberland goes to Ireland—Privy Council Register—State Paper Office—The Gunpowder Plot—Catholic Emancipation—Navarino.

January 28*th*.—Until the Duke of Wellington's commission as First Lord of the Treasury appeared, many people doubted that he would take the office.[1] The Ordnance was offered to

---

[1] [The Duke of Wellington's Cabinet was at first constituted as follows:—

Duke of Wellington, First Lord of the Treasury.
Lord Lyndhurst, Lord Chancellor.
Earl Bathurst, Lord President of the Council.
Earl of Ellenborough, Lord Privy Seal.
Mr. Peel, Home Secretary.
Lord Dudley, Foreign Secretary.
Mr. Huskisson, Colonial Secretary.
Earl of Aberdeen, Duchy of Lancaster.
Mr. Goulburn, Chancellor of the Exchequer.
Mr. Charles Grant, President of the Board of Trade.
Mr. Herries, Master of the Mint.
Viscount Melville, President of the India Board.
Viscount Palmerston, Secretary at War.
Lord Dudley, Mr. Huskisson, Mr. Grant, and Lord Palmerston were the

Lord Rosslyn, who refused it, and then given to Lord Beresford, but without a seat in the Cabinet (as Lord Bathurst told
me) by his own particular desire. Some days have now elapsed,
and time has been afforded for the expression of popular
feeling and opinion on the late changes. Lady Canning
and many of Canning's friends are very much dissatisfied
with Huskisson, and think he deserted his principles and out-
raged the memory of Canning. Lady Canning particularly
is much hurt at what has passed. She has not seen Huskisson, but he is aware of her sentiments, though he says she
has so high an opinion of him that she is sure he is acting for
what he believes to be the best. The majority of Canning's
friends have adhered to the Government. The great body of
the Whigs who belonged to or supported the late Government
are indignant and violent, particularly with Huskisson, who
they think has betrayed them. An interview has taken
place between Huskisson and Lord Lansdowne, in which the
former explained his conduct, and (as far as I can learn) the
latter said but little, neither condemning nor approving.
But the great body of the party are resolved to oppose the
new Government in every way, though without attempting
to form a party, which they do not think feasible in their
present condition. They intend a desultory and harassing
warfare, particularly attacking Huskisson upon Liberal measures, to which he stands pledged, but which they think he
will now be prevented by his colleagues from carrying into
effect. The seceding Whigs are triumphant, because they
assert that what has happened is a full justification of their
conduct. They forget, however, that all this is mainly attribu-
table to them and to Canning's death, which occurred in the
interim. On the other hand the old Tories are not altogether
satisfied, and, though rejoiced at the restoration of the party,
cannot bear to see Huskisson and his friends members of the
Government from abhorrence of Canning and all Liberal

four Canningite members who resigned in May following. They were
replaced by Lord Aberdeen, Sir George Murray, Mr. Vesey Fitzgerald, and
Sir Henry Hardinge respectively.]

principles. However, the principal men have sent in their adhesions in very civil letters to the Duke.

All the Ministers (old and new) were at Windsor the other day; but it was contrived that they should not meet, the *ins* being in one room and Lansdowne and Carlisle in another, and it was afterwards discovered that in a third room by himself was Goderich. This Lord Sefton told me, and he had it from Lord Lansdowne, who had it from the King and confirmed by Lord Conyngham. His Majesty was remarkably civil to Lords Lansdowne and Carlisle. The King had a scene with the Duke of Devonshire, whom he could not persuade to stay in his place, though he tried hard. Scarlett has resigned the Attorney-Generalship, but not very willingly. He wrote to Milton and asked his advice. Milton advised him to resign, and so he did. One thing that has angered the Tories is the Duke's not having consulted Lord Eldon, nor offered him any place; and it seems he is extremely mortified, for though he did not want the seals again, he would have been very glad to take office as President of the Council.

February 25th.—There is one advantage in writing at intervals of some time instead of keeping a regular diary; I can take a more bird's-eye view of events, and avoid falling into many errors, which it would be afterwards necessary to correct. I went to Newmarket and stayed there three weeks for my health. While I was there Huskisson made his speech at Liverpool.[1] The Tories were furious, and in the

---

[1] [The speech made by Mr. Huskisson on his re-election at Liverpool on the 5th of February, 1828, is printed in vol. iii. of his 'Collected Speeches,' p. 673. It contains a full account of these transactions. The passage which gave so much offence to the Tories was that ' if the Government was such as satisfied the view I took of the interests of the country, and provided such arrangements were made in its construction *as afforded a guarantee* that the principle I approved should not be departed from, I was not precluded from joining it;' and again, 'The presence in office of such men as Lord Dudley, Lord Palmerston, Mr. Grant, and Mr. Lamb is the most satisfactory of all guarantees that the general principles of our foreign and commercial system would remain unchanged, and that Ireland would be governed with the strictest impartiality in respect to the Catholic question.'

These declarations of Mr. Huskisson had a material effect on the occurrences which not long afterwards took place.]

House of Lords the Duke of Wellington contradicted it, or
rather said he did not believe it was faithfully reported, for
all that he was reported to have said about *the guarantee* was
untrue.   I returned to town in time for the House of Commons, and found the greatest excitement, curiosity, and violence generally prevailing. As to Huskisson, he had offended
the Tories, the Whigs, and Lady Canning, and everybody
condemned him.   Parties were split to pieces, there was no
Opposition, and no man could tell what were the politics of
his neighbour, scarcely what his own.   Lady Canning was
in a state of great rage and resentment, and had inspired
George Bentinck with the same sentiments.   Clanricarde
had been sent down by her to the House of Lords furnished
with extracts of Canning's letters to throw in the teeth of
his old friends and his old enemies, and she threatened fresh
disclosures and fresh documents which were to confound all
whom she deemed worthy of her indignation.   A very angry
colloquy took place at a dinner at Warrender's between Lord
Seaford and George Bentinck, in which the latter violently
attacked Mr. Canning's friends for joining the present
Government, and quoted Huskisson's declaration that he
would never act with the men who had abandoned him. Lord
Seaford grew angry, and asked George what he knew of that
declaration and what his authority was for quoting it.   To
which George replied that he had it from himself—from
Lord Seaford at Paris. This confounded the noble Lord, and
altogether there was a pretty violent altercation, which
greatly annoyed both him and Howard, who was present,
and was regretted by all their common friends.   Two days
after this came on the debate in the House of Commons
and the explanations of Huskisson and Herries.   Their
speeches were both satisfactory enough till Tierney spoke,
who entirely knocked over their cases, or at least that of
Herries, for against Huskisson he proved nothing, except
that he might perhaps have been more communicative,
though I think this reproach applies more to Lord Goderich
than to him.   The impression left with regard to Herries
was as unfavourable as possible.

The great event of the night was Duncombe's[1] speech, which was delivered with perfect self-possession and composure, but in so ridiculous a manner that everybody laughed at him, although they were amused with his impudence and at the style and objects of his attack. However, the next day it was discovered that he had performed a great exploit; he was loudly applauded and congratulated on all sides, and made into the hero of the day. His fame was infinitely increased on a subsequent night, when Herries again came before the House and when Tommy fired another shot at him. The newspapers were full of his praises. The Whigs called at his door and eagerly sought his acquaintance. Those who love fun and personality cheered him on with loud applause, and he now fancies himself the greatest man going, and is ready to get up and abuse anybody on the Treasury bench. To me, who knew all the secret strings that moved this puppet, nothing can be more amusing.

The history of Tom Duncombe and his speech is instructive as well as amusing, for it is a curious proof of the facility with which the world may be deceived, and of the prodigious effect which may be produced by the smallest means, if they are aided by some fortuitous circumstances and happily applied. Tommy came to Henry de Ros and told him that his constituents at Hertford were very anxious he should make a speech, but that he did not know what to say, and begged Henry to supply him with the necessary materials. He advised him to strike out something new, and having received his assurance that he should be able to recollect anything that he learned by heart, and that he was not afraid of his courage failing, Henry composed for him the speech which Duncombe delivered. But knowing the slender capacity of his man, he was not satisfied with placing the speech in his hands, but adopted every precaution which his ingenuity suggested to avert the danger of his breaking

[1] [Thomas Slingsby Duncombe, nephew of the first Lord Feversham, distinguished for his Radical opinions, M.P. for Finsbury after the Reform Bill. He sat at this time for Hertford; and the incident related in the text appears to have been his *début* in political life.]

down. He made him learn the speech by heart, and then made him think it over again and put it into language of his own, justly fearing that if he should forget any of the more polished periods of the original it would appear sadly botched by his own interpolations. He then instructed him largely as to how and when he was to bring it in, supplying him with various commonplace phrases to be used as connecting links, and by the help of which he might be enabled to fasten upon some of the preceding speeches. I saw Henry de Ros the day before the debate, when he told me what he was doing, and asked me to suggest anything that occurred upon the subject, and at the same time repeated to me the speech with which he had armed his hero. I hinted my apprehensions that he would fail in the delivery, but though he was not without some alarm, he expressed (as it afterwards appeared a well-grounded) confidence in Duncombe's extraordinary nerve and intrepidity.

His speech on the second night was got up precisely in the same manner, and although it appeared to arise out of the debate and of those which preceded it, the matter had been all crammed into him by his invisible Mentor. The amusement to him and to me (especially at the honours that have been thickly poured upon him and the noise which he has made in the world) is indescribably pungent.

Thus Duncombe and his speech have made what is called a great sensation, and he has the reputation (no matter whether justly or not) of having thrown the enemy's camp into greater confusion by the boldness of his language than anybody has ever done, because nobody has ever before dared to mention those whom he dragged forward. To the ignorant majority of the world he appears a man of great promise, of boldness, quickness, and decision, and the uproar that is made about him cannot fail to impress others as well as himself with a high notion of his consequence.

Knighton is gone abroad, I have very little doubt, in consequence of what passed, and as nobody enquires very minutely into the real causes of things where they get apparent ones with ease, it is said and believed at once tha'

Duncombe is the man who has driven him out, and that he has given the first blow to that secret influence which has only been obscurely hinted at before and never openly attacked. These are great and important matters, far exceeding any consequences which the authors of the speech anticipated from its delivery at the time. And what are the agents who have produced such an effect? A man of ruined fortune and doubtful character, whose life has been spent on the race-course, at the gaming-table, and in the green-room, of limited capacity, exceedingly ignorant, and without any stock but his impudence to trade on, only speaking to serve an electioneering purpose, and crammed by another man with every thought and every word that he uttered.

June 12th.—We have now got a Tory Government, and all that remained of Canning's party are gone.[1] The case of the Duke of Wellington and Huskisson is before the world, but nobody judges fairly. Motives are attributed to both parties which had no existence, and the truth is hardly ever told at first, though it generally oozes out by degrees. After the explanations in February the Government went on to all appearance very well, but there lurked under this semblance of harmony some seeds of jealousy and distrust, not I believe so much in the mind of the Duke as in those of his Tory colleagues, and the Canningites on their side certainly felt no cordiality even towards the Duke himself. They said that he never could nor would understand anything; that he said a thing one day and forgot it the next,

---

[1] [Bills had been brought into Parliament for the disfranchisement of the boroughs of Penryn and East Retford, and the transfer of those seats to Manchester and Birmingham. On the East Retford case, which came before the House of Commons on the 19th of May, Mr. Huskisson felt bound in honour to support the measure, and voted against his colleagues. On his return home after the debate he wrote a hasty letter to the Duke of Wellington, in which he said that he 'owed it to the Duke and to Mr. Peel to lose no time in affording them an opportunity of placing his office in other hands.' The Duke regarding this as a formal act of resignation, laid it before the King and filled up the appointment. The correspondence is published in the Duke of Wellington's 'Correspondence,' New Series, vol. iv. p. 449. The resignation of Lord Palmerston, Charles Grant, and Lord Dudley followed. The details of this transaction are sufficiently alluded to in the text.]

and instead of that clearness of intellect for which he had
credit, nothing could be more puzzled and confused than
he was; that nothing could absolve him from the suspicion
of duplicity and insincerity but the conviction that his ambiguous conduct on various occasions arose from a confusion
of ideas. On the other hand, Lord Bathurst told my father
that he thought they (Huskisson and his friends) were too
much disposed to act together as a party in the Cabinet; and
it is clear that the Duke thought so too, and that this feeling
and the resentment it engendered in his mind are the real
reasons of his conduct on the late occasion.

There had been a dispute in the Cabinet about the Corn
Bill, which occasioned the discussion of it to be put off for a
few days at the time, and upon that occasion Grant resigned
his office. The matter was made up and he stayed. But
when upon the East Retford affair Huskisson resigned, and
in such an extraordinary manner, the Duke felt that there was
a disposition to embarrass him by these perpetual tenders
of resignation, which he believed they thought he would
not venture to accept. Upon receiving Huskisson's letter
he went to Lord Bathurst and consulted him, and Lord
Bathurst advised him to take him at his word. Everybody
looks for some cause which does not appear for important
events, and people with difficulty admit of very simple
solutions and very trifling causes, though such are not
unfrequently the real ones. I believe that Huskisson had
no intention of embarrassing the Duke and none of resigning; but for a cool and sensible man his conduct is most
extraordinary, for he acted with the precipitation of a
schoolboy and showed a complete want of all those qualities
of prudence and calm deliberation for which he has the
greatest credit. But though this breach might have been
avoided, from the sentiments which have been expressed by
both parties, it is evident other differences would have arisen
which must have dissolved the Government before long. After
putting aside the violent opinions on both sides, the conclusion is that Huskisson acted very hastily and imprudently,
and that his letter (say what he will) was a complete resig-

nation, and that the Duke had a right so to consider it; that in the Duke's conduct there appeared a want of courtesy and an anxiety to get rid of him which it would have been more fair to avow and defend than to deny; that on both sides there was a mixture of obstinacy and angry feeling, and a disposition to treat the question rather as a personal matter than one in which the public interests were deeply concerned. But the charge which is made on one side that Huskisson wanted to embarrass the Duke's Government and enhance his own importance, and that on the other of the Duke's insincerity, are both unfounded.

Some circumstances, however, contributed to place the Duke's conduct in an unfavourable point of view. These were the extravagant and unconcealed joy of the High Tories and of his immediate friends, and his attending at the same time the Pitt dinner and sitting there while Lord Eldon gave his famous ' one cheer more' for Protestant ascendency. That he treated Huskisson with some degree of harshness there is no doubt, but he was angry, and not without reason; the former brought it all upon himself. During the debate upon East Retford, when Huskisson was called upon by Sandon to redeem his pledge, he told Peel that he could not help himself, and must vote against him; but he begged him to put off the question till the following week, that it might be considered again. This Peel refused; had he acceded, all this would not have taken place.

When the King saw Huskisson he was extremely gracious to him, expressed the utmost regret at losing him, and said that he had wished not to see him at first, that he might avoid receiving his resignation, and in hopes that the matter would have been arranged.[1] However, the other party say that the King is very glad to have got rid of him and his party.

In the middle of all this Madame de Lieven is supposed to have acted with great impertinence if not imprudence,

---

[1] [Huskisson solicited an audience, which his Majesty refused for some days to grant; he would not see him until he had written again to the Duke of Wellington.]

and to have made use of the access she has to the King to
say all sorts of things against the Duke and the present
Government. Her dislike to the Duke has been increasing
ever since that cessation of intimacy which was caused by
Canning's accession to power, when she treated him very
uncivilly in order to pay court to Canning. Esterhazy told
me last night that although her position here was now
greatly changed, and that it was far from being so agreeable
as it was, he could not accuse her of imprudence in having
taken the part she had done, because he thought that it
had answered very well, and that the objects of her Court
had been in great measure accomplished through her
means.

June 18th.—The Duke of Wellington's Speech on the
Catholic question is considered by many to have been so
moderate as to indicate a disposition on his part to concede
emancipation, and bets have been laid that Catholics will
sit in Parliament next year. Many men are resolved to see
it in this light who are anxious to join his Government,
and whose scruples with regard to that question are removed
by such an interpretation of his speech. I do not believe
he means to do anything until he is compelled to it,
which if he remains in office he will be ; for the success of
the Catholic question depends neither on Whigs nor Tories,
the former of whom have not the power and the latter not
the inclination to carry it. The march of time and the
state of Ireland will effect it in spite of everything, and its
slow but continual advance can neither be retarded by its
enemies nor accelerated by its friends. In the meantime
men affect to consider his expressions as of importance
enough to influence their conduct in taking or refusing office.
Frankland Lewis,[1] who refused the Irish Secretaryship, said
that after that speech he regretted his refusal and would be
glad to take it, and now he wants to join the Government
again. Certainly at this moment the Tories are triumphant,

---

[1] [Right Hon. T. Frankland Lewis, a member of the Grenville and
Canning section of the Tory party; made a baronet by Sir Robert Peel;
the father of the Right Hon. Sir George Cornewall Lewis.]

and so far from the Duke's Government having any difficulty
in standing, there does not appear to be a disposition in any
quarter to oppose it.   Not only in Parliament there is no
Opposition, but the press is veering round and treating him
with great civility.   The Government seem well disposed to
follow up the Liberal policy, to which they have been suspected of being adverse, and have already declared that they
do not intend to deviate either in their foreign or domestic
policy from the principles on which the Government was
understood to act previous to the separation.   Arbuthnot
told my father yesterday that they all regret now having
resigned in 1827, and Huskisson owned to A. that he had
acted with unfortunate precipitancy.

June 29th.—I dined yesterday with the King at St.
James's—his Jockey Club dinner.   There were about thirty
people, several not being invited whom he did not fancy.
The Duke of Leeds told me a much greater list had been
made out, but he had scratched several out of it.   •We
assembled in the Throne Room, and found him already there,
looking very well and walking about.   He soon, however,
sat down, and desired everybody else to do so.   Nobody
spoke, and he laughed and said, 'This is more like a Quaker
than a Jockey Club meeting.'   We soon went to dinner,
which was in the Great Supper Room and very magnificent.
He sat in the middle, with the Dukes of Richmond and
Grafton on each side of him.   I sat opposite to him, and he
was particularly gracious to me, talking to me across the
table and recommending all the good things; he made me
(after eating a quantity of turtle) eat a dish of crawfish soup,
till I thought I should have burst.   After dinner the Duke
of Leeds, who sat at the head of the table, gave 'The King.'
We all stood up, when his Majesty thanked us, and said he
hoped this would be the first of annual meetings of the sort
to take place, there or elsewhere under his roof.   He then
ordered paper, pens, &c., and they began making matches
and stakes; the most perfect ease was established, just as
much as if we had been dining with the Duke of York, and
he seemed delighted.   He made one or two little speeches,

one recommending that a stop should be put to the exporta-
tion of horses. He twice gave ' The Turf,' and at the end
the Duke of Richmond asked his leave to give a toast, and
again gave 'The King.' He thanked all the gentlemen, and
said that there was no man who had the interests of the
turf more at heart than himself, that he was delighted at
having this party, and that the oftener they met the better,
and he only wanted to have it pointed out to him how he
could promote the pleasure and amusement of the turf, and
he was ready to do anything in his power. He got up
at half-past twelve and wished us good night. Nothing
could go off better, and Mount Charles told me he was sure
he was delighted.

I dined with the Chancellor [Lord Lyndhurst] three
days ago ; he talked to me a great deal about his acceptance
of the Great Seal and of the speculation it was. He was
Master of the Rolls with 7,000*l.* a year for life when it
was offered to him ; he debated whether it was worth while
to give this up to be Chancellor for perhaps only one year,
with a peerage and the pension. He talked the matter over
with his wife, and they agreed that if it only lasted one
year (which he evidently thought probable) it was worth
while, besides the contingency of a long Chancellorship.
He asked me if the Government was popular and reckoned
strong. I told him it was apparently popular and reckoned
strong, because there was no Opposition and little chance
of any. I said that however hazardous his speculation
might have been, it had turned out well, for he had a good
chance of being Chancellor as long as his predecessor had
been, there being so few candidates for the office. He said
this was true, and then he talked of his Court, and said it
was impossible for one man to do the business of it. In
talking of the speculation he had made, political opinions
and political consistency seemed never to occur to him, and
he considered the whole matter in a light so business-like
and professional as to be quite amusing. He talked of the
Duke, said he was a good man to do business with, quick
and intelligent, and ' how well he managed that little cor-

respondence with Huskisson,' which was droll enough, for Huskisson dined there and was in the room.

August 6th.—About three weeks ago I went to Windsor to a Council. The King had been very ill for a day or two, but was recovered. Rob Adair[1] was sworn in Privy Councillor, and he remained in the room and heard the speech, which he ought not to have done. The Duke attacked me afterwards (in joke) for letting him stay; but I told him it was no business of mine, and his neighbour ought to have told him to go. That neighbour, however, was Vesey Fitzgerald, who said it was the first time he had attended a Council, and he could not begin by turning another man out. I brought Adair back to town, and he told me a great many things about Burke, and Fox, and Fitzpatrick, and all the eminent men of that time with whom he lived when he was young. He said, what I have often heard before, that Fitzpatrick was the most agreeable of them all, but Hare the most brilliant. Burke's conversation was delightful, so luminous and instructive. He was very passionate, and Adair said that the first time he ever saw him he unluckily asked him some question about the wild parts of Ireland, when Burke broke out, ' You are a fool and a blockhead; there are no wild parts in Ireland.' He was extremely terrified, but afterwards Burke was very civil to him, and he knew him very well.

He told me a great deal about the quarrel between Fox and Burke. Fox never ceased to entertain a regard for Burke, and at no time would suffer him to be abused in his presence. There was an attempt made to bring about a reconciliation, and a meeting for that purpose took place of all the leading men at Burlington House. Burke was on the point of yielding when his son suddenly made his appearance unbidden, and on being told what was going on said, ' My father shall be no party to such a compromise,' took Burke aside and persuaded him to reject the overtures. That son Adair

---

[1] [Right Hon. Sir Robert Adair, the friend of Fox, formerly ambassador at Constantinople and Vienna. It was he whom Canning styled in one of the *jeux d'esprit* of the ' Anti-Jacobin,' Bobra-Dara-Adul-Phoola.]

described as the most disagreeable, violent, and wrong-headed of men, but the idol of his father, who used to say that he united all his own talents and acquirements with those of Fox and everybody else. After the death of Richard Burke, Fox and Burke met behind the throne of the House of Lords one day, when Fox went up to Burke and put out both his hands to him. Burke was almost surprised into meeting this cordiality in the same spirit, but the momentary impulse passed away, and he doggedly dropped his hands and left the House.

Adair told me that Lord Holland has written very copious memoirs of his own time, and particularly characters of all the eminent men who have died, in the delineation of which he excels. Soon after Pitt's resignation in 1801 there was an attempt made to effect a junction between Pitt and Fox, to which they were neither of them averse. The negotiation was, however, entrusted to subordinate agents, and Adair said that he had always regretted that they had not met, for if they had he thought the matter would have been arranged. As it was the design was thwarted by the King through the intervention (I think he said) of Lord Loughborough.

There was another Council about a week ago. On these occasions the King always whispers to me something or other about his racehorses or something about myself, and I am at this moment in high favour. We had Howley and Bloomfield[1] at this Council, with the latter of whom I made acquaintance, to the great amusement of the Duke. He laughed at seeing me conversing with this bishop.

I hear from Frederick Lamb that the Duke is greatly alarmed about Ireland. By-the-bye he, Frederick,[2] is come back from Portugal, thinking that our Government have acted very ill and very foolishly, first encouraging and then abandoning these wretched Constitutionalists to their fate, and he is no particular friend to Liberalism.

August 14th.—Just returned from Goodwood, where I

[1] [The Archbishop of Canterbury and the Bishop of London.]
[2] [Sir Frederick Lamb, afterwards created Lord Beauvale, and who became Lord Melbourne on the death of his brother William.]

went on the 11th, and heard on arriving that the Lord
High Admiral had resigned, but no particulars. It is a very
good thing at all events.

August 16th.—The Lord High Admiral was turned out.[1]
The Duke told him that he must go, but that he might
resign as if of his own accord. The Duke is all-powerful.
It is strongly reported that Peel will resign, that the Duke
means to concede the Catholic question and to negotiate a
concordat with the Pope. Many people think Lord Grey
will join the Government, and that he will be First Lord of
the Admiralty. The Duke gave his brother Dr. Bloomfield's
living without any solicitation. Esterhazy told me to-night
that Palmella entertains from twenty to thirty of his
countrymen at dinner every day, of whom there are several
hundred in London, of the best families, totally destitute.
All Palmella's property is sequestrated, but he receives the
appointment of Portuguese Minister from the Brazilian
Government.

August 22nd.—Went to Stoke on the 19th and came
back yesterday. There were the Dowager Lady Salisbury,
Duchess of Newcastle, Worcester and Lady W. Russell,
Giles, Billy Churchill. On the 18th Dawson's speech[2] at
Derry reached us, and I never remember any occurrence which
excited greater surprise. The general impression was that
he made the speech with the Duke's knowledge and concurrence, which I never believed. I thought from what he
said to me just before he went to Ireland that he had
changed his own opinion, and now many people say they
knew this; but I was little prepared to hear of his making

---

[1] [The King's letter dismissing the Duke of Clarence from the office of
Lord High Admiral was dated the 11th of August, 1828. It is published in
the Duke of Wellington's ' Correspondence,' New Series, vol. iv. p. 595.]

[2] [Mr. Peel's confidential letter to the Duke of Wellington, stating his
reluctant conviction that it was indispensably necessary for the Government
to change its policy on the Catholic question, was written on the 11th of
August, 1828. The letter is published in Sir Robert Peel's ' Posthumous
Memoirs,' vol. i. p. 189. It is a remarkable circumstance that Mr. Dawson's
speech at Derry was made *just one week afterwards* ; but there is no evidence
that he knew of the change in his brother-in-law's opinion. See for further
details as to the effect of Dawson's speech *infra.*]

such a speech at such a place as Derry, and on such an occasion as a ''Prentice Boy' commemoration. The rage and
fury of the Orangemen there and of the Orange press here
are boundless, and the violence and scurrility of their abuse
are the more absurd because Dawson only described in
glowing colours, and certainly without reserve, the actual
state of Ireland, but did not argue the question at all further
than leaving on his hearers the inevitable inference that he
thought the time for granting emancipation was come. The
truth is that the conversion of one of the most violent anti-
Catholics must strike everybody as a strong argument in
favour of the measure, and they know not by how many and
by whom his example may be followed. The Orangemen
are moving heaven and earth to create disturbances, and
their impotent fury shows how low their cause is sunk. The
Catholics, on the contrary, are temperate and calm, from
confidence in their strength and the progressive advance of
their course.   But although I think the Catholics are now
in a position which renders their ultimate success certain, I
am very far from participating in the sanguine expectations
of those who think the Duke of Wellington is convinced that
the question must be settled directly, and that he will carry
it through in the ensuing session.   In the first place I see
clearly that the Government are extremely annoyed at
Dawson's speech.   I saw Goulburn to-day, and though he
did not say much, what he did say was enough to satisfy me
of this : 'he hoped that it had been incorrectly reported.'
Dawson has written to the Duke,[1] and the letter was sent
to him to-day. But what has put me in despair about it
is a letter of the Duke's which Drummond read to me
to-day addressed, I do not know to whom, but upon that
subject.   It began, ' My dear sir,' and after other matter
proceeded nearly as follows :—' This subject has been more
discussed and more pamphlets have been written upon it in

---

[1] [This letter is published in the Duke of Wellington's ' Correspondence',
New Series, vol. iv. p. 633. The Duke said, ' Dawson's speech is too bad.
Surely a man who does such things ought to be put in a strait waistcoat.'
Ibid. p. 636.]

the course of the last twenty-five years than any other that
I can remember. No two people are agreed upon what
ought to be done, and yet the Government is expected at
once to settle the question.' This is the old argument, as if
after thirty years.' discussion in every shape it was not time
to settle the question. As if those who undertake to govern
the country were not the men who are bound to find the
means of settling it and allaying the irritation it causes.
And as if, instead of no two persons being agreed upon the
subject, all the ablest and wisest men in the country were not
cordially agreed that complete emancipation is the only
remedy for the evils that exist, and that they are opposed by
the most despicable faction which ever existed, animated by
the most base and sordid motives. This letter was read to
me as conveying the Duke's opinions, which his secretary
thought were very sound and sensible, and which I think
evinced a degree of anility quite pitiable, and proves how
little there is to expect from any liberality and good sense on
his part.

I do not yet know the whole truth of the Lord High
Admiral's resignation, but it seems that it is not yet certain.
Negotiations on the subject are still going on. I believe
he quarrelled with his council, particularly Cockburn, and
the Government took part with Cockburn. The Duke of
Clarence wants to promote deserving officers, but they oppose
it on account of the expense, and they find in everything great
difficulty in keeping him in order. His resignation will be very
unpopular in the navy, for his system of promotion was more
liberal and impartial than that of his predecessor, whose
administration was one perpetual job, and who made the
patronage of the Admiralty instrumental to governing Scotland. Hitherto the appointments of Government have not
been the most judicious—Lord Belmore to Jamaica, because
he is a Lord, and a very dull one; Lord Strangford to the
Brazils, though the Duke knows as well as anybody that he
cannot be trusted, and was recalled by Canning because he
said and did all sorts of things at Constantinople for which
he had no authority, and they found that no reliance what-

ever was to be placed in him. Lord Stuart de Rothesay, too, is sent back to Paris, though personally obnoxious to the King and universally disliked.

Stoke, August 25th.—Went to Windsor to-day for a Council and came on here after it. There were the Chancellor, Peel, Fitzgerald, Ellenborough, Sir G. Murray, the Archbishop, and Bishop of London, who came to do homage. The King gave the Chancellor a long audience, and another to Peel, probably to talk over Dawson's speech and Orange politics. After the Council the King called me and talked to me about racehorses, which he cares more about than the welfare of Ireland or the peace of Europe. We walked over the Castle, which is nearly finished, but too gaudy. The King told me he would go to Egham races to-morrow. I talked to Fitzgerald about Dawson's speech. He said he believed Dawson had never told the Duke or Peel what he meant to do, that he thought he was very bold and imprudent. However, he was glad of it, as it must assist the cause, and the moral effect in Ireland would be produced before the Duke's sentiments could be known. Lord Mount Charles told me the day before yesterday that the reason the Duke of Clarence had resigned was, that he had in many instances exceeded his powers, which had produced remonstrances from the Duke of Wellington, whereupon the Duke of Clarence tendered his resignation, and the Duke immediately carried it to the King without asking him to stay.[1] Afterwards there were some negotiations, when the Duke of Clarence refused to stay if Cockburn did. They would not,

---

[1] [A letter from the Duke of Wellington to Sir Robert Peel, dated the 13th of August, 1828, explains the circumstances that led to the removal of the Duke of Clarence from the office of Lord High Admiral. This letter is published in the first volume of Sir Robert Peel's ' Posthumous Memoirs on the Catholic Question and the Repeal of the Corn Laws,' p. 269. The Duke of Wellington says, 'He behaved very rudely to Cockburn. I saw Cockburn and Croker, and both agreed in stating that the machine could no longer work.' In a subsequent letter the Duke added, 'I quite agree with you that it is very unfortunate the Duke of Clarence has resigned. I did everything in my power to avoid that result, excepting give up Cockburn.' The whole correspondence is published in the fourth volume of the Duke's ' Correspondence,' New Series.]

however, part with Cockburn, but subsequently the Duke shook hands with him and asked him to dine at Bushey on his birthday. He said that his successor was not appointed, but it will probably be Lord Melville. The King has not been well; he goes fishing and dining at Virginia Water, stays out late, and catches cold.

August 29th.—Came from Stoke last night. There were the Lievens, Cowper, Lord Melbourne, Luttrell, Pierre d'Aremberg, Creevy, Russell, Montrond. The King went to Egham races Tuesday and Thursday, was very well received and pleased. He was very gracious to me. Madame de Lieven went over to the Lodge to see Lady Conyngham, who finding she had never seen Clifden, carried her off there, ordered luncheon and the pony carriage, took her all over the place, and then carried her back to Salthill, where the King's carriage met her and took her back to Virginia Water to dinner. Lieven told me they had never expected to find this Turkish expedition an easy business, and had always been prepared for great difficulties, &c., from which I conclude that they have met with some check. I met Bachelor, the poor Duke of York's old servant, and now the King's *valet de chambre*, and he told me some curious things about the interior of the Palace; but he is coming to call on me, and I will write down what he tells me then. There is a report that the Admiralty has been offered to Lord Melbourne. I asked him (at Stoke), and he said he had never heard of it.

London, November 25th.—I have not written anything since I left town, because nothing occurred worth remembering. Yesterday I went to the Council at Windsor. Most of the Ministers were there, the Recorder, two foreign Ministers, and the Duke of Clarence. The King seemed to be very well. The Duke of Wellington did not arrive till late, and before he was come the King sent for Peel and gave him an audience of two hours at least. I thought there must be something in the wind, and was struck with Peel's taking the Duke into one of the window recesses and talking to him very earnestly as soon as he came out. I returned to town after the Council, and in the evening went to the play, and coming out I met Henry de Ros and Frederick Lamb. The former made me go with him in his carriage, when he told me what fully explained the cause of Peel's long audience—that the Duke has at last made up his mind to carry the Catholic question, and that Peel[1] and the rest of the violent anti-Catholics are going out ; that the Duke's present idea is to apply to Huskisson, but that nothing will be done or said till the Ministers assemble in town and hold their cabinets.

He told me also that the French Government have at last agreed to make common cause with us in preventing the Russians from prosecuting the war against Turkey.

December 16th.—A Council at Windsor yesterday ; very few present, and no audiences but Aberdeen for three-quarters of an hour and the Duke for five minutes. I sent for Bachelor and had a long talk with him. He said the King was well, but weak, his constitution very strong, no malady about him, but irritation in the bladder which he could not get rid of. He thinks the hot rooms and want of air and exercise do him harm, and that he is getting every day more averse to exercise and more prone to retirement, which, besides that it weakens his constitution, is a proof that he is beginning to break. Bachelor thinks he is in no sort of danger ; I think he will not live more than two years. He says that his attendants are quite worn out with being always about him, and living in such hot rooms (which obliges them to drink) and seldom getting air and exercise. B. is at present well, but he sits up every other night with the King and never leaves him. He is in high favour, and Sir William Knighton is now as civil and obliging to him as he used to be the reverse. The King instructs him in his

---

[1] [It had not then transpired, nor was it known until long afterwards, that the proposal to carry Catholic Emancipation was made by Mr. Peel to the Duke of Wellington on the 11th of August. Sir Robert Peel states, however, in his 'Memoir,' p. 269, 'At the close of the year 1828 little, if any, progress had been made in removing the difficulties with which the Duke of Wellington had to contend ;' and, p. 274, 'The chief difficulty was the King. At the commencement of the month of January 1829 his Majesty had not yet signified his consent that the whole subject of Ireland, including the Catholic question, should be taken into consideration by his confidential servants.']

duties in the kindest manner, likes to have him about him,
and talks a great deal to him. But his Majesty keeps everybody at a great distance from him, and all about him are
afraid of him, though he talks to his pages with more
openness and familiarity than to anybody. He thinks
Radford (who is dying) is not in such favour as he was,
though he is always there; of O'Reilly the surgeon, who
sees the King every day and carries him all the gossip he can
pick up, Bachelor speaks with very little ceremony. The
King told them the other day that ' O'R. was the damnedest
liar in the world,' and it seems he is often in the habit of
discussing people in this way to his *valets de chambre*. He
reads a great deal, and every morning has his boxes brought
to him and reads their contents. They are brought up by
Knighton or Watson, both of whom have keys of all the
boxes. He says there is not one person about him whom
he likes—Mount Charles pretty well, Taylor better than
anybody, Knighton constantly there and his influence unbounded; he thinks K. can do anything.

December 20*th.*—Hyde Villiers called on me ten days ago
to give me an account of his visit to Ireland. He seems
to have been intimate with several of the leading men,
particularly Sheil, whom all agree in describing as the
cleverest man of his party. He also saw a good deal of the
Lord-Lieutenant;[1] and was struck by his imprudence and
unreserve. He spoke very positively of his determination
not to be a party to any measures contrary to his opinions,
and did not scruple to complain of the little information he
received from the Government here concerning their intentions. He also appears to have been flattered by O'Connell
into entire confidence in him, and told Villiers that he
would trust him implicitly. O'Connell and Sheil detest each
other, though Sheil does not oppose him. Lawless detests
him too, and he does everything he can to thwart and
provoke him, and opposes him in the Association[2] upon all
occasions. Lately in the affair of the ' exclusive dealing ' he

---

[1] [The Marquis of Anglesey was then Lord-Lieutenant of Ireland.]
[2] [The Catholic Association. The ' exclusive dealing ' was a pledge
required of members of the Association not to deal with Orangemen.]

met with such opposition in the Association that it required a great deal of time and management to get rid of that proposition, although in the end he carried the matter very triumphantly. But O'Connell, though opposed by a numerous party in the Association, is all-powerful in the country, and there is not one individual who has a chance of supplanting him in the affections of the great mass of the Catholics. For twenty-five years he has been continually labouring to obtain that authority and consideration which he possesses without a rival, and is now so great that they yield unlimited obedience to his individual will. As an orator he would probably fail in the English House of Commons ; but to a mob, especially an Irish mob, he is perfect, exactly the style and manner which suits their tastes and comprehensions, and consequently his success with them is unbounded. He has a large landed property, is at the head of his profession, an admirable lawyer and manager of a cause, and never for a moment diverted by political or other considerations from the due discharge of his professional duties. He is besides a man of high moral character and great probity in private life, and has been for years in the habit of affording his professional assistance gratis to those of his own religion who cannot afford to pay for it. These are some of the grounds of his popularity, to which may be added his industry and devotion to the Roman Catholic cause ; he rises at three every morning and goes to bed at eight. He possesses a very retentive memory, and is particularly strong in historical and constitutional knowledge. The great object of his ambition is to be at the head of his own profession, and his favourite project to reform the laws, a task for which he fancies himself eminently qualified. To accomplish any particular object he cares not to what charges of partial inconsistency he exposes himself, trusting to his own ingenuity to exonerate himself from them afterwards. Neither O'Connell nor Sheil are supposed to be men of courage, but Lawless is, and he is thought capable of the most desperate adventures. Sheil is of opinion that the Association might be suppressed by law ;

O'Connell thinks it could not, and that if it might legally it could not practically. O'Connell says he can keep the country quiet another year certainly, Doyle thinks not. Doyle is a very able man, a man of the world, dislikes O'Connell, but is obliged to act in concert with him. Doyle, conscious of his own talents, is deeply mortified that no field is open for their display, and he is one of those men who must be eminent in whatever cause they are engaged. Murray[1] is a clever man, but not so ambitious as Doyle; Francis Leveson is extremely cautious, cold in his manners, and therefore conciliates no general regard in Ireland, where they like an exactly opposite character. William Lamb was popular beyond all precedent, but Francis seems to have avoided giving offence to either party, which is perhaps as much as could have been expected from him, and in a country where the rival factions are so exasperated against each other to be able to preserve a character for impartiality is no small praise. I wrote to my brother Henry what I have mentioned under the head of November 21st, and in return he told me that it was in contemplation to put down the Association, and that the law officers in Ireland had reported that it was practicable, and their opinion had come over here, but the decision of the Government had not arrived.

I very soon saw enough to satisfy me that the Duke is endeavouring to prevail on Peel to stay in office, and his repeated conferences with the Bishop of Oxford and other bishops are enough to prove that he is negotiating with the Church, but nothing transpires of his intentions. Not one word has been said to Huskisson or any of his friends. My belief is that in that long conference at Windsor the King tried to prevail on Peel not to go; since which discussions between Peel, the Duke, and the Bishop have been going on to see how the matter can be arranged so as to make Peel's acquiescence palatable to the Church and the Bruns-

---

[1] [Dr. Murray, Roman Catholic Archbishop of Dublin. Lord Francis Leveson (afterwards Lord Francis Egerton and Earl of Ellesmere), Mr. Greville's brother-in-law, was then Irish Secretary. William Lamb, afterwards Lord Melbourne, had preceded him in that office. Henry Greville held a place at the Vice-Regal Court.]

wickers, and perhaps to engage the Duke to modify his intended measures accordingly. This is conjecture. The Duke is gone to Wootton and to Middleton; he is always going about.

December 21*st*.—A few days ago I saw Lord Belmore just as he was setting out for Jamaica. I went to talk to him about my place.[1] He was very civil and said he would do all that depended upon him. He does not seem to be bright, but whatever his talents may be, he seems to be left to the free exercise of them, for he told me that he felt his situation to be one of some difficulty, never having received any instructions (except of course the formal instructions given to every governor in writing) as to his conduct from the Secretary of State, having had no conversation with any of the authorities about the state of the colony, nor any intimation of their views and intentions in respect to the principal matters of interest there. He said that as the Assembly of Jamaica is now sitting, he had proposed to postpone his departure till the end of their session, when the Bills they passed would come over here, and he might discuss them with the Government and learn their sentiments and wishes as to the course he should adopt; a very sensible proposition. But he received for answer that he had better go now, for that when these Bills came over here Parliament would be sitting, and Government would not have leisure to attend to the affairs of Jamaica. And this is the way our colonies are governed! Stephen,[2] to whom I told this, said he was not surprised, for that Sir George Murray did nothing—never wrote a despatch

---

[1] [Mr. Greville held the office of Secretary of the Island of Jamaica. The duties of the office were performed by a deputy paid by the Secretary out of the fees received in the island. He never visited Jamaica, and the office held on these conditions was a sinecure; but he occasionally took part in the affairs of Jamaica in this country. The 'place' alluded to in this passage is unknown to me. Somerset, second Earl of Belmore, had just been appointed Governor of Jamaica at this time.]

[2] [James Stephen, Esq., then law adviser of the Colonial Office, and afterwards Under-Secretary of State for the Colonies. Mr. Henry Taylor the accomplished author of 'Philip von Artevelde,' was at 'the head of the West India department of the office. Sir George Murray was Secretary of State.]

—had only once since he has been in office seen Taylor, who has got all the West Indies under his care.

I might as well have put in on the 25th of November what the King said to me, as it seems to have amused everybody. I was standing close to him at the Council, and he put down his head and whispered, 'Which are you for, Cadland or the mare?' (meaning the match between Cadland and Bess of Bedlam); so I put my head down too and said, 'The horse;' and then as we retired he said to the Duke, 'A little bit of Newmarket.'

December 30th.—Hyde Villiers brought me on Thursday or Friday last a copy of the Duke's letter to Dr. Curtis,[1] which had been sent to him from Dublin under strict injunction of not showing it. The next day it appeared in all the newspapers, O'Connell having read it to the Association. It has made a great noise, and being as usual ambiguous, both parties affect to consider it to be in their favour. I fancy the Duke is very angry at its publication, at least judging from what his secretaries say.

The word *the* in the first paragraph was substituted for *a*, and this alteration these blockheads pretend makes a great difference in the sense. It makes none, and is only worthy of remark because they probably echo what he has said. It is clear enough as to his *opinion*, but nothing more. Curtis was in Spain and imprisoned by the French at Salamanca. After the battle the Duke delivered him and had a good deal

---

[1] [The Duke of Wellington had corresponded with Dr. Curtis, the titular Roman Catholic Primate of Ireland, for many years. Indeed, as appears in the text, he had known him long before at Salamanca, when this prelate was at the Irish College there. Several excellent letters by Dr. Curtis to the Duke are published in the second volume of the Duke's 'Correspondence,' New Series. The letter adverted to in the text was that in which the Duke said (not very wisely) that 'if men could bury the subject (of Catholic Emancipation) in oblivion for a short time, it might be possible to discover a satisfactory remedy.' Curtis put a copy of the letter in O'Connell's hands, and he read it aloud at the Catholic Association. Curtis sent a copy of the letter and his own reply to the Lord-Lieutenant, who answered him in another letter, in which he said that 'he did not before know the precise sentiments of the Duke upon the present state of the Catholic question.' This letter was also made public, and added fuel to the flames.]

of communication with him. He returned to Ireland, and from that period has been in occasional correspondence with the Duke. Curtis had written him a long letter, desiring information about his intentions, and this was the answer. A few days ago Hyde Villiers called on the Duke and placed in his hands the resolutions which were agreed to by a committee of the general meeting to be held in Dublin next month. He took them, but said he must decline saying anything; as Minister of the Crown he could not say a word, as whatever he did must be done in conjunction with his colleagues and with the King; that there was a disposition to draw inferences from everything, as, for example, that a gentleman he had known in Spain had written to him on the subject, and his answer had been handed about, and all sorts of inferences drawn from it, which was very inconvenient, and proved how cautious he must be. No doubt it was the Curtis correspondence to which he alluded.

1829.

January 2nd.—Lord Anglesey was recalled last Sunday. The Duke of Wellington came to see my mother either Saturday or Sunday last, and told her he had been with the King three hours the day before, talking to him about Lord A., that his Majesty was furious with him, thought he took upon himself as if he were King of Ireland, and was indignant at all he said and all he did. The Duke talked a great deal about him, but did not say he was recalled, though his manner was such that he left an impression that he had something in his mind which he would not let out. He gave it to be understood, however, that he had been endeavouring to appease the King, and that Lord A.'s recall was insisted on by his Majesty against his (the Duke's) desire. I enquired warmly whether he had asserted or only implied this, because I don't believe one word of it. I was told that he had only implied it, but had left that impression. But the Duke complained of Lord A.'s conduct to himself; that he had at first written him insolent letters, and latterly had hardly

ever written to him at all. My belief is that the Duke
has for some time wished to get rid of Lord Anglesey, that
these Cabinets have been upon this subject, and that his
recall was settled there. As to the King's dictation and the
Duke's submission, I don't believe a word of it. It has been
clear to me for some time that the Irish Government coul l
not remain in Lord Anglesey's hands. I am very sorry for
it, for I think it will have a bad effect, and have little hope
of its being followed by any measures likely to counteract
the evil it immediately occasions.

January 4th.—I have seen letters from Dublin stating
that the immediate cause of the recall was a letter which
Lord Anglesey had written to the Duke (but what that was I
have not ascertained), and that his imprudence was so great
it was impossible he could have gone on. Certainly the
writing and then publishing this letter of Curtis' is an
enormous act of indiscretion. The consternation in Dublin
seems to have been great, and Henry says that if Lord A.
does not decline all demonstrations of popular feeling towards
him, he will leave Ireland as Lord Fitzwilliam did, attended
by the whole population. Yesterday I asked Fitzgerald[1] if
it was true that Lord A. was recalled. He put on a long
face, and said 'he did not know; *recalled* he certainly was
not.' I saw he was not disposed to be communicative, so
I said no more; he, however, began again of his own
accord, and asked me whether I thought, in the event of
Lord A.'s coming away, that Francis Leveson would remain.
I told him under what conditions he had taken the place,
viz. that he was only to stay while Lord A. did; that circumstances might make a difference, but that I knew nothing.
He said he had done remarkably well, given great satisfaction, and shown great discretion in a difficult situation;
that the rock Lord A. had split upon was his vanity.

January 5th.—The exact history of what took place in
Dublin is as follows :—Lord Anglesey first of all desired

---

[1] [Right Hon. Vesey Fitzgerald, then President of the Board of Trade.
He was raised to the peerage of the United Kingdom in 1835, as Baron
Fitzgerald and Vesci.]

George Villiers would get his letter to Dr. Curtis inserted
in the newspaper.   He took it to Sheil, who agreed to
write as good an article as he could to go with it, and then
he went to Dr. Murray to inform him (as Dr. Curtis's friend)
of the intended publication, as Curtis himself was absent,
and his consent ought to have been previously obtained.   He
went afterwards to the Phœnix Park, and Lord Anglesey
laid the whole case and correspondence before him.   Some
time ago the Duke wrote to Lord Anglesey proposing that
O'Gorman Mahon and Steele should be removed from the
Commission of the Peace on account of their conduct to the
Sheriff of Clare.   Lord Anglesey wrote word that the subject
had engaged his attention, and he had laid the case before
the law officers, who had reported to him that there were
no grounds for any legal proceedings against them.   'How,
therefore,' said the Lord-Lieutenant, 'could I degrade men
against whom my law officers advised me that no charge
could be brought?'   This was one offence; and another, that
he had countenanced Lord Cloncurry, who, being a member
of the Association, was unworthy to receive the King's re-
presentative and the Chancellor.   Lord Anglesey warmly
defended Lord Cloncurry as a magistrate and a man, and
appealed to his known loyalty and respect for the King as
a proof that he would never have done anything derogatory to his own situation.   The Duke's letter he described
to have been overbearing and insolent, Lord Anglesey's [1]
temperate, but firm.   Lord Anglesey declares that these
were all the grounds of offence he had given.   Five weeks
elapsed, during which he heard nothing from the Duke,
and at the end of that time he received his letter of
recall, conceived nearly in these words:—'My dear Lord
Anglesey,—I am aware of the impropriety of having
allowed your letter to remain so long unanswered, but I
wished to consult my colleagues, who were out of town.   I
have now done so, and they concur with me that with such

[1] [The correspondence of Lord Anglesey with the Duke of Wellington on
these charges is now published in the 'Wellington Correspondence,' New
Series, vol. v. p. 244.]

a difference of opinion between the King's Minister and the Lord-Lieutenant of Ireland the government of that country could not be conducted by you with advantage to the public service. I have therefore taken the King's pleasure on the subject, and he commands me to inform you that you will be immediately relieved from your government. I will give you the earliest information of the arrangement which will be made in consequence. Believe me, &c.' This is nearly the letter.[1] From Lord Anglesey George Villiers went to Shiel, and with him to O'Connell, to whom Lord A. desired he would communicate the event. O'Connell was dreadfully dejected, so much so that Shiel and G. Villiers were glad to go home and dine with him in order to calm him. They at length succeeded in doing so, and made him engage to abstain from any discussion of the recall in the Association the next day (a promise which he did not keep). Shiel made a very fine speech in the Association. Nothing, they say, can exceed the general feeling on the subject, and Lord Anglesey appears to be acting with great dignity and reserve ; he wishes to decline all popular honours, and he put off going to the play, which he was to have done.

January 7th.—The Duke wrote to Francis Leveson to say he must not be surprised to hear that a letter would reach Lord Anglesey by that day's post, conveying to him his recall; that the King was so furious with him that he said he would make any sacrifice rather than allow him to remain there five minutes longer. His Secretary had repeatedly remonstrated with the Lord-Lieutenant on his imprudent language in Ireland, and on the tone of his letters to the Duke, but that he always defended both on 'principle. The Duke said that his letters were most offensive towards him, yet he continued to declare that he should have been glad to keep Lord Anglesey on but for the King. The Lord-Lieutenant did not go to the play, but

---

[1] [The letter itself is now published in the ' Wellington Correspondence,' New Series, vol. v. p. 366. Mr. Greville's version of it differs in no material point from the original, though the language is slightly altered.]

his family did, and were received with great applause, although the pit was full of Orangemen. Lord Melville has refused the Lord-Lieutenancy.

January 11*th*.—When George Villiers sent me the accounts of what had passed in Ireland about Lord Anglesey's letter to Curtis I wrote him a long letter, in which I told him why I thought the letter and its publication were unjustifiable and indiscreet, and particularly cautioned him against connecting himself much with the agitator, on account of the harm it would do him here. He wrote me a long answer, defending Lord Anglesey and his measures, but I do not think he makes out a case for him, and if the Lord-Lieutenant makes in the House of Lords the defence which he proposes to make I think he will fail; but if he can keep Lord Plunket on his side, who is now said to be very eager about him, he will do. Plunket is under the influence of Blake, who keeps, as George Villiers says, 'Lord Plunket's mind in his breeches' pocket.' Lord Anglesey has behaved very well since the quarrel, declining all honours and expressions of public feeling.

January 12*th*.—Lord Mount Charles came to me this morning and consulted me about resigning his seat at the Treasury. He hates it and is perplexed with all that has occurred between the Duke and Lord Anglesey. I advised him to resign, feeling as he does about it. He told me that he verily believed the King would go mad on the Catholic question, his violence was so great about it. He is very angry with him and his father for voting as they do, but they have agreed never to discuss the matter at all, and his mother never talks to the King about it. Whenever he does get on it there is no stopping him. Mount Charles attributes the King's obstinacy to his recollections of his father and the Duke of York and to the influence of the Duke of Cumberland. He says that 'his father would have laid his head on the block rather than yield, and that he is equally ready to lay his head there in the same cause.' He is furious with Lord Anglesey, but he will be very much afraid of him when he sees him. Mount Charles was in the room when

Lord Anglesey took leave of the King on going to Ireland, and the King said 'God bless you, Anglesey! I know you are a true Protestant.' Anglesey answered, 'Sir, I will not be considered either Protestant or Catholic; I go to Ireland determined to act impartially between them and without the least bias either one way or the other.' Lord Anglesey dined with Mount Charles the day before he went. The same morning he had been with the Duke and Peel to receive their last instructions, and he came to dinner in great delight with them, as they had told him they knew he would govern Ireland with justice and impartiality, and they would give him no instructions whatever. He showed me a letter from Mr. Harcourt Lees full of invectives against the Duke and lamentations at the recall, to show how the Protestants regretted him as well as the Catholics.

He then talked to me about Knighton, whom the King abhors with a detestation that could hardly be described. He is afraid of him, and that is the reason he hates him so bitterly. When alone with him he is more civil, but when others are present (the family, for instance) he delights in saying the most mortifying and disagreeable things to him. He would give the world to get rid of him, and to have either Taylor or Mount Charles instead, to whom he has offered the place over and over again, but Mount Charles not only would not hear of it, but often took Knighton's part with the King. He says that his language about Knighton is sometimes of the most unmeasured violence—wishes he was dead, and one day when the door was open, so that the pages could hear, he said, 'I wish to God somebody would assassinate Knighton.' In this way he always speaks of him and uses him. Knighton is greatly annoyed at it, and is very seldom there. Still it appears there is some secret chain which binds them together, and which compels the King to submit to the presence of a man whom he detests, and induces Knighton to remain in spite of so much hatred and ill-usage. The King's indolence is so great that it is next to impossible to get him to do even the most ordinary business, and Knighton is still the only man who can prevail on him to sign papers, &c. His greatest delight is to make those who have business to transact with him, or to lay papers before him, wait in his anteroom while he is lounging with Mount Charles or anybody, talking of horses or any trivial matter; and when he is told, 'Sir, there is Watson waiting,' &c., he replies, ' Damn Watson; let him wait.' He does it on purpose, and likes it.

This account corresponds with all I have before heard, and confirms the opinion I have long had that a more con-temptible, cowardly, selfish, unfeeling dog does not exist than this King, on whom such flattery is constantly lavished. He has a sort of capricious good-nature, arising however out of no good principle or good feeling, but which is of use to him, as it cancels in a moment and at small cost a long score of misconduct. Princes have only to behave with common decency and prudence, and they are sure to be popular, for there is a great and general disposition to pay court to them. I do not know anybody who is proof against their seductions when they think fit to use them in the shape of civility and condescension. The great consolation in all this is the proof that, so far from deriving happiness from their grandeur, they are the most miserable of all mankind. The contrast between their apparent authority and the con-tradictions which they practically meet with must be pecu-liarly galling, more especially to men whose minds are seldom regulated, as other men's are, by the beneficial disci-pline of education and early collision with their equals. There have been good and wise kings, but not many of them. Take them one with another they are of an inferior charac-ter, and this I believe to be one of the worst of the kind. The littleness of his character prevents his displaying the dangerous faults that belong to great minds, but with vices and weaknesses of the lowest and most contemptible order it would be difficult to find a disposition more abundantly furnished.

January 16*th.*—I went to Windsor to a Council yesterday. There were the Duke, the Lord Chancellor, Chancellor of the Exchequer, Master of the Mint, Lord President, Lord

Aberdeen, Peel, Melville, Ellenborough. The King kept us waiting rather longer than usual. He looked very well, and was dressed in a blue great coat, all over gold frogs and embroidery. Lord Liverpool was there to give up the late Lord's Garter, and had an audience. He said to me afterwards that the King had asked him all sorts of questions about his family concerns, with which he seemed extraordinarily well acquainted, and to some of which he was puzzled to give an answer. The King is the greatest master of gossip in the world, and his curiosity about everybody's affairs is insatiable. I spoke to Peel about the Council books,[1] which are in the State Paper Office, and he promised they should be restored to the Council Office.

Just before I set off to Windsor I heard from Ireland, and this is an extract of the letter:—' Lord Anglesey received a letter from Peel this morning to the effect " that as he had written and published a letter such as no Lord-Lieutenant was justified in writing, it was his Majesty's pleasure that Lords Justices should be immediately appointed." Francis found him very smiling and glorious, but angry, and declaring that he would do just the same again if he had to choose his line of conduct.'

À propos of Denman's silk gown, Mount Charles told me the other day that Denman wrote a most humble apology to the King, notwithstanding which the Duke of Wellington had great trouble in mollifying him. At last he consented, but wrote himself on the document that in consideration of his humble apology his Majesty forgave him, as he thought it became the King to forgive a subject, but desired this note might be preserved in the Treasury, where Mount Charles says it now is.[2]

January 21st.—The sealed orders with which the ships

---

[1] [At the fire which took place at Whitehall in 1619 several volumes of the ' Council Register ' were lost or dispersed. Some of these missing volumes were in the State Paper Office, and two are still in the British Museum.]

[2] [This curious correspondence has now been published in the fifth volume of the Duke of Wellington's ' Despatches,' New Series, pp. 117 and 153. The cause of the quarrel was a Greek quotation from Dion which Denman had introduced into one of his speeches at the Queen's trial. In

have sailed from Plymouth were orders to prevent the Portuguese (who had been sent away) from landing at Terceira.

Lady Westmeath was the woman meant in the article in the 'Times' from Ireland about the pension to which Lord Anglesey would not agree. The story is very true. There was 700*l*. disposable on the Pension Fund, and the Duke of Wellington desired 400*l*. might be given to Lady Westmeath, which Lord Anglesey and the Secretary both protested against, and were resolved to resign rather than agree to it. They wrote to the Duke such strong remonstrances that he appears to have desisted from the design, for they heard no more of it. It is therefore false that this had anything to do with the recall, though it is by no means improbable that it served to alienate the Duke from the Marquis and to make him desire the more to get rid of him. This happened as long ago as last August, I think.

Yesterday the Duke dined with us, in very good spirits, and agreeable as he always is, though not so communicative and free as he used to be. He had never told Francis Leveson about the Duke of Northumberland[1] till Sunday, when the King's answer to the memorial (which answer was drawn up by the Duke of Wellington) the following passage occurs:—

'The King could not believe that the Greek quotation referred to had occurred to the mind of the advocate in the eagerness and heat of his argument, nor that it was not intended, nor that it had not been sought for and suggested for the purpose of applying to the person of the Sovereign a gross insinuation.' Denman, however, prayed his Majesty to believe that 'no such insinuation was ever made by him, that the idea of it never entered his mind,' &c.

The truth about this quotation is this:—During the Queen's trial Dr. Parr, who was a warm supporter of the Queen and an intimate friend of Denman, employed himself in ransacking books for quotations which might be used in the defence. Thus he lit in Bayle's Dictionary, article 'Octavia,' upon the answer made by Pythias, one of the slaves of Octavia, to Tigellinus, when he was torturing the slaves of the Empress in order to convict her of adultery. The same answer occurs in substance in Tacitus' 'Annals,' book xiv. cap. 60. This Parr sent to Denman, and Denman used it in his speech. The fact is, therefore, that the quotation had been 'sought for and suggested' for the express purpose of saying something personally offensive to the King. The King's resentment against Denman did not end here, as will be seen lower down, where he refused to receive the Recorder's report through the Common Serjeant.]

[1] [Hugh, third Duke of Northumberland, was declared Lord-Lieutenant of Ireland on the recall of Lord Anglesey.]

he wrote to announce the appointment. His Grace seems mightily pleased with it, and fancies that his figure and his fortune are more than enough to make him a very good Lord-Lieutenant. He says he was obliged to coax him a little to get him to accept it.

He said that he was on the best terms with France, talked of Russia and her losses in the war, adding that the notion of her power was at an end. He believed that the Russians were numerically as strong as the Turks in the last campaign, and they were much more numerous than they said : first, *because* they said they were not so ; and secondly, that he had other reasons for believing it ; he thought they had begun the campaign with 160,000 men, and had lost 120,000.[1] They were talking of St. Petersburg and its palaces. The Duke said that the fortunes of the great Russian nobles —the Tolstoys, &c.—were so diminished that they lived in corners of their great palaces ; but this was owing to the division of property and the great military colonies, by which the Crown lands were absorbed, and the Emperors had no longer the means of enriching the nobles by enormous donations as formerly. When to these circumstances are added the amelioration of the condition of the serfs, and the spirit of general improvement, and the growth of Liberal ideas, generated by intercommunication with the rest of Europe, it is impossible to doubt that a revolution must overtake Russia within a short period, and probably the Emperor has undertaken this war in order to give vent to the restless humours which are beginning to work. I said so to Lord Bathurst, and he replied that ' he thought so too, but that the present Emperor was a man of great firmness,' as if any individual authority or character could stem the torrent of determined action impelled by universal revolution of feeling and opinion.

[1] [This seems an extraordinary statement, but it shows how well informed the Duke was. In Major von Moltke's narrative of the campaign of 1828 he estimates the average force of the Russian army at 100,000. But from May 1828 to February 1829 no less than 210,108 men passed through the hospitals, or died in them. So that, as Moltke remarks, in the course of those ten months every man in his army was twice in hospital. Never did an army suffer more severely from sickness.]

He said the late Emperor was so well aware of this that he died of the vexation it had caused him, which was aggravated by the reflection that he was in great measure himself the cause of it. He was so bit by Liberal opinions, and so delighted with the effects he saw in other countries flowing from the diffusion of intelligence and freedom, that he wished to engraft these dangerous exotics upon the rude and unprepared soil of his own slavish community. When he went to Oxford he was so captivated with the venerable grandeur of that University that he declared he would build one when he got home, and it is equally true that he said he 'would have an Opposition.' These follies were engendered in the brain of a very intelligent man by the mixture of such crudities with an unbounded volition, and the whole fermented by a lively imagination and a sincere desire to confer great benefits on his country.

January 25th.—Lord Anglesey's departure from Dublin was very fine, and his answer to the addresses good. I fancy George Villiers had some hand in penning them. The Duke when he dined with us the other day said that a Russian Extraordinary Ambassador was coming here to overhaul Lieven, a M. Matuscewitz. He is the principal writer in their Foreign Office, a clever man. Their despatches are more able than they used to be, but the Duke said that the Turkish officers are better conducted than any, and the Turkish Ministers extremely able. Lord Bathurst told me he had lately read the minutes of a conversation between the Reis-Effendi and the Allied Ministers after the battle of Navarino, when they were ignorant whether the Turk had received intelligence of the event, and that his superiority over them was exceedingly striking. This was the conference in which when they asked him 'supposing such an event had happened, what he should say to it,' he replied 'that in his country they never named a child till its sex was ascertained.'

Everybody thinks the appointment of the Duke of Northumberland a very good one, and that the Duke is in great luck to get him. It is surprising that he should have consented to go, but he probably likes to do something and display his magnificence. He is a very good sort of man, with a very narrow understanding, an eternal talker, and prodigious bore. The Duchess is a more sensible woman, and amiable and good-humoured. He is supposed to be ruled in all things by her advice; he has no political opinions, and though he has hitherto voted against the Catholics, he is one of the people who pin their faith on the Duke, and who are made to vote in any way and upon anything as he may please to desire them.

This pension of Lady Westmeath's makes a great noise, and it is generally believed that when Lord Anglesey refused to grant it the Duke got the King's sign manual for it, and the job was done. The truth is that Lord Anglesey had at first refused, or rather expressed his disapprobation, and asked the Duke if the King had commanded it, to which the Duke sent an angry answer that he might have been sure he should not have recommended it but by the King's commands. M—— told me the pension (400l.) was granted four months ago, for he signed the warrant himself.

Polignac is gone to Paris, but the Duke thinks not to be Minister. Polignac told him that he wished to return here, as he thought he could do more good here than there.

Yesterday I went with Amyot to the State Paper Office to look after my Council books. I found one book belonging to my office and nearly thirty volumes of the 'Register of the Council of State,'[1] which I mean to ask for, but which I suppose they will refuse. Amyot suggests that as all the acts of the Council of State were illegal and of no authority they cannot be considered as belonging to the Council Office, and are merely historical records without an official character. I shall try, however, to get them. Mr. Lemon showed us a great many curious papers. When he first had the care of the State papers they were in the greatest confusion, and he has been diligently employed in reducing them to order.

[1] [Of the time of the Commonwealth. The 'Privy Council Register' extends from the last years of Henry VIII. to the present time, not including the Commonwealth.]

Every day has brought to light documents of importance and interest, which as they are successively found are classed and arranged and rendered disposable for literary and historical purposes.

Lemon has found papers relating to the Powder Plot alone sufficient to make two quarto volumes, exceedingly curious; all Garnett's original papers, and I hope hereafter they will be published.[1] We saw the famous letter to Lord Mounteagle, of which Lemon said he had, he thought, discovered the author. It has been attributed to Mrs. Abington, Lord Mounteagle's sister, but he thinks it was written by Mrs. Vaux, who was a friend of hers, and mistress, probably, of Garnett; it is to her that many of Garnett's letters are addressed. It seems that Mrs. Vaux and Mrs. Abington were both present at the great meeting of the conspirators at Hendlip, and he thinks that the latter, desirous of saving her brother's life, prevailed on Mrs. Vaux to write the letter, for the handwriting exactly corresponds with some other writing of hers which he has seen. There is a remarkable paper written by King James with directions what questions should be put to Guy Faux, and ending with a recommendation that he should be tortured first gently, and then more severely as might be necessary. Then the depositions of Faux in the Tower, which had been taken down (contrary to his desire) in writing, and which he was compelled to sign upon the rack; his signature was written in faint and trembling characters, and his strength had evidently failed

[1] [The substance of these papers has since been published by the late David Jardine, Esq., in his excellent 'Narrative of the Gunpowder Plot.' (Murray, London, 1857.) Some of the particulars here referred to by Mr Greville are not strictly accurate, or at least have not been confirmed by subsequent investigation. It is not probable that the letter to Lord Mounteagle was written by Mrs. Abington or by Mrs. Vaux, nor is it at all certain that either of these ladies had any knowledge of the Plot. Mr. Jardine ascribes the letter to Tresham ('Narrative,' &c., p. 83). Garnett's admissions are printed in Jardine's Appendix. His knowledge of the Plot was derived from Greenway, a priest to whom Catesby had revealed it in confession. The Pope was probably not privy to the Plot. The celebrated 'Treatise on Equivocation' was found in Tresham's desk. The identical copy with Garnett's notes is still in the Bodleian; it was reprinted in 1851.]

in the middle, for he had only written 'Guido.' There is a
distinct admission in the Plot papers in Garnett's own hand
that he came to a knowledge of the Plot otherwise than by
the Sacrament of Confession, which oversets Lingard; a
paragraph by which it is clear that the Pope knew of it;
and a curious paper in which, having sworn that he had
never written certain letters, which letters were produced
when he was taxed with the false oath, Garnett boldly justifies himself, and says that they ought not to have questioned
him on the subject, having the letters in their hands, and
that he had a right to deny what he believed they could not
prove—a very remarkable exposition of the tenets of his
order and the doctrines of equivocation.

When I came away from the State Paper Office I met
George Dawson, and we had a long conversation about Irish
affairs, from which I gathered what is to be done. The
Catholic question is to be conceded, the elective franchise
altered, and the Association suppressed. This latter is, I
take it, to be a preliminary measure, and I suspect the
Duke went to the King on Monday with the resolution
of the Cabinet on the subject, and I think so the more
because the Archbishop was sent for post-haste just before
he went. Dawson talked to me a great deal about his
speech at Derry, and said that so many of his friends
were aware of the change in his opinions that he thought
it more fair and manly to declare them at once in public
than to use any dissimulation with his constituents and
leave them to be guessed at, as if he dared not own them;
that he had made a great sacrifice, for he had risked his
seat, which was very secure before, and had quarrelled with
Peel, with his family, and with all his old political friends
and associates. We talked a great deal about Peel, and I
see clearly that he has given way; probably they have compromised the business, and he agrees to the Emancipation
part, in order to have the Association suppressed and the
40s. freeholders disfranchised. Lord Anglesey always said
that his removal would facilitate the business, for the Duke
wished to have all the credit of it to himself, and had no

mind to divide it with him, whereas if Lord Anglesey had
remained the chief credit would have fallen to his share.

I met Sir Edward Codrington in the morning, and walked
with him to Downing Street, where he was going to talk to
the Duke about his Navarino business.   He is mightily
incensed, thinks he has been scandalously used both by
Dudley and Aberdeen, is ready to tell his story and show
his documents to anybody, and says he is resolved the whole
matter shall come out, and in the House of Commons if he
can produce it.   God knows how his case will turn out, but
I never saw a man so well satisfied with himself.   He says
that the action at Navarino was, as an achievement, nothing
to the affair at Patras, when with one line-of-battle ship,
one frigate, and a corvette he drove before him Ibrahim
and four Turkish admirals and a numerous fleet.

February 4th.—Went to Middleton last Friday; very
few people.   I returned by Oxford, and called on Dr.
Bandinell, who took me to the Bodleian.   I could not
find any Council books, but I had not much time to de-
vote to the search.   Dr. Bandinell promised to inform me
if he could find any books or manuscripts relating to my
office.   I was surprised to find in the Bodleian a vast
number of books (manuscripts) which had belonged to Pepys.
I came to town on Monday night, and found that the con-
cession of Catholic Emancipation was generally known; the
'Times' had an article on Friday which clearly announced it.
The rage and despair of the Orange papers is very amusing.
I have not yet heard how the King took it all.   Glad as I
am that the measure is going to be carried, the conduct of
all those who are to assist in it (the old anti-Catholics) seems
to me despicable to the greatest degree; having opposed it
against all reason and common sense for years past, now
that the Duke of Wellington lifts up his finger they all obey,
and without any excuse for their past or present conduct.
The most agreeable event, if it turns out to be true, is the
defection of Dr. Philpots, whose conduct and that of others
of his profession will probably not be without its due effect
in sapping the foundations of the Church.   All the details

that I have yet learnt confirm my opinion that the spirit in
which the Duke and his colleagues approach this great
measure is not that of calm and deliberate political reasoning,
but a fearful sense of necessity and danger, to which they
submit with extreme repugnance and with the most miserable feelings of pique and mortification at being compelled
to adopt it. The Duke and Peel wrote to Francis Leveson,
complaining of my brother's having met Shiel at dinner,
and they were so enraged with George Villiers [1] that they
seriously meditated turning him out of his office. Wretched
and contemptible to the greatest degree! They are now
exceedingly annoyed because it is discovered that Woulffe
was once a member of the Association, and would willingly
have him turned out of the place of Assistant-Barrister, which
has just been given to him; but Francis is resolved to maintain him in it. They say the Duke sent a copy of the King's
Speech to Lord Eldon.

February 5th.—Went to Brookes' yesterday, and found
all the Whigs very merry at the Catholic news. Most of
them were just come to town and had heard nothing till
they arrived. The old Tories dreadfully dejected, but obliged
to own it was all true ; intense curiosity to hear what Peel
will say for himself. The general opinion seems to be that the
Duke has managed the matter extremely well, which I am
disposed to think too, but there is always a disposition to
heap praise upon him whenever it is possible. Nobody yet
knows who are converted and who are not; they talk of
nine bishops; I think he will have them all, and I expect a
very great majority in the House of Lords. Many people
expect that Wilmot's plan will be adopted, restraining the
Catholics from voting in matters concerning the Church,
which I do not believe, for Wilmot is at a discount and his

---

[1] [Mr. George Villiers, then an Irish Commissioner of Customs (afterwards Earl of Clarendon), had cultivated the society of Shiel and invited
him to dinner. Such an attention from an English official to an Irish
Catholic was at that time an unheard-of innovation. Shiel told his host
that he had never dined in a Protestant house before. The Duke of Wellington took great umbrage at what he considered an unwarrantable breach
of official decorum.]

plan is absurd and impracticable. Lord Harrowby, however, is all for it. I hear many of the Liberals are exceedingly provoked, and not unnaturally, at the Duke's effecting this measure, at which they have been so long labouring in vain, and give as many spiteful flings at him as they can about the insincerity of his letter to Curtis. It matters very little now whether he was sincere or not. It evidently was part of his plan to keep it all secret till it was matured, and as Curtis chose to ask him questions he was quite right to throw dust in his eyes.

CHAPTER V.

February 6th.—Parliament met yesterday; a very full
attendance and intense interest and curiosity. The King's
Speech, which was long and better written than usual, was
not quite satisfactory to the Catholics. I met Lord Harrowby coming from the House of Lords, and he said they did not
like it at all; the previous suppression of the Association
was what they disliked. However, all discontent was removed by Peel's speech, which was deemed (as to the intentions of Ministers) perfectly satisfactory even by those

who were most prejudiced before against Government. I was in the House of Commons. Peel was very feeble, and his case for himself poor and ineffective; all he said was true enough, but it was only what had been said to him over and over again for years past, and he did not urge a single argument for acquiescing now which was not equally applicable to his situation two years ago. However, everybody was so glad to have the measure carried that they did not care to attack Peel or his speech, though if there had been a Brunswicker of any talent in the House he might have cut it up finely; two or three of them spoke, but wretchedly ill, and Lord Chandos was not at all violent, which I expected he would have been. Lord Eldon was violent but impotent, in the House of Lords, and Lord Bathurst made a sort of explanation which was very poor.

On leaving the House of Commons I fell in with Burdett, Lord Sefton, and G. Bentinck, and they all owned that the business is very handsomely done; and Morpeth and many others whom I saw afterwards at the Club are quite satisfied. They would have preferred that the Catholic Relief Bill and the suppression of the Association should have gone together, but do not make any difficulties on this head, and acknowledge (which is the truth) that the Duke was probably obliged to do something to cajole the Tories, and give some colour to their conduct. I sat next to Fitzgerald in the House, who is not yet re-elected, and he told me that this was absolutely necessary. He was of course delighted and said, 'How right Lord Francis was to trust to the Duke,' which, however, is all nonsense. He had no reason to trust to him at all, and I really believe would not have continued in office as Irish Secretary unless he had adopted this measure. He owned as Peel was speaking that he was not doing it well; he was feeble and diffuse in the beginning, and too full of civilities and appeals to Bankes and his old associates. However, thank God, the event is accomplished, no matter how; probably it could not have been done without the concurrence of these Tories, who have, I think, certainly lost their character by their conduct; and there is this evil in the history of the measure, that a blow will have been given to the reputation of public men in general which will, I strongly suspect, have an important though not immediate effect upon the aristocratic influence in this country, and tend remotely to increase the democratic spirit which exists. In all these proceedings there has been so little of reason, principle, or consistency; so much of prejudice, subserviency, passion, and interest, that it is impossible not to feel a disgust to parties in general. The conduct of those idiots the Brunswickers is respectable in comparison with such men as the High Churchmen; and the Whigs and Catholic supporters, however they may have suffered before, in this matter stand clear and have only grounds for exultation. They accept the measure with great moderation, and are not disposed to mar the success of it by the introduction of any topics likely to create ill blood, nor to damp the ardour of new converts by throwing their former follies in their faces.

Now, then, the Duke is all-powerful, and of course he will get all the honour of the day. Not that he does not deserve a great deal for having made up his mind to the thing; he has managed it with firmness, prudence, and dexterity; but to O'Connell and the Association, and those who have fought the battle on both sides of the water, the success of the measure is due. Indeed, Peel said as much, for it was the Clare election which convinced both him and the Duke that it must be done, and from that time the only question was whether he should be a party to it or not. If the Irish Catholics had not brought matters to this pass by agitation and association, things might have remained as they were for ever, and all these Tories would have voted on till the day of their death against them.

Mahony, who is here, has written over to O'Connell, as have all the other Catholics, to implore him to use his whole influence to procure the dissolution of the Association, and it is said that O'Connell had an idea of resigning his seat for Clare to Vesey, on the ground that, having turned him out because he had joined a Government hostile

to their claims, he owed him this reparation on finding it
not to be the case. But I doubt whether this scheme is
practicable ; still, I think if O'Connell could do it it would be a
good thing, and serve to reconcile the people here to him, and
give a great lift to his character. I expect to hear that the
Association has dissolved itself on receiving intelligence of
the proceedings in the House of Commons. Lord Anglesey
spoke very well, but nobody will care for his case now;
besides, I doubt his making out a good one. The fact is
that they laid a trap for him, and that he fell into it; that
the Duke's letters became more insulting, and that a prudent
man would have avoided the snare into which his high spirit
and passion precipitated him.

February 8th.—Peel spoke on Friday night better than he
did on Thursday. Huskisson made a spiteful speech, and
George Dawson one which I heard Huskisson say he thought
one of the neatest speeches he had ever heard. I dined
yesterday with all the Huskissonians at Grant's. There were
there Lords Granville, Palmerston, and Melbourne, Huskisson,
Warrender, and one or two more. Huskisson is in good
humour and spirits, but rather bitter; he said that if Peel
had asked the advice of a friend what he should do, the
advice would have been for his own honour to resign. I said
I did not think Peel would have got credit by resigning. He
said, 'But don't you think he has quite lost it by staying in?'
He owned, however, that the Duke could not have carried
it without Peel, that his influence with the Church party
is so great that his continuance was indispensable to the
Duke.

This affair of the Portuguese at Terceira [1] (which certainly,

[1] [In December 1828 an expedition, consisting of 652 Portuguese
refugees of the party of the Queen, sailed from England for Terceira in four
vessels, under the command of Count Saldanha. The British Government
ordered Captain Walpole, of the 'Ranger,' to stop this expedition off
Terceira, which he did by firing a gun into Saldanha's ship. The ground
taken by the Duke of Wellington in defence of this measure was his resolution to maintain the neutrality of England between the two parties then
contending for the Crown of Portugal. But the proceeding was vehemently
attacked in Parliament and elsewhere.]

unless it can be explained, seems a gross outrage) they all
fell upon very severely, and Lord Harrowby told me afterwards he could not understand it, and thought for the honour
of the country it should be explained forthwith.

We are now beginning to discover different people's
feelings about this Catholic business, and it is clear that
many of the great Tories are deeply offended that the Duke
was not more communicative to them, principally, it seems,
because they have continued to talk in an opposite sense
and in their old strain up to the last moment, thereby com-
mitting themselves, and thus becoming ridiculous by the
sudden turn they are obliged to make. This they cannot
forgive, and many of them are extremely out of humour,
although not disposed to oppose the Duke. The Duke of
Rutland means to go to Belvoir, and not vote at all. The
Duke of Beaufort does not like it, but will support the
measure. Lowther has been to the King, and it is supposed
he has resigned. They complain that the Duke has thrown
them over; still nobody doubts that he will have great
majorities in both Houses. It was asserted most positively
at Brookes' yesterday that Peel's offer of resigning his seat
at Oxford had been accepted. In Dublin the moderate
people are furious with O'Connell for his abuse of everybody.
There is no getting over the fact that he it is who has
brought matters to this conclusion, and that but for him the
Catholic question would never have been carried ; but his
violence, bad taste, and scurrility have made him 'lose the
lustre of his former praise.'

February 9th.—I called at Devonshire House in the
morning, and there found Princess Lieven very eloquent and
very angry about the Terceira business, which certainly requires explanation. She is very hostile to the Duke, which
is natural, as he is anti-Russian, and they have never got
over their old quarrel. Saldanha got up a *coup de théâtre*
on board his ship. When Walpole fired on him a man was
killed, and when the English officer came on board he had
the corpse stretched out and covered by a cloak, which was

suddenly withdrawn, and Saldanha said, ' Voilà un fidèle sujet de la Reine, qui a toujours été loyal, assassiné,' &c.

Went from thence to Mrs. Arbuthnot, who declaimed against O'Connell and wants to have a provision in the Bill to prevent his sitting for Clare, which I trust is only her folly, and that there is no chance of such a thing. The Duke came in while I was there. He said he had no doubt he should do very well in the House of Lords, but up to that time he could only (that he knew of for certain) reduce the majority of last year to twenty. He did not count bishops, of whom he said he knew nothing, but the three Irish bishops would vote with him. There were many others he did not doubt would, but he could only count upon that number. He held some proxies, which he said he would not make use of, such as Lord Strangford's, as he could not hear from him in time, and would not use anybody's proxy for this question who had voted against it before. I told him how peevish the Duke of Rutland, and Beaufort, and others of the High Tories were, but he only laughed. In the evening Fitzgerald told me that the Convocation at Oxford had accepted Peel's resignation of his seat for the University, but left the time to him. It seems to me that this affair was mismanaged. In the first instance Peel wrote to the Dean of Christ Church, but he and Lloyd[1] agreed that he ought to write to the Vice-Chancellor, which he did. The Vice-Chancellor did not read his letter till after they had voted the address to Parliament by three to one, after which it was difficult for them to express anything but disapprobation of Peel's conduct; whereas if the Vice-Chancellor had read it first, probably the petition would not have been carried, or at any rate not by so large a majority. He had better have carried his Bill through and then resigned, when I have no doubt he would have been re-elected; very likely he may be as it is.

Tom Duncombe is going to make another appearance

[1] [The Bishop of Oxford, one of Sir Robert Peel's most intimate friends.]

on the boards of St. Stephen's, on the Terceira business, and he is to give notice to-night. He has been with Palmella and Frederick Lamb, who are both to assist in getting up his case, and he expects to be supported by some of the Whigs and by the Huskissonians, which latter are evidently anxious to do anything they can to embarrass the Government. I know nothing of the case, which, *primâ facie*, appears much against Government; but the moment is so ill-chosen, in the midst of this great pending affair, that I think they will make nothing of it. Palmella is a great fool for his pains, for in clamouring against the Duke he is only kicking against the pricks. As to Duncombe, he is egged on by Lambton and instructed by Henry de Ros, who cares nothing about the matter, and only does it for the fun of the thing. I have no idea but that Duncombe must cut a sorry figure when he steps out of the line of personal abuse and impertinence.

February 11*th*.—Nothing is thought of or talked of but the Catholic question; what Peers and bishops will vote for it? who voted before against it? There is hardly any other feeling than that of satisfaction, except on the part of the ultra-Tories, who do not attempt to conceal their rage and vexation; the moderate Tories, who are mortified at not having been told of what was going on; and Huskisson's party, who would have been glad to have a share in the business, and who now see themselves in all probability excluded for ever. O'Connell arrived yesterday; it is supposed he will not take his seat, but he does not seem inclined to co-operate with Government in keeping things quiet. However, his real disposition is not yet known, and probably he has not made up his mind what to do, but waits for events. Notwithstanding the declaration of the bishops, I do not believe they will vote against Government. Peel spoke very well last night, and severely trimmed old Bankes, which gives me great pleasure, so much do I hate that old worn-out set. How this change of measures changes one's whole way of thinking; though I have nothing to do with politics, I cannot help being influenced to an extraordinary degree by

what has passed, and can understand from my own feelings
how those who are deeply engaged may be biassed by the
prejudices and attachments of party without any imputation against their sincerity or judgment. When we see men
pursuing a course of which we greatly disapprove, all their
actions and motives are suspected by us, and *vice versâ*. We
lend a willing ear to imputations of vanity, interest, and
other unworthy motives, and when we cannot explain or
comprehend the particulars of men's conduct, we judge
them unfavourably while we are opposed to their measures;
but when they do what we wish, we see the same things very
differently, and begin to hesitate about the justice of our
censures and the suspicions which we previously entertained.
It is pretty clear that the Duke will have a good majority
in the House of Lords, and that many Peers and bishops will
find excuses between this and then for voting with him or
remaining neutral.

A ridiculous thing happened the other day in the Vice-
Chancellor's Court. Sugden had taken a brief on each side
of a case without knowing it. Horne, who opened on one
side and was followed by another lawyer, was to be answered
by Sugden; but he, having got hold of the wrong brief,
spoke the same way as Horne. The Vice-Chancellor said
coolly, 'Mr. Sugden is with you?' 'Sir,' said Horne, 'his
argument is with us, but he is engaged on the other side.'
Finding himself in a scrape, he said 'it was true he held
a brief for the other party, but for no client would he ever
argue against what he knew to be a clear rule of law.' However, the Court decided against them all.

February 13*th.*—Still the Catholic question and the
probable numbers in the House of Lords; nobody talks of
anything else. Lord Winchelsea makes an ass of himself,
and would like to be sent to the Tower, but nobody will mind
anything such a blockhead says. Lord Holland talks of a
majority of sixty in the Lords. I walked with Ebrington
to O'Connell's door the other day; he went in. The next day
I asked him what had passed. He said that he had pressed
him strongly to dissolve the Association; O'Connell said he

could not press it himself, but would write to Ireland that it was the unanimous opinion of all the friends of the cause here that it should be done. The fact is, he does not dare to acquiesce in all the measures of Government, though there is little doubt but that he desires to see an end to associations and agitations. Lady Jersey affects to be entirely in the Duke's confidence. She said to Lord Granville at Madame de Lieven's the other night that 'she made it a rule never to talk to the Duke about affairs in public,' and she said to me last night that she had known what was to be done about the Catholics all along. Certainly she contrives to make the Duke see a great deal of her, for he calls on her, and writes to her perpetually, but I doubt whether he tells her much of anything. Some of the household have made a struggle to be exempted from the general obligation on all members of Government to vote for the Bill, but the Duke will not stand it, and they must all vote or go out. The Privy Seal was offered to Lord Westmoreland, but he refused, and his answer was good—that if he had been in the Cabinet, he might possibly have seen the same grounds for changing his mind on the Catholic question that the other Ministers did; but not having had those opportunities, he retained his former opinions, and therefore could not accept office.

February 22nd.—Went to Newmarket last Sunday and came back on Thursday. Still the Catholic question and nothing else. Everybody believed that the Duke of Cumberland would support Government till he made this last speech. He went to the King, who desired him to call on the Duke, and when he got to town he went uninvited to dine with him. There has been nothing of consequence in either House, except the dressing which Lord Plunket gave Lord Eldon, though that hard-bitten old dog shows capital fight. Peel has got a most active and intelligent committee at Oxford, and they consider his election safe. Inglis's committee, on the contrary, is composed of men not much better than old women, except Fynes Clinton, the chairman. Every day the majority promises to be greater in the House of Lords, but it is very ridiculous to see the faces many of these Tory

Lords make at swallowing the bitter pill.   Too great a noise
is made about Peel and his sacrifices, but he must be supported and praised at this juncture.   It is not for those who
have been labouring in this cause, and want his assistance,
to reject him or treat him uncivilly now that he tenders it.
But as to the body of the High Tories, it is impossible not to
regard their conduct with disgust and contempt, for now they
feel only for themselves, and it is not apprehension of those
dangers they have been constantly crying out about that
affects them, but the necessity they are under of making
such a sudden turn, and bitter mortification at having
been kept in total ignorance, and, consequently, having
been led to hold the same violent language up to the last
moment.   If Canning had lived, God knows what would
have happened, for they never would have turned round for
him as they are now about to do for the Duke.   The circumstances of the case are just the same ; since 1825 the same
game has been going on in Ireland, and in the same manner,
and the Clare election was only what had happened at
Waterford before.   All this has given a blow to the aristocracy, which men only laugh at now, but of which the effects
will be felt some day or other.   Who will have any dependence hereafter on the steadiness and consistency of public
men, and what credit will be given to professions and declarations?   I am glad to see them dragged through the
mire, as far as the individuals are concerned, but I am sorry
for the effect that such conduct is likely to produce.   There
was a capital paper of Cobbett's yesterday, in his best style.
Many Liberals are uneasy about what are called the securities, and when the Duke tells Lord Colchester that if he
will wait he will be satisfied with the Bill, it is enough to
make them so ; but my hopes predominate over my fears.
Yesterday Vesey Fitzgerald said that ' we had not yet seen
what some people might consider the objectionable parts of the
measure, but that, though certain things might be necessary,
the Government are impressed with the paramount necessity
of not leaving the Catholic question behind them, and that
the Duke was a man of too firm a mind not to go through

with it;' and I think he said distinctly that Catholics and
Protestants must be placed on an equal footing, or something
to that effect. He went off into a panegyric on the Duke, and
said that seeing him as he did for several hours every day,
he had opportunities of finding out what an extraordinary
man he was, and that it was remarkable what complete
ascendancy he had acquired over all who were about him.
The English of this is (what everybody knew) that he dictates to his Cabinet. The fact is, he is a man of great
energy, decision, and authority, and his character has been
formed by the events of his life, and by the extraordinary
circumstances which have raised him to a situation higher
than any subject has attained in modern times. That his
great influence is indispensable to carry this question, and
therefore most useful at this time, cannot be doubted, for
he can address the King in a style which no other Minister
could adopt. He treats with him as with an equal, and the
King stands completely in awe of him. It will be long
before a correct and impartial estimate is formed of the
Duke's character and abilities ; his talents, however, must be
of a very superior, though not of the most shining description. Whatever he may be, he is at this moment one of the
most powerful Ministers this country has ever seen. The
greatest Ministers have been obliged to bend to the King, or
the aristocracy, or the Commons, but he commands them
all. M—— told me that he had not seen the King, but
that he heard he was as sulky as a bear, and that he was
sure he would be very glad if anything happened to defeat
this measure, though he is too much afraid of the Duke to do
anything himself tending to thwart it.

The Emperor of Russia is extremely disgusted at the
language of the newspapers here, and desired his Minister
to complain of it, and the Duke wrote the answer himself, in
which he entered at great length into the character and
utility of the press in this country, a dissertation affording a
proof certainly of his quickness and industry, overwhelmed
as he is with business. The Duke of Richmond offered to
give up his Garter, but the Duke would not take it back.

February 26*th.*—The debate on Monday night in the House of Lords was very amusing. It was understood the Duke of Clarence was to speak, and there was a good deal of curiosity to hear him. Lord Bathurst was in a great fright lest he should be violent and foolish. He made a very tolerable speech, of course with a good deal of stuff in it, but such as it was it has exceedingly disconcerted the other party. The three royal Dukes Clarence, Cumberland, and Sussex got up one after another, and attacked each other (that is, Clarence and Sussex attacked Cumberland, and he them) very vehemently, and they used towards each other language that nobody else could have ventured to employ; so it was a very droll scene. The Duke of Clarence said the attacks on the Duke [of Wellington] had been *infamous*; the Duke of Cumberland took this to himself, but when he began to answer it could not recollect the expression, which the Duke of Clarence directly supplied. 'I said "infamous."' The Duke of Sussex said that the Duke of Clarence had not intended to apply the word to the Duke of Cumberland, but if he chose to take it to himself he might. Then the Duke of Clarence said that the Duke of Cumberland had lived so long abroad that he had forgotten there was such a thing as freedom of debate.

February 27*th.*—They say Plunket made one of the best speeches he ever delivered last night, and Lord Anglesey spoke very well. There was hardly anybody in the House. Peel's election [Oxford University] is going on ill. The Convocation presents a most disgraceful scene of riot and uproar. I went to the Committee Room last night at twelve, and found nobody there but Dr. Russell, the head-master of the Charterhouse, who was waiting for Hobhouse and amusing himself by correcting his boys' exercises. He knew me, though he had not seen me for nearly twenty years, when I was at school. I shall be sorry if Peel does not come in, not that I care much for him, but because I cannot bear that his opponents should have a triumph.

Lady Georgiana Bathurst told me she had had a great scene with the Duke of Cumberland. She told him not to

be factious and to go back to Germany; he was very angry,
and after much argument and many reproaches they made
it up, embraced, and he shed a flood of tears.

I met with these lines in 'The Duke of Milan' (Massinger),
which are very applicable to the Duke in his dealings with
his Cabinet and his old friends the Tories :—

> You never heard the motives that induced him
> To this strange course ?   No ; these are cabinet councils,
> And not to be communicated but
> To such as are his own and sure.   Alas !
> We fill up empty places, and in public
> Are taught to give our suffrages to that
> Which was before determined.

March 1st.—As the time draws near for the development
of the plans of Government a good deal of uneasiness and
doubt prevails, though the general disposition is to rely on
the Duke of Wellington's firmness and decision and to hope
for the best.   Peel's defeat at Oxford,[1] though not likely to
have any effect on the general measure, is unlucky, because
it serves to animate the anti-Catholics; and had he succeeded, his success would have gone far to silence, as it must
have greatly discouraged, them.   Then the King gives the
Ministers uneasiness, for the Duke of Cumberland has been
tampering with him, and through the agency of Lord Farn-
borough great attempts have been made to induce him to
throw obstacles in the way of the measures.   He is very well
inclined, and there is nothing false or base he would not do
if he dared; but he is such a coward, and stands in such awe
of the Duke, that I don't think anything serious is to
be apprehended from him.   There never was anything so
mismanaged as the whole affair of Oxford.   First the letter
Peel wrote was very injudicious ; it was a tender of resignation, which being received just after the vote of Convocation,

---

[1] [Upon the 4th of February Mr. Peel resigned his seat for the University of Oxford, in consequence of the change of his opinions on the Catholic question.   A contest ensued, Sir Robert Harry Inglis being the candidate
opposed to Peel.   Inglis was returned by a majority of 146.   Mr. Peel sat
for the borough of Westbury during the ensuing debates.]

they were obliged to accept it. Then he should never have
stood unless he had been sure of success, and it appears now
that his canvass never promised well from the beginning.
He should have taken the Chiltern Hundreds, and immediately informed them that he had done so. Probably no
opposition would have been made, but after having accepted
his resignation they could not avoid putting up another man.
It appears that an immense number of parsons came to vote
of whose intentions both parties were ignorant, and they
almost all voted for Inglis.

Codrington was at Brookes' yesterday, telling everybody
who would listen to him what had passed at an interview,
that I have mentioned before, with the Duke of Wellington,
and how ill the Duke had treated him. He said the Duke
assured him that neither he nor any of his colleagues, nor the
Government collectively, had any sort of hostility to him, but,
on the contrary, regarded him as a very meritorious officer,
&c. He then said, ' May I, then, ask why I was recalled ? '
The Duke said, ' Because you did not understand your
instructions in the sense in which they were intended by
us.' He replied that he had understood them in their plain
obvious sense, and that everybody else who had seen them
understood them in the same way—Adam, Ponsonby, Guille-
minot, &c.—and then he asked the Duke to point out the
passages in which they differed, to which he said, ' You
must excuse me.' All this he was telling, and it may be
very true, and that he is very ill-used; but if he means to bring
his case before Parliament, he is unwise to chatter about it
at Brookes', particularly to Lord Lynedoch, to whom he
was addressing himself, who is not likely to take part with
him against the Duke.

March 2nd.—Saw M—— yesterday ; he has been at
Windsor for several days, and confirmed all that I had heard
before about the King. The Duke of Cumberland has
worked him into a state of frenzy, and he talks of nothing
but the Catholic question in the most violent strain. M——
told me that his Majesty desired him to tell his household
that he wished them to vote against the Bill, which M—— of

course refused to do. I asked him if he had told the Duke of Wellington this; he said he had not, but that the day the Ministers came to Windsor for the Council (Thursday last, I think) he did speak to Peel, and told him the King's violence was quite alarming. Peel said he was afraid the King was greatly excited, or something to this effect, but seemed embarrassed and not very willing to talk about it. The result, however, was that the Duke went to him on Friday, and was with him six hours, and spoke to his Majesty so seriously and so firmly that he will now be quiet. Why the Duke does not insist upon his not seeing the Duke of Cumberland I cannot imagine. There never was such a man, or behaviour so atrocious as his—a mixture of narrow-mindedness, selfishness, truckling, blustering, and duplicity, with no object but self, his own ease, and the gratification of his own fancies and prejudices, without regard to the advice and opinion of the wisest and best informed men or to the interests and tranquillity of the country.

March 3rd.—Called on H. de Ros yesterday morning, who told me that the Duke of Cumberland and his party are still active and very sanguine. Madame de Lieven is in all his confidence, who, out of hatred to the Duke, would do anything to contribute to his overthrow. The Duke of Cumberland tells her everything, and makes her a medium of communication with the Huskisson party, who, being animated by similar sentiments towards the Duke, the Tories think would gladly join them in making a party when the way is clear for them. The Chancellor went to Windsor on Sunday, and on to Strathfieldsaye at night, where he arrived at three in the morning. Yesterday the Duke came to town, but called at Windsor on his way. Dawson, however, told me that he believed the Duke in *his* interview on Friday had settled everything with the King, and had received most positive assurances from him that no further difficulties should be made; but it is quite impossible to trust him.

March 4th.—Nothing could exceed the consternation which prevailed yesterday about this Catholic business. The advocates of the Bill and friends of Government were in indescribable alarm, and not without good cause. All yesterday it was thought quite uncertain whether the Duke's resignation would not take place, and the Chancellor himself said that nothing was more likely than that they should all go out. On Sunday the King sent for the Chancellor; he went, and had an audience in which the King pretended that he had not been made aware of all the provisions of the Bill, that the securities did not satisfy him, and that he could not consent to it. The Chancellor could do nothing with him ; so instead of returning to town he went on to Strathfieldsaye, where the Duke was gone to receive the Judges. There he arrived at three in the morning, had a conference of two hours with the Duke, and returned to town quite exhausted, to be in the House of Lords at ten in the morning. The Duke called at Windsor on his way to town on Monday, and had a conversation with the King, in which he told him it was now impossible for him to recede, and that if his Majesty made any more difficulties he must instantly resign. The King said he thought he would not desert him under any circumstances, and tried in vain to move him, which not being able to do, he said that he must take a day to consider his final determination, and would communicate it. This he did yesterday afternoon, and he consented to let the Bill go on. There was a Cabinet in the morning, and another in the evening, the latter about the details of the Bill, for Francis Leveson and Doherty were both present.

I met Lord Grey at dinner, and in the evening at Brookes' had a great deal of conversation with Scarlett, Duncannon, and Spring Rice. They are all much alarmed, and think the case full of difficulties, not only from the violence and wavering of the King, but from the great objections which so many people have to the alteration of the elective franchise. Duncannon says nothing shall induce him to support it, and he would rather defeat the whole measure than consent to it ; Spring Rice, on the contrary, is ready to swallow anything to get Emancipation. The object of the anti-Catholics is to take advantage of this disunion and of the various circumstances which throw difficulties in the way of Government, and they think, by availing themselves of them dexterously, they will be able to defeat the measure. They all seem to think that the Oxford election has been attended with most prejudicial effects to the cause. It has served for an argument to the Cumberland faction with the King, and has influenced his Majesty very much.

Huskisson made a speech last night which must put an end to any hopes of assistance to the Opposition from him and his party, which it is probable they looked to before, and I dare say the Duke of Cumberland has held out such hopes to the King. The correspondence between the Duke of Wellington and the Duke of Cumberland was pretty violent, I believe, but the Duke of Cumberland misrepresents what passed both in it and at their interview. He declared to the Duke that he would not interfere in any manner, but refused to leave the country; to Madame de Lieven he said that the Duke had tried everything—entreaties, threats, and bribes—but that he had told him he would not go away, and would do all he could to defeat his measures, and that if he were to offer him 100,000*l.* to go to Calais he would not take it. The degree of agitation, alternate hopes and fears, and excitement of every kind cannot be conceived unless seen and mixed in as I see and mix in it. Spring Rice said last night he thought these next four days to come would be the most important in the history of the country of any for ages past, and so they are. I was told last night that Knighton has been co-operating with the Duke of Cumberland, and done a great deal of mischief, and that he has reason to think that K. is intriguing deeply, with the design of expelling the Conyngham family from Windsor. This I do not believe, and it seems quite inconsistent with what I am also told —that the King's dislike of Knighton, and his desire of getting rid of him, is just the same, and that no day passes that he does not offer Mount Charles Knighton's place, and, what is more, that Knighton presses him to take it.

March 5th.—Great alarm again yesterday because the

Duke, the Chancellor, and Peel went down to Windsor again. Dined at Prince Lieven's. In the evening we learned that everything was settled—that as soon as the King found the Duke would really leave him unless he gave way, he yielded directly, and that if the Duke had told him so at first he would not have made all this bother. The Duke of Cumberland was there (at Lieven's), but did not stay long. I sat next to Matuscewitz (the Russian who is come over on a special mission to assist Lieven), and asked him if he did not think we were a most extraordinary people, and seeing all that goes on, as he must do, without any prejudices about persons or things, if it was not marvellous to behold the violence which prevailed in the Catholic discussion. He owned that it was inconceivable, and, notwithstanding all he had heard and read of our history for some years past, he had no idea that so much rage and animosity could have been manifested and that the anti-Popery spirit was still so vigorous. The day, however, is at last arrived, and to-night the measure will be introduced. But the Duke of Cumberland and his faction by no means abandon all hopes of being able to throw over the Bill in its progress, and they will leave no stone unturned to effect their purpose and to work on the King's mind while it is going on.

March 6th.—Peel brought on the Catholic question last night in a speech of four hours, and said to be far the best he ever made. It is full of his never-failing fault, egotism, but certainly very able, plain, clear, and statesmanlike, and the peroration very eloquent. The University of Oxford should have been there in a body to hear the member they have rejected and him whom they have chosen in his place. The House was crammed to suffocation, and the lobby likewise. The cheering was loud and frequent, and often burst upon the impatient listener without. I went to Brookes' and found them all just come from the House, full of satisfaction at Peel's speech and the liberality of the measure, and in great admiration of Murray's. The general disposition seemed to be to support both the Bills, and they argued justly who said that those who would have supported the whole measure if it had been in one Bill ought not to take advantage of there being two to oppose the one they dislike. The part that is the most objectionable is making the measure so far prospective ('hereafter to be elected') as to exclude O'Connell from Clare, more particularly after the decision of the Committee in his favour. Six weeks ago Mrs. Arbuthnot told me that it was intended to exclude him, but I did not believe her. It seemed to me too improbable, and I never thought more about it. If they persist in this it is nothing short of madness, and I agree with Spring Rice, who said last night that instead of excluding him you should pay him to come into Parliament, and rather buy a seat for him than let him remain out. If they keep him out it can only be from wretched motives of personal spite, and to revenge themselves on him for having compelled them to take the course they have adopted. The imprudence of this exception is obvious, for when pacification is your object, and to heal old wounds your great desire, why begin by opening new ones and by exasperating the man who has the greatest power of doing mischief and creating disturbance and discontent in Ireland? It is desirable to reconcile the Irish to the measures of disfranchisement, and to allow as much time as possible to elapse before the new system comes into practical operation. By preventing O'Connell from taking his seat his wrongs are identified with those of the disfranchised freeholders. He will have every motive for exasperating the public mind and exciting universal dissatisfaction, and there will be another Clare election, and a theatre for the display of every angry passion which interest or revenge can possibly put in action. It is remarkable that attacks, I will not say upon the Church, but upon Churchmen, are now made in both Houses with much approbation. The Oxford parsons behaved so abominably at the election that they have laid themselves open to the severest strictures, and last night Lord Wharncliffe in one House and Murray in the other commented on the general conduct of Churchmen at this crisis with a severity which was by no means displeasing except to the bishops. I am convinced that very few years will elapse before the Church will really be in danger. People will grow tired of paying so dearly for so bad an article.

March 8th.—Yesterday the list came out of those who had voted on the Catholic question, by which it appeared that several people had voted against the Government (particularly all the Lowthers) who were expected to vote with them, and of course this will be a test by which the Duke's strength and absoluteness may be tried, so much so that it is very generally thought that if he permits them to vote with impunity he will lose the question. It was said in the evening that Lowther and Birkett had resigned, but Lord Aberdeen, whom I met at dinner, said they had not at five o'clock yesterday evening. It is, I think, impossible for the Duke to excuse anybody who votes against him or stays away. Dined at Agar Ellis's and met Harrowbys, Stanleys, Aberdeen, &c. Lord Harrowby thought Peel's speech extremely able and judicious. He said that Lord Eldon had asserted that Mr. Pitt's opinions had been changed on this question, which was entirely false, for he had been much more intimate with Mr. Pitt than Lord Eldon ever was, and had repeatedly discussed the question with him, and had never found the slightest alteration in his sentiments. He had deprecated bringing it on because at that moment he was convinced that it would have driven the King mad and raised a prodigious ferment in England. He talked a great deal of Fox and Pitt, and said that the natural disposition of the former was to arbitrary power and that of the latter to be a reformer, so that circumstances drove each into the course the other was intended for by nature. Lord North's letter to Fox when he dismissed him in 1776 was, ' The King has ordered a new commission of the Treasury to be made out, in which I do not see your name.' How dear this cost him, and what an influence that note may have had on the affairs of the country and on Fox's subsequent life ! They afterwards talked of the ' Cateatonenses ' written by Canning,

Frere, and G. Ellis. Lady Morley has a copy, which I am to see.[1]

March 9th.—It was reported last night that there had been a compromise with Lowther, who is to retain his seat and to vote for the Bill in all its other stages. But he dined at Crockford's, and told somebody there that he had tendered his resignation and had received no answer. I do not understand this indecision; they must deprive those who will not support them thoroughly. 'Thorough,' as Laud and Strafford used to say, must be their word.

Evening.—I asked Lord Bathurst to-day if Lowther, &c., were out, and he said nothing had been done about it, that there was plenty of time. Afterwards met Mrs. Arbuthnot in the Park, and turned back with her. She was all against their being turned out, from which I saw that they are to stay in. We met Gosh, and I walked with them to the House of Commons. We renewed the subject, and he said that he had been just as much as I could be for the adoption of strong measures, but that the great object was to carry the Bill, and if the Duke did not act with the greatest prudence and caution it would still be lost. He hinted that the difficulties with the King are still great, and that he is in a state of excitement which alarms them lest he should go mad. It is pretty clear that the Duke cannot venture to turn them out. In the meantime the Duke of Cumberland continues at work. Lord Bathurst told me that he went to Windsor on Saturday, that he had assured the King that great alarm prevailed in London, that the people were very violent, and that the Duke had been hissed by the mob in going to the House of Lords, all of which of course he believes. The Duke is very unwell. I think matters do not look at all well, and I am alarmed.

March 11th.—The Duke was much better yesterday, went

[1] [The 'Musæ Cateatonenses,' a burlesque narrative of a supposed expedition of Mr. George Legge to Cateaton Street in search of a Swiss chapel. Nothing can be more droll. The only copy I have seen is still at Saltram. This *jeu d'esprit* (which fills a volume) was composed by Canning and his friends one Easter recess they spent at Ashbourne.]

to the House, and made a very good and stirring speech in
answer to Lord Winchelsea, who disgusted all his own party
by announcing himself an advocate for reform in Parliament.
It is now clear that Lowther, &c., are not to quit their
places unless something fresh occurs. The reason supposed
is that the King supports them, and that the Duke does not
venture to insist on their dismissal. The real reason is
that he has got an idea that the Whigs want to make him
quarrel with his old friends in order to render him more
dependent upon them, and he is therefore anxious (as he
thinks he can) to carry through the measure without
quarrelling with anybody, so that he will retain the support
of the Tories and show the Whigs that he can do without
them, a notion which is unfounded, besides being both unwise
land iliberal. He has already given some persons to understand that they *must* support him on this question, and now
he is going to grant a dispensation to others, nor is there
any necessity for *quarrelling* with anybody. Lowther himself evidently felt that he could not hold his office and oppose
the measure, and consequently resigned. The Duke might
accept his resignation with a very friendly explanation on
the subject; eventually he would be certain to join Government again, for to what other party could he betake himself?
These great Tory borough-mongering Lords have no taste
for opposition. Arbuthnot told my father that this was his
feeling, and when I told Mrs. Arbuthnot what a bad moral
effect the Duke's lenity had, she said, ' Oh, you hear that from
the Opposition.' Last night in his speech, when he said he
had the cordial support of his Majesty, he turned round with
energy to the Duke of Cumberland. Several Peers upon one
pretext or another have withdrawn the support they had
intended to give to the Duke's Bill. Fourteen Irish bishops
are coming over in a body to petition the King against this
Bill, and most foolish they. The English bishops may by
possibility be sincere and disinterested in their opposition
(not that I believe they are), but nobody will ever believe
that the Irish think of anything but their scandalous reve-
nues. The thing must go; the only question is when and

how. The Kent petition to the King is to be presented, I
believe, by Lords Winchelsea and Bexley; they would not
entrust it to Peel. Lord W. wanted to march down to
Windsor at the head of 25,000 men.

March 14*th*.—Arbuthnot told the Duke what was said
about not turning out the refractory members, and he
replied, 'I have undertaken this business, and I am determined to go through with it. Nobody knows the difficulties
I have in dealing with my royal master, and nobody knows
him so well as I do. I will succeed, but I am as in a field
of battle, and I must fight it out my own way.' This would
be very well if there were not other motives mixed up with
this—jealousy of the Whigs and a desire to keep clear of
them, and quarrel with them again when this is over.
Herries told Hyde Villiers that *their* policy was conservative,
that of the Whigs subversive, and that they never could act
together. All false, for nobody's policy is subversive who
has much to lose, and the Whigs comprise the great mass of
property and a great body of the aristocracy of the country.
Nobody seems to doubt that the Bill will pass. The day
before yesterday the Duke of Newcastle went to Windsor
and had an audience. Lord Bathurst told me that they had
reason to believe his Grace had told the King his own sentiments on the Catholic question, but that the King had made
no answer. But as nobody was present they could not
depend on the truth of this (which they had from his
Majesty himself, of course), and he begged me to find out
what account the Duke gave of it.

March 15*th*.—The Duke of Newcastle was with the King
an hour and a half or two hours. After he had presented
his petitions he pulled out a paper, which he read to the
King. His Majesty made him no answer, and desired him
if he had any other communications to make to him to send
them through the Duke of Wellington. I dare say this is
true, not because he says so, but because there has been no
notice taken of the Duke's visit in any of the newspapers.
They now talk of thirteen bishops, and probably more,

voting with Government. I suppose the majority will be very large.

March 16*th.*—17*th.*—I received a message from the King, to tell me that he was sorry I had not dined with him the last time I was at Windsor, that he had intended to ask me, but finding that all the Ministers dined there except Ellenborough, he had let me go, that Ellenborough might not be the only man not invited, and 'he would be damned if Ellenborough ever should dine in his house.' I asked Lord Bathurst afterwards, to whom I told this, why he hated Ellenborough, and he said that something he had said during the Queen's trial had given the King mortal offence, and he never forgave it. The King complains that he is tired to death of all the people about him. He is less violent about the Catholic question, tired of that too, and does not wish to hear any more about it. He leads a most extraordinary life—never gets up till six in the afternoon. They come to him and open the window curtains at six or seven o'clock in the morning; he breakfasts in bed, does whatever business he can be brought to transact in bed too, he reads every newspaper quite through, dozes three or four hours, gets up in time for dinner, and goes to bed between ten and eleven. He sleeps very ill, and rings his bell forty times in the night; if he wants to know the hour, though a watch hangs close to him, he will have his *valet de chambre* down rather than turn his head to look at it. The same thing if he wants a glass of water; he won't stretch out his hand to get it. His valets are nearly destroyed, and at last Lady Conyngham prevailed on him to agree to an arrangement by which they wait on him on alternate days. The service is still most severe, as on the days they are in waiting their labours are incessant, and they cannot take off their clothes at night, and hardly lie down. He is in good health, but irritable, and has been horribly annoyed by other matters besides the Catholic affair.

18*th.*—I was at Windsor for the Council and the Recorder's report. We waited above two hours; of course his

Majesty did not get up till we were all there. A small attendance in Council—the Duke, Bathurst, Aberdeen, Melville, and I think no other Cabinet Minister. I sent for Batchelor, the King's *valet de chambre*, and had a pretty long conversation with him; he talked as if the walls had ears, but was anxious to tell me everything. He confirmed all I had before heard of the King's life, and said he was nearly dead of it, that he was in high favour, and the King had given him apartments in the Lodge and some presents. His Majesty has been worried to death, and has not yet made up his mind to the Catholic Bill (this man knows, I'll be bound). But what he most dwelt on was Sir William Knighton. I said to him that the King was afraid of the Duke. He replied he thought not; he thought he was afraid of nobody but of Knighton, that he hated him, but that his influence and authority were without any limit, that he could do anything, and without him nothing could be done; that after him Lady Conyngham was all-powerful, but in entire subserviency to him; that she did not dare have anybody to dine there without previously ascertaining that Knighton would not disapprove of it; that he knew everything, and nobody dared say or do a thing of any sort without his permission. There was a sort of mysterious awe with which he spoke of Knighton, mixed with dislike, which was curious. He is to call on me when he comes to London, and will, I dare say, tell me more. Returned to town at night, and heard of Sadler's speech[1] and read it. It is certainly very clever, but better as reported than as it was delivered. He sent the report to the 'Morning Journal' himself, and added some things and omitted others, and thereby improved it. He is sixty-seven years old, and it is his maiden speech; certainly very remarkable and indicative of much talent. Lord Harrowby told me he heard it, and was greatly struck by it.

19*th*.—Last night the debate ended, with a very ex-

---

[1] [Mr. Sadler, who had never sat in Parliament before, was returned by the Duke of Newcastle at this time for the express purpose of opposing the Catholic Relief Bill, which he did with considerable ability.]

cellent speech from Robert Grant,[1] and a speech from Lord
Palmerston which astonished everybody.   The Attorney-
General was violent and brutal, and Peel's reply very good;
he was bursting with passion, but restrained himself.   I
met Tierney, and told him that there was great disappointment that he had not answered Sadler.   He said he could
not speak for coughing, that Sadler's speech was clever, but
over-rated, nothing like so good as they talked of.   Robert
Grant's was very good indeed, the best for matter; Palmerston's the most brilliant, ' an imitation of Canning, and not
a bad one.'   Though the Opposition gained eight in this
division, they are disappointed and disheartened, and will
make but little fight on the other stages (as it is thought).
Nine bishops are to vote.   The meeting at Lambeth took
place the day before yesterday, but it came to nothing.   They
separated agreeing to meet again, and in the meantime that
each should take his own line.   Tierney talked of the Duke's
management of this business with great admiration, as did
Lord Durham last night in the same strain; but after all
what was it but the resolution of secresy (which I think was
a most wise and judicious one) ? for he did nothing but keep
the secret.   However, the thing has been well imagined and
well executed.   Tierney thinks Peel will resign when it is
all over, and at his father's death will be made a Peer.   I
should not wonder ; he must be worn to death with the
torrents of abuse and invective with which his old friends
assail him on every occasion.   I presume that if he could
have anticipated their conduct he would not have been so
civil to them in the beginning, and would have taken another
turn altogether; it would have been better for him.   Lady
Worcester told me to-day what adds to many other proofs
that the Duke is a very *hard* man ; he takes no notice of any
of his family ; he never sees his mother, has only visited
her two or three times in the last few years ; and has not now
been to see Lady Anne, though she has been in such affliction
for the death of her only son, and he passes her door every

---

[1] [Robert Grant, Esq., M.P., brother of Mr. Charles Grant. He was
afterwards appointed Governor of Bombay.]

time he goes to Strathfieldsaye. He is well with Lady
Maryborough, though they quarrelled after Lord M. was
driven from the Cabinet; Lord Wellesley is seriously affronted
with him at the little consideration the Duke shows for him,
and for having shown him no confidence in all this business,
especially as the Catholic question was the only political
difference that existed between them. He is a very extraordinary man certainly, and with many contradictions in his
character; in him, however, they are so much more apparent
than in any other man, for he is always before the world—all
his actions, his motives, and even his thoughts.

March 21*st, at night.*—This morning the Duke fought a
duel with Lord Winchelsea. Nothing could equal the astonishment caused by this event. Everybody of course sees the
matter in a different light; all blame Lord W., but they are
divided as to whether the Duke ought to have fought or not.
Lord W.'s letter appeared last Monday, and certainly from
that time to this it never entered into anybody's head that
the Duke ought to or would take it up, though the expressions in it were very impertinent. But Lord Winchelsea
is such a maniac, and has so lost his head (besides the
ludicrous incident of the handkerchief[1]), that everybody
imagined the Duke would treat what he said with silent
contempt. He thought otherwise, however, and without
saying a word to any of his colleagues or to anybody but
Hardinge, his second, he wrote and demanded an apology.
After many letters and messages between the parties (Lord
Falmouth being Lord Winchelsea's second) Lord Winchelsea
declined making any apology, and they met. The letters on
the Duke's part are very creditable, so free from arrogance or
an assuming tone; those on Lord Winchelsea's not so, for one
of them is a senseless repetition of the offence, in which he
says that if the Duke will deny that his allegations are true
he will apologise. They met at Wimbledon at eight o'clock.
There were many people about, who saw what passed. They
stood at a distance of fifteen paces. Before they began

---

[1] [The incident of the handkerchief is related below, p. 198.]

Hardinge went up to Lords Winchelsea and Falmouth, and
said he must protest against the proceeding, and declare
that their conduct in refusing an apology when Lord Winchelsea was so much in the wrong filled him with disgust.
The Duke fired and missed, and then Winchelsea fired in the
air.   He immediately pulled out of his pocket the paper
which has since appeared, but in which the word 'apology'
was omitted.   The Duke read it and said it would not do.
Lord Falmouth said he was not come there to quibble about
words, and that he was ready to make the apology in whatever terms would be satisfactory, and the word 'apology' was
inserted on the ground.   The Duke then touched his hat,
said 'Good morning, my Lords,' mounted his horse, and rode
off.   Hume was there, without knowing on whose behalf till
he got to the ground.   Hardinge asked him to attend, and
told him where he would find a chaise, into which he got.
He found there pistols, which told him the errand he was on,
but he had still no notion the Duke was concerned; when he
saw him he was ready to drop.   The Duke went to Mrs.
Arbuthnot's as soon as he got back, and at eleven o'clock she
wrote a note to Lord Bathurst, telling him of it, which he
received at the Council board and put into my hands.   So
little idea had he of Lord Winchelsea's letter leading to anything serious that when on Wednesday, at the Council at
Windsor, I asked him if he had read it, he said, laughing,
'Yes, and it is a very clever letter, much the wisest thing he
ever did; *he has got back his money.*   I wish I could find some
such pretext to get back mine.'   At twelve o'clock the Duke
went to Windsor to tell the King what had happened.   Winchelsea is abused for not having made an apology when it
was first required; but I think, having committed the folly of
writing so outrageous a letter, he did the only thing a man
of honour could do in going out and receiving a shot and
then making an apology, which he was all this time prepared
to do, for he had it ready written in his pocket.   I think the
Duke ought not to have challenged him; it was very juvenile,
and he stands in far too high a position, and his life is so
much *publica cura* that he should have treated him and his

letter with the contempt they merited; it was a great error in judgment, but certainly a venial one, for it is impossible not to admire the high spirit which disdained to shelter itself behind the immunities of his great character and station, and the simplicity, and almost humility, which made him at once descend to the level of Lord Winchelsea, when he might, without subjecting himself to any imputation derogatory to his honour, have assumed a tone of lofty superiority and treated him as unworthy of his notice. Still it was beneath his dignity; it lowered him, and was more or less ridiculous. Lord Jersey met him coming from Windsor, and spoke to him. He said, 'I could not do otherwise, could I?'

I met the Bishop of Oxford in the Park this morning; he said nine bishops, and probably ten, would vote for the Bill. He said he was not at the meeting at Lambeth, but the Archbishop sent for him, and despatched him to the Duke with an account of their proceedings. The Archbishop summoned the bishops to consult upon the course they should pursue, and see if there was any chance of their acting with unanimity. Finding this was not possible, they resolved that each should take his own line; and a proposal to address the King, which was urged by one or two of the most violent (he did not name them), was overruled. The anti-Catholic papers and men lavish the most extravagant encomiums on Wetherell's speech, and call it ' the finest oration ever delivered in the House of Commons,' 'the best since the second Philippic.' He was drunk, they say. The Speaker said ' the only lucid interval he had was that between his waistcoat and his breeches.' When he speaks he unbuttons his braces, and in his vehement action his breeches fall down and his waistcoat runs up, so that there is a great interregnum. He is half mad, eccentric, ingenious, with great and varied information and a coarse, vulgar mind, delighting in ribaldry and abuse, besides being an enthusiast. The first time he distinguished himself was in Watson's trial, when he and Copley were his counsel, and both made very able speeches. He was then a trading lawyer and politician, till the Queen came over, when he made a very powerful speech in the House of

Commons, full of research, in favour of inserting her name
in the Liturgy. He was then engaged by Chancellor Eldon
for the Court, soon after made Solicitor-General, much
abused for ratting, became Attorney-General, and resigned
when Canning became Minister. He was restored when the
Duke was made Prime Minister, and now he will have to
retire again.

March 26th.—Everything is getting on very quietly in the
House of Commons, and the Opposition are beginning to
squabble among themselves, some wishing to create delay, and
others not choosing to join in these tricks, when they know
it is useless. The Duke came here the night before last, but
I was not at home. He talked over the whole matter with his
usual simplicity. The King, it seems, was highly pleased with
the Winchelsea affair, and he said, ' I did not see the letter
(which is probably a lie) ; if I had, I certainly should have
thought it my duty to call your attention to it.' Somebody
added that ' he would be wanting to fight a duel himself.'
Sefton said, ' He will be sure to think he has fought one.'
Hume gave the two Lords a lecture on the ground after the
duel, and said he did not think there was a man in England
who would have lifted his hand against the Duke. Very un-
called for, but the Duke's friends have less humility than he
has, for Lord Winchelsea did not lift his hand against him.
It is curious that the man who threw the bottle at Lord Wellesley in Dublin (and who is a Protestant fanatic) has been
lurking constantly about the House of Lords, so much so that
it was thought right to apprise Peel of it, and the police have
been desired in consequence to keep a strict watch over him,
and to take care that he does no mischief. The Duke after
the duel sent Lord Melville to the Duke of Montrose with a
message that his son-in-law had behaved very much like a
gentleman. The women, particularly of course Lady Jersey,
have been very ridiculous, affecting nervousness and fine
feeling, though they never heard of the business till some
hours after it was over. Mrs. Arbuthnot was not so foolish,
but made very light of it all, which was in better sense and
better taste.

M—— told me two days ago that, although he is more
quiet, the King is not at all reconciled to the Catholic question. His Majesty was very much annoyed at his speech
the other day, having always hoped that he was at heart
too indifferent about it to take a decided line or express
publicly a strong opinion. It is supposed that either Sugden
or Alderson will be Solicitor-General. O'Connell has done
himself great credit by his moderation in the Committee.
Grattan wanted to move an amendment omitting the words
by which O'Connell is excluded from taking his seat for
Clare, when Rice and Duncannon begged him to withdraw
it, and said they were charged with the expression of
O'Connell's wish that his individual case should not be
thought of, as he would not have it be any impediment
to the success of the measure. This, of course, greatly
annoys those who have inveighed against him, and who have
always contended that he only wished for confusion, and
would be very sorry to see the question settled.

The other day Jack Lawless[1] called on Arbuthnot to ask
him some question about the Deccan prize money, in which
a brother of his has an interest. He entered upon politics, was
very obsequious in his manner, extravagant in praise of the
Duke, quite shocked that he should have fought a duel, and
said, 'Sir, we are twelve of us here, and not one but what
would fight for him any day in the week.' He said that some
years ago, when he heard the Duke speak, he was distressed
at his hesitation, but that now he spoke better than anyone;
that in the Lords he heard Eldon, and Plunket, and Grey,
and then up got the Duke and answered everybody, and
spoke better than they all.' Arbuthnot says he was bowing
and scraping, and all humility and politeness, with none of
the undergrowl of the Association.

March 26th, at night.—Just met M——, who had returned that moment from Windsor, where he had left the
King in such an ill humour that he would not stay and dine
there. The Duke of Cumberland never goes there without
unsettling his mind, and yesterday evening Lord Mansfield

[1] [A prominent member of the Catholic Association in Dublin.]

had been to the Castle and had an audience. Lord Eldon prevails on all these Peers to exercise their right and demand audiences. Lord Mansfield had no petition to present, and only went to remonstrate about the Catholic question and tell the King that all the Protestants looked to him to save them from the impending danger. The King declares he only listens to what they say, and replies that he must leave everything to his Ministers; but it is impossible for him to listen (and not talk himself) for an hour and a quarter together. He is very angry at the Bishop of Winchester's speech, and at the declaration in favour of the Bill by both of the brothers.[1] He accused M—— of having influenced the Bishop, which he denied, and told him that he would not have been biassed by anybody. The King still is in hopes that the Bill will not pass, and said that the Ministers had only a majority of five, and with that they would not carry it through. M—— replied that they had above fifty, and after such a majority as there had been in the Commons it must pass. All this he received as sulkily as possible, and it is clear that if he dared, and if he could, he would still defeat the measure. His dislike to it is the opposition of a spoiled child, founded on considerations purely personal and selfish and without any reason whatever.

March 29th, at night.—Dined at Lady Sandwich's, and met Madame de Lieven, who is grown very gracious, craving for news, and probably very malignant. Lieven told me (which she did not) that Lord Eldon was with the King yesterday for four hours. She confirmed it after dinner, and said that Halford had told her, but added that he had done no harm.[2] Lieven also told me that Stratford Canning is coming home, and Robert Gordon going to Constantinople. He is a dull,

---

[1] [The two Sumners. Dr. John Bird Sumner (afterwards Archbishop of Canterbury) had been raised to the see of Chester in 1828. They owed their advancement to the especial favour of George IV. The bishop adverted to in the next sentence was the Bishop of Winchester.]

[2] [This was the celebrated interview related in Lord Eldon's 'Memoirs, vol. iii., when, however, the King gave Lord E. a very erroneous account of the transaction, subsequently corrected by Sir Robert Peel in his 'Memoirs.']

heavy man, and not able, I should think, to cope with the
Turkish Ministers, if they are (as the Duke says) the ablest
diplomatists in Europe. I don't know why Stratford Canning
is coming home, whether *nolens* or *volens*.

I have, I see, alluded to Lord Winchelsea's handkerchief
story,[1] but have not mentioned the circumstances, which I
may as well do. Lord Holland came home one night from
the House of Lords, and as soon as he had occasion to blow
his nose pulled his handkerchief out of his pocket; upon which
my Lady exclaimed (she hates perfumes), 'Good God, Lord
H., where did you get that handkerchief? Send it away
directly.' He said he did not know, when it was inspected,
and the letter *W* found on it. Lord H. said, 'I was sitting
near Lord Winchelsea, and it must be his, which I took up
by mistake and have brought home.' Accordingly the next
day he sent it to Lord Winchelsea with his compliments.
Lord Winchelsea receiving the handkerchief and the message,
and finding it marked *W*, fancied it was the Duke's, and that
it was sent to him by way of affronting him; on which he went
to the Duke of Newcastle and imparted to him the circumstances, and desired him to wait on Lord Holland for an ex-.
planation. This his Grace did, when the matter was cleared
up and the handkerchief was found to be the property of
Lord Wellesley. The next day Lord Winchelsea came up
laughing to Lord Holland in the House of Lords, and said
he had many apologies to make for what had passed, but that
he really was in such a state of excitement he did not know
what he said and did.[2]

April 4th.—On the third reading of the Catholic Bill in
the House of Commons Sadler failed, and Palmerston made
a speech like one of Canning's. The Bill has been two
nights in the House of Lords. They go on with it this
morning, and will divide this evening. The Chancellor made

---

[1] [*Supra*, p. 192.]

[2] [Lord Winchelsea was in the habit of flourishing a white pocket handkerchief while he was speaking in the House of Lords. This peculiarity,
associated with his sonorous tones, his excited action, and his extravagant
opinions, gave point to the incident.]

a very fine speech last night, and the Bishop of Oxford spoke very well the night before, but the debate has been dull on the whole; the subject is exhausted. The House of Lords was very full, particularly of women; every fool in London thinks it necessary to be there. It is only since last year that the steps of the throne have been crowded with ladies; formerly one or two got in, who skulked behind the throne, or were hid in Tyrwhitt's box, but now they fill the whole space, and put themselves in front with their large bonnets, without either fear or shame.

April 5th.—The question was put at a little before twelve last night, and carried by 105—217 to 112 (a greater majority than the most sanguine expected)—after a splendid speech from Lord Grey and a very good one from Lord Plunket. Old Eldon was completely beat, and could make no fight at all; his speech was wretched, they say, for I did not hear it. This tremendous defeat will probably put an end to anything like serious opposition; they will hardly rally again.

I dined at Chesterfield House, but nobody came to dinner. Chesterfield and his party were all at the House of Lords. I found myself almost alone with Vesey Fitzgerald, with whom I had much talk after dinner. He said that it would be a long time before all the circumstances and all the difficulties relating to their proceedings were known, but when they were it would be seen how great had been the latter, how curious the former; that the day the Chancellor, the Duke, and Peel were with the King they actually were out (all of which I knew), and that he believes if the other party could have made a Government with a chance of standing, out they would have gone; but that it was put to them (this I did not know), and they acknowledged they could not. They held consultations on the subject, and the man they principally relied on was the Duke of Richmond; they meant he should be either First Lord of the Treasury or Lord-Lieutenant of Ireland. Lord Winchelsea said to Ellenborough, 'Why, he speaks better than the Duke of Wellington any day.' He happens to have his wits, such as they are, about him, and has been quick and neat in one or two little speeches,

though he spoke too often, and particularly in his attack on
the Bishop of Oxford the other night. Last year, on the
Wool question, he did very well, but all the details were got
up for him by George Bentinck,[1] who took the trouble.
Besides, his fortune consists in great measure of wool, he
lives in the country, is well versed in rural affairs and the
business of the quarter sessions, has a certain calibre of
understanding, is prejudiced, narrow-minded, illiterate, and
ignorant, good-looking, good-humoured, and unaffected, tedious, prolix, unassuming, and a duke. There would not
have been so much to say about him if they had not excited
an idea in the minds of some people of making him Prime
Minister and successor to the Duke of Wellington.

Vesey told me that Dawson's speech at Derry very nearly
overturned the whole design. The King heard of it the day
of a Council at Windsor (which I well remember). The
Chancellor was with him for a long time, but it was almost
impossible to persuade the King that Dawson knew nothing
of the intention of the Government, and that his speech was
not made in concert with Peel and the Duke. This it was
which caused them such excessive annoyance, because it
raised difficulties which well-nigh prevented the accomplishment of the design. It must be owned that the King might
well believe this, and although it is very certain that Dawson
knew nothing, and that his making such a speech ought to
have been a proof that he was in ignorance, it will always
be believed that he was aware of the intended measure, and
that his speech was made with the Duke's concurrence. It is
curious enough that his opinion had been long changed, and
that he had intended to pronounce his recantation when
Brownlow did, but as Brownlow got the start of him he
would not. For two years after this he persevered in the
old course, and when Canning came in, and the Catholic
question was the great field on which he was to be fought,

---

[1] [It deserves remark that Lord George Bentinck was thus early em-
ploying his singular talents in mastering details, although he took no conspicuous part in politics until the proposal for the repeal of the Corn Law
in 1845.]

Dawson reverted vigorously to his old opinions, and spoke vehemently against emancipation. Such is party !

The circumstances that Vesey talked of are in fact pretty well known or guessed at, nor has there ever been any secret as to the main fact of the King's opposition and dislike to the measure. He told me that after Eldon's visit of four hours the Duke remonstrated, and told the King what great umbrage it gave his Ministers to see and hear of these long and numerous interviews with their opponents. The King declared that he said nothing and that nothing passed calculated to annoy them, which they none of them believed, but of course could make no reply to.

April 8th.—I have mentioned above (March 4th[1]), p. 180, the Chancellor, the Duke, and Peel going to the King, and the alarm that prevailed here. That day the Catholic question was in great jeopardy. They went to tell the King that unless he would give them his real, efficient support, and not throw his indirect influence into the opposite scale, they would resign. He refused to give them that support; they placed their resignations in his hands and came away. The King then sent to Eldon, and asked him if he would undertake to form a Government. He deliberated (then it was that it was question of the Duke of Richmond being First Lord or Lord-Lieutenant), but eventually said he could

---

[1] [It was on the 3rd of March that this interview took place, as related by Sir R. Peel himself in his ' Memoir' (vol. i. p. 343). The King asked his Ministers to explain the details of the measure they proposed to bring in. They informed his Majesty that it would be necessary to modify in the case of the Roman Catholics that part of the oath of supremacy which relates to the ecclesiastical jurisdiction and supremacy of the Pope. To this the King said he could not possibly consent. Upon this Mr. Peel and his colleagues informed his Majesty that they must resign. His Majesty accepted the resignations, and the Ministers returned to London (after an audience of five hours) under the full persuasion that the Government was dissolved. In the interval some attempt was made to form a Protestant Cabinet; but on the evening of the following day, the 4th of March, the King wrote a letter to the Duke of Wellington, informing him that his Majesty anticipated so much difficulty in the attempt to form another Administration that he could not dispense with his Ministers' services, and that they were at liberty to proceed with the measures of which notice had been given in Parliament.]

202 REIGN OF GEORGE IV. [Chap. V.

not undertake it. On his refusal the King yielded, and the Bill went on; but if Eldon had accepted, the Duke and his colleagues would have been out, and God knows what would have happened. It was, of course, of all these matters that the King talked to Eldon in the long interview they had the other day. He is very sulky at the great majority in the House of Lords, as I knew he would be.

Lady Jersey is in a fury with Lord Anglesey, and goes about saying he insulted her in the House of Lords the other night. She was sitting on one of the steps of the throne, and the Duchess of Richmond on the step above. After Lord Anglesey had spoken he came to talk to the Duchess, who said, ' How well you did speak;' on which he said, ' Hush! you must take care what you say, for here is Lady Jersey, and she reports for the newspapers;' on which Lady Jersey said very angrily, ' Lady Jersey is here for her own amusement; what do you mean by reporting for news-papers?' to which he replied with a profound bow, ' I beg your Ladyship's pardon; I did not mean to offend you, and if I did I beg to make the most ample apology.' This is his version; hers, of course, is different. He says that he meant the whole thing as a joke. It was a very bad joke if it was one, and as he knows how she abuses him, one may suspect that there was something more than joking in it.

The other night Lord Grey had called Lord Falmouth to order, and after the debate Falmouth came up to him with a menacing air and said, ' My Lord Grey, I wish to inform you that if upon any future occasion you transgress in the slightest degree the orders of the House, I shall most cer-tainly call you to order.' Lord Grey, who expected from his air something more hostile, merely said, ' My Lord, your Lordship will do perfectly right, and whenever I am out of order I hope you will.' Last night old Eldon got a dressing again from the Chancellor.

April 9th.—Met O'Connell at dinner yesterday at William Ponsonby's. The only Irish (agitators) were he and O'Gorman Mahon;——, he said, was too great a blackguard, and he would not invite him. O'Connell arrived from Ireland that day;

there is nothing remarkable in his manner, appearance, or
conversation, but he seems lively, well bred, and at his ease.
I asked him after dinner 'whether Catholics had not taken
the oath of supremacy till it was coupled with the declaration;'
he said, ' in many instances in the reigns of Elizabeth, James,
and Charles, because at that time it was considered to apply
to the civil supremacy of the Pope only, and that the Government admitted of that interpretation of it, but that no
Catholic could take it now, because that construction is never
given to the oath.' Duncannon told me that O'Connell has
no wish to be in Parliament, that he makes so much money
by his profession that it is a great loss to him to attend
Parliament at all. What they want is a compromise with
Vesey Fitzgerald, by which he may be admitted to take his
seat in this Parliament on an understanding that he will
not oppose Vesey in the next; not that I see how that is to
be done, except by an Act of Parliament (which would never
pass) in his favour. Besides, the Duke detests him, and
Vesey likewise. They cannot forgive him for all he has done
and all he has made them do. O'Gorman, the secretary of
the Catholic Association, appears a heavy, civil, vulgar man.
I sat next to Stanley, who told me a story which amused me.
Mackintosh, in the course of the recent debates, went one day
to the House of Commons at eleven in the morning to take
a place. They were all taken on the benches below the gang-
way, and on asking the doorkeeper how they happened to be
all taken so early, he said, ' Oh, sir, there is no chance of
getting a place, for Colonel Sibthorpe sleeps at a tavern close
by, and comes here every morning by eight o'clock and takes
places for all the saints.'

April 13th.—On Friday last the Catholic Bill was read
a third time, after a very dull debate. Lord Eldon attempted to rally, and made a long and wretched speech which
lasted two hours. Nobody spoke well. The Duke in his
reply dropped all the terms of courtesy and friendship he had
hitherto used in speaking of old Eldon, and broke off with
him entirely. He is disgusted at his opposition out of doors,
and at his having been the constant adviser of the Duke of

Cumberland and all the foolish Lords who have been pestering
the King at Windsor; and he is acquainted with all his
tricks and underhand proceedings, probably with more of
them than we know of. He thanked the Opposition for their
support—thanks which they well merit from him—but of
course nobody is satisfied. He was before accused of ingrati-
tude in never taking notice of their conduct, and even it is
said that he gave them to understand he had no more need
of their services, and wished to make them his bow. I don't
believe he meant any such thing; he intended to thank them
simply, though it is probably true that he does not wish to
continue in alliance with them, and is anxious to see the
Tories put themselves under his orders again. On Saturday
he sent the commission down to Windsor for the King's
signature, with other papers as a matter of course; he would
not go himself, that there might be no fresh discussion between them.

I went on Friday morning to the Old Bailey to hear the
trials, particularly that of the women for the murder of
the apprentices; the mother was found guilty, and will be
hanged to-day—has been by this time.[1] The case exhibited a
shocking scene of wretchedness and poverty, such as ought
not to exist in any community, especially in one which pretends to be so flourishing and happy as this is. It is, I suppose, one case of many which may be found in this town,
graduating through various stages of misery and vice. These
wretched beings were described to be in the lowest state of
moral and physical degradation, with scarcely rags to cover
them, food barely sufficient to keep them alive, and working
eighteen or nineteen hours a day, without being permitted
any relaxation, or even the privilege of going to church on
Sunday. I never heard more disgusting details than this

[1] [Two wretched women named Hibner were tried, and one of them
convicted for the murder of a parish apprentice named Francis Colepitts by
savage ill-treatment. The elder prisoner was found guilty and executed on
the 13th of April. No such concourse of people had assembled to witness
an execution since that of Fauntleroy. The details of the crime were horrible, and had excited great sympathy for the victim amongst all classes.—
Ann. Regist. for 1829, *Chronicle,* p. 71.]

trial elicited, or a case which calls more loudly for an investigation into the law and the system under which such proceedings are possible. Poverty, and vice, and misery must always be found in a community like ours, but such frightful contrasts between the excess of luxury and splendour and these scenes of starvation and brutality ought not to be possible; but I am afraid there is more vice, more misery and penury in this country than in any other, and at the same time greater wealth. The contrasts are too striking, and such an unnatural, artificial, and unjust state of things neither can nor ought to be permanent. I am convinced that before many years elapse these things will produce some great convulsion.

After the Old Bailey I went and dined at the Covent Garden Theatrical Fund dinner. The Duke of Clarence could not come, so they put Lord Blessington in the chair, who made an ass of himself. Among other toasts he was to give 'The memory of the Duke of York,' who was the founder of the institution. He prefaced this with a speech, but gave ' The health,' &c., on which Fawcett, who sat opposite, called out in an agony, ' The memory, my Lord !' He corrected himself, but in a minute after said again ' The health.' ' The memory, my Lord !' again roared Fawcett. It was supremely ridiculous. Francis Leveson sat on his right, Codrington on his left, and Lawless the agitator just opposite; he is a pale, thin, common-looking little man, and has not at all the air of a patriot orator and agitator.

May 14*th.*—I have been at Newmarket for three weeks, and have had no time to write, nor has anything particular occurred. The King came to town, and had a levee and drawing-room, the former of which was very numerously, the other shabbily attended. At the levee he was remarkably civil to all the Peers, particularly the Duke of Richmond, who had distinguished themselves in opposition to Government in the late debates, and he turned his back on the bishops who had voted for the Bill. O'Connell and Sheil were both at the levee ; the former had been presented in Ireland, so had not to be presented again, but the King took no notice of him,

and when he went by said to somebody near him, 'Damn
the fellow ! what does he come here for ?'—dignified.

There was an odd circumstance the day of the drawing-
room. The Duke of Cumberland, as Gold Stick, gave orders
at the Horse Guards that no carriages should be admitted
into the Park, and Peel and the Duke of Wellington, when
they presented themselves on their way to Court, were refused
admission. The officer on guard came to the Duke's carriage
and said that such were his orders, but that he was sure
they were not meant to extend to his Grace, and if he would
authorise him he would order the gates to be opened. The
Duke said, ' By no means,' and then desired his carriage to go
round the other way. Many people thought that this was a
piece of impertinence of the Duke of Cumberland's, but the
Duke says that the whole thing was a mistake. Be this as
it may, the Duke of Cumberland and the Duke of Wellington
do not speak, and whenever they meet, which often happens
in society, the former moves off.

Yesterday morning Batchelor called on me, and sat with
me for an hour, telling me all sorts of details concerning the
interior of Windsor and St. James's.   The King is well in
health, except that since last September he has been afflicted
with a complaint in his bladder, which both annoys and
alarms him very much. There is no appearance of stone or
gravel, but violent irritation, which is only subdued by
laudanum, and always returns when the effect of the opiate
is gone off. The laudanum, too, disagrees much with his
general health. He is attended by Sir Henry Holland, Brodie,
and O'Reilly. Sir A. Cooper, who did attend him, is not now
consulted, in consequence (Batchelor thinks) of some petty
intrigue in some quarter. This O'Reilly, who has gradually
insinuated himself into the King's confidence, and by constantly attending him at Windsor, and bringing him all the
gossip and tittle-tattle of the neighbourhood (being on the
alert to pick up and retail all he can for the King's amusement), has made himself necessary, and is not now to be
shaken off, to the great annoyance of Knighton, who cannot
bear him, as well as of all the other people about the King,
who hate him for his meddling, mischievous character. The

King's *valets de chambre* sit up alternately, and as he sleeps very ill he rings his bell every half-hour. He talks of everybody and everything before his valets with great freedom, except of politics, on which he never utters a word in their presence, and he always sends them away when he sees anybody or speaks on business of any kind. Batchelor thinks that this new disorder is a symptom of approaching decay, and that the King thinks so himself.

In the meantime the influence of Knighton and that of Lady Conyngham continue as great as ever; nothing can be done but by their permission, and they understand one another and play into each other's hands. Knighton opposes every kind of expense, except that which is lavished on her. The wealth she has accumulated by savings and presents must be enormous. The King continues to heap all kinds of presents upon her, and she lives at his expense; they do not possess a servant; even Lord Conyngham's *valet de chambre* is not properly their servant. They all have situations in the King's household, from which they receive their pay, while they continue in the service of the Conynghams. They dine every day while in London at St. James's, and when they give a dinner it is cooked at St. James's and brought up to Hamilton Place in hackney coaches and in machines made expressly for the purpose; there is merely a fire lit in their kitchen for such things as must be heated on the spot. At Windsor the King sees very little of her except of an evening; he lies in bed half the day or more, sometimes goes out, and sometimes goes to her room for an hour or so in the afternoon, and that is all he sees of her. A more despicable scene cannot be exhibited than that which the interior of our Court presents—every base, low, and unmanly propensity, with selfishness, avarice, and a life of petty intrigue and mystery.

May 16*th*.—O'Connell attempted to take his seat last night, but the business was put off till Monday. His case is exceedingly well got up, but too long. There are many opinions as to his right; many people think he has established it (though he had failed to do so), that a Bill ought to be brought in to enable him to take the new oaths. It was

supposed Government would take no part, but Peel's speech
and the language of some of the Ministers are rather unfavourable to him.   Lord Grey, when he read the case,
thought his argument on the tenth clause of the Bill con-
clusive, but when he examined the Bill he thought differently,
and that the context gives a different signification to the
words on which O'Connell relies.   Tierney thinks otherwise,
and this they debated Bill in hand in Lady Jersey's room
yesterday morning.   O'Connell was in a great fright when
he went up to the table.   He got through the necessary
forms in the Steward's office, by means of the Commissioners
whom Duncannon provided, and who were, I believe, Burdett
and Ebrington.   He ought to be allowed to take his seat,
but probably he will not; it is a very hard case.[1]   The Duke
of Orleans is come, and his son, the Duke of Chartres; the
latter was at the opera to-night in Prince Leopold's box.

May 29th.—O'Connell is said to have made a very good
speech at the bar of the House, and produced rather a favourable impression.   He has done himself this good, that whereas it was pretty generally thought that he was likely to
fail in the House of Commons as a speaker, he has now
altered that impression.   There is but one opinion as to the
wretched feeling of excluding him, but the saddle is put upon
the right horse, and though the Government are now obliged
to enforce the provisions of their own Bill, everybody knows
that the exclusion was the work of the King.   O'Connell
goes back to Clare (as he says) sure of his election; there
will be a great uproar, but at present nobody expects any
opposition, and all deprecate a contest.

Yesterday the King gave a dinner to the Dukes of
Orleans and Chartres, and in the evening there was a child's
ball.   It was pretty enough, and I saw for the first time the

---

[1] [O'Connell was excluded from taking his seat as member for Clare, for
which he had been elected before the passing of the Relief Act, because it
was held that he was bound to take the oath which was required by law at
the time of his election, and not the oath imposed on Roman Catholics by
the recent statutes.   He presented himself to be sworn at the table of the
House of Commons on the 15th of May, and there refused to take the former
oath, which was tendered to him by the Clerk.   The House divided 190 to
116 against his admission without taking the oath of supremacy on the 18th,
Mr. O'Connell having previously been heard at the bar in person in support
of his claim.]

Queen of Portugal [1] and our little Victoria. The Queen was finely dressed, with a riband and order over her shoulder, and she sat by the King. She is good-looking and has a sensible Austrian countenance. In dancing she fell down and hurt her face, was frightened and bruised, and went away. The King was very kind to her. Our little Princess is a short, plain-looking child, and not near so good-looking as the Portuguese. However, if nature has not done so much, fortune is likely to do a great deal more for her. The King looked very well, and stayed at the ball till two. There were very few people, and neither Arbuthnot nor Mrs. A. were asked. I suspect this is owing to what passed in the House about opening the Birdcage Walk. It puts the King in a fury to have any such thing mentioned, not having the slightest wish to accommodate the public, though very desirous of getting money out of their pockets.

The day before yesterday there was a review for the Duke of Orleans, and the Duke of Wellington, who was there at the head of his regiment, contrived to get a tumble, but was not hurt. Last night at the ball the King said to Lord Anglesey, 'Why, Paget, what's this I hear? they say you rolled off your horse at the review yesterday.'[2] The Duke as he left the ground was immensely cheered, and the people thronged about his horse and would shake hands with him. When Lord Hill went to the King the day before to give him an account of the intended review and the dispositions that had been made, he said, ' Hill, if I can throw my leg over your Shropshire horse, don't be surprised if you see me amongst you.'

The new law appointments have just been announced, and have created some surprise.[3]

---

[1] [Donna Maria II. da Gloria, Queen of Portugal, on the abdication of her father, Don Pedro, succeeded to the throne on the 2nd of May, 1826 She was born on the 4th of April, 1819, and was consequently but a few weeks older than the Princess Victoria.]

[2] [This was probably intended as a hit at the Duke, for the King knew very well it was not Lord Anglesey but the Duke who had the fall. Another version of the story is that the King said, ' Paget, you are not the man to fall off at the head of your regiment.'

[3] [The Attorney-General, Sir Charles Wetherell, had resigned in consequence of his violent opposition to the Catholic Relief Bill, and was suc-

June 11*th.*—I have been at Epsom for a week; the Duke
of Grafton, Lords Wilton, Jersey, and Worcester, Russell,
Anson, Irby, and myself took Down Hall for the races and
lived very well. Nothing particular has occurred. Lord
and Lady Ellenborough are separated, and he is supposed to
have behaved very handsomely to her. They say he does not
now know the whole story of her intrigue with Felix Schwarz-
enberg; that hero is gone to the Russian army. All the
new appointments were declared when I was out of town,
and they excited some surprise and more disapprobation.
They have made Best a Peer, who is poor and has a family,
by which another poor peerage will be added to' the list;
and he is totally unfit for the situation he is to fill—that of
Deputy-Speaker of the House of Lords, and to assist the
Chancellor in deciding Scotch causes, of which he knows
nothing whatever; and as the Chancellor knows nothing
either, the Scotch law is likely to be strangely administered
in that great court of appeal. They would have done better
to have made Alexander [1] a Peer, who is very old, understands Equity Law, and has no children; but he knows very
little of Common Law (which Best is well versed in), and so
they keep him on the bench and put Best on the Woolsack.
Lord Rosslyn is Privy Seal,[2] and Scarlett Attorney-General,
which looks like a leaning towards the Whigs; but then
Trench and Lord Edward Somerset are put into the Ordnance;
George Bankes goes back to the India Board, and Government supports him in his contest at Cambridge against
William Cavendish. This conduct is considered very unhand-

ceeded by Sir James Scarlett (afterwards Lord Abinger). The Solicitor-
General, Sir Nicholas Conyngham Tindal, was raised on the 9th of June to
the Chief Justiceship of the Common Pleas; and was succeeded in the
Solicitorship by Sir Edward Burtenshaw Sugden (afterwards Lord St.
Leonards). The vacancy in the Common Pleas was caused by the resignation of Sir William Draper Best, who was created Lord Wynford for the
purpose of assisting the Chancellor with the judicial business of the House
of Lords.]

[1] [Sir William Alexander, then Lord Chief Baron of the Exchequer.
The Court of Exchequer still retained its Equity jurisdiction.]

[2] [Lord Rosslyn was considered to be a Whig, and Sir James Scarlett
was better known for the Liberal opinions he once professed than for the Tory
opinions he afterwards assumed.]

some, and Tierney, who was well disposed towards the Government, told me yesterday that if the Duke did not take care he thought he would get swamped with such doings, that the way he went on was neither fish nor flesh, and he would offend more people than he would conciliate. At present there is no party, and if Government have no opponents they have no great body of supporters on whom they can depend; everything is in confusion—party, politics, and all.

The event of last week was Palmerston's speech on the Portuguese question, which was delivered at a late hour and in an empty House, but which they say was exceedingly able and eloquent. This is the second he has made this year of great merit. It was very violent against Government. He has been twenty years in office and never distinguished himself before, a proof how many accidental circumstances are requisite to bring out the talents which a man may possess. The office he held was one of dull and dry detail, and he never travelled out of it. He probably stood in awe of Canning and others, and was never in the Cabinet; but having lately held higher situations and having acquired more confidence, and the great men having been removed from the House of Commons by death or promotion, he has launched forth, and with astonishing success. Lord Granville told me he had always thought Palmerston was capable of more than he did, and had told Canning so, who did not believe it.

Yesterday the King had his racing dinner, which was more numerously attended and just as magnificent as that he gave last year, but not half so gay and joyous. I believe he had some gouty feeling and was in pain, for, contrary to his usual custom, he hardly spoke, and the Duke of Richmond, who sat next to him, told me that the little he did say was more about politics than the turf, and he fancied that something had annoyed him. He looked well enough, and was very cheerful before dinner. When his health was drunk ' as Patron of the Jockey Club, and many thanks to him for condescending to accept that title,' he made a speech, in

which he said that ‘he was much gratified by our kindness,
and he could assure us that in withdrawing himself as he had
done from the Jockey Club he was not influenced by any
unkindness to any member of it, or any indifference to the
interests of the turf.’

June 24th. —Went to Stoke for the Ascot races.   There
was such a crowd to see the cup run for as never was seen
before.   The King was very anxious and disappointed.   I
bought the winner for Chesterfield[1] two hours before the race,
he having previously asked the King’s leave, which he gave
with many gracious expressions.   I have set about making a
reconciliation between the King and Lord Sefton.   Both are
anxious to make it up, but each is afraid to make the first ad-
vances.   However, Sefton must make them, and he will.   The
cause of their quarrel is very old, and signifies little enough
now. . . . They have been at daggers drawn ever since, and
Sefton has revenged himself by a thousand jokes at the
King’s expense, of which his Majesty is well aware.   Their
common pursuit, and a desire on the one side to partake of
the good things of the Palace, and on the other side to be
free from future pleasantries, has generated a mutual disposition to make it up, which is certainly sensible.   The King
has bought seven horses successively, for which he has given
11,300 guineas, principally to win the cup at Ascot, which
he has never accomplished.   He might have had Zinganee,
but would not, because he fancied the Colonel would beat
him; but when that appeared doubtful he was very sorry not
to have bought him, and complained that the horse was not
offered to him.   He is now extravagantly fond of Chesterfield, who is pretty well bit by it.   There is always a parcel of
eldest sons and Lords in possession invited to the Cottage
for the sake of Lady Maria Conyngham.   The King likes to
be treated with great deference but without fear, and that
people should be easy with him, and gay, and listen well.

[1] [George Augustus, sixth Earl of Chesterfield, born in 1805, died in
1866.   He married in 1830 Anne, daughter of Lord Forester.   In 1829 he
was one of the most brilliant of the young men of fashion of that day, having
succeeded to a large rental and large accumulations in his minority.]

There was a grand consultation at the Cottage between the
King, Lieven, Esterhazy, and the Duke of Cumberland as
to the way in which the ladies should be placed at dinner,
the object being that Lady Conyngham should sit next to
his Majesty, though according to etiquette the two Ambas-
sadresses should sit one on each side of him. It was contrived by the Duke of Cumberland taking out one of them
and sitting opposite, by which means the lovely Thais sat
beside him and he was happy.

June 26th.—I met Tierney and Lord Grey at dinner
yesterday; the former wanted to know what passed about
the King's Speech at the Council at Windsor the other day.
I had heard nothing, not having been at the Council, but it
is believed that the Ministers had put in the Speech a sentence expressive of satisfaction and sanguine hopes about
Ireland, and that at the last moment the King would not
agree to this; for after the Duke's audience, which lasted
a good while, there was a Cabinet, and it is supposed they
knocked under, for the paragraph about Ireland is cold
enough. The Duke of Cumberland is thought to have
had a hand in all this, and to have persuaded the King
to be obstinate. We talked a great deal about the situation of the Government and the state of the House of
Commons, and Tierney thinks that unless the Duke
strengthens himself he will not be able to go on; that
Rosslyn and Scarlett are of little use to him, and what
he wants is the support of those who will bring followers
in their train, such as Althorp, who has extensive connections, enjoys consideration, and would be of real use
to him. There is a strong report that Althorp is to be
Chancellor of the Exchequer, Goulburn Speaker, and Sutton[1]
a Peer. At present the Government is anything but strong,
but then there exists no party, nor is there any man of
ability and authority enough to make one. The Duke must
strengthen himself, and have recourse for the purpose either

---

[1] [Right Hon. Manners Sutton, Speaker of the House of Commons. He
retained that office till 1835, when he was beaten on the great contest with
Mr. Abercromby, and raised to the peerage as Lord Canterbury.]

to the Whigs or to Huskisson and his friends.   These latter
he detests, and he knows they hate him and are his bitterest
enemies.   The Whigs he would not dislike so much, but the
King is averse to have them, and the Duke is beset by his
old suspicion that they want to break up the Tory party and
make him dependent on themselves.   At the same time, in
taking in Lord Rosslyn and Scarlett, he has made some ad-
vances towards them, though Lord Grey is displeased at his not
having shown him more deference and communicated to him
his intentions about Rosslyn.   Lord Rosslyn asked Lord Grey's
advice as to accepting, and he advised him to take office,
explaining at the same time that he should not pledge himself to support Government, though he was at present well
disposed to do so, and should be still more disposed when
Lord Rosslyn became a part of it.   Tierney said it was very
lamentable that there should be such a deficiency of talent in
the rising generation, and remarkable how few clever young
men there are now in the House of Commons.   The King
did not like Lord Rosslyn's appointment; he hates all the
Whigs; indeed, he hates the best men of all parties, and
likes none but such as will be subservient to himself.   So
little public spirit has he, and so much selfishness, that
he would rather his Government was weak than strong, that
they may be the more dependent upon him; though he only
wishes to be powerful in order to exercise the most puerile
caprices, gratify ridiculous resentments, indulge vulgar prejudices, and amass or squander money; not one great object
connected with national glory or prosperity ever enters
his brain.   I am convinced he would turn out the Duke to-
morrow if he could see any means of replacing him.   I
don't think I mentioned that when he talked of giving the
child's ball Lady Maria Conyngham said, ' Oh, do, it will be
so nice to see the *two little Queens* dancing together ' (the little
Queen of Portugal and the Princess Victoria), at which he
was beyond measure provoked.

July 10th.—I dined with the Duke of Wellington yesterday; a very large party for Mesdames the Duchesse d'Escars
and Madame du Cayla; the first is the widow of the Duc

d'Escars, who was Premier Maître d'Hôtel of Louis XVIII.,
and who was said to have died of one of the King's good
dinners, and the joke was, ' Hier sa Majesté a eu une indi-
gestion, dont M. le Duc d'Escars est mort.' Madame du
Cayla[1] is come over to prosecute some claim upon this
Government, which the Duke has discovered to be unfounded,
and he had the bluntness to tell her so as they were going
to dinner. She must have been good-looking in her youth ;
her countenance is lively, her eyes are piercing, clear complexion, and very handsome hands and arms ; but the best
part about her seemed to be the magnificent pearls she wore,
though these are not so fine as Lady Conyngham's. All

[1] [Madame du Cayla had been the *soi-disant* mistress of Louis XVIII.,
or rather the favourite of his declining years. ' Il fallait une Esther,' to use
her own expression, ' à cet Assuérus.' She was the daughter of M. Talon,
brought up by Madam Campan, and an early friend of Hortense Beauhar-
nais. Her marriage to an officer in the Prince de Condé's army was an
unhappy one ; and she was left, deserted by her husband, in straitened circumstances. After the assassination of the Duc de Berry, M. de la Rochefoucauld, one of the leaders of the ultra-Royalist party, contrived to throw
her in the way of Louis XVIII., in the hope of counteracting the more
Liberal influence which M. de Cazes had acquired over the King. Madame
du Cayla became the hope and the mainstay of the altar and the throne.
The scheme succeeded. The King was touched by her grace and beauty,
and she became indispensable to his happiness. His happiness was said to
consist in inhaling a pinch of snuff from her shoulders, which were remarkably broad and fair. M. de Lamartine has related the romance of her life
in the thirty-eighth book of his ' Histoire de la Restauration,' and Béranger
satirised her in the bitterest of his songs—that which bears the name of
' Octavie ' :—

> Sur les coussins où la douleur l'enchaîne
>   Quel mal, dis-tu, vous fait ce roi des rois ?
> Vois-le d'un masque enjoliver sa haine
>   Pour étouffer notre gloire et nos lois.
>
> Vois ce cœur faux, que cherchent tes caresses,
>   De tous les siens n'aimer que ses aïeux ;
> Charger de fers les muses vengeresses,
>   Et par ses mœurs nous révéler ses dieux.
>
> Peins-nous ces feux, qu'en secret tu redoutes,
>   *Quand sur ton sein il cuve son nectar*,
> Ces feux dont s'indignaient les voûtes
>   Où plane encor l'aigle du grand César.'

It is curious that in 1829 the last mistress of a King of France should have
visited London under the reign of the last mistress of a King of England.]

king's mistresses seem to have a rage for pearls; I remember Madame Narischkin's were splendid. Madame du Cayla is said to be very rich and clever.

After dinner the Duke talked to me for a long time about the King and the Duke of Cumberland, and his quarrel with the latter. He began about the King's making Lord Aberdeen stay at the Cottage the other day when he had engaged all the foreign Ambassadors to dine with him in London. Aberdeen represented this to him, but his Majesty said 'it did not matter, he should stay, and the Ambassadors should for once see that he was King of England.' 'He has no idea,' said the Duke, ' of what a King of England ought to do, or he would have known that he ought to have made Aberdeen go and receive them, instead of keeping him there.' He said the King was very clever and amusing, but that with a surprising memory he was very inaccurate, and constantly told stories the details of which all his auditors must know to be false. One day he was talking of the late King, and asserted that George III. had said to himself, ' Of all the men I have ever known you are the one on whom I have the greatest dependence, and you are the most perfect gentleman.' Another day he said ' that he recollected the old Lord Chesterfield, who once said to him, " Sir, you are the fourth Prince of Wales I have known, and I must give your Royal Highness one piece of advice: stick to your father; as long as you adhere to your father you will be a great and a happy man, but if you separate yourself from him you will be nothing and an unhappy one;" and, by God (added the King), I never forgot that advice, and acted upon it all my life.' ' We all,' said the Duke, 'looked at one another with astonishment. He is extremely clever and particularly ingenious in turning the conversation from any subject he does not like to discuss.

' I,' added the Duke of Wellington, ' remember calling ' upon him the day he received the news of the battle of ' Navarino. I was not a Minister, but Commander-in-Chief, ' and after having told me the news he asked me what I ' thought of it. I said that I knew nothing about it, was

'ignorant of the instructions that had been given to the
'admiral, and could not give any opinion; but "one thing is
'clear to me, that your Majesty's ships have suffered very
'much, and that you ought to reinforce your fleet directly, for
'whenever you have a maritime force yours ought to be
'superior to all others." This advice he did not like; I saw
'this, and he said, "Oh, the Emperor of Russia is a man of
'honour," and then he began talking, and went on to Venice,
'Toulon, St. Petersburg, all over the Continent, and from one
'place and one subject to another, till he brought me to
'Windsor Castle. I make it a rule never to interrupt him,
'and when in this way he tries to get rid of a subject in
'the way of business which he does not like, I let him talk
'himself out, and then quietly put before him the matter in
'question, so that he cannot escape from it. I remember
'when the Duke of Newcastle was going to Windsor with a
'mob at his heels to present a petition (during the late dis-
'cussions) I went down to him and showed him the petition,
'and told him that they ought to be prevented from coming.
'He went off and talked upon every subject but that which I
'had come about, for an hour and a half. I let him go on till
'he was tired, and then I said, "But the petition, sir; here it
'is, and an answer must be sent. I had better write to the
'Duke of Newcastle and tell him your Majesty will receive it
'through the Secretary of State; and, if you please, I will
'write the letter before I leave the house." This I did,
'finished my business in five minutes, and went away with the
'letter in my pocket. I know him so well that I can deal with
'him easily, but anybody who does not know him, and who is
'afraid of him, would have the greatest difficulty in getting
'on with him. One extraordinary peculiarity about him is,
'that the only thing he fears is ridicule. He is afraid of
'nothing which is hazardous, perilous, or uncertain; on the
'contrary he is all for braving difficulties; but he dreads
'ridicule, and this is the reason why the Duke of Cumber-
'land, whose sarcasms he dreads, has such power over him,
'and Lord Anglesey likewise; both of them he hates in pro-
'portion as he fears them.' I said I was very much sur-

prised to hear this, as neither of these men were wits, or likely to make him ridiculous; that if he had been afraid of Sefton or Alvanley it could have been understood. 'But,' rejoined the Duke, 'he never sees these men, and he does ' not mind anybody he does not see ; but the Duke of ' Cumberland and Lord Anglesey he cannot avoid seeing, and ' the fear he has of what they may say to him, as well as of ' him, keeps him in awe of them. No man, however, knows ' the Duke of Cumberland better than he does ; indeed, all ' I know of the Duke of Cumberland I know from him, ' and so I told him one day. I remember asking him why ' the Duke of Cumberland was so unpopular, and he said, ' " Because there never was a father well with his son, or ' husband with his wife, or lover with his mistress, or a ' friend with his friend, that he did not try to make mischief ' between them." And yet he suffers this man to have con- ' stant access to him, to say what he will to him, and often ' acts under his influence.' I said, 'You and the Duke of ' Cumberland speak now, don't you?' 'Yes, we speak. The ' King spoke to me about it, and wanted me to make him an ' apology. I told him it was quite impossible. "Why," said ' he, "you did not mean to offend the Duke of Cumberland, I ' am sure." " No, sir," said I ; " I did not wish to offend him, ' but I did not say a word that I did not mean. When we meet ' the Royal Family in society, they are our superiors, and we ' owe them all respect, and I should readily apologise for ' anything I might have said offensive to the Duke; but in the ' House of Lords we are their peers, and for what I say there ' I am responsible to the House alone." " But," said the ' King, " he said you turned on him as if you meant to address ' yourself to him personally." "I did mean it, sir," said I, ' " and I did so because I knew that he had been here, that he ' had heard things from your Majesty which he had gone and ' misrepresented and misstated in other quarters, and knowing ' that, I meant to show him that I was aware of it. I am sorry ' that the Duke is offended, but I cannot help it, and I cannot ' make him an apology." '

The Duke went on, 'I was so afraid he would tell the

' Duke that I was sorry for what I had said, that I repeated
' to him when I went away, " Now, sir, remember that I will
' not apologise to the Duke, and I hope your Majesty will
' therefore not convey any such idea to his mind." However,
' he spoke to him, I suppose, for the next time I met the Duke
' he bowed to me. I immediately called on him, but he did
' not return my visit. On a subsequent occasion [I forget what
' he said it was] I called on him again, and he returned my
' visit the same day.'

The Duke then talked of the letter which the Duke of
Cumberland had just written (as Grand Master of the Orange
Lodges) to Enniskillen, which he thought was published with
the most mischievous intentions. However, he said, ' I
' know not what he is at, but while I am conscious of going
' on in a straightforward manner I am not afraid of him, or of
' anything he can do,' which I was surprised to hear, because
it looked as if he was afraid of him. I asked him whether,
with all the cleverness he thought belonged to the King, he
evinced great acuteness in discussing matters of business, to
which he replied, ' Oh, no, not at all, the worst judgment that
' can be.' This was not the first time I had heard the Duke's
opinion of the King. I remember him saying something to
the Duke of Portland about him during the Queen's trial
indicative of his contempt for him.

In the meantime the Duke of Cumberland, instead of returning to Berlin, has sent for the Duchess and his son, and
means to take up his abode in this country, in hopes of prevailing upon the King to dismiss his Ministers and make a
Government under his own auspices ; but however weak the
Government may be, he will not succeed, for the King has an
habitual reliance upon the Duke [of Wellington] which over-
comes the mortification and dislike he feels at being dependent upon him ; and, besides, the materials do not exist out
of which a Government could be formed that would have the
support of the House of Commons. The great want which
this Administration experiences is that of men of sufficient
information and capacity to direct the complicated machinery
of our trade and finances and adjust our colonial differences.

Huskisson, Grant, and Palmerston were the ablest men, and the two first the best informed in the Government. Fitzgerald knows nothing of the business of his office, still less of the principles of trade; he is idle, but quick. Of Murray I know nothing; he is popular in his office, but he has neither the capacity nor the knowledge of Huskisson.

CHAPTER VI.

July 21*st.*—There was a Council last Thursday, and the heaviest Recorder's report that was ever known, I believe; seven people left for execution. The King cannot bear this, and is always leaning to the side of mercy. Lord Tenterden, however, is for severity, and the Recorder still more so. It not unfrequently happens that a culprit escapes owing to the scruples of the King; sometimes he put the question of life or death to the vote, and it is decided by the voices of the majority. The King came to town at one, and gave audiences until half-past four. He received Madame du Cayla, whom he was very curious to see. She told me afterwards that she was astonished at his good looks, and seemed particularly to have been struck with his 'belles jambes et sa perruque bien arrangée;' and I asked her if she had ever seen him before, and she said no, 'mais que le feu Roi lui en avait souvent parlé, et de ses belles manières, qu'en vérité elle les avait trouvées parfaites.' There was a reigning Margrave of Baden waiting for an audience in the room we

assembled in. Nobody took much notice of him, and when
the Duke spoke to him he bowed to the ground, bow after
bow; when he went away nobody attended him or opened
the door for him.

July 24th.—The accounts from Ireland are very bad;
nothing but massacres and tumults, and all got up by the
Protestants, who desire nothing so much as to provoke the
Catholics into acts of violence and outrage. They want a
man of energy and determination who will cause the law to
be respected and impartially administered. If Lord Anglesey
was there, it is very probable these outrages would not have
taken place, but no one cares for such a man of straw as the
present Lord Lieutenant.

The Duke of Cumberland is doing all he can to set the
King against the Duke; he always calls him 'King Arthur,'
which made the King very angry at first, and he desired he
would not, but he calls him so still, and the King submits.
He never lets any of the Royal Family see the King alone;
the Duchess of Gloucester complains bitterly of his conduct,
and the way in which he thrusts himself in when she is with
his Majesty. The other day Count Münster came to the
King, and the Duke of Cumberland was determined he
should not have a private audience, and stayed in the room
the whole time. He hates Lady Conyngham, and she him.
They put about that he has been pressed to stay here by the
King, which is not true; the King would much rather he
went away. The Duke of Wellington told me that he one
day asked the King when the Duke was going, and he said,
'I am sick to death of the subject. I have been told he was
going fifty times, but when he goes, or whether he ever goes
at all, I have not the least idea.' He is now very much
provoked because the King will not talk politics with him.
His Majesty wants to be quiet, and is tired of all the Duke's
violence and his constant attacks.

August 8th.—There is a story current about the Duke of
Cumberland and Lady Lyndhurst which is more true than
most stories of this kind. The Duke called upon her, and
grossly insulted her; on which, after a scramble, she rang

the bell. He was obliged to desist and to go away, but
before he did he said, 'By God, madam, I will be the ruin
of you and your husband, and will not rest till I have
destroyed you both.'

Vesey Fitzgerald has turned out the Chief Clerk in the
Board of Trade, and put in Hume[1] as Assistant Secretary.
He told me it was absolutely necessary, as nobody in the
Office knew anything of its business, which is, I believe,
very true, but as true of himself as of the rest. Hume is a
very clever man, and probably knows more of the principles
of trade and commerce than anybody, but so it is in every
department of Government—great ignorance on the part of
the chiefs, and a few obscure men of industry and ability
who do the business and supply the knowledge requisite,
sic vos non vobis throughout.

O'Connell was elected without opposition ; he was more
violent and more popular than ever. They treat him with
every indignity, and then they complain of his violence ;
besides, he must speak to the Irish in the strain to which
they have been used and which pleases them. Had he
never been violent, he would not be the man he is, and
Ireland would not have been emancipated.

August 18th.—Last Saturday I came back from Goodwood, and called on Lady Jersey, whom I found very
curious about a correspondence which she told me had taken
place between the Duke of Cumberland and the Chancellor
relative to a paragraph which had appeared in the 'Age,'
stating that his Royal Highness had been turned out of Lady
Lyndhurst's house in consequence of having insulted her in
it. She said she was very anxious to see the letter, for she
heard that the Duke had much the best of it, and that the
Chancellor's letter was evasive and Jesuitical. The next
day I was informed of the details of this affair. I found
that the Duke had called upon her and had been denied ;
that he had complained half in jest, and half in earnest, to
the Chancellor of her not letting him in ; that on a subse-

---

[1] [Mr. Deacon Hume, a very able public servant. He remained at the
Board of Trade many years.]

quent day he had called so early that no orders had been
given to the porter, and he was let in; that his manner
and his language had been equally brutal and offensive; that
he afterwards went off upon politics, and abused the whole
Administration, and particularly the Chancellor, and after
staying two or three hours, insulting and offending her in
every way, he took himself off. Soon after he met her somewhere in the evening, when he attacked her again. She
treated him with all possible indignation, and would have
nothing to say to him.

Yesterday I met the Chancellor at the Castle at a
Council. He took me aside, and said that he wished to tell me
what had passed, and to show me the correspondence.   He
then began, and said that after the Duke's visit Lady L. had
told the Chancellor of his abuse of him and the Government,
but had suppressed the rest, thinking it was better not to
tell him, as it would put him in a very embarrassing position,
and contenting herself with saying she would never receive
the Duke again upon the other grounds, which were quite
sufficient; but that some time after reports reached her
from various quarters (Lord Grey, Lord Durham, Lord
Dudley, and several others) that the Duke went about
talking of her in the most gross and impertinent manner.
Upon hearing this, she thought it right to tell the Chancellor
the other part of his conduct which she had hitherto concealed, and this she did in general terms—viz. that he had
been very insolent and made an attack upon her. The
Chancellor was exceedingly incensed, but he said after much
consideration he thought it better to let the matter drop; a
long time had elapsed since the offence was committed; all
communication had ceased between all the parties; and he
felt the ridicule and inconvenience of putting himself (holding the high office he did) in personal collision with a Royal
Duke, besides the annoyance which it would be to Lady
Lyndhurst to become publicly the subject of such a quarrel.
There, then, he let the matter rest, but about a fortnight
ago he received a letter from the Duke enclosing a newspaper to this effect, as well as I can recollect it, for I was

obliged to read the letter in such a hurried way that I could not bring the exact contents away with me, though I am sure I do not err in stating their sense) :—

'My Lord,—I think it necessary to enclose to your Lordship a newspaper containing a paragraph which I have marked, and which relates to a pretended transaction in your Lordship's house. I think it necessary and proper to contradict this statement, which I need not say is a gross falsehood, and I wish, therefore, to have the authority of Lady Lyndhurst for contradicting it.

'   I am, my Lord, yours sincerely,
'   ERNEST.'

This was the sense of the letter, though it was not so worded; it was civil enough. The Chancellor answered :— 'The Lord Chancellor with his duty begs to acknowledge the favour of your Royal Highness's letter. The Lord Chancellor had never seen the paragraph to which your Royal Highness alludes, and which he regards with the most perfect indifference, considering it as one of that series of calumnies to which Lady Lyndhurst has been for some time exposed from a portion of the press, and which she has at length learnt to regard with the contempt they deserve.' He said that he thought it better to let the matter drop, and he wrote this answer by way of waiving any discussion on the subject, and that the Duke might contradict the paragraph himself if he chose to do so. To this the Duke wrote again :—'My Lord,—I have received your Lordship's answer, which is not so explicit as I have a right to expect. I repeat again that the statement is false and scandalous, and I have a right to require Lady Lyndhurst's sanction to the contradiction which I think it necessary to give to it.' This letter was written in a more impertinent style than the other. On the receipt of it the Chancellor consulted the Duke of Wellington, and the Duke suggested the following answer, which the Chancellor sent :—'The Lord Chancellor has had the honour of receiving your Royal Highness's letter of ——. The Lord Chancellor does not conceive it necessary to annoy Lady Lyndhurst by troubling her upon the subject, and with what relates to your Royal Highness the Lord Chancellor has no concern whatever; but with regard to that part which states that your Royal Highness had been excluded from the Lord Chancellor's house, there could be no question that the respect and grateful attachment which both the Chancellor and Lady Lyndhurst felt to their Sovereign made it impossible that any brother of that Sovereign should ever be turned out of his house.' To this the Duke wrote another letter, in a very sneering and impertinent tone in the third person, and alluding to the *loose reports* which had been current on the subject, and saying that ' the Chancellor might have his own reasons for not choosing to speak to Lady Lyndhurst on the subject;' to which the Chancellor replied that ' he knew nothing of any loose reports, but that if there were any, in whatever quarter they might have originated, which went to affect the conduct of Lady Lyndhurst in the matter in question, they were most false, foul, and calumnious.' So ended the correspondence; all these latter expressions were intended to apply to the Duke himself, who is the person who spread the *loose reports* and told the lies about her. When she first denied him, she told Lord Bathurst of it, who assured her she had done quite right, and that she had better never let him in, for if she did he would surely invent some lies about her. Last Sunday week the Chancellor went down to Windsor, and laid the whole correspondence before the King, who received him very well, and approved of what he had done; but of course when he saw the Duke of Cumberland and heard his story, he concurred in all his abuse of the Chancellor. I think the Chancellor treated the matter in the best way the case admitted of. Had he taken it up, he must have resigned his office and called the Duke out, and what a mixture of folly and scandal this would have been, and how the woman would have suffered in it all!

August 22nd.—The day before yesterday Sir Henry Cooke called on me, and told me that he came on the part of the Duke of Cumberland, who had heard that I had seen the correspondence, and that I had given an account of it which was unfavourable to him, that his Royal Highness wished me, therefore, to call on him and hear his statement of the facts. Cooke then entered into the history, and told me that it was he who had originally acquainted the Duke with the reports which were current about him, and had advised him to contradict them, but that he had not found any opportunity of taking it up till this paragraph appeared in the 'Age' newspaper; that the Duke had given him an account of what had passed, which was that Lady Lyndhurst had begged him to call upon her, then to dine with her, and upon every occasion had encouraged him. I heard all he had to say, but declined calling on the Duke. As I wished, however, that there should be no misrepresentation in what I said on the subject, I wrote a letter to Cooke, to be laid before the Duke, in which I gave an account of the circumstances under which I had been concerned in the business, stating that I had not expressed any opinion of the conduct of the parties, and that I did not wish to be in any way mixed up in it. After I had seen Cooke I went to the Chancellor and read my letter to him. I found he had not shown the King the two last letters that had passed; and as Cooke had told me that the Duke meant to go to Windsor the next day and lay the whole correspondence before the King, the Chancellor immediately sent off a messenger with the two letters which the King had not seen. The Chancellor has since circulated the correspondence among his friends, but with rather too undignified a desire to submit his conduct to the judgment of a parcel of people who only laugh at them both, and are amused with the gossip and malice of the thing.

August 25th.—I came to town from Stoke yesterday morning, and found a palavering letter from Cooke, returning mine, saying that the Duke was quite satisfied, and saw that it would be useless to have an interview with me; that he had persuaded his Royal Highness to drop the whole affair; and ended with many protestations of respect for the Chancellor and the purity of his own motives in meddling with the matter. I sent his letter to the Chancellor, together with my own, that he might show them both to the Duke of Wellington.

Melbourne, who is a pretty good judge of Irish affairs, thinks that Government will probably be under the necessity of adopting strong coercive measures there; but whether they are adopted, or a temporary policy of expedients persisted in, nobody is there fit to advise what is requisite. The Duke of Northumberland is an absolute nullity, a bore beyond all bores, and, in spite of his desire to spend money and be affable, very unpopular. The Duchess complains of it and can't imagine why, for they do all they can to be liked, but all in vain.

August 28th.—At Stoke [1] since Tuesday for the Egham races; Esterhazy, Alvanley, Montrond, Mornay, B. Craven, &c. The King came to the races one day (the day I was not there) in excellent health. The weather exceeds everything that ever was known—a constant succession of gales of wind and tempests of rain, and the sun never shining. The oats are not cut, and a second crop is growing up, that has been shaken out of the first. Everybody contemplates with dismay the approach of winter, which will probably bring with it the overthrow of the Corn Laws, for corn must be at such a price as to admit of an immense importation. So much for our domestic prospect here, to say nothing of Ireland.

In the meantime the Sultan with his firmness has brought the Russians to the gates of Constantinople, and not a soul doubts that they are already there, or that they will be directly; there is nothing to resist either Diebitsch or Paskiewitch. Esterhazy talks of it as certain, and so unaccountable does it seem that Austria should have been a passive spectator of the Russian victories, that a strong notion prevails that Metternich has made his bargain with them, and that in the impending partition Austria is to have her share. Still more extraordinary does it appear that the Duke, from whom vigour and firmness might have been expected,

---

[1] [Stoke, near Slough, was at this time the residence of Lord Sefton; but it still belonged, I think, to the Penn family, who afterwards sold the place to Lord Taunton.]

should not have interfered. That cursed treaty of the 6th of
July, and the subsequent battle of Navarino, which were intended to give us a right to arrest the ambition of Russia, have
been rendered nugatory by the obstinacy of the Turks on the
one hand, and the perpetual changes of Administration here
and in France, which have prevented any steady and consistent course of policy from being followed; while the Russians,
availing themselves of both these circumstances, have pushed
on with singleness of purpose and great vigour of execution.
It is quite impossible now to foresee the end of all this, but
the elements are abroad of as fine disturbances as the most
restless can desire.

France is probably too much occupied with her own
affairs to pay much attention to those of Turkey, nor is it
clear that the French would much regret any event which
tended to impair our commercial greatness. So busy are the
French with their own politics, that even the milliners have
left off making caps. Lady Cowper told me to-day that
Madame Maradan complained that she could get no bonnets,
&c., from Paris; for they would occupy themselves with nothing but the change of Administration.[1] Nothing can exceed the violence that prevails; the King does nothing but
cry. Polignac is said to have the fatal obstinacy of a martyr,
the worst sort of courage of the *ruat cœlum* sort. Aberdeen
said at dinner at Madame de Lieven's the other day that he
thought him a very clever man; and that the Duke of Wellington went still further, for he said that he was the ablest
man France had had since the Restoration. I remember
him well when he was courting his first wife, Archy Mac-
donald's sister; and if being first a prisoner, then an emi-
grant, then a miser, and now a saint can make him a good
Minister, he may be one.

August 31*st*.—The Duke, the Chancellor, and Privy Seal
came from Walmer to-day for a Cabinet; and Esterhazy,
who was to have dined with me, sent word that as he had received a courier this morning, and was obliged to send off
Dietrichstein this evening, he could not come. It is said

[1] [The Polignac Ministry took office on the 8th of August.]

that Sir Frederick Gordon has sent word that the Turks are
frightened and wish to treat, but probably it is now too late.

Last night news came that Villa Flor had routed Miguel's
expedition against Terceira, and at the same time the little
Queen is embarking with the Empress for the Brazils. This
probably comes too late; some time ago it might have been
of some use. Miguel will probably be recognised by this
country, and then the game is up. I have long been convinced that the Duke meant eventually to acknowledge
Miguel, or he would not have tolerated Beresford's conduct.
If Lamb is to be believed, Beresford was secretly in it all.

I met the Chancellor this morning, who gave me back my
letter and Cooke's answer. He said, 'There are other reports
afloat now, I hear.' I said, 'What? I have heard none.' 'Oh,'
he said, 'on public matters, and they are put about by that
blackguard,' meaning the Duke of Cumberland. I suppose
he alludes to changes in the Government, but I have heard
of none; they are, in fact, kept in hot water by this fellow's
activity, though I think he cannot do the mischief he would
like.

From what I hear, it is probable that Lord William
Bentinck will be speedily recalled from India. His measures
are of too Liberal a cast to suit the taste of the present
Government. The Duke has never liked him, not since the
war in Spain, when he did not behave quite well to Lord
William, and he seldom forgets old animosities; besides, he
cannot bear anybody who takes a line of their own.

Lord Ellenborough, strong in the concurrence of the Duke,
is inclined to be insolent in his tone to Lord William, which,
I take it, he will not stand. The Duke looks upon Lord
William as a hasty, imprudent man, with bad judgment, and
I am not sure that he is very wrong. He has made himself
popular by the affability and *bonhomie* of his manner, his
magnificence and hospitality, and the liberal and generous
character of his political opinions, but he is far from a
clever man, and I suspect his judgment is very indifferent.

I hear from Ireland that Doherty conducts the trial of
the policeman with consummate skill; the object was that

the trial should appear fair, and that the men should be acquitted. They were acquitted, and the people were furious. There is excitement enough in that wretched country, and every effort is made to keep it up at its highest pitch; the press on each side teems with accusations and invectives, and the Protestants strain every nerve to inflame the spirit of rancorous fury which distinguished the Brunswickers before the Catholic question was carried, and to provoke the Catholics to overt acts of violence. Both sides are to blame, but the Protestants the most. George Villiers wrote me word of a crime that has been perpetrated, the most atrocious I ever heard of. . . . The country in which such an abomination was perpetrated should be visited with the fate of Sodom and Gomorrah. The arm of justice is too slow; public indignation should deal out a rapid and a terrible vengeance.

September 5th.—There is a strong report that the Turks want to treat, and the proclamation of Diebitsch looks as if the Russians were ready to make peace. There is also a hope that the Russian army may have been too bold, and finds itself in a scrape by having advanced too far from its resources, but the former notion is the most likely of the two. Three or four sail of the line are ordered out to the Mediterranean.

Yesterday I went with Amyot to his house, where he showed me a part of Windham's diary; there are twenty-eight little volumes of it, begun in 1784, when he was thirty-four years old, and continued irregularly till his death; it seems to be written very freely and familiarly, and is probably a correct picture of the writer's mind. I only read a few pages, which were chiefly notices of his moving about, where he dined, the company he met, and other trifles, often very trifling and sometimes not very decent; it abounds with expressions of self-reproach for idleness, breach of resolutions, and not taking care of his health; talks of the books he reads and means to read, and constantly describes the state of spirits he is in. There is a paper containing an account of his last interview with Johnson, shortly before Johnson died; he says that he told Johnson how much he reproached himself for not having lived more in his society, and that he had often resolved to be with him as much as he could, but that his not having done so was a proof of the fallacy of our resolutions, that he regretted. In Windham's diary are several Johnsoniana, after the manner of Boswell, only much shorter, his opinions on one or two subjects briefly given, some quotations and criticisms. I was much struck with his criticisms on Virgil, whom he seems to have held in great contempt, and to have regarded as inferior to Ovid. He says, ' Take away his imitation of Homer, and what do you leave him ? ' Of Homer his admiration was unbounded, although he says that he never read the whole of the ' Odyssey ' in the original, but that everything which is most admirable in poetry is to be found in Homer. I care the less about remembering these things because they will probably appear in print before long.[1]

Windham told Johnson that he regretted having omitted to talk to him of the most important of all subjects on which he had often doubted. Johnson said, ' You mean natural and revealed religion,' and added that the historical evidences of Christianity were so strong that it was not possible to doubt its truth, that we had not so much evidence that Cæsar died in the Capitol as that Christ died in the manner related in the Bible ; that three out of four of the Evangelists died in attestation of their evidence, that the same evidence would be considered irresistible in any ordinary historical case. Amyot told me, as we were coming along, that Windham had questioned Johnson about religion, having doubts, and that Johnson had removed them by this declaration: if, then, the commonest and hundred times repeated arguments were sufficient to remove such doubts as were likely to occur to a mind like Windham's, it may be counted a miracle, for I am sure, in the ordinary affairs of life, Windham would not have been so easily satisfied. It has always appeared to me questionable whether Johnson was a believer (I mean whether his clear and unbiassed judgment was

---

[1] [A selection from Mr. Windham's journals was published by Mrs. Henry Baring in 1866. The Johnsoniana had previously been published by Mr. Croker in his edition of Boswell's ' Life of Johnson.']

satisfied) in Christianity; he evidently dreaded and disliked
the subject, and though he would have been indignant had
anybody hinted that he had doubts, his nervous irritation at
any religious discussion betokened a mind ill at ease on the
subject.   I learnt one thing from Windham's diary which I
put into immediate practice, and that is, to write mine on one
side only, and leave the other for other matters connected
with the text; it is more convenient certainly.

September 16th.—Went to Brighton on Saturday last to
pay Lady Jersey a visit and shoot at Firle.   Jersey and I
shot 376 rabbits, the greatest number that had ever been
killed on the hills.   The scenery is very fine—a range of
downs looking on one side over the sea, and on the other
over a wide extent of rich flat country.   It is said that Firle
is the oldest park in England.   It belongs to Lord Gage.

I heard at Brighton for the first time of the Duke of
Wellington's prosecution of the ' Morning Journal,' which
was announced by the paper itself in a paragraph quite as
scurrilous as those for which it is attacked.   It seems that
he has long made up his mind to this measure, and that he
thinks it is a duty incumbent on him, which I do not see,
and it appears to me to be an act of great folly.   He stands
much too high, has performed too great actions, and the
attacks on him were too vulgar and vague to be under the
necessity of any such retaliatory measure as this, and he
lowers his dignity by entering into a conflict with such an
infamous paper, and appearing to care about its abuse.   I
think the Chancellor was right, and that he is wrong.   There
is a report that the King insists upon the Duke of Cumberland being Commander-in-Chief, and it is extraordinary how
many people think that he will succeed in turning out the
Duke.   Lord Harrington died while I was at Brighton, and
it is supposed that the Duke of Cumberland will try and get
the Round Tower,[1] but probably the King will not like to
establish him so near himself.   The King has nearly lost
his eyesight, and is to be couched as soon as his eyes are in

[1] Lord Conyngham got the Round Tower, and Lord Combermere the
regiment.—[C. C. G.]

a proper state for the operation. He is in a great fright with his father's fate before him, and indeed nothing is more probable than that he will become blind and mad too ; he is already a little of both. It is now a question of appointing a Private Secretary, and Knighton, it is supposed, would be the man; but if he is to abstain from all business, there would seem to be no necessity for the appointment, as he will be as little able to do business with his Private Secretary as with his Minister.

I have been living at Fulham at Lord Wharncliffe's villa for six or seven weeks; I have lived here in idleness and luxury, giving dinners, and wasting my time and my money rather more than usual. I have read next to nothing since I have been here ; I am ashamed to think how little—in short, a most unprofitable life.

September 23rd.—At Fulham till Friday, when I came to town. Went to Stoke on Saturday, and returned yesterday; old Lady Salisbury, Giles, E. Capel, and Conroy. There is always something to be learnt from everybody, if you touch them on the points they know. Giles told me about the letter to his sister written by Francis,[1] and which was supposed to have afforded another proof that he was Junius. Many years ago Francis was in love with his sister, Mrs. King (at Bath), and one day she received an anonymous letter, enclosing a copy of verses. The letter said that the writer had found the verses, and being sure they were meant for her, had sent them to her. The verses were in Francis' handwriting, the envelope in a feigned hand. When the discussion arose about Francis being Junius, Giles said to his sister one day, 'If you have kept those verses which Francis wrote to you many years ago at Bath, it would be curious to examine the handwriting and see if it corresponds with that of Junius.' She found the envelope and verses, and, on comparing them, the writing of the envelope was

---

[1] [Sir Philip Francis, the reputed author of the 'Letters of Junius.' This anecdote has since been verified with great minuteness by Mr. Twisleton in his researches on the authorship of 'Junius.' The copy of verses and the envelope in a feigned hand are still in existence. I have seen them. The feigned hand appears to be identical with that of Junius.]

identical with that of Junius as published in Woodfall's book.

Old Creevey is rather an extraordinary character. I know nothing of the early part of his history, but I believe he was an attorney or barrister; he married a widow, who died a few years ago; she had something, he nothing; he got into Parliament, belonged to the Whigs, displayed a good deal of shrewdness and humour, and was for some time very troublesome to the Tory Government by continually attacking abuses. After some time he lost his seat, and went to live at Brussels, where he became intimate with the Duke of Wellington. Then his wife died, upon which event he was thrown upon the world with about 200*l.* a year or less, no home, few connections, a great many acquaintance, a good constitution, and extraordinary spirits. He possesses nothing but his clothes, no property of any sort; he leads a vagrant life, visiting a number of people who are delighted to have him, and sometimes roving about to various places, as fancy happens to direct, and staying till he has spent what money he has in his pocket. He has no servant, no home, no creditors; he buys everything as he wants it at the place he is at; he has no ties upon him, and has his time entirely at his own disposal and that of his friends. He is certainly a living proof that a man may be perfectly happy and exceedingly poor, or rather without riches, for he suffers none of the privations of poverty and enjoys many of the advantages of wealth. I think he is the only man I know in society who possesses nothing.

Captain Dickinson's trial[1] ended last week, with a sentence which was levelled against Codrington, and which called the charges groundless, frivolous, and vexatious. It

[1] [Captain Dickinson fought the 'Genoa' at the battle of Navarino after Captain Bathurst, the commander of the ship, was killed. A quarrel afterwards took place between him and Sir Edward Codrington, and Dickinson was tried by court-martial for not making proper use of the springs ordered by the Admiral to be placed on the anchors, the consequence of which was that her broadside was not directed against the enemy, but fired into the 'Albion.' Captain Dickinson was honourably acquitted of all the charges, and it was proved that Sir Edward Codrington's recollection of what had passed was inaccurate in some particulars.]

is generally thought that this sentence might have been
spared, though the acquittal was proper; that Codrington
behaved very foolishly, and in ever mentioning the round
robin after he had forgiven it, very inexcusably; but that,
on the other hand, the Admiralty had displayed a spirit of
hostility and rancour against him which is very disgusting,
and that Blackwood was sent down to the court-martial for
the express purpose of bullying and thwarting him.   I saw
him after the sentence; he seemed annoyed, but said that
such a sentence made it necessary the matter should not
stop there, and that it must be taken up in Parliament.   I
cannot see what he is to gain by that; he may prove that the
Ministry of that day (which was not the Duke's) behaved
very ill, but that has nothing to do with the court-martial.

The whole press has risen up in arms against the Duke's
prosecution of the ' Morning Journal,' which appears to me,
though many people think he is right, a great act of weakness and passion.   How can such a man suffer by the attacks
of such a paper, and by such attacks, the sublime of the
ridiculous ?—' that he is aiming at the Crown, but *we* shall
take care that he does not succeed in this.'   The idea of the
Duke of Wellington seeking to make himself King, and his
ambition successfully resisted by the editor of a newspaper,
' flogs ' any scene in the ' Rehearsal.'   I saw the Duke
yesterday morning; he was just come from Doncaster, where
he told me he had been very well received.   He was with
Chesterfield, who was to have had a large party.   Afterwards
I rode with him and he took me to see his house, which is
now excellent.   He told me that both the King's eyes were
affected, the left the most, and that he would have the
operation performed when they were fit for it; he said that
the King never evinced any fear upon these occasions, that
he was always perfectly cool, and neither feared operations
or their possible consequences; that he remembered when
he had a very painful and dangerous operation performed
some time ago upon his head, that he was not the least
nervous about it, nor at all afraid of dying, for they told him
that he would very likely not recover.   I said, ' Then, after

all, perhaps he who has the reputation of being a coward
would prove a very brave man if circumstances occasioned
his showing what he is.' He said, 'Very likely;' that he
seemed to have but one fear, that of ridicule: he cannot bear
the society of clever men, for fear of ridicule; he cannot
bear to show himself in public, because he is afraid of the
jokes that may be cut on his person.

In the evening I met Matuscewitz, who is all glorious at
the Russian successes. He, Montrond, and I talked the
matter over, and he said that they should make peace, but
of course (I had said, 'Vous serez modestes, n'est-ce pas?')
they should profit by circumstances; that the Allied
Ministers would not be permitted to interfere, and they
should grant such terms as they pleased without consulting
them. This was a lie,[1] for Bandinell had told me in the
morning that the negotiations were going on in concert
with the Ambassadors of the Allies.

November 4th.—Left London the last week in September,
and, after visiting at several country houses, slept at Har-
borough, and went to Bretby to breakfast; got there at twelve
and found nobody up. In process of time they came down
to breakfast, the party consisting of the Chancellor and Lady
Lyndhurst, the Worcesters, Mrs. Fox, and Williams, the
chaplain, and his wife. I saw very little of the place, which
seems pretty, but not large; a very large unfinished house.
I stayed two or three hours, and went on to Chatsworth,[2]
where I arrived just as they were going to dinner, but was
not expected, and so there was no room at the table. The
party was immense; 40 people sat down to dinner every day,
and about 150 servants in the steward's room and servants'
hall; there were the Lievens, Cowpers, Granvilles, Wharn-

---

[1] It was not a lie though after all, for I don't believe the Allied
Ministers had any concern in the matter. (December 5th.)—[C. C. G.]

[2] [The hospitality of Chatsworth in the lifetime of William Spencer
Cavendish, sixth Duke of Devonshire, was princely. The Duke of Port-
land, Mr. Greville's grandfather, married Dorothy, only daughter of
William, fourth Duke of Devonshire, from whom Mr. Greville derived his
second name of Cavendish. He was therefore second cousin of the sixth
Duke and of Lady Granville and Lady Carlisle.]

cliffes, Granthams, Wiltons, Stanleys, Belfasts, Newboroughs, Dawsons, Matuscewitz, Clanwilliams, G. Anson, H. de Ros, &c. Nothing could be more agreeable from the gaiety of numbers and the entire liberty which prevails ; all the resources of the house—horses, carriages, keepers, &c.—are placed at the disposal of the guests, and everybody does what they like best. In the evening they acted charades or danced, and there was plenty of whist and *écarté* high and low. It was in the middle of that party that news came of the negotiations being begun between the Russians and Turks,[1] and I received a letter from Robert Grosvenor, which Madame de Lieven was ready to devour, and she was very angry that I would not let her see the whole of it. Our Russians were of course triumphânt, and the Princess's good humour was elevated to rapture by a very pretty compliment which was paid her in the shape of a charade, admirably got up as a *pièce de circonstance*, and which has since made some noise in the world. The word was Constantinople, which was acted : *Constant*, Penelope and the suitors ; *Inn*, a tavern scene ; and *Opal*, the story in ' Anne of Geierstein.' The whole represented the Divan, the arrival of Diebitsch's Ambassadors, a battle between the Turks and Russians, the victory of the latter, and ended by Morpeth as Diebitsch laying a crown of laurel at Madame de Lieven's feet. She was enchanted, and of course wrote off an account of it to the Empress. The whole thing is abused as a *bassesse* by her enemies, but it was very amusing, and in the Duke's house, who is a friend of the Emperor, a not unbecoming compliment.

I returned to Newmarket on the 11th of October. At the end of the week I had a fall from my horse, which con-fined me to my room for ten days. The Arbuthnots were at Newmarket, having come from Sudbourne, where Lord Hertford had brought the Duke and Huskisson together. Nothing seems to have passed between them beyond the common civilities of society, but Huskisson has suffered

[1] [The negotiations for the peace of Adrianople, which terminated the Russo-Turkish war.]

greatly from a universal opinion that the meeting was sought by him for the purpose of re-ingratiating himself with the Duke, and, if possible, getting into office on any terms. It is a proof of the low estimation in which his character is held even by those who rate his talents the highest that all his former political adherents think this of him. With such a reputation his political efficacy never can be great again. There was a strong report that he was to join the Government, which is now dying away. The Duke is very fortunate, for his most formidable opponents always do something to lower their own characters and render themselves as little formidable to him as possible.

The trials in Ireland are just over, and the Government have been defeated, which I find they think may be productive of very important consequences to the peace of the country. The obstinacy of one man, who held out against the other eleven, in the second batch of conspirators who were tried, obliged them at length to dismiss the jury, and the prisoners will be tried at the next assizes; the others were acquitted, though the evidence against them was the same as that on which Leary, &c., were convicted. The exertions of O'Connell, who appears to have acted with great ability, produced this result. The Government say, of course, that he has acted very ill, but as the Judge, at the conclusion of the trial, said publicly that the defence had been conducted with perfect regard to the due administration of the laws, we may conclude that while he availed himself of every advantage, he did not overstep the legitimate duty of an advocate to his client. It is, however, agreed on all hands, notwithstanding these excesses, that the state of the country is improving, and the Emancipation Bill producing fresh benefits every day.

November 9th.—Dined to-day with Byng and met Tom Moore, who was very agreeable; he told us a great deal about his forthcoming 'Life of Byron.' He is nervous about it; he is employed in conjunction with Scott and Mackintosh to write a history of England for one of the new publications like

the Family Library.[1] Scott is to write Scotland, Mackintosh
England, and Moore Ireland; and they get 1,000*l.* apiece;
but Scott could not compress his share into one volume, so he
is to have 1,500*l.* The republication of Scott's works will
produce him an enormous fortune; he has already paid off
30,000*l.* of the Constable bankruptcy debt, and he is to pay
the remaining 30,000*l.* very soon. A new class of readers is
produced by the Bell and Lancaster schools, and this is the
cause of the prodigious and extensive sale of cheap publications. Moore had received a letter from Madame de Guiccioli
to-day; he says she is not handsome. Byron's exploits,
especially at Venice, seem to have been marvellous. Moore
said he wrote with extraordinary rapidity, but his correc-
tions were frequent and laborious. When he wrote the
address for the opening of Drury Lane Theatre, he corrected
it repeatedly.

I saw Miss Fanny Kemble for the first time on Friday,
and was disappointed. She is short, ill made, with large
hands and feet, an expressive countenance, though not handsome, fine eyes, teeth, and hair, not devoid of grace, and with
great energy and spirit, her voice good, though she has a
little of the drawl of her family. She wants the pathos and
tenderness of Miss O'Neill, and she excites no emotion; but
she is very young, clever, and may become a very good,
perhaps a fine actress. Mrs. Siddons was not so good at her
age. She fills the house every night.

The King, who was to have gone to Brighton, has given it
up, nobody knows why, but it is supposed that the Marchioness
is not well. This morning the Duke and my brother were
occupied for half an hour in endeavouring to fold a letter
to his Majesty in a particular way, which he has prescribed,
for he will have his envelopes made up in some French fashion.

---

[1] Dr. Lardner's 'Cyclopædia.' Moore told me that the editor of one of
the annuals offered him 600*l.* to write two articles for his work, but 'that he
loathed the task' and refused, though the money would have been very
acceptable. The man said he did not care about the merit of the performance, and only wanted his name; when Moore refused, the editor raked out
some old and forgotten lines of his to Perry, and inserted them with his
name.—[C. C. G.]

I hear he thinks that he rode Fleur de Lis for the cup at
Goodwood, which he may as well do as think (which he does)
that he led the heavy dragoons at Salamanca.

O'Connell has been making a most infamous speech at
Youghal, and is moving heaven and earth to begin a fresh
agitation about the Union, and to do all the mischief he can.
Francis Leveson is to meet Sheil at dinner to-morrow for the ·
first time; he did not dare do this without asking leave of
Peel.   Peel answered his letter that he 'rather inclined
himself to do anything to win him, but stating that the
Duke would urge the difficulties of their position, and also
the King's horror of the man,' &c.   The King's horror is in
consequence of his speech about the Duke of York.   I am
told Greece is to be erected into a kingdom, with a boundary
line drawn from Volo to Arta, and that the sovereignty is to
be offered to Prince Frederick of Orange, and, if he refuses
it, to Leopold.

November 12th.—At Roehampton at Lord Clifden's from
Tuesday, the 10th, till to-day; Sir James Mackintosh, Moore,
Poodle Byng,[1] and the Master of the Rolls.   It was uncommonly agreeable.   I never was in Mackintosh's society for
so long before, and never was more filled with admiration.
His prodigious memory and the variety and extent of his
information remind me of all I have heard and read of
Burke and Johnson; but his amiable, modest, and unassuming character makes him far more agreeable than they
could either of them (particularly Johnson) have been,
while he is probably equally instructive and amusing.   Not
a subject could be mentioned of which he did not treat with

---

[1] [Honble. Frederick Byng, formerly of the Foreign Office, was universally known in society as 'the Poodle.'   There has been some discussion as
to the origin of this nickname, and one of the critics of this work asserts
that it was given him, 'notoriously, because when tilburys were the fashion,
he used to drive out with a poodle seated by his side.'   I am now informed
on indisputable authority, that the name was given him in early life by
Lady Bath and Georgiana, Duchess of Devonshire, who used to call him
'their poodle,' on account of his thick curly head of hair.   This was Mr.
Byng's own account of the matter.]

equal facility and abundance, from the Council of Trent to
Voltaire's epistles ; every subject, every character, every work,
all were familiar to him, and I do not know a greater treat
than to hear him talk.

Mackintosh said he was a great reader of novels ; had read
' Old Mortality ' four times in English and once in French.
Ellis said he preferred Miss Austen's novels to Scott's.
Talked of the old novelists—Fielding, little read now,
Smollett less ; Mackintosh is a great admirer of Swift, and does
not think his infamous conduct to Vanessa quite made out.
Talked of the articles of our religion, and said that they
were in almost exact conformity with certain doctrines laid
down in the Council of Trent. The Jansenists differ very
little from our Church, except as to the doctrine of the Real
Presence. Speaking of India, Mackintosh said that it was very
remarkable that we had lost one great empire and gained
another in the same generation, and that it was still a moot
point whether the one really was a gain or the other a loss.
Called America the second Maritime Power. Franklin wept
when he quitted England. When he signed the treaty at
Paris, he retired for a moment and changed his coat. It was
remarked, and he said he had been to put on the coat in
which he had been insulted by Lord Loughborough at the
English Council Board. Madame de Staël, he said, was more
agreeable in *tête-à-tête* than in society ; she despised her
children, and said, ' Ils ne me ressemblent pas.' He told her
she did not do them justice, particularly her daughter. She
said, ' C'est une lune bien pâle.' She took an aversion to
Rogers, but when she met him at Bowood, and he told her
anecdotes, she liked him. She had vanquished Brougham,
and was very proud of those conquests.

Moore told several stories which I don't recollect, but
this amused us :—Some Irish had emigrated to some West
Indian colony ; the negroes soon learnt their brogue, and
when another shipload of Irish came soon after, the negroes
as they sailed in said, ' Ah, Paddy, how are you ?' ' Oh,
Christ ! ' said one of them, ' what, y're become black already !'

Moore, without displaying the astonishing knowledge of
Mackintosh, was very full of information, gaiety, and humour.

Two more delightful days I never passed. I could not help reflecting what an extraordinary thing success is in this world, when a man so gifted as Mackintosh has failed completely in public life, never having attained honours, reputation, or wealth, while so many ordinary men have reaped an abundant harvest of all. What a consolation this affords to mediocrity! None can approach Mackintosh without admiring his extraordinary powers, and at the same time wondering why they have not produced greater effects in the world either of literature or politics. His virtues are obstacles to his success; he has not the art of pushing or of making himself feared; he is too *doucereux* and complimentary, and from some accident or defect in the composition of his character, and in the course of events which have influenced his circumstances, he has always been civilly neglected. Both Mackintosh and Moore told a great many anecdotes, but one morning at breakfast the latter related a story which struck us all. Mackintosh said it was enough to furnish materials for a novel, but that the simple narrative was so striking it ought to be written down without exaggeration or addition. I afterwards wrote it down as nearly as I could recollect it. It was Crampton, the Surgeon-General, who told it to Moore, and Crampton *loquitur.*

‘ Some years ago I was present at a duel that was fought between a young man of the name of MacLoughlin and another Irishman. MacLoughlin was desperately wounded; his second ran up to him, and thought to console him with the intelligence that his antagonist had also fallen. He only replied, " I am sorry for it if he is suffering as much as I do now." I was struck by the good feeling evinced in this reply, and took an interest in the fate of the young man. He recovered, and a few years after my interest was again powerfully excited by hearing that he had been arrested on suspicion of having murdered his father-in-law, his mother's second husband. He was tried and found guilty on the evidence of a soldier who happened to be passing in the middle of the night near the house in which the murder was committed. Attracted by a light which gleamed through the lower part of the window, he approached it, and through an opening between the shutter and the frame was able to look into the room. There he saw a man in the act of lifting a dead body from the floor, while his hands and clothes were stained all over with blood. He hastened to give information of what he had seen; MacLoughlin and his mother were apprehended, and the former, having been identified by the soldier, was found guilty. There was no evidence against the woman, and she was consequently acquitted. MacLoughlin conducted himself throughout the trial with determined calmness, and never could be induced to acknowledge his guilt. The morning of his execution he had an interview with his mother; none knew what passed between them, but when they parted he was heard to say, "Mother, may God forgive you!" The fate of this young man made a deep impression on me, till time and passing events effaced the occurrence from my mind. It was several years afterwards that I one day received a letter from a lady (a very old and intimate acquaintance) entreating that I would immediately hasten down to the assistance of a Roman Catholic priest who was lying dangerously ill at her house, and the symptoms of whose malady she described. Her description left me doubtful whether the mind or the body of the patient was affected. Being unable to leave Dublin, I wrote to say that if the disease was bodily the case was hopeless, but if mental I should recommend certain lenitives, for which I added a prescription. The priest died, and shortly after his death the lady confided to me an extraordinary and dreadful story. He had been her confessor and intimate friend, and in moments of agony and doubt produced by horrible recollections he had revealed to her a secret which had been imparted to him in confession. He had received the dying confession of MacLoughlin, who, as it turned out, was not the murderer of his father-in-law, but had died to save the life and honour of his mother, by whom the crime had been really committed. She was a woman of violent passions; she had quarrelled with her husband in the middle of the night, and after throwing him from the bed had despatched him by repeated blows. When she found he was dead she was seized with terror, and hastening to the apartment of her

son, called him to witness the shocking spectacle and to
save her from the consequences of her crime. It was at this
moment, when he was lifting the body and preparing to
remove the bloody evidence of his mother's guilt, that the
soldier passed by and saw him in the performance of his
dreadful task. To the priest alone he acknowledged the
truth, but his last words to his mother were now explained.'

November 20*th*.—Roehampton. Only Moore and myself;
Washington Irving and Maclane, the American Minister,
come to-morrow. Moore spoke in the highest terms of
Luttrell, of his wit and information, and of his writings, to
which he does not think the world does justice, particularly
the 'Advice to Julia,' but he says Luttrell is too fearful of
giving offence. Moore was very agreeable, told a story
of Sir —— St. George in Ireland. He was to attend a
meeting at which a great many Catholics were to be present
(I forget where), got drunk and lost his hat, when he went
into the room where they were assembled and said, ' Damna-
tion to you all; I came to emancipate you, and you've stole
my hat.' In the evening Moore sang, but the pianoforte
was horrid, and he was not in good voice ; still his singing
' va dritto al cuore,' for it produces an exceeding sadness,
and brings to mind a thousand melancholy recollections, and
generates many melancholy anticipations. He told me as
we came along that with him it required no thought to write,
but that there was no end to it; so many fancies on every
subject crowded on his brain; that he often read what he
had written as if it had been the composition of another,
and was amused; that it was the greatest pleasure to him to
compose those light and trifling pieces, humorous and satiri-
cal, which had been so often successful. He holds Voltaire
to have been the most extraordinary genius that ever lived,
on account of his universality and fertility ; talked of Scott
and his wonderful labour and power of composition, as well
as the extent to which he has carried the art of book-making ;
besides writing this history of Scotland for Dr. Lardner's
' Encyclopædia,' he is working at the prefaces for the republication of the Waverley Novels, the ' Tales of a Grandfather,' and has still found time to review Tytler, which he

has done out of the scraps and chips of his other works. A
little while ago he had to correct some of the proofs of the
history of Scotland, and, being dissatisfied with what was
done, he nearly wrote it over again, and sent it up to the
editor.   Some time after finding another copy of the proofs,
he forgot that he had corrected them before, and he rewrote
these also and sent them up, and the editor is at this moment
engaged in selecting from the two corrected copies the best
parts of each.

Yesterday I met the Chancellor at dinner at the Master
of the Rolls', when he told me about the King and Denman.[1]
The King would not have the Recorder's report last week,
because the Recorder was too ill to attend, and he was resolved not to see Denman.   The Duke went to him, when he
threw himself into a terrible tantrum, and was so violent and
irritable that they were obliged to let him have his own way
for fear he should be ill, which they thought he would otherwise certainly be.   He is rather the more furious with Denman from having been forced to consent to his having the silk
gown, and he said at that time that he should never set his
foot in any house of his ; so that business is at a standstill,
and the unfortunate wretches under sentence of death are
suffered to linger on, because he does not choose to do his
duty and admit to his presence an officer to whom he has
taken an aversion. As the Chancellor said to me, ' the fact is,
he is mad.'   The fact is that he is a spoiled, selfish, odious
beast, and has no idea of doing anything but what is agreeable to himself, or of there being any duties attached to the
office he holds.   The expenses of the Civil List exceed the
allowance in every branch, every quarter ; but nobody can
guess how the money is spent, for the King makes no show
and never has anybody there.   My belief is that —— and
—— —— plunder him, or rather the country, between them,
in certain stipulated proportions.   Among other expenses

[1] [Thomas Denman, afterwards Lord Denman and Lord Chief Justice
of England, was at this time Common Serjeant of the City of London.
George IV. hated him for the part he had taken on the Queen's trial, and
did all he could to prevent his having a silk gown. *Vide supra*, p. 156.]

his tailor's bill is said to be 4,000*l*. or 5,000*l*. a year. He is now employed in devising a new dress for the Guards.

November 21*st.*—Maclane, the American Minister, could not come, but Irving did. He is lively and unassuming, rather vulgar, very good-humoured. We went to Strawberry Hill to-day—Moore, Ellis, Lady Georgiana, and I. Ellis is an excellent cicerone; everything is in the state in which old Horace Walpole left it, and just as his catalogue and description describe it. He says in that work that he makes that catalogue to provide against the dispersion of his collections, and he tied up everything as strictly as possible. Moore sang in the evening and was very agreeable the whole day. He said that Byron thought that Crabbe and Coleridge had the most genius and feeling of any living poet. Nobody reads Crabbe now. How dangerous it is to be a story-teller, however agreeable the manner or amusing the budget, for Moore to-day told a story which he told here last week! However, they all laughed just the same, except me, and I moralised upon it thus. Clifden is a very odd man, shrewd and well informed, and somewhat sarcastic, but very gay and good-humoured, fond of society and the ' Times' newspaper, a great enemy to the Church, and chuckles over its alarms and its dangers, but I was amused with a comical contradiction. Somebody told a story about an erratum in an Irish paper, which said that such a one had abjured the errors of the Romish Church and embraced those of the Protestant, at which he was greatly diverted, and said, ' That is just what I should have said myself;' and to-day after dinner, all of a sudden, he said grace (he says grace on Sunday only).

Moore gave an account this morning of his being examined in Trinity College, Dublin, when a boy, during the rebellion. Many of the youths (himself, and he says he is pretty sure Croker, among the number) had taken· the oath of the United Irishmen [1] (Emmett [2] and some others who were in the College had absconded). The Chancellor (Lord Clare)

---

[1] He did not take the oath till after this examination.

[2] He had lived in intimacy with Emmett.

came to the College, erected his tribunal, and examined all
the students upon oath. He asked first if they had belonged
to any society of United Irish, and, if the answer was in the
affirmative, he asked whom they had ever seen there and
what had passed. Contumacy was punishable by expulsion
and exclusion from every profession. At the end of the
first day's examination Moore went home to his parents, and
told them he could not take an oath which might oblige him
to criminate others (as he should be forced to answer any
question they might choose to put), and though they were
poor, and had conceived great hopes of him, they encouraged
him in this resolution. The next day he was called forth,
when he refused to be sworn, stating his reasons why. The
Chancellor said he did not come there to dispute with him,
but added that they should only ask him general questions,
on which he took the oath, but reserved to himself the
power of declining to answer particular questions. They only
asked him such questions as he could conscientiously answer
(they had got all the information they wanted, and were
beginning to relax), but when they had done with him Lord
Clare asked him why he had demurred to answer. He said
he was afraid he might be called on to criminate others, and
that he had never taken an oath before, and naturally felt
some reluctance and dread on such an occasion.

Moore told a story of an Irishman who saw from the
pit a friend of his acting Othello, and he called out, ' Larry,
Larry, Larry, there's the least taste in life of your linen
hanging out! ' One day in America near the falls of Niagara
Moore saw this scene:—An Indian whose boat was moored
to the shore was making love to the wife of another Indian;
the husband came upon them unawares; he jumped into
the boat, when the other cut the cord, and in an instant
it was carried into the middle of the stream, and before he
could seize his paddle was already within the rapids.
He exerted all his force to extricate himself from the
peril, but finding that his efforts were vain, and his canoe
was drawn with increasing rapidity towards the Falls, he
threw away his paddle, drank off at a draught the contents
of a bottle of brandy, tossed the empty bottle into the air, then

quietly folded his arms, extended himself in the boat, and awaited with perfect calmness his inevitable fate. In a few moments he was whirled down the Falls and disappeared for ever.

Washington Irving wants sprightliness and more refined manners. He was in Spain four years, at Madrid, Seville, and Grenada. While at the latter place he was lodged in the Alhambra, which is excellently preserved and very beautiful; he gives a deplorable description of the ignorance and backward state of the Spaniards. When he returned to France he was utterly uninformed of what had been passing in Europe while he was in Spain, and he says that he now constantly hears events alluded to of which he knows nothing.

December 1st.—After I left Roehampton last week came to town and dined with Byng, Moore, Irving, Sir T. Lawrence, and Vesey Fitzgerald; very agreeable. No news but the failure of the Spanish expedition against Mexico, which capitulated, and the soldiers promised never to bear arms against Mexico again. On Friday went to see Lord Glengall's comedy, with a prologue by F. Mills and an epilogue by Alvanley.[1] It succeeded, though the first two acts went off heavily; not much novelty in it, but the characters well drawn and some of the situations very good: it amused me very well, and was exceedingly well acted. Glengall came to me afterwards to get criticisms on his play. I told him some of the faults, and he was not in the Sir Fretful line, but took it all very thankfully. At Roehampton on Sunday; Byng, Sir Robert Wilson, Sharpe,[2] and Luttrell. There is a joke of Luttrell's about Sharpe. He was a wholesale hatter formerly; having a dingy complexion, somebody said he had transferred the colour of his hats to his face, when Luttrell said that ' it was *darkness which might be felt.*' Wilson has written to the Sultan a letter full of advice, and he says the Turks will be more powerful than ever. Wilson is always full of opinions

---

[1] [A comedy by the Earl of Glengall, entitled 'The Follies of Fashion.']

[2] [Richard Sharpe, Esq., well known by the *sobriquet* of 'Conversation Sharpe.']

and facts; the former are wild and extravagant, the latter generally false.

No Council yet; the King is employed in altering the uniforms of the Guards, and has pattern coats with various collars submitted to him every day. The Duke of Cumberland assists him, and this is his principal occupation; he sees much more of his tailor than he does of his Minister. The Duke of Cumberland's boy, who is at Kew, diverts himself with making the guard turn out several times in the course of the day to salute him.

December 3rd.—Came from Roehampton. Lady Pembroke and her daughter, Luttrell and I, and the Lievens, dined there one day. Lady Pembroke was Countess Woronzow; Lord Pembroke pleaded poverty all his life, and died leaving each of his five daughters 20,000*l.*, and his wife 200,000*l.*, to do what she liked with. Old Woronzow was Ambassador here many years, has lived here ever since, and never learnt a word of English. His son Michel is one of the most distinguished officers in the Russian army, and now Governor of Odessa and the province of which that city is the capital.

I went to see Glengall's play again, which was much better acted than the first time, and, having been curtailed, went off very well. Henry de Ros, Glengall, and I went together. I was very much amused (but did not venture to show it) at a point in one of the scenes between Lureall and Sir S. Foster: the latter said, 'Let me tell you, sir, that a country gentleman residing on his estate is as valuable a member of society as a man of fashion in London who lives by plundering those who have more money and less wit than himself;' when De Ros turned to Glengall and said, 'Richard, there appears to me to be a great deal of twaddle in this play; besides, you throw over the good cause.'

December 5th.—This morning the Duke of Wellington sent for me about the Council on Monday, and after settling that matter he began talking about the King's conduct with reference to the Recorder's report. I told him it was thought very extraordinary. He said, 'You have no idea what a scene I had with him; there never was anything like it.

I never saw him so violent.' He then rang the bell, when
Drummond (his secretary) appeared, and the Duke desired
him to bring the correspondence with the King about the
Recorder, which was done. He then said, ' I came to town
on the Monday for the Council and report, which was to
have been on Tuesday, and which he had himself settled,
without consulting me; in the afternoon Phillips came to me
and said that the Recorder could not attend, and that they
did not know if his Majesty would receive Denman. I
wrote to the King directly this letter.' He then read the
letter, which was to this effect : that he informed the King
that the Recorder was ill, and therefore the Common Serjeant, Mr. Denman, would have the honour of making the
report to his Majesty ; that he thought it right to apprise
him of this, and if he had any objection to receive Mr.
Denman, it would be better to put off the Council, as no
other person could now lay the report before him. ' To this
the King wrote an answer, beginning " My dear Duke,"
not as usual,' the Duke said, ' " My dear Friend," that the
state of his eyes would not allow him to write by candle-
light, and he was therefore obliged to make use of an
amanuensis. The letter was written by Watson, and signed
by the King, " Your sincere Friend, G. R." It was to
the effect that he was quite surprised the Duke should have
made him such a proposal ; that he had been grossly insulted by Denman, and would never admit him to his
presence ; that it had been settled the Deputy-Recorder,
Arabin, in the absence of the Recorder, should make the
report, and that he had already done so ; that he was surprised, knowing as the Duke must do the firmness of his
character, that he should think him capable of yielding
on this subject ; that he never would do so, and desired
the Council might take place, and the report be made by
Arabin.' His letter was much longer, but this was the
pith of it. On the receipt of this the Duke held a consultation with Peel and the Chancellor, when they determined to put off the Council, which was done, and the Duke
wrote to the King, as nearly as I can recollect, as follows.

This was an admirable letter—business-like, firm, and
respectful:—'That upon the receipt of his Majesty's letter he
had thought it his duty to consult the Chancellor, and that
they had come to the resolution of postponing the Council
and report; that the making of this report was the privilege
of the City of London, and that the Recorder in the execution
of this duty, being unable to attend, had placed it in the
hands of the Common Serjeant, whose duty it then became
to present it; that it was now in his hands, and could not
be withdrawn without his consent; that the only occasion on
which it had been presented by Mr. Serjeant Arabin had been
when the Common Serjeant was on the circuit; that as his
Majesty objected to admit Mr. Denman to his presence, they
had thought it best to put off the Council, as if Mr. Arabin
was summoned he could have no report to present, and there
would probably arise some discussion between the Common
Serjeant and him, which would be a proceeding such as ought
not to take place in his Majesty's palace, and that he would
wait upon his Majesty the next morning and take his
commands upon the subject.' The next day, he continued,
he went to Windsor, where he had a grand scene with his
Majesty. 'I am sure,' said the Duke, 'that nobody can
manage him but me.' He repeated all he had said in his
letter, and a great deal more; represented to him that having
given his sanction to the official appointment of Denman
since the Queen's trial, he could not refuse to receive him in
the execution of his duty without alleging legal objections
for so doing; to which the King replied that Lord Liverpool
had behaved very ill to him, and had made him do this; and
then he became very violent, and cursed and swore, and said
he never would see him. The Duke said that he might put
off the report; that there were three men who must be
hanged, and it did not signify one farthing whether they were
kept in prison a little longer or shorter time (he forgets that
there are others lying under sentence of death, probably
several), and that he had better put it off than have the
Common Serjeant come down to a scene in his palace. After
letting him run on in his usual way, and exhaust his violence,

he left him, and the report stands over once more ; but the Duke told me that it could not stand over after this, and if the Recorder is not well enough when the time arrives for the next report, his Majesty must receive Denman whether he will or no, and that he shall insist upon it. He told me the whole history in great detail mixed with pretty severe strictures on the King. I have put down all I could carry away. I have not such a memory (or such an invention) as Bourrienne.

The Duke then told me that he had made strong remonstrances about the excess of expenditure on the Civil List ; that in the Lord Steward's department there had been an excess of 7,000*l.*, in that of the Master of the Horse of 5,000*l.*, and that of the Master of the Robes (the tailor's bill) of 10,000*l.* in the last half-year ; [1] that he had stated that unless they could save the difference in the next half-year, or pay it out of the Privy Purse, he must go to Parliament, which would bring the whole of the expenses of the Civil List under discussion. He said it was very extraordinary, that the King's expenses appeared to be nothing ; his Majesty had not more tables than he (the Duke) had.

I asked him about Brummell and his Consulship. He said Aberdeen hesitated ; that he had offered to take all the responsibility on himself ; that he had in Dudley's time proposed it to him (Dudley), who had objected, and at last owned he was afraid the King might not like it, on which he had spoken to the King, who had made objections, abusing Brummell—said he was a damned fellow and had behaved very ill to him (the old story, always himself—*moi, moi, moi*)— but after having let him run out his tether of abuse, he had at last extracted his consent ; nevertheless Dudley did not give him the appointment. The Duke said he had no acquaintance with Brummell.

---

[1] I am not sure that I am correct in the sums, but very nearly so.— [C. C. G.]

CHAPTER VII.

December 7th.—At Windsor for a Council; the Duke was
there, and Lord Aberdeen, Murray, Lord Rosslyn, the Chancellor, and Herries. There was a chapter of the Bath, when
the Duke of Clarence was installed Grand Master, Stratford
Canning and Robert Gordon Grand Crosses. The King looked
very well, but was very blind. The Council was by candle-
light, but he could not see to read the list, and begged me to
read it for him. However, I was so good a courtier that I held
the candle in such a way as to enable him to read it himself.
He saw the Duke for a short time, and the Chancellor for a
long time. I asked the latter if the King had been *Denman-
ising*, and he said 'Oh, yes—" I said when I consented to that
fellow's having the silk gown that I would never admit him,"
&c.' I was amused with old Conyngham, who told me
his wife had been in danger, 'so they tell me,' talking of
her as if she were somebody else's wife. The Duke went
from the Council to Stowe; we all returned to town.

December 9th.—Dined with Prince Lieven; a great

dinner—Laval,[1] Granvilles, Aberdeen, Montrond, &c. The Duc de Dino, who came here to amuse himself, has been arrested, and Montrond and Vaudreuil begged Laval to put him on his list of *attachés* at the Foreign Office, which would release him from the sponging-house. He was afraid and made difficulties; they were excessively provoked, but at last induced him to speak to Lord Aberdeen about it, which he said he would do after dinner. In the meantime Montrond got me to tell the story to Aberdeen, which I did, and got him to encourage Laval to do the business. He then told Laval that I had *aplani* the matter, at which the Ambassador was rather affronted, but I suppose the thing will be done and Dino will get out. The Duc de Dino is Talleyrand's nephew, and his son has married Mademoiselle de Montmorency, a relation of the Duc de Laval.

December 10*th.*—Last night Miss Kemble acted Belvidera for the first time, and with great success.

December 18*th.*—At Roehampton last Saturday to Monday; Granvilles, Byng, Lord Ashley, and I. Dino was extricated from prison by Laval's paying the money, which he did very handsomely; he thought it wrong to have him in prison and wrong to attach him fictitiously to his Embassy, so he paid the debt, and Dino is gone back to France.

Despatches were received from Gordon yesterday giving an account of a ball he had given to the Divan; the Turks came, and the Reis-Effendi waltzed with a Mrs. Moore. After supper they drank King George IV.'s health in bumpers of champagne. This story was told to Lord Sidmouth as a good joke; but he said with a face of dismay, ' Good God, is it possible? To what extent will these innovations be carried ? '

December 19*th.*—There is a review in the ' Foreign Quarterly ' (the last number) on Greece, which is a remarkably able critique of the conduct of our Government in the affairs of that State. The writer, whoever he may be, has been amply supplied with documents and information, probably from Paris. Nothing can be more just than his

---

[1] [The Duc de Laval had succeeded Prince Polignac as French Ambassador in London.]

remarks on our miserable policy, or more severe. I showed
it to Lord Granville, who told me that it was generally
correct, though containing some errors; for instance, that
it was not true that we had engaged to afford the Greeks
pecuniary aid, which we never did promise, but that he had
been himself the person to negotiate with M. de la Ferronnays,
then Minister for Foreign Affairs at Paris, for the more
limited boundary, and to dissuade the French from sending
their expedition to the Morea; that there had been a violent
contest in the English Cabinet on that subject, Huskisson
and Dudley being in favour of the French expedition, and
the Duke and the rest against it, but that the moment
Huskisson and his party resigned the Duke gave way and
agreed to the measure. This affords another example of his
extraordinary mode of proceeding, that of opposing the
views and plans of others violently, and when he finds
opposition fruitless, or likely to become so, turning short
round and adopting them as his own, and taking all the
credit he can get for doing so. He did so in the case of the
recognition of the South American colonies, of the Test and
Corporation Acts, the Catholic question, and in this instance.
Then his conduct on the Corn Bill is only the converse of
the same proposition—begins by being a party to it and then
procures its rejection. Greece and Portugal, if well handled,
would afford two great cases against the Duke's foreign
policy, and they serve as admirable commentaries on each
other. The raising the siege of Previsa, and the respect
paid to Miguel's blockade, and compulsion exercised on the
Terceira people are enough to prove everything.

Ashley told me a curious thing about Sir Thomas Lawrence the other day. His father kept the inn at Devizes,[1]
and when Lord Shaftesbury's father and mother were once
at the inn with Lord Shaftesbury, then a boy, the innkeeper
came into the room and said he had a son with a genius
for drawing, and, if they would allow him, his little boy

[1] [Sir Thomas Lawrence's father at one time kept the 'Black Bear' at
Devizes. In 1775 Lord and Lady Kenyon had the young prodigy (as he
was called) introduced to them there. Lawrence was then only six years old.]

should draw their little boy's picture; on which the little Lawrence was sent for, who produced his chalk and paper, and made a portrait of the young Lord.

December 21st.—At Roehampton from Saturday; Maclane, the American Minister, Washington Irving, Melbourne, Byng, and on Sunday the Lievens to dinner. Maclane a sensible man, with very good American manners, which are not refined. Even Irving, who has been so many years here, has a bluntness which is very foreign to the tone of good society. Maclane gave me a curious account of Gallatin. He was born at Geneva, and went over to America early in life, possessed of nothing; there he set up a little huxtering shop—in I forget what State—and fell in love with one of the daughters of a poor woman at whose house he lodged, but he was so destitute that the mother refused him. In this abject condition accident introduced him to the celebrated Patrick Henry, who advised him to abandon trade, and go into the neighbouring State and try to advance himself by his talents. He followed the advice, and soon began to make himself known.[1]

December 22nd.—Dined with Byng yesterday and met Moore, Fitzgerald, and Luttrell. Luttrell is a great lover of conundrums, which taste he acquired from Beresford, the author of the 'Miseries of Human Life,' who has invented some very curious but elaborate conundrums. They are not worth repeating. Moore told a story of an Irishman at the play calling out, ' Now boys, a clap for Wellington ! ' which being complied with, ' And now silence for the rest of the family ! '

[1] [This story of M. Gallatin, which was thus related by Mr. Maclane to Mr. Greville, is completely untrue. M. Gallatin belonged to one of the best families in Geneva. He was left an orphan early, inheriting considerable property from both his parents. He started for America in 1780, furnished with a letter of introduction from Benjamin Franklin, and on his arrival there he raised a company of troops to serve in the American army, paid them out of his own funds, and eventually purchased considerable estates in Virginia. These facts have been communicated to me by M. Gallatin's family, and I have no doubt at all of their accuracy. It is most extraordinary that Mr. Maclane should have related to Mr. Greville a story so much at variance with the truth, and it gives me great pleasure to correct this erroneous statement.]

He complained that all the humour which used to break out in an Irish audience is extinct.

Fitzgerald told me that the King had been annoying them as much as he could, that he took pleasure in making his Government weak, that the money matter (which the Duke told me of before) had been settled by ' contrivances,' or that they must have gone to Parliament for the amount; that he has just ordered plate to the amount of 25,000*l.* Fitzgerald is so ill that he can scarcely carry on the business of his office, and yet he does not like to give it up, for fear of embarrassing the Government; he complained that the other offices had thrown much of their business on the Board of Trade, a custom which had grown up in Huskisson's time, who was the most competent man and who took it all. Probably Huskisson was not sorry, by making himself very useful, to make himself nearly indispensable, and thought that he was so; and so he was *de jure*, but the Duke would not let him be so *de facto*.

December 23rd.—Went to the Court of King's Bench this morning to prove that the Duke of Wellington is a Privy Councillor, on the trial of the action which the Duke brought against the ' Morning Journal.' The action brought by the Chancellor had been tried the day before. Scarlett was feeble; Alexander again defended himself in a very poor speech; the jury retired for three hours, and I thought would have said ' Not guilty; ' but they brought in a verdict which is tantamount to a defeat of the prosecution on this charge, and amply proves the folly of having instituted it at all. I did not hear the second trial, on which they gave a verdict of guilty, after consulting for about half an hour. The jury in each case consisted of eight special jurors and four talesmen. The prosecution finished with the trial of Bell (of the ' Atlas '), who made a very good speech (it was about Lord and Lady Lyndhurst), and the jury found him guilty of publishing only, which I take to be an acquittal; the point, however, will not be tried probably, for it is not likely that he will be brought up for judgment. He will be contented to get off, and they will not like to stir such a question.

The result of the trials proves the egregious folly of having
ever brought them on, especially the Duke's. One of the
verdicts is, as far as he is concerned, an acquittal; the
author showed himself to be so contemptible that he had
better have been treated with indifference. He has been
converted into a sort of martyr, and whatever may have been
thought of the vulgar scurrility of the language, ruin and
imprisonment will appear to most people too severe a punishment for the offence. Then the whole press have united
upon this occasion, and in some very powerful articles have
spread to every corner of the country the strongest con-
demnation of the whole proceeding. The Government, or
rather the Duke, is likely to become unpopular, and no good
end will have been answered. I do not believe that these
prosecutions originate in a desire to curb the press, but
merely in that of punishing a writer who had so violently
abused him; not, however, that he would be sorry to adopt
any measure which should tend to fetter free discussion, and
subject the press to future punishment. But this would be
a fearful war to wage, and I do not think he is rash enough
to undertake such a crusade.

 December 27*th.*—At Panshanger since the 24th; Lievens,
J. Russell, Montrond, M. de la Rochefoucauld, F. Lamb. On
Christmas Day the Princess [Lieven] got up a little *fête*
such as is customary all over Germany. Three trees in
great pots were put upon a long table covered with pink
linen; each tree was illuminated with three circular tiers of
coloured wax candles—blue, green, red, and white. Before
each tree was displayed a quantity of toys, gloves, pocket-hand-
kerchiefs, workboxes, books, and various articles—presents
made to the owner of the tree. It was very pretty. Here it
was only for the children; in Germany the custom extends
to persons of all ages. The Princess told us to-day about the
Emperor of Russia's relapse and the cause of it. He had
had a cold which he had neglected, but at length the
physicians had given him some medicine to produce per-
spiration, and he was in bed in that state, the Empress
sitting by him reading to him, when on a sudden a dreadful
noise was heard in the next (the children's) room, followed

by loud shrieks. The Empress rushed into the room, and the Emperor jumped out of bed in his shirt and followed her. There the children, the governess, and the nurses were screaming out that Constantine (the second boy, of two years old) was destroyed; a huge vase of porphyry had been thrown down and had fallen over the child, who was not to be seen. So great was the weight and size of the vase that it was several minutes before it could be raised, though assistance was immediately fetched, and all that time the Emperor and Empress stood there in ignorance of the fate of the child, and expecting to see the removal of the vase discover his mangled body, when to their delight it was found that the vase had fallen exactly over him, without doing him the least injury, but the agitation and the cold brought on a violent fever, which for some time put the Emperor in great danger. The Princess said she was surprised that it did not kill the Empress, for she is the most nervous woman in the world, ever since the conspiracy at the time of his accession, when her nerves were *ébranlés* by all she went through. That scene (of the revolt of the Guards) took place under the window of the Palace. The whole Imperial Family was assembled there and saw it all, the Emperor being in the middle of men by whom they expected him to be assassinated every moment. During all that time—many hours—the young Empress never spoke, but stood ' pâle comme une statue,' and when at length it was all over, and the Emperor returned, she threw herself on her knees and began to pray.

December 29th.—At Osterley;[1] Lady Euston, Mrs. Sheridan and her son; a very fine house, which is thrown away, as they hardly ever live there. They spent 200,000*l.* in building Middleton, which is the worst place in England, and now they regret it, but Lord Jersey hates Osterley and likes Middleton. This place belonged to Sir Thomas Gresham, but the present house is modern. It was here that Sir Thomas Gresham feasted Queen Elizabeth, and pulled down a wall in the night which she had found fault with, so that in the morning she found it was gone.

---

[1] [Lord Jersey's seat near Hanwell, Middlesex.]

1830.

January 2nd.—At Roehampton; William Howard, Baring Wall, and Lady Pembroke's son;[1] the best sort of youth I have seen for a long while, and he will have 12,000*l.* a year, besides what his mother may leave him. Vesey Fitzgerald is so ill that it is doubtful if he will recover, and, at all events, almost impossible that he should remain in office. It will be very difficult for the Duke to fill his place. There is not a man in office now who is fit for it, and where is he to look for anyone else? Yet I think almost anybody would take it; for although the late prosecutions are blamed, and the foreign policy is thought by most people to have been very miserable, there is an extensive disposition to support the Duke and to keep him at the head of affairs. Huskisson is the man whose knowledge and capacity would be of the greatest service just now, but the Duke will not like to apply to him in a moment of distress, because he would probably take advantage of that distress to make better terms for himself; at the same time, I should not be surprised if the Duke were to invite him to return to the Cabinet, and that he accepted the Chancellorship of the Exchequer or one of the Secretaryships without any conditions. Vesey will be a great loss, for he is clever and ready in debate, and by great diligence and application, and the powerful assistance of Hume and Stephen, he has made considerable progress in the science of trade and commerce.

January 5th.—There are many speculations about Vesey's successor; some think Lord Chandos or Herries; I think Frankland Lewis, but that Lord Chandos will have some

---

[1] [Sidney Herbert, afterwards Lord Herbert of Lea, whose life and character did not belie the promise of his youth.]

place before long; the Duke has a great hankering after that set. In the meantime all accounts concur in admitting the great and increasing distress; and, as such a state of things not unnaturally produces a good deal of ill-humour, the Duke is abused for gadding about, visiting, and shooting while the country is in difficulty, and it is argued that he must be very unfeeling and indifferent to it all to amuse himself in this manner. Nothing can be more unjust than such accusations as these. The sort of relaxation he takes is necessary to his health, and, all things considered, it is not extraordinary he should prefer other people's houses to his own, particularly when everyone invites him in the most pressing manner. But these visits by no means interrupt the course of his official business; all his letters are regularly sent to him, and as regularly answered every day, and it is his habit to open his letters himself, to read them all, and to answer all. He never receives any letter, whatever may be the subject or the situation of the writer, that he does not answer, and that immediately, to a degree which is not only unprecedented, but quite unnecessary, and I think unwise, although certainly it contributes to his popularity. It is another proof of that simplicity of character and the absence of all arrogance which are so remarkable in him, especially as he has long been used to command and to implicit obedience, and the whole tenour of his conduct since he has been in office shows that he is covetous of power and authority, and will not endure anybody who will not be subservient to him; still in his manner and bearing there is nothing but openness, frankness, civility, and good-humour. As to his supposed indifference to the public distress, I firmly believe that his mind is incessantly occupied with projects for its relief, and that when unwarped by particular prejudices, partialities, and antipathies, which have had a stronger and more frequent influence over him than befits so great a man, he is animated with a sincere desire to reform abuses of any kind, and is not diverted from his purpose by any personal considerations or collateral objects. The King is preparing for a new battle with him (stimulated, I presume, by the Duke of Cumberland) about the appointment of sheriffs. He has taken it into his head that he will not appoint any Roman Catholic sheriff; and as several have been named, and these generally first on the list, according to the usual practice, they must be chosen. The King will be obliged to give way, but it is an additional proof of his bad disposition and his pleasure in thwarting his Ministers on every possible occasion.

January 7th.—Stapleton's 'Memoirs of Canning' are coming out directly, but he is prevented from making use of all the documents he, or rather Lady Canning, has. She has had an angry correspondence with the Foreign Office. Every Minister takes away a *précis* of all he has done while in office, but Canning's *précis* was not finished when he died. She wrote and demanded that what was incomplete should be furnished to her, but claimed it as a right, and said it was for the purpose of vindicating him. Lord Aberdeen declined giving it, and I think very properly. The reason he assigned was that a Minister who was furnished with such documents for his own justification was bound by his oath of secrecy not to reveal the contents, but the secrets of the State could not be imparted to any irresponsible person, who was under no such restraint.

Vesey Fitzgerald is better, but will hardly be able to do any business. Some think he will have leave of absence, that Dawson will exchange offices with Courtenay, and do the business of the Board of Trade; others, that Herries will succeed Vesey, or Frankland Lewis. The revenue has fallen off one million and more. The accounts of distress from the country grow worse and more desponding, and a return to one pound notes begins to be talked of.

Roehampton, January 9th.—Yesterday morning died Sir Thomas Lawrence after a very short illness. Few people knew he was ill before they heard he was dead. He was *longè primus* of all living painters, and has left no one fit to succeed him in the chair of the Royal Academy. Lawrence was about sixty, very like Canning in appearance, remarkably gentlemanlike, with very mild manners, though rather too *doucereux*, agreeable in society, unassuming, and not a great talker; his mind was highly cultivated, he had a taste for every kind of literature, and was enthusiastically devoted to his art; he was very industrious, and painted an enormous number of portraits, but many of his later works are still unfinished, and great complaints used to be made of his exacting either the whole or half payment when he began a picture, but that when he had got the money he could never be prevailed on to complete it. Although he is supposed to have earned enormous sums by his paintings, he has always been a distressed man, without any visible means of expense, except a magnificent collection of drawings by the ancient masters, said to be the finest in the world, and procured at great cost. He was, however, a generous patron of young artists of merit and talent. It was always said that he lost money at play, but this assertion seems to have proceeded more from the difficulty of reconciling his pecuniary embarrassments with his enormous profits than from any proof of the fact. He was a great courtier, and is said to have been so devoted to the King that he would not paint anybody who was personally obnoxious to his Majesty; but I do not believe this is true. He is an irreparable loss; since Sir Joshua there has been no painter like him; his portraits as pictures I think are not nearly so fine as Sir Joshua's, but as likenesses many of them are quite perfect. Moore's was the last portrait he painted, and Miss Kemble's his last drawing.

The King has been very ill; lost forty ounces of blood. Vesey is better, but has no chance of going on with his office. The general opinion seems to be that Herries will succeed him. I do not believe he knows anything of the business of the Board of Trade. Charles Mills told me yesterday that a proposal was lately made by Government to the East India Company to reduce their dividends, and that at the very time this was done Rothschild, who had 40,000*l.* East India Stock, sold it all out, and all his friends who held any did the same. The matter was eventually dropped, but he says nobody doubts that N—— gave notice to Rothschild of the proposed measure. The Company are mightily satisfied with Lord William Bentinck, who has acted very handsomely by them in this business by the reduction of the pay of the troops. He has written some very trimming letters to Lord Combermere, who is coming home, and if he had not been, would probably have been recalled. The Duke, as well as the Company, is furious with Combermere for the part he has acted in the affair.

Leopold's election to the throne of Greece seems to be settled, and while everybody has been wondering what could induce him to accept it, it turns out that he has been most anxious for it, and has moved heaven and earth to obtain it; that the greatest obstacle he has met with has been from the King, who hates him, and cannot bear that he should become a crowned head. He may think it ' better to reign in hell than serve in heaven,' but I should have thought he had a better prospect here, with 50,000*l.* a year and as uncle to the heiress apparent, than to go to a ruined country without cities or inhabitants, and where everything is to be created, and to sit on such a wretched throne as the nominee of the Allied Powers, by whom he will be held responsible for his acts ; however, ' il ne faut pas disputer des goûts.'

George Bentinck told me that Lady Canning is not satisfied with Stapleton's book, particularly with that part of it in which he attempts to answer Lord Grey's speech, which she thinks poor and spiritless; he is not disposed to be very severe on Lord Grey, being in a manner connected with him. She is persuaded that that speech contributed to kill Canning; his feelings were deeply wounded that not one of his friends said a word in reply to it, although some of them knew that the facts in Lord Grey's speech were incorrect. He vehemently desired to be raised to the peerage, that he might have an opportunity of answering it, and he had actually composed and spoken to Mrs. Canning the speech which he intended to make in the House of Lords. A great part of this she remembers. It seems, too, that to the day of his death this was the ruling desire of his mind, and he had declared that the following year, when he should have carried the Corn Bill through the House of Commons, he would go to the House of Lords and fight the battle there.

January 17*th.*—Charles Mills told me the other day that the Chancellor of the Exchequer has been making enquiries as to the fact of Rothschild having sold his India stock at the time he did. The two Grants (Charles and Robert) are always together, and both very forgetful and unpunctual. Somebody said that if you asked Charles to dine with you at six on Monday, you were very likely to have Robert at seven on Tuesday.

Edward Villiers (who has been living with Malcolm on board his ship in the Mediterranean) writes word that Malcolm told him that he had orders, in the event of Diebitsch's marching upon Constantinople, to destroy the Russian fleet. If this is true, it would have been a great outrage, and a most extraordinary piece of vigour, after so much long-suffering and endurance.

The country gentlemen are beginning to arrive, and they all tell the same story as to the universally prevailing distress and the certainty of things becoming much worse; of the failure of rents all over England, and the necessity of some decisive measures or the prospect of general ruin. Of course they differ as to the measures, but there appears to be a strong leaning towards the alteration in the currency and one pound notes. It really does appear, from many representations, that a notion prevails of the Duke of Wellington's indifference to the state of the country, and of his disposition to treat the remonstrances and petitions of the people, as well as their interests and feelings, with contempt, which I believe most false and unjust. He has an overweening opinion of his own all-sufficiency, and that is his besetting sin, and the one which, if anything does, will overturn his Government, for if he would be less dictatorial and opinionated, and would call to his assistance such talents and information as the crisis demands, he would be universally voted the best man alive to be at the head of the Government; but he has such a set of men under him, and Peel will never get over the Catholic question. [Peel got over it, but not before he had expiated his conduct by being turned out.]

January 20th.—The Duke and Lord Bathurst dined here yesterday, the former not in good spirits. The battle about Leopold and Greece is still going on between his Majesty and his Ministers. The Duke was talking about the robbery at Brussels of the Princess of Orange's jewels, and that there is reason to believe that Pereira, the Prince's friend, had some concern in it; many people suspect that both he and the Prince were concerned. The Princess was in the country, and only one maid-servant in the house where such valuable property was left. The jewels were in a case, and the key of the case was kept in a cabinet, which was opened, the key taken, and the large case or chest opened by it. Small footsteps (like those of Pereira, who has very small feet) were traced in the house or near it, and the day of the robbery the porter was taken by Pereira's servant to his house and there made drunk. The robbery was discovered on Friday morning, but no steps were taken to inform the police till Sunday night.

January 22nd.—I believe it to be impossible for a man of squeamish and uncompromising virtue to be a successful politician, and it requires the nicest feeling and soundest judgment to know upon what occasions and to what extent it is allowable and expedient to diverge from the straight line. Statesmen of the greatest power, and with the purest intentions, are perpetually counteracted by prejudices, obstinacy, interest, and ignorance ; and in order to be efficient they must turn, and tack, and temporise, sometimes dissemble. They who are of the *ruat cœlum* sort, who will carry everything their own way or not at all, must be content to yield their places to those who are certainly less scrupulous, and submit to the measures of those who are probably less wise. But though it is possible that the less rigid and austere politician may be equally virtuous and disinterested, the whole context of

his life must be such as to endure the most scrutinising
enquiry, which unfortunately it will very seldom do, in order
to establish a character for integrity. If Canning had had
a fair field, he would have done great things, for his lofty
and ambitious genius took an immense sweep, and the
vigour of his intellect, his penetration and sagacity, enabled
him to form mighty plans and work them out with success;
but it is impossible to believe that he was a high-minded
man, that he spurned everything that was dishonest, un-
candid, and ungentlemanlike; he was not above trick and
intrigue, and this was the fault of his character, which was
unequal to his genius and understanding. However, notwithstanding his failings he was the greatest man we have
had for a long time, and if life had been spared to him, and
opposition had not been too much for him, he would have
raised our character abroad, and perhaps found remedies for
our difficulties at home.   What a difference between his
position and that of the Duke of Wellington! Everybody
is disposed to support the latter and give him unlimited
credit for good intentions. The former was obliged to
carry men's approbation by storm, and the moment he
had failed, or been caught tripping, he would have been
lost.

The Duke has lately given audience to the West Indians
who came to complain of their sufferings and taxation and
to implore relief.   Murray and Goulburn were present,
neither of whom, it is said, spoke a word. The Duke cut
them very short, and told them they were not distressed at
all, and that nothing would be done for them. He is like
the philosopher in Molière's play, who says, ' Il ne faut pas
dire que vous avez reçu des coups de bâton, mais qu'il vous
semble que vous en avez reçus.'

Lawrence was buried yesterday; a magnificent funeral,
which will have cost, they say, 2,000*l.* The pall was borne
by Clanwilliam, Aberdeen, Sir G. Murray, Croker, Agar Ellis,
and three more—I forget who.   There were thirty-two
mourning-coaches and eighty private carriages. The ceremony in the church lasted two hours. Pretty well for a man

who died in very embarrassed circumstances. The favourites for the chair of the Academy are Shee and Wilkie, painters, and Westmacott and Chantrey, sculptors.

We were talking of Clanwilliam, who Agar said was the quickest man he had ever known; Luttrell said he and Rogers were 'the *quick* and the *dead.*' Looking over the 'Report of the Woods and Forests and the Cost of the Palaces,' somebody said 'the pensive' (meaning the public: see Rejected Addresses) must pay; Luttrell said 'the public was the pensive and the King the expensive.'

January 26th.—Yesterday afternoon Tierney died. He sank back in his chair and expired suddenly, without any previous illness; he had been in an indifferent state of health for some time, but he had resolved to make one more effort in Parliament and deliver his opinion on the present state of affairs. He is a great loss to all his friends; his political life was already closed.

Shee was elected President of the Royal Academy last night at ten o'clock. He had sixteen or eighteen votes; Sir William Beechey six, who was the nearest to Shee; Wilkie only two. He is an Irishman and a Catholic, a bad painter, a tolerable poet, and a man of learning, but, it is said, florid.

Had a long conversation with Arbuthnot yesterday, who is weak, but knows everything; his sentiments are the Duke's. They are furious with the old Tories, especially Lord Lonsdale, and not well satisfied with Lowther, whom they suspect to be playing a sneaking, underhand part. The Duke is determined not to alter his Government, nor to take anybody in to strengthen it. Arbuthnot said that the Duke had shown he did not mean to be exclusive when he had taken in Scarlett and Calcraft, and that 'his friends' would not have borne any more extensive promotion from that party; that of all Ministers he was the one who least depended upon Parliamentary influence and the assistance of the great families; and that if Lord Lonsdale and all his members were to leave him to-morrow, he would not care a straw. Still he pays them, if not court, great deference, and he keeps Lowther,

though he suspects him. Arbuthnot said that as soon as
the Duke became Minister he said to him, ' Now, Duke, for
God's sake settle that question ' (the Catholic), which was
as much as to say, ' Now that you have got rid of every
enemy and every rival, now that you can raise your own
reputation, and that you will share the glory with no one,
do that which you would never let anybody else do, and fight
for the measure you have been opposing all your life.' It
may be imagined he would not have said this unless he had
been fully aware of the Duke's sentiments on the subject.
This speech was made to him eight months after Canning
came into office, when they *all* went out, *on the Catholic
question*. He says it is utterly false that the Duke is unconscious of or indifferent to the distress, but that it is
exaggerated, and the Duke attributes it to temporary and
not to permanent causes ; that he labours incessantly on the
subject, and his thoughts are constantly occupied with
devising a remedy for it, which he thinks he can do. He
adverted to the difficulties with the King, who is never to be
depended upon, as his father was. He remembers upon
some occasion, when Perceval was Minister, and thought the
difficulties of his situation great, he represented to George
III. his sense of them in a letter ; Perceval showed him the
King's answer, which was in these words :—' Do you stand
by me as I will stand by you, and while we stand by each
other we have nothing to fear.'

I told Arbuthnot it was reported that the Duke had
given a very rough answer to the West Indian deputations,
and that if he had it was unwise, as, though he might not
adopt such measures of relief as they desired, he could treat
them with soft language. He said that, so far from it, Lord
Chandos had returned to the Duke the next day, and apolo-
gised for their conduct to him, assuring him that he was
ashamed and tired of his connection with them, and should
withdraw from it as soon as possible. This I mentioned at
Brooks's, but Gordon (a West Indian) said that they had all
been shocked at the manner in which he had used them,
that some of them had declared they would never go to him

again; and Spring Rice said that old George Hibbert, who
has been their agent these thirty years, and had attended
deputations to every Prime Minister since Pitt, had told him
that he never saw one so ill received before. It is customary
for every deputation to draw out a minute of their conversation with the Minister, which they submit to him to admit
its correctness. They did so, but the Duke destroyed their
minute, and sent them back one drawn out by himself,
which, however, they declare was not so correct as that
which had been transmitted to him; which I can well believe, but they had no right to complain of this, on the
contrary.

January 30*th.*—Laid up with the gout these last three
days. George Bankes has resigned, and John Wortley is
appointed Secretary to the Board of Control. He was of the
Huskisson party, as it is called (though it does not deserve
the name), and previously to the offer of this place being
made to him was rather inimical to the Government; but
the Duke proposed, and he accepted. I doubt his being of
much use to them. Lord Ellenborough's letter to Sir John
Malcolm, which appeared in the 'Times' a few days ago,
has made a great deal of noise, as it well may, for a more
flippant and injudicious performance has seldom been seen.[1]

The greatest curiosity and interest prevail about the
transactions in the ensuing session—whether there will be
any opposition, and from what quarter, how Peel will
manage, how the country gentlemen will act and what
language they will hold, and whether the Duke will produce
any plan for alleviating the distress. I think there will be
a great deal of talking and complaining, a great many half-
measures suggested, but no opposition, and that the Duke

---

[1] [This letter, which excited much attention at this time, will be found
in the 'Life of Sir John Malcolm,' by Mr. (now Sir John) Kaye, vol. ii.
p. 528. It had been written a year before, and by some indiscretion obtained publicity in India. A warm dispute had broken out between Sir
John Malcolm, then Governor of Bombay, and the Judges of the Supreme
Court there. Lord Ellenborough took Malcolm's part with great eagerness,
and said of Sir J. P. Grant, one of these Judges, that he 'would be like a
wild elephant led away between two tame ones.' This expression was long
remembered as a joke against Lord Ellenborough.]

will do nothing, and get through the session without much difficulty. There was to have been a Council on Thursday to prick the sheriffs, but it was put off on account of my gout, and I was not able to attend at the dinner at the Chancellor's on Wednesday for the same reason. I remember once before a Council was put off because I was at Egham for the races ; that was a Council in '27, I think, to admit foreign corn.

February 1st.—Stapleton's book on Mr. Canning is not to appear. Douglas was sent to him by Aberdeen to tell him that if anything appeared in it which ought not to be published he would be turned out of his office. He wrote to Lady Canning accordingly, who sent him a very kind answer, desiring him by no means to expose himself to any such danger, and consenting to the suppression of the work. I am glad of it on all accounts.

February 3rd.—Brougham has given up Lord Cleveland's borough, and comes in for Knaresborough, at the Duke of Devonshire's invitation. He is delighted at the exchange. I see by the ' Gazette' there has been a compromise with the King about the Catholic sheriffs; only one (Petre for Yorkshire) is chosen, the others, though first on the list and no excuses, passed over : they were Townley for Lancashire and Sir T. Stanley for Cheshire. It is childish and ridiculous if so; but no matter, as the principle is admitted.

I have just finished the first volume of Moore's ' Life of Byron.' I don't think I like this style of biography, half-way between ordinary narrative and self-delineation in the shape of letters, diary, &c. Moore's part is agreeably and feelingly written, and in a very different style from the ' Life of Sheridan '—no turgid diction and brilliant antitheses. It is, however, very amusing; the letters are exceedingly clever, full of wit, humour, and point, abounding in illustration, imagination, and information, but not the most agreeable sort of letters. They are joined together by a succession of little essays upon his character. But as to life, it is no life at all; it merely tells you that the details of his life are not tellable, that they would be like those of Tilly or Casanova, and so indecent, and compromise so many people, that we must be content to look at his life through an impenetrable veil. Then in the letters and diary the perpetual hiatus, and asterisks, and initials are exceedingly tantalising; but altogether it is very amusing. As to Byron, I have never had but one opinion about his poetry, which I think of first-rate excellence; an enormous heresy, of course, more particularly with those whose political taste rests upon the same foundation that their religious creed does—that of having been taught what to admire in the one case as they have been enjoined what to believe in the other. With regard to his character, I think Moore has succeeded in proving that he was far from deficient in amiable qualities; he was high-minded, liberal, generous, and good-natured, and, if he does not exaggerate his own feelings, a warm-hearted and sincere friend. But what a wretch he was! how thoroughly miserable with such splendid talents! how little philosophy!—wretched on account of his lame foot; not even his successes with women could reconcile him to a little personal deformity, though this is too hard a word for it; then tormenting himself to death nobody can tell why or wherefore. There never was so ill-regulated a mind, and he had not even the talent of making his pleasures subservient to his happiness—not any notion of *enjoyment*; all with him was riot, and debauchery, and rage and despair. That he very sincerely entertained a bad opinion of mankind may be easily believed; but so far from his pride and haughtiness raising him above the influence of the opinion of those whom he so despised, he was the veriest slave to it that ever breathed, as he confesses when he says that he was almost more annoyed at the censure of the meanest than pleased with the praises of the highest of mankind; and when he deals around his fierce vituperation or bitter sarcasms, he is only clanking the chains which, with all his pride, and defiance, and contempt, he is unable to throw off. Then he despises pretenders and charlatans of all sorts, while he is himself a pretender, as all men are who assume a character which does not belong to them, and affect to be something which they are all the time conscious they are not in reality.

But to ‘assume a virtue if you have it not’ is more allowable than to assume a vice which you have not. To wish to appear better or wiser than we really are is excusable in itself, and it is only the manner of doing it that may become ridiculous; but to endeavour to appear worse than we are is a species of perverted vanity the most disgusting, and a very bad compliment to the judgment, the morals, or the taste of our acquaintance. Yet, with all his splendid genius, this sort of vanity certainly distinguished Lord Byron, and that among many other things proves how deeply a man may be read in human nature, what an insight he may acquire into the springs of action and feeling, and yet how incapable he may be of making any practical application of the knowledge he has acquired and the result of which he can faithfully delineate. He gives a list of the books he had read at eighteen which appears incredible, particularly as he says that he was always idle, and eight years after Scott says he did not appear well read either in poetry or history. Swift says ‘some men know books as others do Lords—learn their titles, and then boast of their acquaintance with them,’ and so perhaps at eighteen he knew by name the books he mentions; indeed, the list contains Hooker, Bacon, Locke, Hobbes, Berkeley, &c. It sounds rather improbable; but his letters contain allusions to every sort of literature, and certainly indicate considerable information. ‘Dans le pays des aveugles les borgnes sont rois,’ and Sir Walter Scott might think a man half read who knows all that is contained in the brains of White’s, Brookes’, and Boodle’s, and the greater part of the two Houses of Parliament. But the more one reads and hears of great men the more reconciled one becomes to one’s own mediocrity.

> Say thou, whose thoughts at nothingness repine,
> Shall Byron’s fame with Byron’s fate be thine ?

Who would not prefer any obscurity before such splendid misery as was the lot of that extraordinary man ? Even Moore is not happy. One thinks how one should like to be envied, and admired, and applauded, but after all such men suffer more than we know or they will confess, and their celebrity is dearly purchased.

> Se di ciascun l' interno affanno
> Si leggesse in fronte scritto,
> Quanti guai ch' invidia fanno
> Ci farebbe pietà.

One word more about Byron and I have done. I was much struck by the coincidence of style between his letters and his journal, and that appears to me a proof of the reality and nature which prevailed in both.

February 5th.—Parliament met yesterday; there was a brisk debate and an amendment on the Address in each House. The Duke had very indiscreetly called the distress ' partial ' in the Speech, and the consequence was an amendment moved by Knatchbull declaring it to be general. The result shows that Government has not the slightest command over the House of Commons, and that they have nothing but casual support to rely upon, and that of course will only be to be had ' dum se bene gesserint.' For a long time Holmes and their whippers-in thought that they should be in a minority; but Hume and a large party of Reformers supported them (contrary to their own expectations), so they got a majority of 50 out of 250. The division was very extraordinary, Brougham, Sadler, and O'Connell voting together. It is pretty clear, however, that they are in no danger of being turned out, but that they are wretchedly off for speakers. Huskisson made a shabby speech enough, O'Connell his *début*, and a successful one, heard with profound attention; his manner good, and his arguments attended and replied to. In the Lords there was nothing particular, but nothing was concerted by any party, for the subject of the amendment in the Commons was not even touched upon in the Lords, which is very remarkable. Lord Chandos has refused the Mint, because they will not give him a seat in the Cabinet, but many people think it is because he has been pressed to refuse by his High Tory friends. Charles Ross is the new

Lord of the Admiralty,[1] and Abercromby Chief Baron of
Scotland, which everybody is glad of.

There is a charlatan of the name of Chobert, who calls
himself the Fire King, who has been imposing upon the
world for a year or more, exhibiting all sorts of juggleries in
hot ovens, swallowing poisons, hot lead, &c.; but yesterday
he was detected signally, and after a dreadful uproar was
obliged to run away to avoid the ill-usage of his exasperated
audience. He pretended to take prussic acid, and challenged
anybody to produce the poison, which he engaged to swallow.
At last Mr. Wakley, the proprietor of the 'Lancet,' went
there with prussic acid, which Chobert refused to take, and
then the whole deception came out, and there is an end of it;
but it has made a great deal of noise, taken everybody in, and
the fellow has made a great deal of money. It was to have
been his last performance, but 'tant va la cruche à l'eau
qu'enfin . . . .'

February 13th.—In the House of Lords last night: Lord
Holland's motion on Greece; his speech was amusing, but
not so good as he generally is; Aberdeen wretched, the
worst speaker I ever heard and incapable of a reply; I
had no idea he was so bad. The Duke made a very clever
speech, answering Holland and Melbourne, availing himself with great dexterity of the vulnerable parts of their
speeches and leaving the rest alone. I was sitting by
Robert Grant on the steps of the throne, and said to him,
'That is a good speech of the Duke's,' and he said, 'He
speaks like a great man;' and so he did; it was bold and
manly, and a high tone, not like a practised debater, but a
man with a vigorous mind and determined character.

In the House of Commons Graham spoke for two, hours;
Burdett said not well, but others said the contrary. The
Government resolution moved as an amendment by Dawson
was better than his, so it was adopted without difficulty. Burdett said Peel made the best speech he ever heard him make,
and threw over the Tories. Dined afterwards with Cowper,
Durham, and Glengall. Durham said that Lord Grey's

[1] The appointment has not taken place.

politics were the same as his, and that before Easter he
thought an Opposition would be formed, and that the elements, though scattered, exist of a strong one. I doubt it.

February 16*th*.—Last night the English Opera House was
burnt down—a magnificent fire. I was playing at whist at the
'Travellers' with Lord Granville, Lord Auckland, and Ross,
when we saw the whole sky illuminated and a volume of fire
rising in the air. We thought it was Covent Garden, and
directly set off to the spot. We found the Opera House and
several houses in Catherine Street on fire (sixteen houses),
and, though it was three in the morning, the streets filled by
an immense multitude. Nothing could be more picturesque
than the scene, for the flames made it as light as day and
threw a glare upon the strange and motley figures moving
about. All the gentility of London was there from Princess
Esterhazy's ball and all the clubs; gentlemen in their fur
cloaks, pumps, and velvet waistcoats mixed with objects like
the *sans-culottes* in the French Revolution—men and women
half-dressed, covered with rags and dirt, some with night-
caps or handkerchiefs round their heads—then the soldiers,
the firemen, and the engines, and the new police running
and bustling, and clearing the way, and clattering along, and
all with that intense interest and restless curiosity produced
by the event, and which received fresh stimulus at every
renewed burst of the flames as they rose in a shower of sparks
like gold dust. Poor Arnold lost everything and was not
insured. I trust the paraphernalia of the Beefsteak Club
perished with the rest, for the enmity I bear that society for
the dinner they gave me last year.

February 19*th*.— In the House of Lords last night to
hear Melbourne's motion about Portugal—a rather long
and very bad debate. Melbourne spoke very ill—case very
negligently got up, weakly stated, confused, and indiscreet
—in the same sense as his brother's pamphlet, with part
of which (the first part) none of the members of Canning's
Administration or of Goderich's agree, and consequently it
was answered by Lansdowne and Goderich. The latter made
an excellent speech, the only good one that was made. Aber-

deen was wretched; it is really too bad that a man should
be Secretary for Foreign Affairs who cannot speak better.
The Duke made no case for the Terceira business, and
delivered a very poor speech; but I like his speaking—it is so
much to the point, no nonsense and verbiage about it, and he
says strongly and simply what he has to say. The other
night on Greece there was a very brisk skirmish between
Palmerston and Peel, and the former spoke, they say,
remarkably well; the latter, as usual, was in a passion.

February 21st.—Dined with the Chancellor; Granvilles,
Hollands, Moore, Luttrell, Lord Lansdowne, Auckland, and
one or two more; very agreeable. Lord Holland told stories
of Lord Thurlow, whom he mimicks, they say, exactly.
When Lord Mansfield died, Thurlow said, ' I hesitated a long
time between Kenyon and Buller. Kenyon was very intemperate, but Buller was so damned corrupt, and I thought
upon the whole that intemperance was a less fault in a judge
than corruption, not but what there was a damned deal of
corruption in Kenyon's intemperance.' Lady Holland and
I very friendly; the first time I have met her in company since our separation (for we have never quarrelled).
She is mighty anxious to get me back, for no other reason
than because I won't go. Everybody is surprised at Melbourne's failure the other night; some say he was not well,
some that he did not like the business. I doubt if he is up
to it; he did not speak like a man that has much in him.

February 23rd.—Dined with Lord Bathurst and a dull
party; but after dinner Lady Bathurst began talking about
the King, and told me one or two anecdotes. When the
account of Lord Liverpool's seizure reached the King at
Brighton, Peel was at the Pavilion; the King got into one
of his nervous ways, and sent for him in the middle of the
night, desiring he would not dress; so he went down in his
bedgown and sat by the side of the King's bed. Peel has
got an awkward way of thrusting out his hands while he
talks, which at length provoked the King so much that he
said, 'Mr. Peel, it is no use going on so (taking him off)

and thrusting out your hands, which is no answer to my question.'

Went to Esterhazy's ball; talked to old Rothschild, who was there with his wife and a dandy little Jew son. He says that Polignac's Government will stand by the King's support and Polignac's own courage; offered to give me a letter to his brother, who would give me any information I wanted, squeezed my hand, and looked like what he is.

February 25th.—Yesterday at Windsor for a Council; the first time I have seen one held in the new rooms of the Castle. They are magnificent and comfortable, the corridor really delightful—furnished through its whole length of about 500 feet with the luxury of a drawing-room, and full of fine busts and bronzes, and entertaining pictures, portraits, and curious antiquities. There were the Chancellor, the Duke, three Secretaries of State, Bathurst, and Melville. The King very blind—did not know the Lord Chancellor, who was standing close to him, and took him for Peel; he would not give up the point, though, for when he found his mistake he attributed it to the light, and appealed to Lord Bathurst, who is stone-blind, and who directly agreed.

February 26th.—Intended to go to the House of Lords to hear the debate on Lord Stanhope's motion (state of the nation), but went to see Fanny Kemble in 'Mrs. Beverley' instead. She had a very great success—house crowded and plenty of emotion—but she does not touch me, though she did more than in her other parts; however, she is very good and will be much better.

The debate in the Lords was not lively, and the Duke, they say, made a most execrable speech. The fact is that he is not up to a great speech on a great question; he wants the information and preparation, the discipline of mind, that is necessary, and accordingly he exposes himself dreadfully, and entirely lost all the advantages he had gained by the excellent speeches he had previously made on other and more confined questions. He was very angry with the Duke of Richmond, whose opposition to him is considered by the

Duke's adherents as a sort of political parricide. Old Eldon spoke very well, and Radnor; the rest but moderate.

February 27th.—Dined at Lord Lansdowne's; Moore, Rogers, J. Russell, Spring Rice, Charles Kemble, Auckland, and Doherty; very agreeable, but Rogers was overpowered by numbers and loud voices. Doherty told some good professional stories, and they all agreed that Irish courts of justice afforded the finest materials for novels and romances. The 'Mertons' and 'Collegians' are both founded on facts; the stories are in the 'New Monthly Magazine;' they said the author had not made the most of the 'Collegians' story. Very odd nervousness of Moore; he could not tell that story (of Crampton's), which I begged him to do, and which would not have been lugged in neck and shoulders, because everybody was telling just such stories; he is delighted with my note of it. Charles Kemble talked of his daughter and her success—said she was twenty, and that she had once seen Mrs. Siddons in 'Lady Randolph' when she was seven years old. She was so affected in 'Mrs. Beverley' that he was obliged to carry her into her dressing-room, where she screamed for five minutes; the last scream (when she throws herself on his body) was involuntary, not in the part, and she had not intended it, but could not resist the impulse. She likes Juliet the best of her parts.

February 28th.—Dined yesterday with Lord Stanhope; Murray the bookseller (who published 'Belisarius'), Wilkie the painter, and Lord Strangford; nobody else of note. Wilkie appears stern, and might pass for mad; he said very little. Murray chattered incessantly; talked to me a great deal about Moore, who would have been mightily provoked if he had heard him. An odd dinner, not agreeable, though Lord Stanhope is amusing, so strange in his appearance, so ultra-Tory and anti-Liberal in his politics, full of information and a good deal of drollery. Murray told me that Moore is going to write a 'Life of Petrarch.' Croker would have written Lawrence's Life if Campbell [the poet] had not seized the task before anybody else thought of laying hold of it. He has circulated a command that all persons who have anything to communicate will send their letters to *his secretary*, and not to him.

March 2nd.—To-morrow I set out to Italy, after many years of anxiety to go there, without violent expectations of pleasure, but not thinking of disappointment. I care not for leaving London or anything in it; there are a few people whose society I regret, but as to friends or those who care for me, or for whom I care, I leave few behind.

CHAPTER VIII.

Calais—Beau Brummell—Paris—The Polignac Ministry—Polignac and
  Charles X.—The Duke of Orleans—State of Parties—Talleyrand —Lyons
  —First Impressions of Mountain Scenery—Mont Cenis—Turin—Marengo
  —Genoa—Road to Florence—Pisa—Florence—Lord and Lady Burghersh
  —Thorwaldsen—Lord Cochrane—Rome—St. Peter's—Frascati—Grotta
  Ferrata—Queen Hortense and Louis Napoleon—Coliseum—Death of
  Lady Northampton—The Moses—Gardens—Palm Sunday—Sistine
  Chapel—The Cardinals—Popes—Cardinal Albani—The Farnese Palace
  —A Dead Cardinal—Pasquin—Statue of Pompey—Galleries and Cata-
  combs—Bunsen—The Papal Benediction—Ceremonies of the Holy
  Week—The Grand Penitentiary—A Confession—Protestant Cemetery—
  Illumination of St. Peter's—Torlonia—Bunsen on the Forum.

Paris, March 6th.—I left London at three o'clock on
Wednesday, the 3rd, and arrived at Dover between twelve
and one. Went over in the packet at nine on Thursday, which was not to have sailed till twelve, but did
go at nine, principally because they heard that I had got
despatches, for I had armed myself with three passports
couched in such terms as were most likely to be useful. A
good but rather long passage—near four hours—and the day
magnificent. Landed with difficulty in boats. Detained at
Calais till seven. There I had a long conversation with
Brummell about his Consulship, and was moved by his
account of his own distresses to write to the Duke of
Wellington and ask him to do what he could for him. I
found him in his old lodging, dressing; some pretty pieces
of old furniture in the room, an entire toilet of silver, and a
large green macaw perched on the back of a tattered silk
chair with faded gilding; full of gaiety, impudence, and
misery.

Lord Tweeddale came over in the packet, and we dined

together. He was full of the Duke of Richmond's speech about the Duke of Wellington the other night, which he said had annoyed the Duke of Wellington more than anything that ever happened to him, and that the Duke of Richmond was now equally sorry for what he had said. He (Tweeddale) was employed to carry a message from the one Duke to the other, which, however, the Duke of Wellington did not take in good part, nor does it seem that he is at all disposed to lay aside his resentment. Tweeddale ranks Richmond's talents very highly, and says he was greatly esteemed in the army.

Left Calais at seven; travelled all night—the roads horrid in most parts—and arrived at Paris last night at half-past twelve. Found everything prepared—an excellent apartment, *laquais de place*, and courier. Called on Lady Stewart and old Madame Craufurd, and wandered about the whole day. Paris looking gay and brilliant in the finest weather I ever saw. I find the real business is not to begin in the Chambers till about the 10th, so I shall not wait for it. Polignac is said to be very stout, but the general opinion is that he will be in a minority in the Chambers; however, as yet I have seen nobody who can give good information about the state of parties. For the first time (between Calais and Paris) I saw some new houses and barns building near Abbeville and Beauvais, and the cottages near Monsieur de Clermont-Tonnerre's mansion had a very English look.

It is Lent, and very little going on here. During the Carnival they had a ball for the benefit of the poor, which was attended by 5,000 people, and produced 116,000 francs. Immense sums were given in charity, and well appropriated during the severe weather. There are also nuns (*sœurs de charité*), who visit and tend the sick, whose institution is far more practically useful than anything of which our Protestant country can boast. I shall only stay here a very few days.

March 8th.—It will be difficult to get away from this place if I don't go at once; the plot thickens, and I am in great danger of dawdling on. Yesterday morning I walked

about, visiting, and then went through the Tuileries and the
Carrousel. The Gardens were full of well-dressed and good-
looking people, and the day so fine that it was a glorious sight.
The King is, after all, hardly master of his own palace, for the
people may swarm like bees all around and through it, and
he is the only man in Paris who cannot go into the Gardens.
Dined with Standish, Brooke Greville, Madame Alfred de
Noailles and her daughter, and then went to Madame de Flahault's to see the world and hear politics. After all, nobody
has an idea how things will turn out, or what are Polignac's
intentions or his resources. Lord Stuart[1] told me that he knew
nothing, but that when he saw all the Ministers perfectly
calm and satisfied, and heard them constantly say all would
be well, although all France and a clear majority in both
Chambers seemed to be against them, he could not help thinking they must have some reason for such confidence, and
something in reserve, of which people were not aware. Lady
Keith,[2] with whom I had a long talk, told me that she did
not believe it possible they could stand, that there was no
revolutionary spirit abroad, but a strong determination to
provide for the stability of their institutions, a disgust at
the obstinacy and pretensions of the King, and a desire to
substitute the Orleans for the reigning branch, which was
becoming very general; that Polignac is wholly ignorant of
France, and will not listen to the opinions of those who
could enlighten him. It is supposed that the King is determined to push matters to extremity, to try the Chambers,
and if his Ministry are beaten to dissolve them and govern
par ordonnance du Roi, then to try and influence the elections and obtain a Chamber more favourable than the
present. Somebody told her the other day of a conversation
which Polignac had recently had with the King, in which
his Majesty said to him, 'Jules, est-ce que vous m'êtes très-
dévoué?' 'Mais oui, Sire; pouvez-vous en douter?' 'Jusqu'à
aller sur l'échafaud?' 'Mais oui, Sire, s'il le faut.' 'Alors

[1] [Lord Stuart de Rothesay was then British Ambassador in Paris.]
[2] [Married to Count de Flahault; in her own right Baroness Keith and
Nairn. She died in 1867.]

tout ira bien.' It is thought that he has got into his head
the old saying that if Louis XVI. had got upon horseback
he could have arrested the progress of the Revolution—a piece
of nonsense, fit only for a man 'qui n'a rien oublié ni rien
appris.' It is supposed the Address will be carried against
the Government by about 250 to 130. (It was 221 to 180.
—— has a *tabatière Warin* of that day, with the names of
the 221 on the lid.) All the names presented to the King
yesterday for the Presidency are obnoxious to him, but he
named Royer Collard, who had twice as many votes as any
of the others. It was remarked at the *séance royale* that
the King dropped his hat, and that the Duke of Orleans
picked it up, and they always make a great deal of these
trifles. The Duke of Orleans is, however, very well with the
Court, and will not stir, let what will happen, though he
probably feels like Macbeth before the murder of Duncan—

> If chance will have me King, why let chance crown me
> Without my stir.

March 8th, at night.—Walked about visiting, and heard
all the gossip of Paris from little Madame Graham, who
also invited me to Pozzo di Borgo's box at the Opera. I
don't mean to record the gossip and scandal unless when I
hear something out of the common way and amusing.
Dined with Stuart; Tweeddale, Gurwood, Allen, and some
heavy *attachés*; no French. He appears to live handsomely.
Afterwards to the Opera to see Taglioni, who did not dance;
then to Madame Appony's, to whom I was introduced, and
we had plenty of bowing and smirking and civilities about
my family. Rather bored at the party, and am come home
quite resolved to be off on Thursday, but am greatly puzzled
about my route, for everybody recommends a different
one.

March 9th.—Dined with M. de Flahault; met M. de
Talleyrand, Madame de Dino, General Sébastiani, M. Bertin
de Vaux, Duc de Broglie, and Montrond. Sébastiani and
Bertin de Vaux are Deputies, and all violent Oppositionists.
After dinner M. de Lescure, another man, and the young

Duc de Valençay, Madame de Dino's son, came in. They talked politics all the time, and it was curious enough to me. Bertin is the sort of man in appearance that Tierney was, and shrewd like him; he is brother to the editor, and principal manager himself, of the 'Journal des Débats.' Sébastiani is slow and pompous. The Duc de Broglie is one of the best men in France. They all agreed that the Government cannot stand. Talleyrand is as much against it as any of them. Sébastiani told me they should have 280 against 130. Talleyrand said that it was quite impossible to predict what might be the result of this contest (if the Court pushed matters to extremity) both to France and Europe, and that it was astonishing surrounding nations, and particularly England, did not see how deeply they were interested in the event. He said of us, 'Vous avez plus d'argent que de crédit.' He looks horridly old, but seems vigorous enough and alive to everything. After dinner they all put their heads together and chattered politics as fast as they could. Madame de Flahault is more violent than her husband, and her house is the resort of all the Liberal party. Went afterwards to the Opera and saw Maret, the Duc de Bassano, a stupid elderly bourgeois-looking man, with two very pretty daughters. The battle is to begin in the Chamber on Saturday or Monday on the Address. Talleyrand told me that the next three weeks would be the most important of any period since the Restoration. It is in agitation to deprive him of his place of Grand Chambellan.

Susa, March 15th, 9 o'clock.—Just arrived at this place at the foot of Mont Cenis. Left Paris on the 11th, at twelve o'clock at night. On the last day, Montrond made a dinner for me at a club to see M. des Chapelles play at whist. I saw it, but was no wiser; but I conclude he plays very well, for he always wins, is not suspected of cheating, and excels at all other games. At twelve I got into my carriage, and (only stopping an hour and a half for two breakfasts) got to Lyons in forty-eight hours and a half. Journey not disagreeable, and roads much better than

I expected, particularly after Macon, when they became as good as in England ; but the country presents the same sterile, uninteresting appearance as that between Calais and Paris— no hedges, no trees, except tall, stupid-looking poplars, and no châteaux or farm-houses. I am at a loss to know why a country should look so ill which I do not believe is either barren or ill cultivated. Lyons is a magnificent town. It was dark when I arrived, or rather moonlight, but I could see that the quay we came along was fine, and yesterday morning I walked about for an hour and was struck with the grandeur of the place ; it is like a great and magnificent Bath ; but I had not time to see much of it, and, with beautiful weather, I set off at ten o'clock. The mountains (les Échelles de Savoie) appear almost directly in the distance, but it was long before I could make out whether they were clouds or mountains.

After crossing the Pont de Beauvoisin we began to mount the Échelles, which I did on foot, and I never shall forget the first impression made upon me by the mountain scenery. It first burst upon me at a turn of the road—one huge perpendicular rock above me, a deep ravine with a torrent rushing down and a mountain covered with pines and ilexes on the other side, and in front another vast rock which was shining in the reflected light of the setting sun. I never shall forget it. How I turned round and round, afraid to miss a particle of the glorious scene. It was the liveliest impression because it was the first. I walked nearly to the other post with the most exquisite pleasure, but it was dark by the time I got to La Grotta. I went on, however, all night, very unhappy at the idea of losing a great deal of this scenery, but consoled by the reflection that there was plenty left. As soon as it was light I found myself in the middle of the mountains (the Lower Alps), and from thence I proceeded across the Mont Cenis. Though not the finest pass, to me, who had never seen anything like it, it appeared perfectly beautiful, every turn in the road presenting a new combination of Alpine magnificence. Nothing is more striking than the patches of cultivation in the midst of the tremendous rocks and precipices, and in one or two spots there were plots of grass and evergreens, like an English shrubbery, at the foot of enormous mountains covered with snow.   There was not a breath of air in these valleys, and the sun was shining in unclouded brightness, so that there was all the atmosphere of summer below with all the livery of winter above.

> The altitude of some tall crag
> That is the eagle's birthplace, or some peak
> Familiar with forgotten years, that shows,
> Inscribed as with the silence of the thought
> Upon its bleak and visionary sides,
> The history of many a winter storm
> Or obscure record of the path of fire.
>   There the sun himself
> At the calm close of Summer's longest day
> Rests his substantial orb; between those heights,
> And on the top of either pinnacle,
> More keenly than elsewhere in night's blue vault
> Sparkle the stars, as of their station proud :
> Thoughts are not busier in the mind of man
> Than the mute agents stirring there,—alone
> Here do I sit and watch.

In one place, too, I remarked high up on the side of the rugged and barren mountain two or three cottages, to arrive at which steps had been cut in the rock.   No sign of vegetation was near, so exactly the description of Goldsmith :—

> Dear is that shed to which their souls conform,
> And dear that hill that lifts them to the storm ;

In another place there was a cluster of houses and a church newly built.   Not far from Lans-le-Bourg (at the foot of Mont Cenis) is a very strong fort, built by the King of Sardinia, which commands the road.   It has a fine effect perched upon a rock, and apparently unapproachable.   A soldier was pacing the battlement, and his figure gave life to the scene and exhibited the immensity of the surrounding objects, so minute did he appear.   At Lans-le-Bourg they put four horses and two mules to my carriage, but I took my courier's horse and set off to ride up the mountain with a

guide who would insist upon going with me, and who
proposed to take me up a much shorter way by the old
road, which, however, I declined; he was on foot, and made
a short cut up the hill while I rode by the road, which winds
in several turns up the mountain.   Fired with mountainous
zeal, I had a mind to try one of these short cuts, and giving
my horse to Paolo (my *valet de chambre*) set off with my guide
to climb the next intervening ascent; but I soon found that
I had better have stuck to my horse, for the immensity of
the surrounding objects had deceived me as to the distance,
and the ground was so steep and slippery that, unprepared
as I was for such an attempt, I could not keep my footing.
When about half-way up, I looked ruefully round and saw
steeps above and below covered with ice and snow and loose
earth.   I could not get back, and did not know how to get
on.   I felt like the man who went up in a balloon, and when
a mile in the air wanted to be let out.   My feelings were very
like what Johnson describes at Hawkestone in his tour in
Wales.   ' He that mounts the precipices at —— wonders how
he came thither, and doubts how he shall return; his walk
is an adventure and his departure an escape.   He has not
the tranquillity but the horrors of solitude—a kind of turbulent pleasure between fright and admiration.'   My guide,
fortunately, was active and strong, and properly shod; so
he went first, making steps for me in the snow, into which
I put my feet after his, while with one hand I grasped
the tail of his blue frock and with the other seized bits of
twig or anything I could lay hold of; and in this ludicrous
way, scrambling and clambering, hot and out of breath, to
my great joy I at last got to the road, and for the rest of the
ascent contented myself with my post-horse, who had a set
of bells jingling at his head and was a sorry beast enough.
I was never weary, however, of admiring the scenery.   The
guide told me he had often seen Napoleon when he was
crossing the mountain, and that he remembered his being
caught in a *tormento*,[1] when his life was saved by two young

[1] A *tormento* (most appropriate name) is a tempest of wind, and sleet,
and snow, exceedingly dangerous to those who are met by it.

Savoyards, who took him on their backs and carried him to a *rifugio*.[1] He asked them if they were married, and, finding they were not, enquired how much was enough to marry upon in that country, and then gave them the requisite sum, and settled pensions of 600 francs on each of them. One is dead, the other still receives it. As I got near the top of the mountain the road, which had hitherto been excellent, became execrable and the cold intense. I had left summer below and found winter above. I looked in vain for the chamois, hares, wolves, and bears, all of which I was told are found there. At last I arrived at the summit, and found at the inn a friar, the only inhabitant of the Hospice, who, hearing me say I would go there (as my carriage was not yet come), offered to go with me; he was young, fat, rosy, jolly, and dirty, dressed in a black robe with a travelling-cap on his head, appeared quick and intelligent, and spoke French and Italian. He took me over the Hospice, which is now quite empty, and showed me two very decently furnished rooms which the Emperor Napoleon used to occupy, and two inferior apartments which had been appropriated to the Empress Maria Louisa. The N.'s on the *grille* of the door had been changed for V.E.'s (Victor Emmanuel) and M. T.'s (Maria Theresa), and frightful pictures of the Sardinian King and Queen have replaced the Imperial portraits. All sorts of distinguished people have slept there *en passant*, and do still when compelled to spend the night on Mont Cenis. He offered to lodge and feed me, but I declined. I told him I was glad to see Napoleon's bedroom, as I took an interest in everything which related to that great man, at which he seemed extremely pleased, and said, ' Ah, monsieur, vous êtes donc comme moi.' I dined at the inn (a very bad one) on some trout which they got for me from the Hospice—very fine fish, but very ill dressed. The sun was setting by the time I set off, it was dusk when I had got half-way down the descent, and dark before I had reached the first stage. When half-way down the descent, the last rays of the sun were still

[1] A *rifugio* is a sort of cabin, of which there are several built at certain distances all the way up the mountain, where travellers may take shelter.

gilding the tops of the crags above, and the contrast between that light above and the darkness below was very fine. From what I saw of it, and from what I guess, straining my eyes into the darkness to catch the dim and indistinct shapes of the mountains, the Italian side is the finest—the most wild and savage and with more variety. On the French side you are always on the breast of the same mountain, but on the Italian side you wind along different rocks always hanging over a precipice with huge black, snow-topped crags frowning from the other ridge. I was quite unhappy not to see it. Altogether I never shall forget the pleasure of the two days' journey and the first sight of the Alps, exceeding the expectations I had formed, and for years I have enjoyed nothing so much. The descent (at the beginning of which, by-the-bye, I was very nearly overturned) only ends at this place, where I found a tolerable room and a good fire, but the *cameriere* stinking so abominably of garlic that he impregnated the whole apartment.

Turin, March 16th.—Got here early and meant to sleep, but have changed my mind and am going on. A fine but dull-looking town. Found the two Forsters, who pressed me to stay. Made an ineffectual attempt to get into the Egyptian Museum, said to be the finest in the world. It was collected by Drovetti, the French Consul, and offered to us for 16,000*l.*, which we declined to give, and the King of Sardinia bought it. Forster told me that this country is rich, not ill governed, but plunged in bigotry. There are near 400 convents in the King's dominions. It is the dullest town in Europe, and it is because it looks so dull that I am in a hurry to get out of it. This morning was cloudy, and presented fresh combinations of beauty in the mountains when the clouds rolled round their great white peaks, sometimes blending them in the murky vapour, and sometimes exhibiting their sharp outlines above the wreath of mist. I did not part from the Alps without casting many a lingering look behind.

Genoa, March 18th.—Got on so quick from Turin that I went to Alessandria that night, and set off at half-past six

yesterday morning.   Crossed the field of battle of Marengo,
a boundless plain (now thickly studded with trees and houses),
and saw the spot where Desaix was killed.   The bridge over
the Bormida which Melas crossed to attack the French army
is gone, but another has been built near it.   The Austrians
or Sardinians have taken down the column which was
erected to the memory of Desaix on the spot where he fell;
they might as well have left it, for the place will always be
celebrated, though they only did as the French had done
before.   After the battle of Jena they took down the Column
of Rossbach,[1] but that was erected to commemorate the
victory, and this the death of the hero.   I feel like Johnson—
'far from me and my friends be that frigid philosophy
which can make us pass unmoved over any scenes which
have been consecrated by virtue, by valour, or by wisdom'—
and I strained the eyes of my imagination to see all the
tumult of this famous battle, in which Bonaparte had been
actually defeated, yet (one can hardly now tell how) was in
the end completely victorious.   This pillar might have been
left, too, as a striking memorial of the rapid vicissitudes of
fortune : the removal of it has been here so quick, and at
Rossbach so tardy, a reparation of national honour.

The Apennines are nothing after the Alps, but the descent
to Genoa is very pretty, and Genoa itself exceeds everything
I ever saw in point of beauty and magnificence.

> How boldly doth it front us, how majestically—
> Like a luxurious vineyard : the hill-side
> Is hung with marble fabrics, line o'er line,
> Terrace o'er terrace, nearer still and nearer
> To the blue heavens, here bright and sumptuous palaces
> With cool and verdant garden interspersed.
>
> .   .   .   .   .   .
> While over all hangs the rich purple eve.
>
> MILMAN's *Fall of Jerusalem.*

I passed the whole day after I got here in looking into
the palaces and gardens and admiring the prospect on every

---

[1] The battle of Rossbach was gained by Frederick the Great over the
French and Austrians in 1757.

side. You are met at every turn by vestiges of the old
Republic; in fact, the town has undergone very little alteration for hundreds of years, and there is an air of gaiety and
bustling activity which, with the graceful costume of the men
and women, make it a most delightful picture. Genoa appears to be a city of palaces, and although many of the largest
are now converted to humbler uses, and many fallen to
decay, there are ample remains to show the former grandeur
of the princely merchants who were once the lords of the
ocean. Everything bespeaks solidity, durability, and magnificence. There are stupendous works which were done at
the expense of individuals. In every part of the town are
paintings and frescoes, which, in spite of constant exposure
to the atmosphere, have retained much of their brilliancy
and freshness. The palaces of Doria are the most interesting; but why the Senate gave him that which bears still
the inscription denoting its being their gift it is difficult to
say, when his own is so superior and in a more agreeable
situation. The old palace of Andrew is now let for lodgings,
and the Pamfili Doria live at Rome. The walls are covered
with inscriptions, and I stopped to read two on stone slabs
on the spot where the houses of malefactors had formerly
stood, monuments of the vindictive laws of the Republic,
which not only punished the criminal himself, but consigned
his children to infamy and his habitation to destruction;
though they stand together they are not of the same date.
There is no temptation to violate the decree by building
again on the spot, for they are in a narrow, dirty court, to
which light can scarcely find access. The Ducal Palace now
belongs to the Governor. It has been modernised, but in
the dark alleys adjoining there are remains demonstrative of
its former extent—pictures of the different Doges in fresco
on the walls half erased, and little bridges extending from
the windows (or doors) of the palace to the public prisons
and other adjoining buildings. The view from my *albergo*
(*della villa*) is the gayest imaginable, looking over the
harbour, which is crowded with sailors and boats full of ani-
mation.

Evening.—Passed the whole day seeing sights. Called
on Madame Durazzo, and went with her and her niece,
Madame de' Ferrari, to the King's palace, formerly a Durazzo
palace. Like the others, a fine house, full of painting
and gilding, and with a terrace of black and white marble
commanding a view of the sea. The finest picture is a
Paul Veronese of a Magdalen with our Saviour. The
King and Queen sleep together, and on each side of the
royal bed there is an assortment of ivory palms, crucifixes,
boxes for holy water, and other spiritual guards for their
souls. For the comfort of their bodies he has had a machine
made like a car, which is drawn up by a chain from the
bottom to the top of the house; it holds about six people,
who can be at pleasure elevated to any storey, and at each
landing-place there is a contrivance to let them in and out.
From thence to the Brignole Palace (called the Palazzo
Rosso), where I met M. and Madame de Brignole, who were
very civil and ordered a scientific footman to show us the
pictures. They are numerous and excellent, but we could
only take a cursory look at them; the best are the Vandykes,
particularly a Christ and a portrait of one of the Brignoles on
horseback, and a beautiful Carlo Dolce, a small bleeding Christ.
I saw the churches—San Stefano, Annunziata, the Duomo,
Sant' Ambrogio, San Cyro. There are two splendid pictures
in the Ambrosio, a Guido and a Rubens; the Martyrdom in
the San Stefano, by Julio Romano and Raphael, went to Paris
and was brought back in 1814. The churches have a profusion of marble, and gilding, and frescoes; the Duomo is
of black and white marble, of mixed architecture, and highly
ornamented—all stinking to a degree that was perfectly intolerable, and the same thing whether empty or full; it is
the smell of stale incense mixed with garlic and human
odour, horrible combination of poisonous exhalations. I
must say, as everybody has before remarked, that there is
something highly edifying in the appearance of devotion
which belongs to the Catholic religion; the churches are
always open, and, go into them when you will, you see men
and women kneeling and praying before this or that altar,

absorbed in their occupation, and who must have been led there by some devotional feeling. This seems more accordant with the spirit and essence of religion than to have the churches, as ours are, opened like theatres at stated hours and days for the performance of a long service, at the end of which the audience is turned out and the doors are locked till the next representation. Then the Catholic religion makes no distinctions between poverty and wealth—no pews for the aristocracy well warmed and furnished, or seats set apart for the rich and well dressed; here the church is open to all, and the beggar in rags comes and takes his place by the side of the lady in silks, and both kneel on the same pavement, for the moment at least and in that place reduced to the same level.

I saw the Ducal Palace, where there are two very fine halls,[1] the old Hall of Audience and the Hall of Council, the latter 150 by 57 feet; and the Doria Palace, delightfully situated with a garden and fine fountain, and a curious old gallery opening upon a marble terrace, richly painted, gilt and carved, though now decayed. Here the Emperor Napoleon lived when he was at Genoa, preferring Andrew Doria's palace to a better lodging: he had some poetry in his ambition after all. Lastly to the Albergo dei Poveri,[2] a noble institution, built by a Brignole and en-

---

[1] They are left just in the state in which they were in the time of the Republic; the balustrade still surrounds the elevated platform on which the throne of the Doge was placed.

[2] The Albergo dei Poveri and the Scoghetti Gardens pleased me more than anything I saw in Genoa. I am sorry I did not see the Sordi e Muti, which is admirably conducted, and where the pupils by all accounts perform wonders. The Albergo is managed by a committee consisting of the principal nobles in the town. The Scoghetti Gardens are delightfully laid out; there is a shrubbery of evergreens with a cascade, and a summer-house paved with tiles—two or three rooms in it, and a hot and cold bath. It is astonishing how they cherish the memory of 'Lord Bentinck.'* I heard of him in various parts of the town, particularly here, as he lived in the house when first he came to Genoa. The Gardens command a fine view of the city, the sea, and the mountains. The saloon in the Serra is only a very splendid room, glittering with glass, and gold, and lapis lazuli; by no means

---

* [Lord William Bentinck was Mr. Greville's uncle.]

riched by repeated benefactions; like all the edifices of the
old Genoese, vast and of fine proportions. The great staircase and hall are adorned with colossal statues of its benefactors (among whom are many Durazzos), and the sums
that they gave or bequeathed are commemorated on the
pedestals. In the chapel is a piece of sculpture by Michael
Angelo, a dead Christ and Virgin (only heads), and an altar-
piece by Puget. Branching out from the chapel are two
vast chambers, lofty, airy, and light, one for the men, the
other for the women. About 800 men and 1,200 or 1,300
women are supported here. Many of the nobles are said
to be rich—Ferrari, Brignole, Durazzo, and Pallavicini particularly. I forgot to mention the chapel and tomb of
Andrew Doria; the chapel he built himself; his body,
arrayed in princely robes, lies in the vault. There is a Latin
inscription on the chapel, signifying that he stood by the
country in the days of her affliction. It is a pretty little
chapel full of painting and gilding. In the early part of
the Revolution the tomb narrowly escaped destruction, but
it was saved by the solidity of its materials. I gave the
man who showed me this tomb a franc, and he kissed my
hand in a transport of gratitude.

Florence, March 21*st.*—Arrived here at seven o'clock.
Left Genoa on the 19th (having previously gone to see the
Scoghetti Gardens and the Serra Palace), and went to Sestri
to pass that evening and the next morning with William
Ponsonby, who was staying there. The road from Genoa to
Chiavari is one continual course of magnificent scenery,
winding along the side of the mountains and hanging over
the sea, the mountains studded with villages, villas, and
cottages which appear like white specks at a distance, till
on near approach they swell into life and activity. The
villas are generally painted as at Genoa; the orange trees
were in full bloom, and the gardens often slope down to the
very margin of the sea. Every turn in the road and each

deserves to be called, as it is by Forsyth, the finest saloon in Europe. It is
not very large, and not much more gilt than Crockford's drawing-room, but
looks cleaner, though it has been done these seventy years or more.

fresh ascent supplies a new prospect, and the parting view
of Genoa, with the ocean before and the Apennines behind,
cannot be imagined by those who have not seen it. ' Si
quod vere natura nobis dedit spectaculum in hac tellure vere
gratum et philosopho dignum, id semel, mihi contigisse
arbitror, cum ex celsissimâ rupe speculabundus ad oram
maris mediterranei, hinc aequor cæruleum, illinc tractus
Alpinos prospexi, nihil quidem magis dispar aut dissimile
nec in suo genere magis egregium et singulare.' [1]

Chiavari and Sestri are both beautiful, especially the
latter, in a little bay with a jutting promontory, a rocky hill
covered with evergreens, and shrubs, and heather, and
affording grand and various prospects of the still blue sea
and the white and shining coast with the dark mountains
behind—

> A sunny bay
> Where the salt sea innocuously breaks
> And the sea breeze as innocently breathes
> On Sestri's leafy shores—a sheltered hold
> In a soft clime encouraging the soil
> To a luxuriant beauty.

The mountain road from Chiavari to La Spezzia presents the same scenery as far as Massa and Carrara, which
I unfortunately lost by travelling in the night. I crossed
the river in the boat by candle-light, which was picturesque enough, the scanty light gleaming upon the rough
figures who escorted me and plied the enormous poles
by which they move the ferry-boat. Got to Pisa to breakfast (without stopping at Lucca), and passed three hours
looking at the Cathedral, Leaning Tower, Baptistry, and
Campo Santo, the last of which alone would take up the
whole day to be seen as it ought. The Cathedral is under
repair; the pictures have been covered up or taken down,
and the whole church was full of rubbish and scaffolding;
but in this state I could see how fine it is, and admire
the columns which Forsyth praises, and the roof and many
of the marbles. The Grand Duke has ordered it all to be

[1] Burnet's 'Theory of the Earth.'

cleaned, and very little of it to be altered.   One alteration,
however, is in very bad taste; he has taken away the old
confessionals of carved wood, and substituted others of
marble, fixed in the wall, which are exactly like modern
chimney-pieces, and have the worst effect amidst the
surrounding antiquities.   The exterior is rather fantastic,
but the columns are beautiful, and John of Bologna's bronze
doors admirable.   The Campo Santo is full of ancient tombs,
frescoes, modern busts, and morsels of sculpture of all ages
and descriptions.   The Leaning Tower [1] is 190 feet high,
and there are 293 steps to the top of it, which I climbed up
to view the surrounding country, but it was not clear enough
to see the sea and Elba.   Here is the finest aqueduct I have
seen, which continues to pour water into the town.   Part
of the old wall [2] with its towers is still standing.   These
pugnacious republics, who were always squabbling with
each other and wasting their strength in civil broils, erected
very massive defences.   The Pisans are proud of their
ancient exploits.   The San Stefano or Chiesa dei Cavalieri
is full of standards taken from the Turks, and the man who
showed me the Campo Santo said that a magnificent Grecian
vase which is there had been brought from Genoa by the
Pisans before the foundation of Rome.   There are Egyptian,
Etruscan, Roman, and Grecian remains, which have been
plundered, or conquered, or purchased by patriotic Pisans to
enrich their native city.   The frescoes are greatly damaged.
I went to look at the celebrated house 'Alla Giornata,' a
white marble palace on the Arno; the chains still hang over
the door, and there is an inscription above them which looks
modern.   My *laquais de place* told me what I suppose is the
tradition of the place—that the son of the family was taken
by the Turks, and that they had captured a Turk, who was
put in chains; that an exchange was agreed upon, and the
prisoners on either side released, and that the chains were

---

[1] There was another leaning edifice, but the Grand Duke had it pulled
down; it was thought dangerous.

[2] It had been destroyed, but was restored by the Medici or the present
family.

hung up and the inscription added, signifying that the Turk was at liberty to go again into the light of day. But it was a lame and improbable story, and I prefer the mystery to the explanation.

Much as I was charmed with the mountains, I was not sorry, for a change, to get into the rich, broad plain of Tuscany, full of vineyards and habitations along the banks of the Arno. The voice and aspect of cheerfulness is refreshing after a course of rugged and barren grandeur; the road is excellent and the travelling rapid. Yesterday being a holiday, and to-day Sunday, the whole population in their best dresses have been out on the road, and very good-looking they generally are. There are not more beggars than in France, and certainly a far greater appearance of prosperity throughout the north of Italy than in any part of France I have seen, although there are the same complaints of distress and poverty here that are heard both there and in England. Thorwaldsen, the sculptor, is in this inn, and the King of Bavaria left it this morning. The book of strangers is rather amusing; the entries are sometimes remarkable or ridiculous. I found ' La Duchesse de Saint-Leu et le Prince Louis-Napoléon; Lord and Lady Shrewsbury and family; Miss Caroline Grinwell, of New York; the King of Bavaria (not down in the book though); Thorwaldsen.' Tuscany seems to be flourishing and contented; the Government is absolute but mild, the Grand Duke enormously rich.

March 23rd.—Yesterday morning breakfasted with Lord Normanby, who has got a house extending 200 feet in front, court, garden, and stables for about 280*l.* a year, everything else cheap in proportion, and upon 2,000*l.* a year a man may live luxuriously. His house was originally fitted up for the Pretender, and C. R.'s are still to be seen all over the place. Called on Lord Burghersh,[1] who was at breakfast—the table covered with manuscript music, a pianoforte, two fiddles, and a fiddler in the room. He was full of composition and getting up his opera of ' Phædra ' for to-morrow night. The Embassy

[1] [Lord Burghersh, afterwards Earl of Westmoreland, was then British Minister at Florence.]

is the seat of the Arts, for Lady Burghersh has received the gift of painting as if by inspiration, and she was in a brown robe in the midst of oils, and brushes, and canvas; and a model was in attendance, some part of whose person was to be introduced into a fancy piece. She copies pictures in the Gallery, and really extraordinarily well if it be true that till a year ago she had never had a brush in her hand, and that she is still quite ignorant of drawing.

Went into two or three of the churches, then to the Gallery, and sat for half an hour in the Tribune, but could not work myself into a proper enthusiasm for the 'Venus,' whose head is too small and ankles too thick, but they say the more I see her the more I shall like her. I prefer the 'Wrestlers,' and the head of the 'Remontleur' is the only good *head* I have seen, the only one with expression. 'Niobe' is fine, but I can't bear her children, except one. Then to the Cascine on horseback to see the town and the world: it seems a very enjoyable place. This morning again dropped into some of the churches, after which I have always a hankering, though there is great sameness in them, but I have a childish liking for Catholic pomp. The fine things are lost amidst a heap of rubbish, but there is no lack of marble, and painting, and gilding in most of them. They are going on with the Medici Chapel, on which millions have been wasted and more is going after, for the Grand Duke is gradually finishing the work. The profusion of marble is immense, and very fine and curious if examined in detail; the precious stones are hardly seen, and when they are, not to be recognised as such. To the Pitti Palace, of which one part is under repair and not visible, but I saw most of the best pictures. I like pictures better than statues. It is a beautiful palace, and well furnished for show. Nobody knows what Vandyke was without coming here. To the Gabinetto Fisico, and saw all the wax-works, the progress of gestation, and the representation of the plague, incomparably clever and well executed. I saw nothing disgusting in the wax-works in the museum, which many people are so squeamish about.

Before dinner yesterday called upon Thorwaldsen, who

was in the inn, to tell him Lord Gower likes his 'Ganymede.'
He was mighty polite, squeezed my hand, and reconducted me
to my own door.   At night went to the Opera and heard
David and Grisi in ' Ricciardo e Zoraida.'   She is like Pasta
in face and figure, but much handsomer, though with less
expression.   She is only eighteen.   He has lost much of his
voice, and embroiders to make up for it, but every now and
then he appears to find it again, and his taste and expression
are exquisite.   To-night at a child's ball at Lady William-
son's, where I was introduced to Lord Cochrane, and had a
great deal of talk with him; told him I thought things
would explode at last in England, which he concurred in,
and seemed to like the idea of it, in which we differ, owing
probably to the difference of our positions; he has nothing,
and I everything, to lose by such an event.

   March 25th.—Went yesterday morning to Santa Croce to
hear a Mass on the completion of a monument which has
been erected to Dante ; very crowded and the music indifferent.   Afterwards to the Gallery and saw all the cabinets,
but we were hurried through them too rapidly.   I began to
like the ' Venus ' better, best of all the statues.   The ' Niobe '[1]
cannot have been a group, nor the children have belonged
to the mother.   Rode to Normanby's villa at Sesto, five
miles from Florence ; a large and agreeable house, gardens
full of fountains, statues, busts, orange and lemon trees,
shrubs and flowers.   He pays 600 dollars a year for it, exclusive of the race-ground.   In the evening to Burghersh's
opera, which was very well performed ; pretty theatre,
crowded to suffocation.   All the actors amateurs ;[2] chorus

---

[1] The 'Niobe' is supposed to have been a group upon some temple

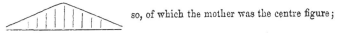 so, of which the mother was the centre figure ;

this makes it more probable, but the difficulty to this hypothesis is, that
there do not appear to be the necessary gradations in the size or altitude
of the other figures ; the sons in the ' Laocoon ' are certainly little men.

[2]

Phædra	Miss Williams	Soprano.
Hippolytus	Madame Vigano	Contralto.
The Girl	Madame de Bombelles	Soprano.
Theseus	Goretti	Tenor.
Attendant	Franceschini	Bass.

composed of divers ladies and gentlemen of Florence, principally English. Here all the society of Florence was assembled in nearly equal proportions of Italians, English, and other foreigners. Nothing can be worse than it is, for there is no foundation of natives, and the rest are generally the refuse of Europe, people who come here from want of money or want of character. Everybody is received without reference to their conduct, past or present, with the exception, perhaps, of Englishwomen who have been divorced, whose case is too notorious to allow the English Minister's wife to present them at Court.

March 26th.—Yesterday morning to a Mass at the Annunziata, to which the Grand Duke came in state, with his family and Court. The piazza was lined with guards ; seven coaches-and-six with his *guardia nobile* and running footmen ; the Mass beautifully performed by his band, Tacchinardi (father of Madame Persiani, I believe) singing and Manielli directing. Then rode to Lord Cochrane's villa, where we found them under a matted tent in the garden, going to dinner. He talks of going to Algiers to see the French attack it. He has made 100,000*l.* by the Greek bonds. It is a pity he ever got into a scrape; he is such a fine fellow, and so shrewd and good-humoured. To the Certosa, on a hill two miles from Florence ; very large convent, formerly very rich. and had near forty monks, now reduced to seven residents, though there are a few more who belong to it, but who are absent. It is in good repair, but looks desolate. There is an old monk, Don Fortunatus by name, who understands English and speaks it tolerably, delights in English people and books, received us in his cell, which consists of two or three little apartments, not uncomfortable, and commanding a beautiful view ; talked with great pleasure of his English acquaintance, and showed all their cards, which he treasured up. A very lively, good-humoured old friar. Returned to ride in the Corso, which is a narrow street going from the Duomo to the Annunziata, to drive up and down which is one of the ceremonies of the day (Lady Day), as the people are supposed to go and pay their respects to the Virgin. In the evening to the Opera and heard David again.

Rome, March 29*th.*—Set off yesterday morning at half-past seven from Florence, and arrived here at six this evening in a fine glowing sunset, straining my eyes to catch interesting objects, and trying in vain to make out the different hills. The last two days at Florence I went to the Gallery and Pitti Palace again with the Copleys. Half the rooms were shut up when I was at the Pitti before, but we now saw them all, and probably the finest collection of pictures in the world. The Raphaels, Rubens, Andrea del Sartos, and Salvators I liked the best. On Saturday evening went to Court and was presented to the Grand Duke, who is vulgar-looking and has bad manners ; but the whole thing is rather handsome. Stopped at Siena to see the cathedral; very fine, the ancient fount beautiful. The mutilated Graces I am not connoisseur enough to appreciate, but the illuminated Missals of the thirteenth century I thought admirable, both for the colouring and the drawing, and as exquisitely finished as any miniature. The entrance to Rome through the Porta del Popolo appeared very fine, but I was disappointed in the first distant view of the city from the hill above Viterbo. I passed Radicofani in the dark, and saw little to admire in the Lake of Bolsena or the surrounding country. The women throughout Italy appeared very handsome, one quite beautiful at Siena.

March 30*th.*—This morning I awoke very early and could not rest till I had seen St. Peter's ; so set off in a hackney coach, drove by the Piazza Colonna and the Castle, of St. Angelo (which burst upon me unexpectedly as I turned on the bridge), and got out as soon as St. Peter's was in sight. My first feeling was disappointment, but as I advanced towards the obelisk, with the fountains on each side, and found myself in that ocean of space with all the grand objects around, delight and admiration succeeded. As I walked along the piazza and then entered the church, I felt that sort of breathless bewilderment which was produced in some degree by the first sight of the Alps. Much as I expected I was not disappointed. St. Peter's sets criticism at defiance; nor can I conceive how anybody can do anything but admire and wonder there, till time and familiarity with its glories shall have subjected the imagination to the judgment. I then came home and went with Morier to take a cursory view of the city and blunt the edge of curiosity. In about five hours I galloped over the Forum, Coliseum, Pantheon, St. John Lateran, Santa Maria Maggiore, the Vatican, and several arches and obelisks. I cannot tell which produced the greatest impression, St. Peter's or the Coliseum; but if I might only have seen one it should be the Coliseum, for there can be nothing of the same kind besides.[1]

They only who have seen Rome can have an idea of the grandeur of it and of the wonders it contains, the treasures of art and the records of antiquity. Of course I had the same general idea of there being much to see that others have, but was far from being prepared for the reality, which exceeds my most sanguine expectations. The Vatican alone would require years to be examined as it deserves. It is remarkable, however, how the pleasure of the imagination arising from antiquities depends upon their accidents. The busts, statues, columns, tombs, and fragments of all sorts are heaped together in such profusion at the Vatican that the eyes ache at them, the senses are bewildered, and we regard them (with some exceptions) almost exclusively as objects of art, and do not feel the interest which, separately, they might inspire by their connection with remote ages, whereas there is scarcely one of those, if it were now to be discovered, that would not excite the greatest curiosity, and be, in the midst of the ruins to which it belongs, an object of far greater interest than a finer production which had taken its splendid but frigid position in this collection. We went to the Sistine Chapel, and saw Michael Angelo's frescoes, which Sir Joshua Reynolds says are the finest paintings in the world, and which the unlearned call great rude daubs. I do not pretend to the capacity of appreciating their merits, but was very much struck with the ease, and

---

[1] Of the same kind there is at Pompeii, but not near so fine; more perfect as a specimen, far less beautiful as an object. And the amphitheatre at Verona, but that is very inferior.

grace, and majesty of some of the figures; it was, however, too dark to see the ' Last Judgment.' I ended by St. Peter's again, where there were many devout Catholics praying round the illuminated tomb of the Apostle, and many foolish English poking into it to stare and ask questions, the answers to which they did not understand. I have but one fault to find, and that is with the Glory, a miserable transparency in the great window opposite the entrance, throwing a yellow light upon the Dove, which has the most paltry effect, and is utterly unworthy of the grandeur of such a place.

April 1st.—Yesterday morning at nine o'clock went with Edward Cheney and George Hamilton to Frascati to dine with Henry Fox, who has got a villa there. As soon as we arrived Cheney and I walked over to Grotta Ferrata to see Domenichino's frescoes. The convent is about a mile and a half off, large, formerly rich, full of monks, and a fortress; also the scene of various miracles performed by St. Nilo, the founder and patron saint; now tenanted by a few beggarly friars, and part of it let to Prince Gagarin, the Russian Minister, as a villa. Domenichino sought and found an asylum there in consequence of some crime he had committed or debt he had incurred; he stayed there two years, and in return for the hospitality of the monks adorned their chapel with (some think) the finest frescoes in the world. They are splendid pictures, and all painted by his own hand.

At dinner we had Hortense, the ex-Queen of Holland, her son, Prince Louis Napoleon, her lady in waiting, Lady Sandwich and her daughter, Cheney, Hamilton, Lord Lovaine, and Fordwich. We dined in the garden, but there was too much wind for a *fête champêtre*. Hortense is not near so ugly as I expected, very unaffected and gay, and gives herself no royal airs. The only difference between her and anybody else was that, after dinner, when she rose from table, her own servant presented her with a finger-glass and water, which nobody else had. She is called Madame.

We returned by moonlight, and though I did not go into the Coliseum, because the moon was not full enough, it looked fine, and the light shining through the lower arches had a

beautiful effect. This morning went a long round of sights—
Cæsar's Palace, of which there are no remains but fragments
of walls; it really does 'grovel on earth in indistinct decay.' Caracalla's Baths, which are stupendous ; the *custode*
showed us a room in which were heaped up bits of marble of
all sorts and sizes, fragments of columns and friezes ; and he
told us that they never excavated without finding something.
And Titus's Baths, less magnificent but equally curious, because they contain the remains of the Golden House of Nero,
on which Titus built his Thermæ. The ruins are, in fact, part
of the Golden House, for the Thermæ have been altogether
destroyed. Then to the Capitol, Forum, Temple of Vesta,
Fortuna Virilis, and other places with Morier. The Capitol
contains an interesting collection of busts and statues of
all the Emperors, most famous characters of ancient Rome
and Greece together, with various magnificent objects of art.
By dint of repeatedly seeing their effigies, one becomes
acquainted with the faces of these worthies. These tastes
grow upon one strangely at Rome, and there is a sort of elevation arising from this silent intercourse with the 'great
of old.'

> Proud names, who once the reins of empire held,
> In arms who triumphed, or in arts excell'd,
> Chiefs graced with scars, and prodigal of blood,
> Stern patriots who for sacred freedom stood,
> Just men by whom impartial laws were given,
> And saints who taught, and led the way to heaven.
>
> TICKELL.

There has been a wrangle about the Borghese Gardens
which the Prince ordered to be shut up ; the Government
remonstrated, and a correspondence ensued which ended in
their being reopened to the public, whom he has no right
to exclude. Paul V. gave the Borghese Gardens to his
nephew (Aldobrandini) with a condition that they should
always be open to the public, which they have been from
then till now. They were a part of the Cenci property,
which was immense, and confiscated by an enormous piece
of injustice.

April 3rd.—Went on Thursday to Lady Mary Deerhurst's and the Duchess Torlonia's, where all the English in Rome (or rather all the most vulgar) were assembled. Yesterday morning to the Colonna Palace, Museum of the Capitol, Baths of Diocletian, now Church of Santa Maria degli Angeli, which are very remarkable because built on the baths, of which it has preserved the form ; San Pietro in Vincoli, San Bernardo, all built on the site and amidst the ruins of Titus's and Vespasian's Baths ; in various parts the old pavement is preserved, which shows how magnificent they must have been, for it is all of giallo, verd antique, porphyry, &c.   To the garden of the Maronite Convent to see the Coliseum, whence there is the finest view of it in Rome. Then to the Coliseum, and walked all over the ruins while a parcel of friars with covered faces were chanting and praying at each of the altars in succession round the circle below (called the Via Crucis).

I called yesterday morning on M. de la Ferronnays, the French Ambassador, who was very civil and obliging. Dined in the evening with Lord Haddington, Lovaine, Morier, Prince Gagarin the Russian Minister, Cheney, and M. Dedel. After dinner George Hamilton came in and said that Lady Northampton had died suddenly at five o'clock. I never saw her, but they say she was a very good sort of woman, and remarkably clever, which good sort of women seldom are. She had written a poem full of genius and imagination. Lord Northampton was absent at a *scavo* he has forty miles off.

There has been no rain here for two months, and the clouds of dust are insupportable ; as it is the town in Europe best supplied with water (there are three aqueducts ; the ancients had sixteen) so it is the worst watered. The excavations which are going on (though languidly) are always producing something. Two busts, said to be fine, were found the day before yesterday at the Borghese Villa at Frascati.

I saw yesterday at San Pietro in Vincoli Michael Angelo's famous Moses. It may be very fine, but to my eye is merely a colossal statue ; the two horns are meant to represent rays of light ; but how can rays of light be represented in marble,

x 2

any more than the breath? It is impossible to make marble imitate that which is impalpable. The beard is ropy and unnatural; it is, however, an imposing sort of figure. But I am more sensible to painting than to sculpture. I delight in almost everything of Domenichino's, who is only inferior (if inferior) to Raphael. As to Michael Angelo, he speaks a language the unlearned do not understand; his merit, acknowledged to be transcendent as it is by all artists, cannot be questioned; but he must serve as a model to form future excellence, and not be expected to produce present delight, except to those who, by long study, have learnt to comprehend and appreciate him.

Evening.—This morning to the tomb of the Scipios, Catacombs, Cecilia Metella (from which I wonder they don't take the battlements), the Circus of Maxentius, Temple of Bacchus, the Fountain of Egeria, San Stefano Rotondo, Temple of Pallas, Arches of Drusus and Dollabella, and the Borghese Villa and Gardens. The ruins of the Gaetani Castle are rather picturesque, but they spoil the tomb, which would be far finer without its turrets. The Circus is as curious as anything I have seen, for it looks like a fresh ruin. Old Torlonia furbished it up at his own expense, and brought to light the inscription which proved it to be Maxentius's instead of Caracalla's Circus. The remains are so perfect that it is easy to trace the whole arrangement of the ancient games. Forsyth says very truly that the Fountain of Egeria is a mere trough; but everybody praises the water, which is delicious, and it falls with a murmur which invites to idleness and contemplation. This fountain has been beautifully sung, but it is a miserable ruin, ill deserving of such strains.

> In vallem Egeriæ descendimus et speluncas
> Dissimiles veris—quanto præstantius esset
> Numen aquæ, viridi si margine clauderet undas
> Herba, nec ingenuum violarent marmora tophum.
>
> JUVENAL.

A little wood of firs, and pines, and ilexes about thirty or forty years old is pointed out as the grove in which Numa

used to meet the nymph. In all the views on one side So-
racte is a striking object, as it

> From out the plain
> Heaves like a long-swept wave about to break
> And on the curl hangs pausing.

I like this side of Rome, where the aqueducts stride over
the Campagna, and the ruins of the mighty Claudian tower
over the pigmy arches of the Pope, like the genius of
ancient over that of modern Rome. The Borghese is the
beau idéal of a villa; lofty, spacious apartments, adorned with
statues, busts, and marbles, painting and gilding, and magnificent gardens; but deserted by its owner, who has only
been there once in the last thirty years, and untenable in
the summer from malaria, which is very unaccountable, for
it is close to Rome, high, and full of trees; but nobody
knows anything about the malaria. The Gardens are the
fashionable lounge, but after June nobody can walk there.
Though the Prince never comes here, he has just bought a
large piece of ground between the Porta del Popolo and the
Gardens, and is making a handsome entrance, has already
built gates and some ugly Egyptian imitations, and is
making a waterfall. I dined with Lady William Russell,
and set off to go to Queen Hortense in the evening, but
found so few carriages in the court that we would not go in.

April 4th. —To the Sistine Chapel for the ceremonies of
Palm Sunday; we got into the body of the chapel, not without
difficulty; but we saw M. de la Ferronnays in his box, and he
let us in (Morier and me). It was only on a third attempt I
could get there, for twice the Papal halberdiers thrust me
back, and I find since it is lucky they did not do worse; for
upon some occasion one of them knocked a cardinal's eye
out, and when he found who he was, begged his pardon, and
said he had taken him for a bishop. Here I had a fine opportunity of seeing the frescoes, but they are covered with
dirt, the 'Last Judgment' neither distinguishable nor in-
telligible to me. The figures on the ceiling and walls are
very grand even to my ignorance. The music (all vocal)

beautiful, the service harmoniously chanted, and the re-
sponsive bursts of the chorus sublime. The cardinals appeared a wretched set of old twaddlers, all but about three
in extreme decrepitude—Odescalchi, who is young and a
good preacher, Gregorio, Capellari [afterwards Pope Gregory
XVI.]. On seeing them, and knowing that the sovereign
is elected by and from them, nobody can wonder that the
country is so miserably governed. These old creatures, on
the demise of a Pope, are as full of ambition and intrigue
as in the high and palmy days of the Papal power. Rome
and its territory are certainly worth possessing, though
the Pontifical authority is so shorn of its beams; but the
fact is that the man who is elected does not always govern
the country,[1] and he is condemned to a life of privation and
seclusion. An able or influential cardinal is seldom elected.
The parties in the Conclave usually end by a compromise,
and agree to elect some cardinal without weight or influence, and there are not now any Sixtus the Fifths to
make such an arrangement hazardous. Austria, Spain, and
France have all vetos, and Portugal claims and exercises one
when she can. To this degradation Rome is now obliged to
submit. The most influential of the cardinals is Albani.[2] At
the last election the Papal crown was offered to Cardinal
Caprara, but Albani stipulated that he should make him
Secretary of State; Caprara refused to promise, and Albani
procured the election of the present Pope (who did not desire or expect the elevation), became Secretary of State

---

[1] This, from what I have heard since, was not true of the last Pope,
Leo XII., who was an odious, tyrannical bigot, but a man of activity, talent,
and strength of mind, a good man of business, and his own Minister. He
was detested here, and there are many stories of his violent exertions of
authority. He was a sort of bastard Sixtus V., but at an immense distance
from that great man, 'following him of old, with steps unequal.' He used,
however, to interfere with the private transactions of society, and banish
and imprison people, even of high rank, for immorality.

[2] Albani holds the Austrian veto, and is supported by her authority.
But I have heard that since Clement XI., who was an Albani, there has
always been a powerful Albani faction in the Conclave. This cardinal is
enormously rich and the head of his house. The Duke of Modena is his
nephew, and it is generally thought will be his heir.

(being eighty), and governs the country. He is rich and
stingy. The great Powers still watch the proceedings of
the Conclave with jealousy; and though it is difficult to conceive how the Pope can assist any one of them to the detri-
ment of another, an Ambassador will put his veto upon any
cardinal whom he thinks unfavourable to his nation; this
produces all sorts of trickery, for when the Conclave want to
elect a man who is obnoxious to Austria, for example, they
choose another whom they think is equally so (but whom they
do not really wish to elect), that the veto may be expended
upon him, for each Government has one veto only. The last
veto absolutely put was on Cardinal ——, who was elected
on the death of Pius VII. He had behaved very rudely to
the Empress Maria Louisa when she took refuge in the north
of Italy after the downfall of Napoleon, thinking it was a
good moment to bully the abdicated Emperor's wife. She
complained to her father, who promised her the Cardinal
never should be Pope. He was a young and ambitious man,
and the veto killed him with vexation and disappointment.

Went and walked about St. Peter's, and was surprised to
find how very little longer it is than St. Paul's. To the Farnese Palace, built by Paul III. out of the ruins of the Coliseum, which now, with all the Farnese property, belongs to
the King of Naples, and is consequently going to decay.
It got into his hands by the marriage of a King of Naples
with the last heiress of the house of Farnese. The Neapolitan property here consists of the Farnese and Farnesina
Palaces, the Orti Farnesiani, and the Villa Madama, all in a
wretched state; and the Orti, in which there are probably
great remains, they will not allow to be excavated. Many
of the fine things are gone to Naples, but a few remain,
most of which came out of the Thermæ of Caracalla, and
originally from the Villa of Adrian. These two, principally
the one through the other, have been the great mines from
which the existing treasures of art were drawn. The
frescoes in this palace are beautiful—a gallery by Annibal
and Agostino Caracci, with a few pictures by Domenichino,
Guido, and Lanfranco. Annibal Caracci's are as fine as any

I have seen; also a little cabinet picture painted entirely by Annibal, which is exquisite.

As we were going to this palace we drove by the Cancellaria (which was likewise built out of the Coliseum), and heard by accident that a dead cardinal (Somaglia) was lying in state there. Somaglia was Secretary of State in Leo's time. Having seen all the living cardinals, we thought we might as well complete our view of the Sacred College with the dead one, and went up. After a great deal of knocking we were admitted to a private view half an hour before the public was let in. He had been embalmed, and lay on a bed under a canopy on an inclined plane, full dressed in cardinal's robes, new shoes on, his face and hands uncovered, the former looking very fresh (I believe he was rouged), his fingers black, but on one of them was an emerald ring, candles burning before the bed, and the window curtains drawn. He was 87 years old, but did not look so much, and had a healthier appearance in death than half the old walking mummies we had seen with palms in their hands in the morning.

Took a look at Pasquin, who had nothing but advertisements pasted upon him. I had seen Marphorius in the Capitol; there has long been an end to the witty dialogues of the days of Sixtus V., so quaintly told by Leti; they are so little 'birds of a feather' (for Pasquin is a mutilated fragment, Marphorius a colossal statue of the ocean) that, residing as they did at different parts of the town, it is difficult to understand how they ever came to converse with each other at all. I remember one of the best of his stories. Sixtus V. made his sister a princess, and she had been a washerwoman. The next day Pasquin appeared with a dirty shirt on. Marphorius asks him 'why he wears such foul linen;' and he answers 'that his washerwoman has been made a princess, and he can't get it washed.'

To the Farnesina: Raphael's frescoes, the famous Galatea, and the great head which Michael Angelo painted on the wall, as it is said as a hint to Raphael that he was too minute. There it is just as he left it. Here Raphael painted the Transfiguration, and here the Fornarina was shut up with

him that he might not run away from his work. It might
be thought that to shut up his mistress with him was not the
way to keep him to his work.   Be that as it may, the plan
was a good one which produced these frescoes and the Transfiguration.

I very nearly forgot to mention the Palazzo Spada, where
we went to see the famous statue of Pompey, which was
found on the spot where the Senate House formerly stood,
and which is (as certainly as these things can be certain)
the identical statue at the foot of which Cæsar fell.

> Muffling his face within his robe
> Ev'n at the base of Pompey's statue,
> Which all the while ran blood, great Cæsar fell.

People doubt this statue, because it is not like his busts.
There is certainly no resemblance to the bust I have seen,
which represents Pompey as a fat, vulgar-looking man with
a great double chin.   It is impossible for the coldest imagination to look at this statue without interest, for it calls up
a host of recollections and associations, standing before you
unchanged from the hour when Cæsar folded his robe round
him and 'consented to death' at its base.   Those who cannot feel this had better not come to Rome.   Cardinal Spada
was Secretary of State when this statue was found, and Julius
III. (Giocchi Del Monte, 1550) made him a present of it.

The Temple of Bacchus is one of the most remarkable objects in Rome; it is not in the least altered, merely turned
into a Christian church, and some saints, &c., painted on the
walls.   The mosaic ceiling and the pavement are just the same
as when it was devoted to the worship of the jolly god.   The
mosaics are beautiful, and perfect models of that sort of
ceiling.   The pavement is covered with names and other
scribblings cut out upon it, all ancient Roman.   Not a
column has been removed or mutilated.   The fact is, Rome
possesses several complete specimens of places of heathen
worship; this temple, the Pantheon, and San Stefano Rotondo
are perfect in the inside, the Pantheon within and without,
Vesta and Fortuna Virilis perfect on the outside.

In the Rospigliosi Palace is the famous Aurora of Guido. It is in excellent preservation, and three artists were copying it in oils. One copy was just finished, and admirably done, for which the painter asked forty louis. I begin to like frescoes better than oils; there is such a life and brilliancy about them. At the Quirinal, which was fitted up for the King of Rome and inhabited by the Emperor of Austria, we saw everything but the Pope's apartments. It is a delightful house, and commands a charming view of Rome. The Pope always goes there the last day of the Holy Week, and stays there all the summer. Nothing can be more melancholy than his life as described by the *custode*; he gets up very early, lives entirely alone and with the greatest simplicity. In short, it shows what a strange thing ambition is, which will sacrifice the substantial pleasures of life for the miserable shadow of grandeur. Coming home we stopped by accident at the Capuchins, and looked in to see Guido's St. Michael, with which I was disappointed till I looked at it from a distance. We then went to their catacombs, the most curious place I ever saw. There are a series of chapels in the cloisters, or rather compartments of one chapel, entirely fitted up with human bones arranged symmetrically and with all sorts of devices. They are laid out in niches, and each niche is occupied by the skeleton of a friar in the robes of his order; a label is attached to it with the name of the skeleton and the date of his death. Beneath are mounds of earth, each tenanted by a dead friar with similar labels. When a friar dies, the oldest buried friar, or rather his skeleton, is taken up and promoted to a niche, and the newly defunct takes possession of his grave; and so they go on in succession. I was so struck by this strange sight that, when I came home at night, I ventured on the following description of it :—

THE CATACOMBS IN THE CAPUCHIN CONVENT.

In yonder chapel's melancholy shade,
  Through which no wandering rays of daylight peep,
In strange and awful cemetery laid,
  The ancient Fathers of the convent sleep.

No storied marble with monastic pride
  Records the actions of their tranquil life,
Or tells how, fighting for their faith, they died
  Unconquer'd martyrs of religious strife.

They are not laid in decent shroud and pall,
  To wait, commingling with their kindred earth,
Th' Archangel's trumpet, whose dread blast shall call
  The whole creation to a second birth.

But midst the mouldering relics of the dead
  In shapes fantastic, which the brethren rear,
Profaned by heretic's unhallowed tread,
  The monkish skeletons erect appear.

The cowl is drawn each ghastly skull around,
  Each fleshless form's arrayed in sable vest,
About their hollow loins the cord is bound,
  Like living Fathers of the Order drest.

And as the monk around this scene of gloom
  The flick'ring lustre of his taper throws,
He says, ' Such, stranger, is my destined tomb ;
  Here, and with these, shall be my last repose.'

At night I went with a party of English to see the
Coliseum, but the moon was as English as the party, and
gave a faint and feeble light. Still, with this dim moon it
was inconceivably grand. The exquisite symmetry of the
building appears better, and its vast dimensions are more
developed by night. I long to see it with an Italian sky
and full moon; but not with a parcel of chattering girls,
who only ' flout the ruins grey.'

April 9th.—On Wednesday called on Bunsen, the Prussian Minister, who lives at the top of the Tarpeian Rock, in
a house commanding one of the best views of Rome. He has
devoted himself to the study of Roman history and antiquities, and has the whole subject at his fingers' ends. He is
really luminous, and his conversation equally amusing and
instructive. He is about to publish a book about ancient and
modern Rome, which, from what I hear, will be too minute

and prolix. I then went to look at the Tarpeian Rock, but the accumulation of earth has diminished its height—there is the Rock, but in a very obscure hole. It was probably twice as high as it is now. I think it is now about forty feet. Bunsen says that though the antiquaries pretend to point out the course of the ancient triumphal way, he does not think it can ever be ascertained. The only remains (only bits of foundations) of the temple of the Capitoline Jupiter, to which the conquerors ascended, are in the garden under his windows. He thinks the population of ancient Rome may be taken at two millions at its most flourishing period. It is curious that there are hardly any houses on the hills on which ancient Rome was built, and that there were none formerly where modern Rome stands —no private houses, only public buildings and temples.

To the Mamertine Prisons, probably not a stone of which has been changed from the time that Jugurtha was starved in them. The tradition about St. Peter and the well of course is not to be believed; but it is very odd there should be a well there when there are so few in Rome. To the Sistine Chapel with M. de la Ferronnays, and very much disappointed with the music, which was not so good as on Sunday; nor was the ceremony accompanying the Miserere at all imposing. Yesterday morning to the Sistine again; prodigious crowd, music moderate. As soon as it was over we set off to see the benediction; and, after fighting, jostling, and squeezing through an enormous crowd, we reached the *loggia* over one side of the colonnade. The Piazza of St. Peter's is so magnificent that the sight was of necessity fine, but not near so much so as I had fancied. The people below were not numerous or full of reverence. Till the Pope appears the bands play and the bells ring, when suddenly there is a profound silence; the feathers are seen waving in the balcony, and he is borne in on his throne; he rises, stretches out his hands, blesses the people—URBI ET ORBI—and is borne out again. A couple of indulgences were tossed out, for which there is a scramble, and so it ends. Off we scampered, and by dint of tremendous exertions, reached the hall in which the feet of the pilgrims are washed. The Pope could not attend, so the Cardinal Deacon officiated. No ceremony can be less imposing, but none more clean. Thirteen men are ranged on a bench—the thirteenth represents the angel who once joined the party—dressed in new white caps, gowns, and shoes; each holds out his foot in succession; an attendant pours a few drops of water on it from a golden jug which another receives in a golden basin; the cardinal wipes it with a towel, kisses the foot, and then gives the towel, a nosegay, and a piece of money to the pilgrim—the whole thing takes up about five minutes—certain prayers are said, and it is over. Then off we scampered again through the long galleries of the Vatican to another hall where the pilgrims dine. The arrangements for the accommodation of the Ambassadors and strangers were so bad that all these passages were successive scenes of uproar, scrambling, screaming, confusion, and danger, and, considering that the ceremonies were all religious, really disgraceful. We got with infinite difficulty to another box, raised aloft in the hall, and saw a long table at which the thirteen pilgrims seated themselves; a cardinal in the corner read some prayers, which nobody listened to, and another handed the dishes to the pilgrims, who looked neither to the right nor the left, but applied themselves with becoming gravity to the enjoyment of a very substantial dinner. The whole hall was filled with people, all with their hats on, chattering and jostling, and more like a ring of blacklegs and blackguards at Tattersall's than respectable company at a religious ceremony in the palace of the Pope. There remained the cardinals' dinner, but I had had more than enough, and came away hot, jaded, and disgusted with the whole affair.

.In the evening I went to St. Peter's, when I was amply recompensed for the disappointment and bore of the morning. The church was crowded; there was a Miserere in the chapel, which was divine, far more beautiful than anything I have heard in the Sistine, and it was the more effective because at the close it really was night. The lamps were extinguished at the shrine of the Apostle, but one altar—the altar of the Holy Sepulchre—was brilliantly illuminated. Presently the Grand Penitentiary, Cardinal Gregorio, with his train entered, went and paid his devotions at this shrine, and then seated himself on the chair of the Great Confessional, took a golden wand, and touched all those who knelt before him. Then came a procession of pilgrims bearing muffled crosses ; penitents with faces covered, in white, with tapers and crosses ; and one long procession of men headed by these muffled figures, and another of women accompanied by ladies, a lady walking between every two pilgrims. The cross in the procession of women was carried by the Princess Orsini, one of the greatest ladies in Rome. They attended them to the church (the Trinità delle Pellegrine) and washed their feet and fed them. A real washing of dirty feet. Both the men and the women seemed of the lowest class, but their appearance and dresses were very picturesque. These processions entered St. Peter's, walked all round the church, knelt at the altars, and retired in the same order, filing along the piazza till they were lost behind the arches of the colonnades. As the shades of night fell upon the vast expanse of this wonderful building it became really sublime; 'the dim religious light' glimmering from a distant altar, or cast by the passing torches of the procession, the voices of the choir as they sang the Miserere swelling from the chapel, which was veiled in dusk, and with no light but that of the high taper half hid behind the altar, with the crowds of figures assembled round the chapel moving about in the obscurity of the aisles and columns, produced the most striking effect I ever beheld. It was curious, interesting, and inspiring—little of mummery and much of solemnity. The night here brings out fresh beauties, but of the most majestic character. There is a colour in an Italian twilight that I have never seen in England, so soft, and beautiful, and grey, and the moon rises 'not as in northern climes obscurely bright,' but with far-spreading rays around her. The figures, costume, and attitudes that you see in the

churches are wonderfully picturesque. I went afterwards to
the Jesù, where there was a tiresome service (the Tre Ore),
and heard a Jesuit preaching with much passion and em-
phasis, but could not understand a word he said. So then I
called on Cheney and saw his mother's illustrations of Milton,
which are admirable, full of genius.

At night.—To St. Peter's, where the Miserere was not so
good as last night. It was reported that the Pope was
coming to St. Peter's, and the Swiss Guards lined the nave,
but he did not arrive. Formerly, when the Cross was illuminated, he used to come with all the cardinals to adore it.
Now the cardinals (or rather some of them) came and adored
the Cross and the relics belonging to the church, which
were exhibited in succession from one of the balconies—a
bit of the true Cross, Santa Veronica's bloody handkerchief,
and others. There were, as the night before, several fra-
ternities of penitents, some in black, others in white or
brown, all disguised by long hoods, but there was to-night
one of the most striking and remarkable exhibitions I ever
beheld.

The Grand Penitentiary, Cardinal Gregorio, again took
his seat in the chair of the Great Confessional. All those
who have been absolved after confession by their priest,
and who present themselves before him, are touched with
his golden wand, in token of confirmation of the absolution; and here again that quality which I have so often
remarked as one of the peculiar characteristics of the Catholic
religion is very striking. Men and women, beggars and
princesses, present themselves indiscriminately; they all
kneel in a row, and he touches them in succession. In the
churches there seem to be no distinctions of rank; no one,
however great or rich, is contaminated by the approximation
of poverty and rags. But to return to the Confessional.
There are some crimes of such enormity that absolution
for them can only be granted by the Pope himself, who de-
legates his power to the Grand Penitentiary, and he receives
such confessions in the chair in which he was seated to-day.
They are, however, very rare; but this evening, after he had

finished touching the people, a man, dressed like a peasant in a loose brown frock, worsted stockings, and brogues, apparently of the lowest order, dark, ill-looking, and squalid, approached the Confessional to reveal some great crime. The confession was very long, so was the admonition of the Cardinal which followed it. The appearance of the Cardinal is particularly dignified and noble, and, as he bent down his head, joining it to that of this ruffian-like figure, listening with extreme patience and attention, and occasionally speaking to him with excessive earnestness, while the whole surrounding multitude stood silently gazing at the scene, all conscious that some great criminal was before them, but none knowing the nature of the crime, it was impossible not to be deeply interested and impressed with such a spectacle. Nothing could exceed the patience of the Cardinal and the intensity with which he seemed absorbed in the tale of the penitent. When it was over he wiped his face, as if he had been agitated by what he heard. It was impossible not to feel that be the balance for or against confession (which is a difficult question to decide, though I am inclined to think the balance is against) it is productive of some good effects, and, though susceptible of enormous abuses, is a powerful instrument of good when properly used. I have no doubt it is largely abused, but it is the most powerful weapon of the Romish Church, the one, I believe, by which it principally lives, moves, and has its being. That penitence must be real, and of a nature to be worked upon, which can induce a man to come forward in the face of multitudes and exhibit himself as the perpetrator of some atrocious though unknown crime.

At night I went to the Trinità dei Pellegrini to see the pilgrims at supper. The washing of the feet was over; a cardinal performs it with the men, and ladies with the women, but it is no mere ceremony as at the Vatican; they really do wash and scrub the dirty feet perhaps of about a dozen of them each night. I saw the room in which they were just clearing away the apparatus and collecting piles of dirty towels. The pilgrims sit on benches; under their feet

are a number of small wooden tubs, with cocks to turn the
water into them, and there they are washed. Afterwards they
go to supper, and then to bed. The men sup in a very long
hall—most curious figures, and natives of half the world.
The Cardinal Camerlengo[1] says grace and cuts the meat.
They are waited upon by gentlemen and priests, and have
a very substantial meal. The women are treated in the same
way.[2] No men are admitted to their hall, but we contrived
to get to the door and saw it all. The Princess Orsini and
a number of Roman ladies were there (who had been washing
feet) with aprons on, waiting upon them at supper. Their
dormitories were spacious, clean, and sweet, though the beds
were crowded together. The pilgrims are kept there from
Palm Sunday to Easter Sunday, when they are dismissed.
Their numbers are generally about 250 or 300. The funds
of the establishment are supplied by private subscriptions,
legacies, and donations, the names of the benefactors, with
the amount of their contributions, being recorded on boards
hung up in the hall. There were a great many spectators,
but the whole ceremony was ordered with regularity and
decency, which is more than can be said for those of the
Vatican. I walked to-night to St. Peter's, to look at it by
moonlight. From every point of view it is magnificent; the
stillness of the night is broken only by the waters of the foun-

---

[1] Minister of the Interior and Chamberlain; but Consalvi deprived the
Camerlengo of his Ministerial functions, and joined them to the Secretaryship of State, and so it has since remained.

[2] I met Lady ——, a very tiresome woman, a day or two after, who had
been to see this ceremony, and was most devoutly edified by the humility
and charity of the ladies. She told me a very old woman put out her foot
to her, thinking she was one of them, and begged her to be very careful, as
she had got some sores produced by the itch; but as it formed no part of
her Protestant duty, she turned her over to the Princess Orsini, who handled
this horrid old leg with great tenderness; and afterwards, when the same
Princess was handed into the other apartment to see the male pilgrims at
supper, by an attendant in the livery which they all wore, this attendant
turned out to be Prince Corsini. It sounds very fine, but after all I don't
think there is much in it. It is ostentatious charity and humility, and
though rather disgusting and disagreeable, it is the fashion, and those who
do it are set up in a capital stock of piety and virtue. It may be both cause
and effect of great moral excellence, but I think it questionable.

tains, which glitter in the moonbeams like sheets of molten silver. The obelisk, the façade, the cupola, and the columns all contribute to the grandeur and harmony of the scene : but everything at Rome should be seen at night. The Castle of St. Angelo, the Tiber, and the Bridge are all wonderfully fine in these bright nights.

April 10*th.*—In the morning to St. John Lateran, where, as my *laquais de place* said, ' converted Jews, or Turks, or *Lutherans* ' were baptised ; got too late for the baptism, which I believe is a farce regularly got up, but heard the High Mass. The churches were crowded all this week with pilgrims, whose appearance is always very picturesque. Went into the cloisters, and was shown by the monk or priest (whichever he was) some very remarkable articles that they possess—a bit of the column on which the cock stood when he crowed after Peter's three denials ; a slab showing the exact height of Jesus Christ, as He could just stand under it,[1] and two halves which had once been a whole column, but which was broken when the veil of the Temple was rent on the death of Christ. The column is adorned with sculpture, which they say is Jewish, and was brought to Rome with the Holy Stairs. Then to Santa Croce in Gerusalemme, where they were performing High Mass, with many assistants and a full choir, but without a congregation ; there were not six people in the church. To Minerva Medica, a questionable and uninteresting ruin, and besides falling to pieces. To the Barberini Palace, where there is little besides the Cenci, which is worth going any distance to see. To the Doria, a magnificent palace, with an immense number of pictures, and some very fine ones, which I was hurried through. To the Pyramid of Caius Cestius, which is in the middle of the wall of Aurelian, and forms the back of a very pretty Protestant burial ground, the greatest number of those who have been buried there being of course English. It is on the side of a hill with high, turreted walls behind it. There are two rows of white marble tombs, whose diminutive proportions form a contrast with the enormous sepulchre of

[1] He must have been just six feet high.

the Roman. Round some of the tombstones rose-trees and other shrubs have been planted, and all but one adorned with epitaphs and inscriptions in Latin, English, German, and Italian. That one is the tomb of the pretty Miss Bathurst who was drowned in the Tiber. Her mother was to have returned to Rome and supply the epitaph, but she has never come, and it has not even her name inscribed upon it. I copied the following, which are apparently intended for Latin verses, from one of the tombs—of Frederica Ursulina Arabella de Montmorency, by her father, Colonel Raymond Henry de Montmorency, whose feelings set quantity at defiance:—

> Frederica quæ claris fueram prælata puellis
>   Illa ego hoc brevi condita sum tumulo;
> Cui formam pulcherrimam, charites tribuere decoram
>   Quam Deus cunctis artibus erudiit.

Clambered up Monte Testaccio, from which the view is beautiful, and then went on to the ruins of San Paolo fuori le Mure. The church, which was the finest in Rome except St. Peter's, was entirely destroyed by fire; but although it is near three miles from the gates, and not the least wanted, and that there are hundreds of churches, half of which seldom or never have congregations to fill them, they are already rebuilding this at an enormous cost, and the priest told me, to my great disgust, that they had got all the materials ready, and in ten years they expected the work to be finished. There are plenty of fools found to contribute to the expense, the greatest part of which, however, is supplied by the Government. It is to be built just as it was before, but they cannot replace the enormous marble columns which were its principal ornament. To a church to hear the Armenian Mass. The priests arrived in splendid oriental dresses, but I did not stay it out. Walked to the Borghese Gardens, the fine weather being something of which no description can convey an idea, and in it the beauty of Rome and its gardens and environs are equally indescribable. Groups of pilgrims in their odd dresses, with staves, and great bundles on their heads, were lounging about, or lying under the trees. At night to the Coliseum (but the moon never will shine properly), and back by the Forum and the Capitol. The columns in the Forum look beautiful, but St. Peter's gains at least as much as the ancient ruins by the light of the moon. The views from different hills, and sunset from the Pincian in such weather as this, and with spring bursting in every direction, are things never to be forgotten.

Sunday.—High Mass in St. Peter's, which was crowded. I walked about the church to see the groups and the extraordinary and picturesque figures moving through the vast space. They are to the last degree interesting : in one place hundreds prostrate before an altar—pilgrims, soldiers, beggars, ladies, gentlemen, old and young in every variety of attitude, costume, and occupation. The benediction was much finer than on Thursday, the day magnificent, the whole piazza filled with a countless multitude, all in their holiday dresses, and carriages in the back-ground to the very end. The troops forming a brilliant square in the middle, the immense population and variety of costume, the weather, and the glorious locality certainly made as fine a spectacle as can possibly be seen. The Pope is dressed in white, with the triple crown on his head ; two great fans of feathers, exactly like those of the Great Mogul, are carried on each side of him. He sits aloft on his throne, and is slowly borne to the front of the balcony. The moment he appears there is a dead silence, and every head is bared. When he rises, the soldiers all fall on their knees, and some, but only a few, of the spectators. The distance is so great that he looks like a puppet, and you just see him move his hands and make some signs. When he gives the blessing— the sign of the cross—the cannon fires. He blesses the people twice, remains perhaps five minutes in the balcony, and is carried out as he came in.

The numbers who come to the benediction are taken as a test of the popularity of the Pope, though I suppose the weather has a good deal to do with it. Leo XII. was very unpopular from his austerity, and particularly his shutting up the wine shops. The first time he gave the benediction after that measure hardly anybody came to be blessed.

At night.—The illumination of St. Peter's is as fine as I was told it was, and that is saying everything. I saw it from the Pincian, from the windows of the French Academy and Horace Vernet's room. He is established in the Villa Medici; a very lively little fellow, and making a great deal of money as director of the Academy and by his paintings. His daughter is very pretty. Here I met Savary, the Duc de Rovigo, a tall, stout, vulgar-looking man. We were introduced and conversed on French politics. Afterwards drove down to the piazza and round it. The illumination is more effective at a distance, but I think it looks best from the entrance to the piazza and the Bridge of St. Angelo; the blaze of light, the crowd, and the fountains, covered with a red glare, made altogether the most splendid sight in the world. (One poor devil was killed, and there is almost always some accident.) Eight hundred men are employed in illuminating St. Peter's; the first pale and subdued light, which covers the whole church, is brought out by the darkness of night, the little lamps being lit in the day-time. The blazing lights which succeed are made by large pots of grease with wicks in them; there is one man to every two lamps. On a given signal, each man touches his two lamps as quick as possible, so that the whole building bursts into light at once by a process the effect of which is quite magical—literally, as the Rejected Addresses say, 'starts into light, and makes the lighter start.'

April 12th.—At night at Torlonia's to see the girandola, which is as fine as fireworks can be, but nothing will do after the illumination of St. Peter's. All the world was there at an assembly after the ceremony, at which I was introduced to Don Michele Gaetani, said to be the cleverest man in Rome, and I had a long conversation with Monsignore Spada, who is a young layman with ecclesiastical rank and costume, and a judge. A Monsignore holds ecclesiastical rank at Rome, as a Lady of the Bedchamber at St. Petersburg holds military rank, where she is a major-general; there is no other. He is free to marry, and I presume to do anything else, but he must preserve a certain orthodox gravity of dress and conduct; he is a curious nondescript, about an equal mixture of the cardinal and the dandy. This Monsignore is a very clever, agreeable man, and gave me some information about the administration of law in this country. There seems to be a good deal of laxity in it, for a man was condemned for stabbing another (with premeditation) a little while ago to six months' imprisonment, or more perhaps; and having been George Hamilton's *laquais de place*, his family came to him and begged him to try and get him off. He applied to Spada, and got the punishment commuted to some trifling imprisonment, and when he got out he came, with all his family, to kiss Hamilton's hand.

April 13th.—Breakfasted with Bunsen at the Capitol; Lovaine, Morier, Haddington, Hamilton, Kestner, Falck, G. Fitzclarence, Sir W. Gell, a little Italian servant, and Mr. Hall, Bunsen's brother-in-law. Haddington told the story of Canning's sending to Bagot a despatch in cipher, containing these lines:—

> In matters of commerce the fault of the Dutch
> Is giving too little and asking too much;
> With equal protection the French are content:
> So we'll lay on Dutch bottoms just twenty per cent.
> > *Chorus of Officers.*—We'll lay, &c.
> > *Chorus of Douaniers.*—Nous frapperons Falck avec
> > Twenty per cent.

He received the despatch at dinner, and sent it to be deciphered. After some hours they brought him word they did not know what to make of it, for it seemed to be in verse, when he at once saw there was a joke.

Went to see the excavations in the Via Triumphalis and the Temple of Concord, and heard Bunsen's theory of the Forum. Bunsen gives different names to the remains of the temples in the Forum from those which have been usually given, and by which they are known, and on very plausible grounds, drawn chiefly from accounts in different Roman authors and peculiarities in the buildings themselves. The

Temple of Fortune he thinks was the Basilica of Augustus, and the Temple of Jupiter Tonans the Temple of Saturn; but all his reasons I need not put down if I could remember them, for are they not written in the voluminous work he is going to publish in four or six volumes octavo?

Bunsen's history is rather curious. He was a poor German student destined for the Church; came to Rome, and got employed by Niebuhr, from whom he first got a taste for antiquities. The King of Prussia came to Rome and saw him; he was struck with his knowledge and the character he heard of him, and consulted him about a new Liturgy he wished to introduce into Prussia. Bunsen gave him so much satisfaction in that matter, as well as in some others which were entrusted to him, that on Niebuhr's return to Prussia he was appointed to succeed him, and has been at Rome ever since—thirteen years. Some say he is not a profound man, and that his speculations about the ruins are all wrong. He talks English, French, and Italian like his own language.

The part of the triumphal road was discovered by accident in digging for a drain; and an attempt is being made to procure the permission of the Government to excavate all that can be found of it, and ascertain its exact course. It was in the Temple of Concord that Cicero assembled the Senate and pronounced one of his orations against Catiline. The building must have been large and magnificent, from the remains now visible, which are of the finest marble. The pavement is in a state of considerable preservation. Then we went to the old Tabularium, standing on the Intermontium, an undoubted work of the Republic. This was the place where the records of the Senate were kept. It is very perfect. Nibby, the great authority here, differs, however, about this place; the antiquaries are at daggers drawn upon the subject of the ruins, remains, and discoveries. They have all different systems, which they support with great vehemence and obstinacy, and perhaps ingenuity, but the ignorant and curious traveller is only perplexed with their noisy and discordant assertions. They will insist upon know-

ing everything, whereas there are many things here which
are so doubtful, that they can only conjecture about them;
but when once they have published a theory they will not
hear of its being erroneous, and oppose any fresh discovery
likely to throw discredit upon it.   After his lecture in the
Forum we went to San Nicolo in Carcere, an old church built
on three old temples, or two and a prison, but not much to
see.   The prison of San Nicolo in Cercera is said to be the
scene of the story of the Roman daughter, which it probably
is not.   Over the Bridge of Fabricius to the Basilica of Saint
Bartholomew and Temple of Esculapius ; small remains, but
curious ; and very pretty view of the Tiber and Temple of
Vesta.   To the Villa Lanti, a delicious villa belonging to
Prince Borghese, who never goes there, and will neither let
nor lend it.   One of the finest views of Rome is from the
terrace, and Julio Romano's frescoes adorn the ceilings.
When Raphael was painting the Vatican, he and Julio
Romano used to retire every night to the Villa Lanti, and
the ceilings are covered with frescoes painted by both of
them.   Just below is a terrace, and on it a beautiful tree
called Tasso's Oak, because under it he used to sit and compose when he lived in the Convent of San Onofrio, which is
close by, and where he died.   This convent is remarkably
clean, airy, and spacious.   In the library is a bust of Tasso,
a mask taken from his face just after he died ; in the chapel
his tomb.

> And Tasso is their glory—
> Hark to his strain and then survey his cell.
>   Byron.

In the cloister are some frescoes of the universal Domenichino.
I like the Convent of San Onofrio.   To Santa Maria in
Trastevere, a very fine church ; splendid ceiling with a
Domenichino in the middle.   Immense granite columns of
various orders taken from God knows what temples, and
mosaic floor rich to a degree.   Large pieces of porphyry and
verd antique eternally trodden by the Trasteverine mob, and
never even cleaned.   It is a basilica, and at the end is an

ancient stone chair, which was evidently the old justice-seat, though they of the Church do not know it.

April 14*th.*—Set off early to make up an arrear of churches. First to Santa Maria sopra Minerva, and lit upon the funeral of a cardinal (Bertazzoli), which I was obliged to see instead of Michael Angelo's Christ. All the cardinals attended; the church hung with black and gold; guards, tapers, mob, &c. Then to the SS. Apostoli, Araceli (built where the Citadel stood, and is a corruption of Arx, but with a legend); a curious church enough, with some fine frescoes of Pinturicchio, and the Chapel of the Virgin with hundreds of ex voto's hung round it, almost all wretched daubs of pictures, and principally representing accidents in gigs, carriages, or carts, broken heads or limbs. To Santa Anastasia, Santa Maria in Cosmedin, Santa Sabina. Santa Maria in Cosmedin, or the Bocca della Verità, built in and on the ruins of an old temple (di Pudicizia), is one of the best worth seeing in Rome; the columns, if freed from the modern church, would present as perfect a front as the temples in the Forum. To Monte Aventino to see the view of Rome and the Chapel of the Order of Malta, where Cardinal Zurla as Grand Prior has a most agreeable residence. The garden contains immense orange-trees and a very large palm. To San Gregorio to see the famous rival frescoes of Guido and Domenichino, which are much impaired. I began by liking Guido's and ended by liking the other best. The view of the Palatine from this convent is magnificent. To San Gregorio and San Paolo, and saw the ruins, which must have belonged to the Coliseum, for the architecture is exactly similar, and they have every appearance of having been the Vivarium from their shape. To the Corsini Palace, containing one of the best collections of pictures, of which the finest are two portraits of cardinals by Raphael and Domenichino. The palace is very fine, and the villa joins it on the opposite hill of the Janiculum, but both are affected by the malaria. Then to the Vatican and saw all the frescoes and pictures; the collection of pictures is very small, but they are all masterpieces. To the gallery below to see the mosaics and the process of copying the great pictures. The coloured bits are numbered, and though there are not above six or seven colours, the sub-divisions of various shades amount to 18,000. This art is in a great degree mechanical, but requires ingenuity, attention, and some knowledge of painting. On the large pictures, such as those which are in St. Peter's, several men are employed at the same time, but on the lesser only one. It is very tedious, requiring years to copy one of the largest size. All the pictures in St. Peter's are in mosaic, except one, and they are at work on one which is to replace this single oil-piece. The studio appeared in good order, but there were only two men at work, as the Government spends very little money upon it at present. From one of the open galleries we (Morier and I) saw a thunderstorm, with gusts of wind, flashes of lightning, and rain. It was amazingly grand from that place as it swept over the city and made us 'sharers in its fierce delight.' Then to the Borghese Gardens, and back to one of those sunsets from the Pincian which will long be remembered among the smoke and fogs in which I am destined to live.

CHAPTER IX.

Velletri, April 15*th.*—Left Rome at nine o'clock this morning; at Albano procured an ancient rural cicerone, a boy, and two donkeys, and set out on the grand *giro* of the place. The road over the Campagna is agreeable, because the prospect roundabout is so fine, and the aqueducts stretching over the plain so grand. After climbing up to the Capuchin Convent, close to which are the remains of what is called Domitian's Theatre, we came to the lake, which is beautiful, but does not look large, and still less as if it had ever threatened Rome with destruction. There is a road called the Upper Gallery, shaded by magnificent ilexes which leads to the Villa Barberini, a delicious garden, once Clodius's and afterwards part of Domitian's Villa, containing many remains of former magnificence. This villa was probably the scene of the council described by Juvenal (Fourth Satire).

> Misso proceres exire jubentur
> Concilio, quos Albanam Dux magnus in arcem
> Traxerat attonitos.

I could not make out that any excavations have ever been made here, though they would be certain of finding marbles. The road passes along the hill which overhangs the margin of the lake to Castel Gandolfo, and thence a path leads to the bottom, where are the Emissarium, the Nymphæum (called the Baths of Diana), and a beautiful view of the lake, Monte Albano, and its towns. There is nothing more curious than the Emissarium, built with a solidity which has defied the effect of time, for it has never required reparations, and performs its office still as it did more than 2,000 years ago (393 years before the Christian era). Nothing is so incomprehensible as the magnitude and grandeur of the works of the Republic before it had acquired power, territory, or population. The Romans built as if they had an instinctive prescience of future greatness, and not even the pressure of immediate danger could induce them to sacrifice solidity to haste. After wondering at their enterprise and industry we may go and admire their subsequent luxury in the Baths of Diana, as the place is called, but which is evidently a natural cave improved into a delicious retreat by some inhabitant of one of the villas above. We mounted the hill and went by another road (called the Lower Gallery, shaded by the finest ilexes, elms, and oaks, which 'high over-arch'd embower,' and where there is one ilex which twelve men can hardly embrace) to the Doria Villa, once Pompey's and likewise Domitian's, who included both Clodius's and Pompey's in his own. There are no remains here, but some arabesques in a sort of grotto, which I suspect are modern. All their villas command views of the Campagna, the sea, Rome, and the mountains. It is no wonder Hannibal was deeply mortified when he looked down on Rome from these hills (the hills at least close by called the Prati d'Annibale) at having twice just missed taking it. Poetry and history contribute alike to the interest of this beautiful scenery. We met an Englishman, a single bird who had lost his covey, and had procured a guide who could not understand what he said. He wanted to go to Albano, and the man was taking him to the Emissarium. We put him right, but his fury in mixed Italian, French, and English was exceedingly comical. It was unlucky that we met him at the top instead of the bottom of the hill.

The road to Aricia, where Horace got such a bad dinner—

Egressum magnâ me excepit Aricia Româ
Hospitio modico—

is beautiful, and close to Genzano we went to look at the
Lake of Nemi, which is very pretty, but not so grand as
Albano. The peasantry are a fine race in these parts, and
we met many men driving carts or riding asses who would
not disgrace the most romantic group of banditti. The
people were all working in the open air, and seemed very
gay. There were few beggars, and not much rags and
wretchedness.

Started from Velletri at six in the morning; went very
quick over the Pontine Marshes (which form an avenue of
about twenty miles, quite straight, shaded with trees, and
with vegetation of remarkable luxuriance on each side) to
Terracina (Anxur), where we breakfasted in a room looking
upon the sea. The place is extremely pretty. Thence to
Mola di Gaeta, which is very beautiful, but where we did
not stop; and, after a very tiresome journey, got to Naples
at two o'clock in the morning. Vesuvius was so obliging as
to emit some flames as we passed by, just to show us his
whereabouts. They were, however, his first and his last while
I was at Naples.

Naples, April 18th.—I am disappointed with Naples. I
looked for more life and gaiety, a more delicious air, beautiful
town, and picturesque lazaroni, more of Punch, more smoke
and flame from Vesuvius. It strikes me as less beautiful
than Genoa, but these are only first impressions. The Bay
and the Villa Reale, a garden along the sea, full of sweets
and sea breezes and shade, are certainly delightful. All the
people seem anxious to cheat as much as they can, from the
master of the inn to the driver of the hackney coach. At
present I don't feel disposed to stay here, and when I
have seen Pæstum, Pompeii, and the environs I shall be
glad to get back to Rome. Sir Henry Lushington said
at dinner yesterday he had seen at Naples a 'Courier'
newspaper of that day week, produced by Rothschild and
brought by one of his couriers. It came very fast, but was
236 hours on the road, including 20 hours' stoppage. This

is 168 hours, which appears incredible, but ' gold imp'd by Jews can compass hardest things.'

April 19*th.*—I retract all I said about disappointment, for I have since seen Naples, and it is the most beautiful and the gayest town in the world. Yesterday morning with Morier I walked up to the Castle of St. Elmo and the Certosa ; went over the chapel, which is full of costly marbles, and fine pictures, both in oil and fresco, particularly one by Spagnolet as fine as any at Rome or anywhere. Tasted the *custode's* lachryma Christi, which, if it be as good of the sort as he pretends, is middling stuff, but not bad with water. Saw all the views, which are magnificent. Walked down to the Villa Reale, which was crowded with people, and the Chiaja with carriages. Dined with Hill—half English and half foreigners—and went to the Opera ; a very indifferent opera of Rossini, ill sung, called the ' Siege of Corinth.'

This morning at half-past eight we went to the Court of Justice to hear an extraordinary trial which excites great interest here. The proceedings of the day happened to be very uninteresting, not that it made much difference, for I could not understand a word anybody said, but I had an opportunity of seeing the manner in which they conduct trials in this country, and the behaviour of the judges, the counsel, and the prisoners. Nothing can be less analogous than the proceedings here to those which prevail in our courts ; and although it is possible that ours might be better, it is not possible that theirs could be worse.

I soon left the Court, and walked up the Strada di Toledo— the finest and liveliest street in the world, I believe—crowded with people. An Italian proverb says, ' Quando Dio onni- potente è tristo, prende una finestra nel Toledo.' Then to the Museum, of which everything was shut but the library and the papyri. The former contains 180,000 volumes, but is deficient in modern (particularly foreign) books. They showed us the process of deciphering the papyri, which is very ingenious. The manuscript (which is like a piece of charcoal) is suspended by light strings in a sort of frame ; gum and goldbeater's skin are applied to it as it is unrolled, and, by extreme delicacy of touch, they contrive to unravel without destroying a great deal of it, but probably they have been discouraged by the small reward which has attended their exertions; for there are several black-looking rolls which have never yet been touched, and very few men at work. The gentlemen who explained to us the process said that Sir Humphrey Davy had attended them constantly, and had taken great pains to contrive some better chemical process for the purpose, but without success.

April 20th.—A delightful drive (made by Murat) to the Marquis di Gallo's villa on the Capo di Monte, which far surpasses all the villas I saw at Rome. The entrance is about half a mile from the house, through a wood, one part of which is a vineyard; the vines hanging in festoons from cherry trees, and corn growing underneath. The house is not large, but convenient; a wide terrace runs along the whole front of it with a white marble balustrade; below this is a second terrace covered with rose-trees; below that a third, planted with vines, and oranges, and myrtles. From the upper terrace the view is beautiful. Naples lies beneath, and the Bay stretches beyond with the opposite mountains, and all the towns and villages from Portici to Sorrento. On the right the Castle of St. Elmo and the Certosa, and Vesuvius on the left. There is a large wood on one side, cut into shady walks and laid out with grottoes, and on the other a vineyard, through which there is also a walk under a treillage of vines for nearly half a mile. The ground extremely diversified, and presenting in every part of it views of the surrounding country—

> Umbrageous grots and caves
> Of cool recess, o'er which the mantling vine
> Lays forth her purple grape, and gently creeps
> Luxuriant.

It is always let, and, till he went away, was occupied by Stackelberg, the Russian Ambassador.

In the evening went to a ball at the Duchesse d'Eboli's; very few people, and hardly any English, and those not the best—only four, I think: Sir Henry Lushington, the Consul;

a Mr. Grieve, of whom I know nothing but that his father was a physician at St. Petersburg, and that he killed his brother at Eton by putting a cracker into his pocket on the 5th of November, which set fire to other crackers and burnt him to death; Mr. Auldjo, the man who made a very perilous ascent of Mont Blanc, of which he published a narrative; Mr. Arbuthnot, who levanted from Doncaster two years ago—but most of the Italian women were there, and I was surprised at their beauty. Acton, who introduced me to some of them, assured me that they were models of conduct, which did not precisely tally with my preconceived notions of Neapolitan society. They danced, but with no music but a pianoforte. This is one of the few houses here which is habitually open, for they have not the means of doing much in the way of society and gaiety; they are poor, and the Government (the worst in the world) interferes. The Duchesse d'Eboli is poor, but she was a beauty, and has had adventures of various sorts.

April 21st.—Dined with Keppel Craven yesterday; Acton, Morier, Duchesse d'Eboli, and some other people.

The day was so disagreeable yesterday I could not go out—not cold, but a hurricane and clouds of dust. The principal topic of conversation at dinner was the trial, which goes on every day, has already lasted a month, and is likely to last two or three more. The Code Napoléon is in force here, so that there may probably be something like a certain and equal administration of justice between man and man; but this is a Government prosecution, and therefore exempted from ordinary rules. The history of this trial exemplifies the state of both the law and the Government of this country. The accused are five in number; the principal of them, Matteis, was an *intendente*, or governor, of a province; 2nd, the advocate-general of the province; 3rd, Matteis's secretary; and 4th and 5th, two spies. These men united in a conspiracy to destroy various persons who were obnoxious to them in the province, some of them actuated by political motives, and others in order to get possession of the property of their victims. The bugbear of the Court is Carbonarism, and Matteis pretended that there was a Carbonari plot on foot, in which several persons were implicated. He employed the spies to seduce the victims into some imprudence of language or conduct, and then to inform against them; in this way he apprehended various individuals, some of whom were tortured, some imprisoned or sent to the galleys, and some put to death. These transactions took place eight or nine years ago, and such was the despotism of this man and the terror he inspired, that no resistance was made to his proceedings, or any appeal against them ever sent to Naples. At last one of his own secretaries made some disclosures to Government, and the case appeared so atrocious that it was thought necessary to institute an immediate enquiry. The *intendente* was ordered to Naples, and commissioners were sent to obtain evidence in the province and sift the matter to the bottom. After much delay they made a report confirming the first accusations and designating these five men as the criminals. As soon as the matter was thus taken up, the public indignation burst forth, and a host of witnesses who had been deterred by fear from opening their lips came forward to depose against Matteis and his associates. They were arrested in the year 1825 and thrown into prison, but owing to the difficulties and delay which they contrived by their influence to interpose, and to the anomalous character of the prosecution, five years elapsed before the proceedings began. At length a royal order constituted a Court of Justice, composed of all the judges of the Court of Cassation (about twenty), the highest tribunal in the kingdom, and they have just been enjoined not to separate till the final adjudication of the case. Although the offences with which the criminals are charged are very different in degree, they are all arraigned together; a host of witnesses are examined, each of whom tells a story or makes a speech, and the evidence is accordingly very confused, now affecting one and now another of them. They have counsel and the right of addressing the Court themselves, which the *intendente* avails himself of with such insolence that they are obliged to begin the proceedings of each day by reading an order to the prisoners to behave themselves decently to the Court. Their counsel are assigned by the Court, and it is not one of the least extraordinary parts of this case that the advocate of Matteis is his personal enemy, and a man whom he displaced from an office he once held in the province. They say, however, that he defends him very fairly and zealously. The day I was there the proceedings were uninteresting, but yesterday they were very important. An officer was examined who had been imprisoned and ill-treated in prison, and who deposed to various acts of cruelty. They on their part hardly deny the facts, but attempt to justify them by proving that the sufferers really were Carbonari, that other governors had done the same thing, and that they were doing a service to the Government by these pretended plots and consequent executions. Though their guilt is clear, it is by no means so clear that they will be condemned, or at least all of them. The public indignation is so great that they must sacrifice some of them, and the spies, it is said, will certainly be hanged. Matteis has interest in the Court, but, as a majority of votes will decide his fate, it is most likely he will be condemned.

April 22*nd.*—Yesterday to Pompeii, far better worth seeing than anything else in Italy. Who can look at other ruins after this? At Rome there are certain places consecrated by recollections, but the imagination must be stirred up to enjoy them; here you are actually in a Roman town. Shave off the upper storey of any town, take out windows, doors, and furniture, and it will be as Pompeii now is: it is marvellous. About one-fifth part of the town has been excavated, and the last house found is the largest. It is said 1,000 men would clear it in a year, and there are thirty at work. The road is a bed of dust, and infested with blind beggars, each led by a boy. There are habitations almost uninterruptedly along the road between Naples and Pompeii, built apparently for no other reason than because they are exposed to eruptions of the mountain, for any other part of the Bay would be just as agreeable, and safe from that danger.

This morning we went to an Ursuline convent to see two

girls take the veil. The ceremony was neither imposing, nor interesting, nor affecting, nor such as I expected. I believe all this would have been the case had it been the black veil, but it was the white unfortunately. I thought they would be dressed splendidly, have their hair cut off in the church, be divested (in the convent) of their finery, and reappear to take leave of their relations in the habit of the order. Not at all. I went with A. Hill and Legge, who had got tickets from the brother of one of the *sposine*; we were admitted to the grating, an apartment about ten feet long by five wide, with a very thick double grating, behind which some of the nuns appeared and chattered. A turning box supplied coffee and cakes to the company. I went to the door of the parlour (which was open), but they would not admit me. There the ladies were received, and the nuns and novices were laughing and talking and doing the honours. Their dress was not ugly—black, white, and a yellow veil. The chapel was adorned with gold brocade, and blue and silver hangings, flowers, tapers; a good orchestra, and two or three tolerable voices. It was as full as it could hold, and soldiers were distributed about to keep order; even by the altar four stood with fixed bayonets, who when the Host was raised presented arms—a military salute to the Real Presence! The brother of one of the girls did the honours of the chapel, placing the ladies and bustling about for chairs, which all the time the ceremony was going on were handed over heads and bonnets, to the great danger of the latter. It was impossible not to be struck with this man's gaiety and *sang-froid* on the occasion, but he is used to it, for this was the fourth sister he has buried here. When the chapel was well crammed the *sposine* appeared, each with two *marraines*. A table and six chairs were placed opposite the altar; on the table were two trays, each containing a Prayer Book, a pocket-handkerchief, and a white veil. The girls (who were very young, and one of them rather pretty) were dressed in long black robes like dressing-gowns, their hair curled, hanging down their backs and slightly powdered. On the top of their

z 2

heads were little crowns of blue, studded with silver or dia-
monds. The ladies attending them (one of whom was Princess
Fondi and another Princess Bressano) were very smart, and
all the people in the chapel were dressed as for a ball. There
was a priest at the table to tell the girls what to do. High
Mass was performed, then a long sermon was delivered by a
priest who spoke very fluently, but with a strange twang and
in a very odd style, continually apostrophising the two girls
by name, comparing them to olives and other fruit, to *cande-
labri*, and desiring them to keep themselves pure that 'they
might go as virgins into the chamber of their beloved.' When
the Sacrament was administered the ladies took the crowns
off the girls, who were like automata all the time, threw the
white veils over them, and led them to the altar, where the
Sacrament was administered to them; then they were led
back to their seats, the veils taken off and the crowns replaced. After a short interval they were again led to the
altar, where, on their knees, their profession was read to
them; in this they are made to renounce the world and their
parents; but at this part, which is at the end, a murmuring
noise is made by the four ladies who kneel with them at the
altar, that the words may not be heard, being thought too
heart-rending to the parents; then they are led out and taken
into the convent, and the ceremony ends. The girls did not
seem the least affected, but very serious; the rest of the
party appeared to consider it as a *fête*, and smirked and gos-
siped; only the father of one of them, an old man, looked
as if he felt it. The brother told me his sister was eighteen;
that she would be a nun, and that they had done all they
could to dissuade her. It is a rigid order, but there is a still
more rigid rule within the convent. Those nuns who embrace
it are for ever cut off from any sort of communication with the
world, and can never again see or correspond with their own
family. They cannot enter into this last seclusion without
the consent of their parents, which another of this man's
four sisters is now soliciting.

We afterwards drove through the Grotto of Pausilippo,
that infernal grotto which one must pass through to get

out of Naples on one side; it is a source of danger, and the ancient account of it is not the least exaggerated :—

Nihil isto carcere longius, nihil illis faucibus obscurius, quo nobis præstant non ut per tenebras videamus sed ut ipsas.

There are a few glimmering lamps always obscured by dust, and it is never hardly light enough to avoid danger except at night; in the middle it is pitch dark.

Then round the Strada Nuova, Murat's delightful creation, and walked in the Villa Reale, where I found Acton, who had been all the morning at the trial, which was very interesting. A woman was examined, who deposed that her husband was thrown into prison and ill-treated by Matteis because he would not give some false evidence that he required of him; that she went to Matteis and entreated him to release him, and that he told her he would if she would bring her daughter to him, which she refused, and he was put to death. On this evidence being given, the examining judge dropped the paper, and a murmur of horror ran through the audience. The accused attacked the witness and charged her with perjury, and said he was ill in bed at the time alluded to. The woman retorted, ' Canaglia, tu sai ch' egli è vero,' and there was a debate between the counsel on either side, and witnesses were called who proved that he was in good health at the time. They think the evidence of to-day and the apparent disposition of the judges must hang him.

Salerno, April 24th.—Here Morier and I are going to pass the night on our way to Pæstum, and as he is gone to bed (at half-past eight) I must write. Yesterday morning Morier, St. John, Lady Isabella, and I went to Pozzuoli, embarked in a wretched boat to make the *giro* of Baiæ.

> Ante bonam Venerem gelidæ per litora Baiæ
> Illa natare lacu cum lampade jussit amorem,
> Dum natat, algentes cecidit scintilla per undas,
> Hinc vapor ussit aquas, quicumque natavit, amavit.
>
> Venus bade Cupid on fair Baiæ's side
> Plunge with his torch into the glassy tide;

As the boy swam the sparks of mischief flew
And fell in showers upon the liquid blue ;
Hence all who venture on that shore to lave
Emerge love-stricken from the treacherous wave.

I was disappointed with the country, which is bare and
uninteresting; but the line of coast, with the various bays
and promontories and the circumjacent islands, is extremely
agreeable, and the Bay of Baiæ, with the Temple of Venus,
delightful. The Temple of Mercury is also worth seeing.
The Cave of the Sibyl, Lake Avernus, and Temple of Apollo
are not worth seeing, but as they are celebrated by Virgil
they must be visited, though the embellishments of Virgil's
imagination and the lapse of time have made disappointment
inevitable. Nature indeed no longer presents the same
aspect; for there is a mountain more (Monte Nuovo) and a
wood less about the lake than in Virgil's time. We found
two ridiculous parties there, one English, the other French,
the latter the most numerous and chattering, and mounted on
asses, so as to make a long cavalcade. There was a fat old
gentleman just coming puffing out of the cave, and calling
with delight to his ladies, 'Ah, mesdames, êtes-vous
noires?' as they certainly were, for all one gets in the cave
is a blackened face from the torches. There was another
gaunt figure of the party in a fur cap, who was playing the
flute—

His reedy pipe with music fills,
To charm the God who loves the hills
And rich Arcadian scenery.

We landed from our boat in various places, but declined
going down the Cento Camerelle to have a second face-
blackening. All the ruins, said to be of Cæsar's and Marius's
Villas, Agrippina's Tomb, Caligula's Bridge, &c., may be
anything; they are nothing but shapeless fragments, only
on a rock I saw a bit of marble or stucco in what they call
Cæsar's Villa. The Stygian Lake presented no horrors, nor
the Elysian Fields any delights; the former is a great round
piece of water, and the latter are very common-looking
vineyards. When well wooded, which in the time of the

Romans it was, this coast must have been a most delicious and luxurious retreat, so sequestered and sheltered, such a calm sea, and soft breezes.

> Mira quies pelagi; ponunt hic lassa furorem
> Æquora, et insani spirant clementius Austri.

We went up to look at the old harbour of Misenum, where, instead of a Roman fleet, were a few fishing-boats, and walked back through fields in which spring was bursting forth through endless varieties of cultivation—figs, mulberries, and cherry trees, with festoons of vines hanging from tree to tree, and corn, peas, and beans springing up underneath.

Our boatmen, as we rowed back, were very proud of their English, and kept on saying, 'Pull away,' 'Now boys,' and other phrases they have picked up from our sailors. This morning we set off to come here [to Salerno] with Vetturino horses; the dust intolerable; stopped at Pompeii, and walked half round the walls and to the Amphitheatre. All the ground (now covered with vineyards) belongs to the King (for Murat bought it); the profusion and brilliancy of the wild flowers make it quite a garden—

> Flowers worthy of Paradise, which not nice art
> In beds and curious knots, but nature boon
> Pours forth profuse on hill, and dale, and plain.

If Murat had continued on the throne two or three years longer, the whole town would have been excavated. He, and still more the Queen, took great interest in it, and they both went there frequently. She used to see the houses excavated, and one day they found the skeleton of a woman with gold bracelets and earrings, which were brought to her, and she put them on herself directly. In their time 800 men and 50 cars were at work; now there are 40 men and 6 cars. The expense of 800 men and 50 cars would be about 13,000*l.* a year, but these men will spend nothing. A car costs a scudo, and a man four carlins, a day. (A scudo is ten carlins, a carlin fourpence.) The Royal Family seldom or never come here; the Duke of Calabria has been once. The Amphitheatre, though not to be compared in size or beauty with the Coliseum, is much more perfect. The road here is beautiful, particularly about La Cava. I walked up to the Convent of the Trinità; it stands on the brink of a deep ravine in the middle of the hills, which are tossed into a hundred different shapes and covered with foliage—a magnificent situation. The convent is very large, and well kept; it contains fifty monks, who were most of them walking about the road. Here were all the raw materials requisite for a romance—a splendid setting sun, mountains, convent, flock of goats, evening bell, friars, and peasants. Arrived here, delighted with the outside and disgusted with the inside of the town; but the Bay of Salerno is beautiful, the place gay and populous, all staring at a fire-balloon which was just ascending, and soon after came down in the sea. The inns execrable. We got into one at last, in which there is a wide terrace looking over the sea, and there we ordered our dinner to be laid; but we were soon driven in, not by the cold, but by the flaring of our tallow candles.

We were obliged to write our names down for the police, who are very busy and inquisitive. One man, whose name was just before mine, had added this poetical encomium on the inn :—

> I mention by way of *guidanza*
>   For those who are going to Pæstum,
> They'll find at this inn, the ' Speranza,'
>   A good place to eat and to rest 'em.

I could not concur with this poet, so I added to my name this contradiction :—

> On the ' Hope's ' being such a good treat
>   We must both put our positive vetos;
> We not only got nothing to eat,
>   But ourselves were ate up by mosquitos.

Naples, April 25th.—Started at four o'clock in the morning from Salerno, and got to Pæstum at eight. Tormented to death by beggars and ciceroni (often both characters in one), for in Italy everybody who shows a stranger about is a

1830]   PÆSTUM.   345

cicerone, from Professor Nibby down to a Calabrian peasant.
There is little beauty in the scenery of Pæstum, but the
temples amply repay the trouble of the journey. I agree
with Forsyth that they are the most impressive monuments
I have ever seen. The famed roses of Pæstum have disappeared, but there are thousands of lizards ' nunc virides
etiam occultant spineta lacertos.' No excavations have ever
been made here, but they talk of excavating. There were
some fine Etruscan vases found in a tomb at Pæstum, which
we did not see. The brute of a *custode* knew nothing of it,
nor should I if I had not seen the model in the Museum
afterwards. Thousands of Etruscan vases may be had for
digging; they are found in all the tombs. The peasants
have heaps of little carved images of terra cotta and coins,
which they offer for sale. I believed they were fabricated,
but a man I met there showed me two or three that he had
turned up with his stick, so that they may be genuine.
What treasures Naples possesses, and how unworthy she is
of them! Pæstum[1] long neglected, and Pompeii hardly
touched! At Rome they are always digging and doing
something, and though the Papal Government is neither
active nor rich, I do believe they would not let this town
(Pompeii, I mean) remain buried when a few thousand
pounds would bring it all to light. There seem to be no
habitations near Pæstum, but there is a church, which was
well attended, for the peasants were on their knees all round
it; and while we were breakfasting (in a manger with the
horses out in the air) they came out, strange-looking figures,
rude, uncouth, and sunburnt, and without any of the finery
which they generally wear on a Sunday.

Naples, April 26th.—To the Museum; met the Dalbergs
and Prince and Princess Aldobrandini, a good-looking

---

[1] The authorities of course can't agree when Pæstum was built, and by
whom, or whether one of the temples (the largest) was a temple or a
basilica. The perfect state of these temples, particularly that called of
Neptune, is the more remarkable because there are scarcely any vestiges of
other buildings. Morier thought them inferior to the temples at Athens,
but so they may well be; the Athenian temples are built of white marble
from the Pentelic quarries, and highly ornamented by Phidias.

daughter and two sons. They will have all Prince Borghese's estate. I only went into the Pompeii and Herculaneum part of the collections.

The lazaroni are very amusing. This morning four of
them stripped stark naked under my window, put off in a
boat, and thirty yards from the shore fished for cockle fish,
which they do by diving like ducks, throwing their feet up
in the air as the ducks do their tails. The creatures are
perfectly amphibious; they don't care who sees them, and
their forms are perfect. Then there are little lazaroni who
ape the big ones. Met a christening this morning, and then
a funeral. The wet nurse, full dressed, was carried in a
sedan chair down the middle of the street, and the child,
dressed also, held out of the window in her arms, and so she
was going to church. The funeral was a priest's—a long file
of penitents in white, carrying torches, a bier covered with
crimson and gold, and the priest dressed in robes and exposed
upon it, a ghastly sight, with a chalice in his hand and a
book at his feet, other priests following, the cross borne
before him. When young girls are buried in this way, they
are gaily dressed with chaplets of flowers, a flower in the
mouth, and flowers at their feet.

Rode to the race-course and round the hills; such views
and such an evening! At seven o'clock I could see the houses
at Sorrento, nineteen miles off on the other side of the
Bay. Dined with Acton; none but English. In the evening
went to Toledo, the Spanish Ambassador's. The Duc de
Dalberg talked of an association to excavate at Calabria and
Apulia. The Government reserves four places—Pompeii,
Pæstum, Stabiæ, Herculaneum—for its own use, and anybody may excavate elsewhere who will be at the trouble and
expense.

April 29th.—On Tuesday again to the Museum and
the King's Palace; rather fine, good house, very ridiculous
pictures of the royal families of Naples and Spain. The
Duchess of Floridia's apartment (old Ferdinand's wife) is delightful; the rooms are furnished with blue satin and white
silk, opening upon a terrace covered with orange-trees,

flowers, and shaded walks, and looks over the Bay. A few fine pictures, but not many. There is a bath, built after one of those at Pompeii.

From what I saw at the Museum, I see no reason to doubt that the ancients were as excellent in painting as in sculpture; there are some very exquisite paintings taken from Pompeii. Then we are not to believe that the best have been found, or that a provincial town contained the finest specimens of the art. Painted on walls, they appear deficient in light and shade, but the drawing and expression, and sometimes the colouring (allowing for spoiling), are very good. There are some Cupids playing at games, and driving chariots, very like the Julio Romanos in the Lanti Villa at Rome, which indeed were borrowed from the ancient frescoes discovered in the Baths of Titus. The bronzes taken out of Herculaneum and Pompeii are very interesting, because they display the whole domestic economy of the ancients, and their excellent taste in furniture, sacrificial instruments, &c., but there is nothing particularly curious in the fact of their pots and pans being like our pots and pans, for if they were to boil and stew they could not well have performed those operations with a different kind of utensils. However, all the people marvel at them; they seem to think the Romans must have been beings of a different organisation, and that everything that is not dissimilar is strange. What is really curious is a surgical instrument which was lately found, exactly similar to one invented thirty years ago in France. The lava would not touch bronze; the iron was always encrusted and spoilt, but the bronze things all look like new.

May 2nd.—Went to the Lake of Agnano and the Grotto del Cane; very pretty lake, evidently the crater of a volcano; saw the dog perform; a sight neither interesting nor cruel; the dog did not mind it a bit, and the old woman must make a fortune, for she had eight carlins for it. The grotto is very hot and steaming; a torch goes out held near the ground, and when I put my face down the steam from the earth went up my nose like salts. Virgil's Tomb, which is very

picturesque, and from whence the common view of Naples is
taken; there has been plenty of discussion whether it really
is Virgil's tomb or not.   Forsyth seems to doubt it, with one
of his off-hand flings at the authority for its being so, a sort
of 'Who the Devil, I humbly beg to know, is Donatus?' but
there is tradition in its favour, the fact of Virgil having been
buried here or hereabouts, and the honour being claimed by
no other spot.   When there is probability it is unwise to be
so very sceptical: take away names, and what are the places
themselves?   Here not much, at Rome nothing.

Thursday.—Went a long and most beautiful ride up to
the Camaldoli, from which the view extends over sea and
land to an immense distance in every direction.

> Thus was this place
> A happy rural seat of various views.

The convent was once very rich, but the French stripped
all the convents of their property, which they have never
since recovered.   It is remarkably clean and spacious.   Each
monk has a house of his own containing two or three little
rooms, and a little garden, and they only eat together on particular days.   The old man who took us about said he had
been there since he was eighteen, had been turned out by the
French, but came back as soon as he could, and had never
regretted becoming a monk.   He showed me a bust of the
founder of their order (I think San Romualdo), and when I
asked him how many years ago it was founded, he said,
'Perhaps 2,000.'   I said when I became a monk I would go
to that convent, when he asked very seriously if I was going
to be a monk.   I said, 'Not just yet.'   'Very well,' he said;
'you must pay 120 ducats, and you can come here.'   We
went down a road cut for miles in the mountain, very narrow
and steep, through shady lanes, groves, and vineyards (with
magnificent views), through Pianura to Pozzuoli, entering
by the old Roman road and Street of Tombs.   The *columbaria* in the Street of Tombs are the best worth seeing *ejus
generis* of any.   Went to the Temple of Jupiter Serapis, of
which there are very curious remains.

> Hard by the reverent ruins
> Of a once glorious temple, reared to Jove,
> Whose very rubbish (like the pitied fall
> Of virtue, most unfortunate) yet bears
> A deathless majesty, though now quite rased,
> Hurl'd down by wrath and lust of impious kings,
> So that where holy Flamens wont to sing
> Sweet hymns to Heaven, there the daw and crow,
> The ill-voiced raven, and still chattering pie
> Send out ungrateful sounds.—MARSTON.

To the ruins of the Amphitheatre, from the top of which there is one of the finest views I ever saw of the Bay of Baiæ and the islands; and then to the Solfatara. The ruins scattered about Naples (those at Pozzuoli, for instance) are far more extensive than most of those at Rome, but partly ' carent quia vate sacro,' and partly because there are no well-known names attached to them, the ground is not so holy, and little is said or thought about them. If these temples were at Rome, what an uproar they would cause! The Solfatara is remarkable as a sort of link between the quick and the dead volcanoes; it is considered extinct, but the earth is hot, the sulphur strong, and at a particular spot, when a hole is made, it hisses and throws up little stones and ashes, and exhibits a sort of volcano in miniature, but the surface of the crater is overgrown with vegetation. The road to Naples by the convent of the Jesuits and Chapel of St. Januarius is the most beautiful I ever saw, particularly towards sunset, when the colouring is so rich and varied. It lies over a crest commanding a prospect of the mountains on one side and the sea on the other.

> Quid mille revolvam
> Culmina visendique vices.

May 3rd.—We sailed across the Bay to Resina, to see Herculaneum, the old and new excavations. At the new there are only seven or eight men at work; the old are hardly worth seeing. So much earth and cinders are mixed with the lava in the new part, that they might excavate largely if they would spend money enough; at present they have only excavated one or two houses, but have found some bronzes and marbles. The houses are laid open, just like those at Pompeii.

The next day Morier, Watson, and I set off to ascend Vesuvius; we rode on donkeys from Salvatore's house to the bottom of the last ascent, which was rather less formidable than I expected, though fatiguing enough. Another party went up at the same time: one man of that party, Watson, and I walked up alone; the others were all lugged up. They take the bridles off the donkeys and put them on the men; the luggee holds by this tackle and the guide goes before him. After infinite puffing and perspiring, and resting at every big stone, I reached the top in thirty-five minutes. It was very provoking to see the facility with which the creatures who attended us sprang up. There was one fellow with nothing on but a shirt and half a pair of breeches, who walked the whole way from Resina with a basket on his head full of wine, bread, and oranges, and while we were slipping, and clambering, and toiling with immense difficulty he bounded up, with his basket on his head, as straight as an arrow all the time, and bothering us to drink when we had not breath to answer. I took three or four oranges, some bread, and a bottle of wine of him at the top, and when I asked Salvatore what I should pay him, he said two carlins (eightpence English). I gave him three (a shilling), and he was transported. It was a magnificent evening, and the sunset from the top of Vesuvius (setting in the sea) a glorious sight—

> For the sun,
> Declined, was hastening now with prone career
> To the ocean's isles, and in th' ascending scale
> Of heaven the stars, that usher evening, rose.

The view, too, all round is very grand; the towns round the Bay appear so clear, yet so minute. I had formed to myself a very different idea of the crater, of which the dimensions are very deceitful; it is so much larger than it appears. The bottom of the crater is flat, covered with masses of lava and sulphur, but anybody may walk all about it. At one end stands what looks like a little black hillock, from which smoke was rising, as it was from various crevices in different parts; that little hillock is the crater from which all eruptions burst. The mountain was provokingly still, and only gave one low grumble and a very small emission of smoke and fire while we were there; it has never been more tranquil. The descent is very good fun, galloping down the cinders; you have only to take care not to tumble over the stones; slipping is impossible. The whole ascent of the mountain is interesting, particularly in that part which is like a geat ocean of lava, and where the guides point out the courses of the different eruptions, all of which may be distinctly traced. We got to the Hermitage just as it was dark; there was still a red tint round the western horizon, and the islands were dimly shadowed out, while the course of the Bay was marked by a thousand dancing lights. Salvatore has especial care of the mountain under the orders of Government, to whom he is obliged to make a daily report of its state, and he is as fond of it as a nurse of a favourite child, or a trainer at Newmarket of his best race-horse, and delights in telling anecdotes of old eruptions and phenomena, and of different travellers who have ascended it.

Two years ago an English merchant here laid a bet of 200 napoleons that he would go from Resina [1] to the top in an hour and a half. Salvatore went with him, and they did it in an hour and thirteen minutes. The Englishman rode relays of horses, but the guide went the whole way on foot, and the best part of the ascent had to drag up his companion. He said it nearly killed him, and he did not recover from it for several weeks; he is 53 years old, but a very handsome man. He said, however, that the fatigue of this exploit was not so painful as what he went through in carrying the Duke of Buckingham to the top; he was carried up in a chair by

[1] From Salvatore's house at Resina to the top of the mountain is seven miles; from the Hermitage to the top, 3⅓. It is a mile and 200 feet from the bottom of the ascent (on foot) to the top, 800 feet from the point we first gain to the bottom of the crater; the inner crater (or black hill, as I call it) is 230 feet high and 180 feet in circumference. The miles are Neapolitan miles, about three-fourths of an English mile.

twelve men, and the weight was so enormous that his shoulder was afterwards swelled up nearly to his head. When the Duke got down he gave a great dinner (on the mountain), which he had brought with him to celebrate the exploit. Salvatore said that he continues to write to many scientific men in various parts of Europe when anything remarkable occurs in the mountain, and talked of Buckland, Playfair, and Davy. We got down to Resina about half-past nine, and at ten embarked again and sailed over to Castel-a-Mare, where we arrived at one o'clock.

The next morning Mr. Watson and I got a six-oared boat (with sails) and went to Sorrento. Castel-a-Mare and the whole coast are beautiful. Landed a mile from Sorrento, and walked by a path cut in the rock to the Cocomella, a villa with a magnificent prospect of the Bay exactly opposite Naples.

> Placido lunata recessu
> Hinc atque hinc curvas perrumpunt æquora rupes.
> Dat natura locum, montique intervenit imum
> Litus et in terras scopulis pendentibus exit.

Then to the town to see the curiosities, which are the Piscine, Tasso's house, and some very romantic caverns in a wild dell under the bridge at Sorrento ; all very well worth seeing, but Tasso's house was locked, so we could not get to the terrace. Just as we arrived at Sorrento we found they were performing a ceremony which takes place there every year on the 1st of May, and there only—the benediction of the flowers, the ushering in the may.

> With songs and dance they celebrate the day,
> And with due honours usher in the may.

It was in the Archiepiscopal church, which was gaily adorned with hangings of various colours, gold and silver and flowers, full of people, all in their best attire. A priest in the pulpit opposite the Archbishop's throne called on the representatives of the different parishes (seven in number), who advanced in succession, each bearing a huge cross fifteen or twenty feet high, entirely made of flowers, and adorned with garlands and devices, all likewise of the most brilliant flowers, and, as each came up, a little cannon was fired off. They were blessed in succession, and then deposited around the throne of the Archbishop, who, after this ceremony was concluded, went up to the altar and celebrated High Mass. They told me that this festival had taken place at Sorrento from the remotest time.

After seeing the Piscine we went into a garden above, where there was a profusion of orange and lemon trees, loaded with ripe fruit; the oranges we pulled off the trees and ate; they were excellent, and as red as Morella cherries—

> Whose fruit, burnished with golden rind,
> Hung amiable, Hesperian fables true,
> If true, here only, of delicious taste.

We could not stay long at Sorrento, and were four hours rowing across the Bay to Naples. Dined with Hill at the Villa Belvidere (a delicious villa on the Vomero), with a large, tiresome party, principally English.

Yesterday the miracle of the blood of San Gennaro was performed, and of course successfully; it will be repeated every morning for eight days. I went to-day to the Cathedral, where San Gennaro's silver bust was standing on one side of the altar, surrounded by lights, and the vessel containing the blood on the other. Round the altar were ranged silver heads of various saints, his particular friends, who had ac- companied him there to do him honour, and who will be taken this evening with him in procession to his own chapel. Acton and I went together, and one of the people belonging to the church seeing us come in, and judging that we wanted to see the blood, summoned one of the canons, who was half asleep in a stall, who brought out the blood, which is contained in a glass vase mounted with silver. It liquefies in the morning, remains in that state all day, and congeals again at night. A great many people were waiting to kiss the vessel, which was handed to us first. We kissed it, and then it went round, each person kissing it and touching it with his head, as they do St.

Peter's foot at Rome. San Gennaro and his silver com-
panions were brought in procession from one of the other
churches, all the nobility and an immense crowd attending. I had fancied that the French had exposed and put
an end to this juggle, but not at all. They found the people
so attached to the superstition that they patronised it; they
adorned the Chapel of St. Januarius with a magnificent
altarpiece and other presents. The first time (after they
came to Naples) that the miracle was to be performed the
blood would not liquefy, which produced a great ferment
among the people. It was a trick of the priests to throw
odium on the French, and the French General Championnet
thought it so serious that he sent word that if the blood did
not liquefy forthwith the priests should go to the galleys.
It liquefied immediately, and the people were satisfied.
Acton told me that nobody believed it but the common
people, but that they did not dare to leave it off. It is what
is called a false position to be in, when they are obliged to
go on pretending to perform a miracle in which no men of
sense and education believe, and in which it is well known
they don't any of them believe themselves. Miracles, if
sometimes useful and profitable, are sometimes awkward
incumbrances. Drove round the obscure parts of the town,
and through dense masses of population, by the old palace
of Queen Joan and the market place, which was the scene
of Masaniello's sedition. He was killed in the great church
(in 1646).

May 4th.—To the Museum, and saw the mummies which
have been unrolled; they are like thin, black, shrivelled
corpses; hair and shape of face perfect, even the eyelids.
The canvas fold in which they are wrapped quite fresh-
looking; the best preserved is 3,055 years old. Amongst the
bronzes there is a bust of Livia with a wig. Dined with
Toledo, the Spanish Minister. The women put their knives
into their mouths, and he is always kissing his wife's hand—
an ugly little old woman. Toledo was Romana's aide-de-
camp.

May 5th.—To Cumæ, and dined at the Lake of Fusaro

with the Talbots and Lushingtons; not a pretty lake, but the country near it pretty enough. A splendid sunset, with real purple. ' Lumine vestit purpureo.'

May 7th.—In the morning to the Chapel of St. Januarius, to see the blood liquefy. The grand ceremony was last Saturday at the Cathedral, but the miracle is repeated every morning in the Chapel for eight days. I never saw such a scene, at once so ludicrous and so disgusting, but more of the latter. There was the saint, all bedizened with pearls, on the altar, the other silver ladies and gentlemen all round the chapel, with an abundance of tapers burning before them. Certain people were admitted within the rails of the altar; the crowd, consisting chiefly of women, and most of them old women, were without. There is no service, but the priests keep muttering and looking at the blood to see if it is melting. To-day it was unusually long, so these old Sibyls kept clamouring, ' Santa Trinità !' ' Santa Vergine !' 'Dio onnipotente!' 'San Gennaro !' in loud and discordant chorus; still the blood was obstinate,[1] so the priest ordered them to go down on their knees and to say the Athanasian Creed, which is one of the specifics resorted to in such a case. He drawled it out with his eyes shut, and the women screamed the responses. This would not do, so they fell to abuse and entreaties with a vehemence and volubility, and a shrill clamour, which was at once a proof of their sincerity and their folly. Such noise, such gesticulations. One woman I never shall forget, with outstretched arm, distorted visage, and voice of piercing sharpness. In the meantime the priest handed about the phial to be kissed, and talked the matter over with the bystanders. 'È sempre duro?' 'Sempre duro, adesso v' è una piccola cosa.' At last, after all the handling, praying, kissing, screaming, entreating, and abusing, the blood did melt;[2] when the organ struck up, they

---

[1] I dined at Hill's; sat next to the Duchess de Dalberg, talked of the miracle, which she told me she firmly believed. I fancied none believed it but the lowest of the people, and was (very foolishly) astonished; for what ought ever to produce astonishment which has to do with credulity in matters of religion?

[2] Illarum lacrymæ meditataque murmura præstant.—JUVENAL. 6.

all sang in chorus, and so it ended. It struck me as particularly disgusting, though after all it is not fair to abuse
these poor people, who have all been brought up in the belief
of the miracle, and who fancy that the prosperity of their
city and all that it contains is somehow connected with its
due performance. The priests could not discontinue it but
by acknowledging the imposture, and by an imaginative
people, who are the slaves of prejudice, and attached to it by
force of inveterate habit, the acknowledgment would not be
believed, and they would only incur odium by it; there it is,
and (for some time at least) it must go on.

Went up to Craven's villa (this is the villa at which the
amour between the present Queen of Naples and Captain
Hess was carried on), and sat there doing nothing in the
middle of flowers, and sea breezes, and beautiful views. To
comprehend all the luxury of the *bel far niente* one must
come to Naples, where idleness loses half its evil by losing
all its enervating qualities; there is something in the air so
elastic that I have never been at any place where I have felt
as if I could make exertions so easily as here, and yet it is a
great pleasure to sit and look at the Bay, the mountains, the
islands, and the town, and watch its amusing inhabitants.
At least half an hour of every morning is spent at my
window, while I am dressing, watching the lazaroni, who
fish, work, swim, dress, cook, play, and quarrel under it. At
this moment the scene is as follows :—Half a dozen boats with
awnings and flags moored off the landing-place, a few fishing-
boats with men mending their nets, three fellows swimming
about them, two with red caps on perched upon the wall
playing at cards, two or three more looking on, one on the
ground being shaved by a barber with a basin (the exact
counterpart of Mambrino's helmet), and two or three more
waiting their turn for the same operation—always a certain
number lounging about, others smoking or asleep.

May 8th.—Rode with a large party to Astroni, where
they dined, but I did not. There were the Lushingtons,
Prince and Princess Dentici (he is at the head of the Douane),
Madame and Mademoiselle Galiati (she is remarkably pretty),

Count (I believe) and Countess Rivalvia, her uncle, Lord A.
Chichester, Count Gregorio, and a Mr. Stuart. The park,
or whatever it is called—for it is the King's chase and full
of wild boars—is one of the most beautiful and curious
places about Naples. Milton's description of the approach
to Eden applies exactly to Astroni; if ever he saw it it is
likely that he meant to describe it—

> To the border comes
> Of Eden, where delicious Paradise,
> Now nearer, crowns with her enclosure green,
> As with a rural mound, the champaign head
> Of a steep wilderness, whose hairy sides,
> With thicket overgrown, grotesque, and wild,
> Access denied; and overhead up grew
> Insuperable height of loftiest shade,
> A sylvan scene, and as the ranks ascend
> Shade above shade, a woody theatre
> Of stateliest view.

It is an immense crater of a volcano, the amphitheatre
quite unbroken, and larger than that of Vesuvius, but covered
with wood, and the bottom with very fine trees of various sorts
and with fern—very wild and picturesque. There are several
little hillocks, supposed to have been small craters; but although it is proved that this was a volcano from the lava under
the soil and from its shape, there is no mention of it as an
active volcano, and nobody can tell how many thousand years
ago it was in operation. The King, with his usual good taste,
is cutting down the finest trees, and has made a ride round
the bottom, which he has planted with poplars in a double
row, spoiling as much as he can all the beauty of the place.
They dined in a shady arbour, made on purpose with
branches of trees bound together, and on beds of fern, were
very merry, pelting each other with oranges and cherries,
and dealing about an abundance of manual jests.

Evening.—I have taken my last ride and last look at
Naples, and am surprised at the sorrow I feel at quitting it,
as I fear, for ever. Rode again to Astroni with Morier, and
walked through the wood and tried to scale one of the sides

of the mountain, but lost the path, and could only get half-way up; it is the most beautiful place about Naples. Came back by the Strada Nuova, and saw for the last time that delicious Bay with its coast and its islands, which are as deeply imprinted on my memory as if I had passed my life among them. To-night I have stood once more by the shore, and could almost have cried to think I should never see it again—

> The smooth surface of this summer sea—

nor breathe this delicious air, nor feast my eyes on the scene of gaiety, and brilliancy, and beauty around me. Nobody can form an idea of Naples without coming to it; every gale seems to bring health and cheerfulness with it, and appears ' able to drive all sadness but despair.'

Naples, they tell me, does very well for a short time, but you will soon grow tired of it. To be sure, I have been here only three weeks, but I liked it better every day, and I am wretched at leaving it. What could I ever mean by thinking it was not gay, and less lively than Genoa? To-night, as I came home from riding, the shore was covered with lazaroni and throngs of people, dancing, singing, harping, fiddling—all so merry, and as if the open air and their own elastic spirits were happiness enough. I suppose I shall never come again, for when I have measured back the distance to my own foggy country, there I shall settle for ever, and Naples and her sunny shores and balmy winds will only be as a short and delightful dream, from which I have waked too soon.

CHAPTER X.

Mola di Gaeta, May 9th.—I have dined here on an open terrace (looking over the garden and the delicious Bay), where I have been sitting writing the whole evening. The moon is just rising, and throwing a flood of silver over the sea—

> Rising in cloudless majesty,
> Apparent queen, unveiled her peerless light
> And o'er the dark her silver mantle threw.

We left Naples at half-past seven in the morning, went to Caserta, and walked over the palace, in which nothing struck me but the dimensions, the staircase, and a few of the rooms. The theatre is very well contrived; it is at one end of the palace, and the back of it opens by large folding doors into the garden, so that they can have any depth of stage they please, and arrange any pageants or cavalcades. This

could, however, only be at a theatre in a country house.
Thence to Capua, and went over the Amphitheatre, which is
very remarkable. It is said to be larger than the Coliseum,
but the arena did not appear to me so vast. Here we are
in the land of names again, and it is impossible for the imagination not to run over the grandeur, luxury, and fate of
Capua, for on the very spot on which I was standing (for the
chief places are ascertained) in all probability Hannibal often
sat to see the games.[1]

The Italian postilions, it must be owned, are a comical
set. They sometimes go faster than ever I went in England,
then at others they creep like snails, and stop at the least
inclined plane to put on the *scarpa*. The occasions they
generally select for going fast are when they have six horses
harnessed to the carriage, and so extend about ten yards,
on slippery pavement, through very narrow streets, extremely
crowded with women and children; then they will flog their
horses to full speed, and clatter along without fear or shame.
Nothing happens; I have remarked that nothing ever does
anywhere in Italy.

I have walked over this garden [at Gaeta], which contains
remains of one of Cicero's villas, but they are only arched
rooms like vaults, and not worth seeing but for the name of
Cicero, and the recollection that he was murdered almost on
this spot. He had good taste in his villas, for this bay is as
placid and delicious as that of Baiæ. There is an ancient
bath, which probably belonged to the villa; it is in the sea,
and still available, when cleaned out, which just now it is not.

Rome, May 10th.—Left Mola at half-past seven and got
here at ten minutes after seven. It was so kind as to rain
last night and this morning, and lay the dust all the way.
Stopped at Terracina, and went to see the ancient port,
which is worth seeing. The road is pretty all the way, but
the scenery in Italy wants verdure and foliage. The beauty

---

[1] No such thing. *His* Capua was nearly destroyed, and if it had an amphitheatre it would have been ruined. These ruins must have belonged to
Capua the Second, which was restored by Augustus or Tiberius, and became
as flourishing and populous as the first had been.—[C. C. G.]

of these landscapes consists in the bold outlines, lofty
mountains, abundant vegetation, and bright atmosphere,
and they are always better to look at from a little distance
than very near.   Aricia is pretty well wooded.   I found a
parcel of letters with the London news; but the post is
enough to drive one mad, for I got one of the 23rd of April
and another of the 19th of March on the same day.

ON TAKING LEAVE OF NAPLES.

(Written in a carriage between Naples and Mola di Gaeta.)

' *Nascitur poeta.*'

Though not a spark of true poetic fire
  Beamed at my birth, or on my cradle fell,
Though rude my numbers, and untuned my lyre,
  I will not leave thee with a mute farewell.

I cannot see recede thy sunny shore,
  Nor ling'ring look my last upon thy bay,
And know that they will meet my gaze no more,
  Yet tearless take my unreturning way.

'Tis not that Love laments his broken toys,
  Nor is it Friendship murmurs to depart,
Touching the chords of recollected joys
  Which ring with sad vibration on the heart.

Nor bound am I in Habit's unfelt chain,
  Which o'er the fancy steals with gradual pow'r,
Till local sympathy awakes in pain,
  That slept unconscious till the parting hour.

But 'tis the charm, so great, yet undefin'd,
  That Nature's self around fair Naples throws,
Which now excites and elevates the mind,
  And now invites it to no dull repose.

No exhalations damp the spirits choke,
  That feed on ether temp'rate and serene;
No yellow fogs, or murky clouds of smoke,
  Obscure the lustre of this joyous scene.

The God of Gladness with prolific ray
　Bids the rich soil its teeming womb expand,
While healthful breezes, cooled with Ocean's spray,
　Scatter a dewy freshness o'er the land.

No mountain billow's huge uplifted crest
　Lashes the foaming beach with sullen roar;
The smooth sea sparkles in unbroken rest,
　Or lightly rakes upon the pebbled shore.

The Ocean's Monarch on these golden sands
　Seems the luxurious laws of Love to own,[1]
And yield his trident to Thalassia's hands,
　To rule the waters from the Baian throne.

Here the green olive, and the purple vine,
　The lofty poplar and the elm espouse,
Or round the mulberry their tendrils twine,
　Or creep in clusters through the ilex boughs.

A thousand flow'rs, enameling the fields,
　Declare the presence of returning spring;
A various harvest smiling Ceres yields,
　And all the groves with vocal music sing.

Earth, air, and sea, th' enchantment of the clime,
　Revived that young elation of the breast
When Hope, undaunted, saw the form of Time
　In Fancy's gay, deluding colours drest.

And though those visions are for ever fled
　Which in the morning of existence rose,
And all the false and flatt'ring hopes are dead
　That vainly promised a serener close,

I'll snatch the joys which spite of fate remain
　To cheer life's darkness with a transient ray,
And oft in vivid fancy roam again
　Through these blest regions when I'm far away.

Rome, May 13th.—11th.—Walked about visiting to
announce my return, and found nobody at home. Hired a
horse and rode with Lovaine till near eight o'clock; rode by

---

[1] The Temple of Venus stands upon the shore of the Bay of Baiæ.

the Via Sacra two or three miles along the Street of Tombs—
very interesting and curious—and then cut across to the ruin
of an old villa, where an apartment floored with marble
has lately been discovered, evidently a bath, and a very
large one; on to Torlonia's *scavo* and under the arches of
the Claudian aqueduct. Nothing at Rome delights and
astonishes me more than the aqueducts, the way they stretch
over the Campagna—[1]

> As some earth-born giants spread
> Their mighty arms along th' indented mead.

And when you approach them how admirable are their
vastness and solidity—each arch in itself a fabric, and the
whole so venerable and beautiful. After all my delight at
Naples I infinitely prefer Rome; there is a tranquil magnificence and repose about Rome, and an indefinable pleasure
in the atmosphere, the colouring, and the ruins, which are
better felt than described. We lingered about the aqueducts
till dark, but there is hardly any twilight here; the sun sets,
and in half an hour it is night. Almost everybody is gone
or going, but the heat can't have driven them away, for it is
perfectly cool.

As we set out on our ride we passed a little church called
' Domine, quo vadis ? ' which was built on this occasion :—
St. Peter was escaping from Rome (he was a great coward,
that Princeps Apostolorum), and at this spot he met Christ,
and said to him, ' Domine, quo vadis ? ' ' Why,' replied our
Saviour, ' I am going to be crucified over again, for you are
running away, and won't stay to do my business here ; ' on
which St. Peter returned to suffer in his own person, and the
church was built in commemoration of the event. The
Saint has no reason to be flattered at the character which is
given of him by the pious editors of his Epistles. ' Confidence
and zeal form a conspicuous part of his character, but he

---

[1] The Claudian aqueduct, which is the grandest, and whose enormous
remains form the great ornament of the Campagna, was begun by Caligula,
and finished by Claudius. The structure of the arches is exactly like those
of the Coliseum. The first aqueduct was built by Appius Cæcus, the censor,
the same who laid down the Via Appia, 310 B.C.

was sometimes deficient in firmness and resolution. He had the faith to walk upon the water, but when the sea grew boisterous his faith deserted him and be became afraid. He was forward to acknowledge Jesus to be the Messiah, and declared himself ready to die in that profession, and yet soon after he thrice denied, and with oaths, that he knew anything of Jesus. The warmth of his temper led him to cut off the ear of the High Priest's servant, and by his timidity and dissimulation respecting the Gentile converts at Antioch he incurred the censure of the eager and resolute St. Paul.'

We returned through the Porta di San Giovanni, and by the Scala Santa. There are three flights of steps; those in the middle are covered with wood (that the marble may not be worn out), and these are the holy steps; the other two are for the pious to walk down. I had no idea anybody ever went up on their knees, though I was aware they were not allowed to go up on their feet, and with no small surprise saw several devout females in the performance of this ceremony. They walk up the vestibule, drop upon their knees, rise and walk over the landing-place, carefully tuck up their gowns, drop again, and then up they toil in the most absurd and ridiculous postures imaginable.

> Weak in their limbs, but in devotion strong,
> On their bare hands and feet they crawl along.
>
> DRYDEN, *Juv.* 6.

I suppose there is some spiritual advantage derivable from the action, but I don't know what. Why, however, I should be surprised I can't tell, after all I have seen here. Madame de Dalberg came to my recollection, and San Gennaro; she had owned to me that she believed in the miracle, and we had a long dispute about it, though I have since thought that I am wrong to regard her credulity with such pity and contempt. The case admits of an argument, though not that which she made use of. Many people are right in what they do, but without knowing why; some wrong, with very fair reasons. She, however, is wrong both ways, but she had been brought up in principles of strong religious belief, and she belongs to a church which teaches that miracles have never ceased from the days of the Apostles till now. Those who believe that a miracle ever was performed cannot doubt that another *may* be performed now; the only question is as to the fact. *We* believe that miracles ceased with the Apostles, and we pronounce all that are alleged to have happened since to be fictitious. Believing as she does that miracles have continually occurred, it is more reasonable to believe in the reality of one she sees herself than in those which are reported by others. She sees this done; it is, then, a miracle or it is an imposture; but it is declared to be a miracle by a whole body of men, who must know whether it be so or not, and to whom she has been accustomed to look up with respect and confidence, and who have always been deemed worthy of belief. What is it, then, she believes? The evidence of her own senses, and the testimony of a number of men, and a succession of them, who are competent witnesses, and whose characters are for the most part unblemished, in her opinion certainly. The objection that it is improbable, and that no sufficient reason is assigned for its performance, is quite inadmissible, as all considerations of reason are in matters of revelation.

And when the event only is revealed, it is not for men to dogmatise about the mode or means of its accomplishment, for God's ways are not as our ways, nor His thoughts as our thoughts, and His purposes may be wrought out in a manner that we wot not.—KEITH.

There is nothing of which we are so continually reminded, as that we must not pretend to judge of the reasonableness and fitness of the Divine dispensations, and there may therefore be good cause for the San Gennaro affair, though we cannot fathom it. Still, as the generality of people of education have given it up, one wonders at the orthodox few whose belief lingers on. There are other bloods that liquefy in various places besides San Gennaro's.

12th.—Walked to Santa Agnese, in the Piazza Navona,

a pretty church, but hardly anybody in it; to Santa Maria sopra Minerva, empty likewise, but Michael Angelo's Christ was there—a grand performance, though defective about the legs, which are too thick; he has one golden foot for the devotees, who were wearing out the marble toe, and would soon have had it as smooth as that of Jupiter's in St. Peter's; *ci-devant* Jupiter, now St. Peter.

I went again to the Pantheon, and walked round and round, and looked, and admired; even the ragged wretches who came in seemed struck with admiration. It is so fine to see the clouds rolling above through the roof; it passes my comprehension how this temple escaped the general wreck of Rome. Then to St. Peter's, and went up to the roof and to the ball, through the aperture of which I could just squeeze, though there is plenty of room when once in it. The ball holds above thirty people, stuffed close of course. Three other men were going up at the same time, who filled the narrow ascent with garlicky effluvia. It is impossible to have an idea of the size and grandeur of St. Peter's without going over the roof, and examining all the details, and looking down from the galleries. The ascent is very easy; there are slabs at the bottom taken from the holy gates, as they were successively opened and closed by the different Popes at the Jubilees.[1] At the top were recorded the ascents of various kings and princes and princesses, who had clambered up; there was also an inscription in Latin and Italian, the very counterpart of that which is still seen on the wall in Titus's Baths, only instead of ' Jovem omnipotentem atque omnes Deos iratos habeat,' &c. &c., it runs, ' Iratos habeat Deum omnipotentem et Apostolos Petrum et Paulum,' though I don't see why Paul should care about it. Went afterwards and walked on the Pincian.

---

[1] The Jubilee was established by Boniface VIII. in 1300, and was originally a centenary commemoration, but reduced to fifty years, and afterwards to twenty-five, as it still continues. Hallam remarks that the Court of Rome at the next Jubilee will read with a sigh the description of that of 1300. ' The Pope received an incalculable sum of money, for two priests stood day and night at the altar of St. Peter, with rakes in their hands, raking up the heaps of money.'—MURATORI.

This morning went with the Lovaines and Monsignore Spada to see the library of the Vatican, which was to have been shown us by Monsignore Mai, the librarian, but he was engaged elsewhere and did not come. These galleries are most beautiful, vast, and magnificent, and the painting of the old part interesting and curious, but that which was done by Pius VI. and Pius VII. has deformed the walls with such trash as I never beheld; they present various scenes of the misfortunes of these two Popes, and certain passages in their lives. The principal manuscripts we saw were a history of Federigo di Feltro, Duke of Urbino, and nephew of Julius II., beautifully illuminated by Julio Clovio, a scholar of Giulio Romano. I never saw anything more exquisite than these paintings. Amongst the most curious of the literary treasures we saw was a manuscript of some of St. Augustine's works, written upon a palimpsest of Cicero's ' De Republicâ;' this treatise was brought to light by Mai; the old Latin was as nearly erased as possible, but by the application of gall it has been brought out faintly, but enough to be made out, and completely read: Henry VIII.'s love-letters to Anne Boleyn, in French and English: Henry's reply to Luther, the presentation copy to the Pope (Leo X.), signed by him twice at the end, in English at the end of the book, in Latin at the dedication, which is also written by his own hand, only a line; the pictures representing St. Peter's in different stages of the work are very curious. In the print room there is a celestial globe painted by Julio Romano.

Just before I went to the Vatican I read in ' Galignani' the agreeable intelligence that my mare Lady Emily had beat Clotilde at Newmarket, which I attribute entirely to my *ex voto* of a silver horse-shoe, which I vowed, before I went to Naples, to the Virgin of the Pantheon in case I won the match; and, as I am resolved to be as good as my word, I have ordered the horse-shoe, which is to be sent on Monday, and as soon as it arrives it shall be suspended amongst all the arms, and legs, and broken gigs, and heads, and silver hearts, and locks of hair.

Everybody here is in great alarm about the King (George IV.), who I have no doubt is very ill. I am afraid he will die before I get home, and I should like to be in at the death and see all the proceedings of a new reign; but, now I am here, I must stay out my time, let what will happen. I shall probably never see Rome again, and 'according to the law of probability, so true in general, so false in particular,' I have a good chance of seeing at least one more King leave us.

May 15th.—I rode with Lord Haddington to the Villa Mellini last evening on a confounded high-going old hunter of Lord Lynedoch's, which he gave to William Russell. On my return found Henry de Ros just arrived, having been stopped at Aquapendente and Viterbo for want of a *lascia passare*.

This morning I have been dragging him about the town till he was half dead. The three last days have been the hottest to which Rome is subject—not much sun, no wind, but an air like an oven. The only cool place is St. Peter's, that is delicious. It is the coolest place in summer and the warmest in winter. We went to St. Peter's, Coliseum, gallery of the Vatican, Villa Albani, and Villa Borghese. The Villa Albani I had not seen before; it is a good specimen of a Roman villa, full of fine things (the finest of which is the Antinous), but very ill kept up. The Cardinal has not set his foot in it for a year and a half; there is one walk of ilexes perfectly shady, but all the rest is exposed to the sun. The post brought very bad accounts of the King, who is certainly dying. I have no notion that he will live till I get home, but they tell me there will be no changes. Gagarin told me last night that Lieven is to be governor to the Emperor of Russia's eldest son, that for the present he will retain the title of Ambassador, and that Matuscewitz will be Chargé d'Affaires in London.

May 18th.—Again dragging Henry de Ros about, who likes to see sights, but is not strong enough to undergo fatigue. Yesterday I called on M. de la Ferronays, and had a long conversation about French politics; he is greatly

alarmed at the state of affairs in France, and told me that he
had said everything he could to the King to dissuade him from
changing his Ministry and trying a *coup d'état*, that the
King has always been in his heart averse to a Constitution,
and has now got it into his head that there is a settled design
to subvert the royal authority, in which idea he is confirmed
by those about him, 'son petit entourage.' He anticipates
nothing but disaster to the King and disorder in the country
from these violent measures, and says that France was increasing in prosperity, averse to change, satisfied with its
Government and Constitution, and only desirous of certain
ameliorations in the internal administration of the country,
and of preserving inviolate the institutions it had obtained.
He thinks the success of the expedition to Algiers, if it should
succeed, will have no effect in strengthening the hands of
Polignac; says they committed a capital fault in the beginning by proroguing the Chambers upon their making that
violent Address in answer to the Speech, that they should
immediately have proceeded to propose the enactment of
those laws of which the country stands in need, when if the
Chamber had agreed to them the Ministry would have appeared to have a majority, and would thereby gain moral
strength; and if they had been rejected, the King would
have had a fine opportunity of appealing to the nation, and
saying that as long as they had attacked him personally he
had passed it by, but as they opposed all those ameliorations
which the state of France required, his people might judge
between him and them, and that this would at least have
given him a chance of success and brought many moderate
people to his side. He added that he had also said the same
thing to Polignac, but without success, that he is totally
ignorant of France and will listen to nobody. I told him
that Henry de Ros had been at Lyons when the Dauphin
came, and how ill he was received by the townspeople and
the troops, at which he did not seem at all surprised, though
sorry.

Went to Santa Maria in Trastevere to-day, the Farnese

Palace, the Farnesina and Spada, Portico d'Ottavia and Mausoleo d'Augusto; this last not worth seeing at all. The last time I was at the Spada I did not see the pictures, some of which are very good, particularly a Judith by Guido, and a Dido by Guercino, which is damaged, but beautiful. Then to Santa Maria Maggiore and St. John Lateran, and a ride over the Campagna to the Claudian aqueduct and Torlonia's *scavo*.

May 20*th*.—I breakfasted with Mills at his villa on the Palatine; Madame de Menon, Henry Cheney, Fox, and the Portuguese Chargé d'Affaires; very agreeable: his villa charming; it formerly belonged to Julius II., and one room is painted in fresco by Raphael and his scholars, as they say.

The Portuguese is Donna Maria's officer. The relations of the Holy See with Portugal are rather anomalous, but sensible. The Pope says he has nothing to do with politics, does not acknowledge Don Miguel, but as he is *de facto* ruler of Portugal, he must for the good of the Church (whose interests are not to be abandoned for any temporal considerations) transact business with him, and so he does. This Envoy is very sanguine as to the ultimate success of the Queen's cause.

Went to the Orti Farnesiani and to Livia's Baths, where there is still some painting and gilding to be seen. Then to the Capitol; saw the pictures and statues (again), and called on Bunsen, who told me a colossal head of Commodus could not be Commodus (which stands in the court of the Capitol); he won't allow anything is anything. He is full of politics, and thinks the French will get rid of their domestic difficulties by colonising Africa, and does not see why they should not as well as the Romans; but he seems a better antiquary than politician.

Some pictures in the Capitol are very fine—Domenichino's Sibyl and Santa Barbara, Guercino's Santa Petronella (copied in mosaic in St. Peter's) and Cleopatra and Antony. There are several unfinished Guidos, some only just begun. They say he played, and when he lost and could not pay, painted a picture; so these are the produce of bad nights, and their progress perhaps arrested by better.

To the Borghese Villa. At present I think Chiswick better than any villa here, but they tell me when I get home and see Chiswick and remember these I shall think differently.

May 22*nd.*—Found it absolutely necessary to adopt Roman customs and dine early and go out after dinner; one must dine at four or at nine. Went to Raphael's house, which is painted by his scholars, and one room by himself; a very pretty villa, uninhabited, and belongs to an old man and an old woman, who will neither live in it nor let it. Though close to the Villa Borghese, which is occupied by the malaria, this villa is quite free from it. The malaria is inexplicable. If it was 'palpable to sight as to feeling,' it would be like a fog which reaches so far and no farther. Here are ague and salubrity, cheek by jowl. To the Pamfili Doria, a bad house with a magnificent view all round Rome; fine garden in the regular clipped style, but very shady, and the stone pines the finest here; this garden is well kept. Malaria again; Rome is blockaded by malaria, and some day will surrender to it altogether; as it is, it is melancholy to see all these deserted villas and palaces, scarcely one of which is inhabited or decently kept. I don't know one palace or villa which is lived in as we should live in England; the Borghese Villa is the only one which is really well kept, but Prince Borghese has 70,000*l.* a year; he lives at Florence and never comes here, but keeps collecting and filling his villa. The other morning the ground here was in many parts covered by a thin red powder, which was known to come from an eruption, and everybody thought it was Vesuvius, and so travellers reported, but it turns out to be from Etna or Stromboli. Naples was covered with it, and the sun obscured, but it is much nearer. Rome must be 300 or 400 miles from Etna.

May 23*rd.*—Went to three churches—Nuova, San Giovanni dei Fiorentini, San Agostino; in this latter is Raphael's fresco of the prophet Isaiah, in the style of M. Angelo, but it did not particularly strike me. There is a remarkable Madonna here, a great favourite; her shrine is quite illumi-

nated with lamps and candles, and adorned with offerings
which cover the columns on each side of the church. Numerous devotees were kissing her gilt foot, and the Virgin
and Child were decked with earrings, bracelets, and jewels
and gold in every shape; the Child, which is of a tawny
marble, looked like some favourite little 'nigger,' so bedizened was he with finery. She is a much more popular
Madonna than my friend of the Pantheon, to whom I went,
as in honour bound, and hung up my horse-shoe by a purple
riband (my racing colour) round one of the candlesticks on
the altar, with this inscription—C. C. G., P.G.R.N.A.27,
1830.[1]

Took H. de Ros to see the Cenci and the skeleton
friars, not exactly birds of a feather; was obliged to squabble
with the monk to get a sight of my old friends the skeletons,
who at last let us in, but would not take any money, which
I thought monks never refused, but my *laquais de place* said,
'Lo conosco bene, c'è molto superbo.' Rode along the Via
Appia and to Maxentius's Circus.

May 24th.—Called on Sir William Gell at his eggshell of
a house and pretty garden, which he planted himself ten
years ago, and calls it the Boschetto Gellio. He was very
agreeable, with stories of Pompeii, old walls, and ruined
cities, besides having a great deal to say on living objects
and passing events.

Dined with M. de la Ferronnays—a great party—and was
desired to hand out Madame la Comtesse de Maistre, wife
to the Comte Xavier de Maistre, author of the 'Voyage
autour de ma Chambre' and 'Le Lépreux,' to which works
I gave a prodigious number of compliments. The Dalbergs
and Aldobrandinis dined there, and some French whom I
did not know. The Duc de Dalberg and his wife are a
perpetual source of amusement to me, she with her devotion
and believing everything, he with his air *moqueur* and believing nothing; she so merry, he so shrewd, and so they
squabble about religion. 'Qui est cet homme?' I said to

---

[1] [It has been suggested to me since the publication of the former editions
that these letters stand for 'Charles Cavendish Greville, Pro Gratiâ Receptâ;
Newmarket, April 27th, 1830.']

him when a ludicrous-looking abbé, broader than he was long, came into the room. 'Que sais-je? quelque magot.' 'Ah, je m'en vais dire cela à la Duchesse.' 'Ah, mon cher, n'allez pas me brouiller avec ma famille.'

He had been talking to me about La Ferronnays the day before, and said he was a sensible, right-headed man, 'mais diablement russe;' and last night La Ferronnays gave us an account of the revolt of the Guards on the Emperor Nicholas's accession, of which he had been a witness—of the Emperor's firmness and his subsequent conversations with him, all which was very interesting, and he recounted it with great energy.   He said that the day after the affair of the Guards all the *Corps Diplomatique* had gone to him, that he had addressed them in an admirable discourse and with a firm and placid countenance.   He told them that they had witnessed what had passed, and he had no doubt would give a faithful relation of it to their several Courts; that on dismissing them he had taken him (La Ferronnays) into his closet, when he burst into tears and said, 'You have just seen me act the part of Emperor; you must now witness the feelings of the man.   I speak to you as to my best friend, from whom I conceal nothing.'   He went on to say that he was the most miserable of men, forced upon a throne which he had no desire to mount, having been no party to the abdication of his brother, and placed in the beginning of his reign in a position the most painful, irksome, and difficult; but that though he had never sought this elevation, now that he had taken it on himself he would maintain and defend it.   When La Ferronnays had done, 'L'entendez-vous?' said Dalberg.   'Comme il parle avec goût; cela lui est personnel.   L'Empereur ne lui a pas dit la moitié de tout cela.'

La Ferronnays introduced me to Cardinal Albani, telling him I had brought him a letter from Madame Craufurd, which I did, and left it when I was here before.   He thought I was just come, and asked for the letter, which I told his Eminence he had already received.   He had, however, forgotten all about me, my letter, and old Craaf.   We had a long conversation about the Catholic question, the Duke's duel with Lord Winchelsea (which he had evidently never heard of,) the King's illness, &c.   He is like a very ancient red-legged macaw, but I suppose he is a dandy among the cardinals, for he wears two stars and two watches.   I asked him to procure me an audience of the Pope, which he promised to do.   Escaped at last from the furnace his room was, and went to air in the streets; came home early and went to bed.

This morning got up at half-past six, and went to look out for some *columbaria* I had heard of out of the Porta Pia, and near Santa Agnese.   The drones at Santa Agnese knew nothing about them, but I met La Ferronnays riding as I was returning in despair, and he showed me the way to them.   They have been discovered about six years, and are in a garden.   The excavation may be fifteen feet by about eight or nine, more or less, and is full of broken urns and inscriptions, some of which are very good indeed.   One is upon C. Cargilius Pedagogus :—

> Vixi quandiu potui, sine lite, sine rixâ,
> Sine contentione, sine ære alieno, amicis fidem
> Bonam præstiti, peculio pauper, animo divitissimus,
> Benè valeat is qui hoc titulum perlegit meum.

Another—

> Lucius Virius Sancius æt. xxiii.
> Quod tu mî debebas facere, ego tibi facio, mater pia.

The same idea as in Canning's verses on his son :—

> Whilst I, reversed our nature's kindlier doom,
> Pour forth a father's sorrows o'er his tomb.

And Evander on Pallas :—

> Contra ego vivendo vici mea fata superstes
> Restarem ut genitor.

As I came back I looked into San Bernardo, Santa Maria della Vittoria, and Santa Susanna, and I stopped to look at the ' Moses striking the Rock,' which is certainly very fine, though there is too much of Moses and not enough of rock or water After breakfast to the Vatican library, where the Duc de Dalberg had engaged the Abbé Mai to meet him, and he showed us all the manuscripts, most of which I had already

seen. He is very laborious as well as learned. Mai is said
to undertake too much, and to leave a great deal half examined, and therefore unknown; but somebody (I forget
who) is at daggers drawn with him, so it may be the accusa-
tion of a literary enemy. Went about with the Dalbergs to
several places, to all of which I had been before. At every
church the Duchess and her daughter dropped on their knees
and sprinkled themselves with holy water, and prayed and
curtsied, but nothing could get him down upon his marrow
bones.

May 25th.—Breakfasted with Gell in his Boschetto Gellio
under a treillage of vines, and surrounded by fruits and
flowers. He was very agreeable, and told us a great many
anecdotes of the Queen and her trial. We are just setting
off for Tivoli.

May 27th.—Went to Tivoli. The journey hotter than
flames over the Campagna. It is the most beastly town I
ever saw, more like the Ghetto here than any other place,
full of beggars and children. The inn very moderate, but
Henry and I got a very good apartment, looking over the
country, in a private house. We all dined together.

—— is the merriest of saints, the jolliest of devotees, and
very unlike the ghost in ' Don Juan,' who says, ' Chi si pasce
di cibo celeste non si pasce di cibo mortale,' for though rigor-
ously obedient to the prescribed fasts of the Church, she
devours flesh enough on other days to suffice for those
on which it is forbidden; and on the meagre days she in-
demnifies herself by any quantity of fish, vegetables, and
sucreries of all kinds. It is only like eating her first course
on Thursday and her second on Friday.

After dinner we sent for the most famous guide, with
the magnificent name of Pietro Stupendo, called ' Stupendous ' from his frequent use of that adjective in pointing
out the views. His real name is Barbarossa, which is nearly
as fine. We went to see the sun set from the Villa d'Este ;
a very fine villa, with clipped trees, waterworks, and all the
usual beauties of Italian villas. It belongs to the Duke of
Modena, is uninhabited, and falling to decay for want of

care and attention. Thence to the Temple of the Sibyl or
Vesta[1] (for it goes by both names), which is very airy and
graceful, and perched on the point of a rock, but its effect
spoiled by being embedded in dirty, ugly houses. The fall
below was made by Bernini, and is very pretty, but not
grand, and it looks rather artificial. We saw it from what
is called the Grotto of Neptune. At night I returned again,
but nobody else would stir out. I went down to the fall, and
had bundles of hay lit on the rock above, and some blue
lights called *lumi di Bengala,* a sort of firework, put in the
temple, and the effect was beautiful. The reflected light
upon the cascade, and the light and shade upon the rocks,
and the temple made visible through the darkness by the
soft blue flame, without any of the background of buildings
appearing, were very fine, and in the obscurity it seemed
much more extensive and natural. I saw this first from the
Grotto of Neptune, and then from the opposite height.

Yesterday morning we were to have started on the *giro*
of Tivoli at six, but as women are never ready, and a good
deal of eating and drinking was to be gone through before
we got under weigh, we were not off till near eight. The consequence was that we got into the heat, and lost the colouring
of the early morning, and those lights and shades on which
great part of the beauty of this scenery depends. I was
altogether disappointed; the hills are either quite bare or
covered with olives, the most tiresome of trees; the falls are
all artificial, and though the view at the foot of the largest
(or as near as you can approach it) is beautiful, on the whole
no part of the scenery answered my expectations. The water
falls in eleven separate cascades (above and below), and sinking
into the gulf appears to boil up again in clouds of spray, but
the artificial channel above is distinctly visible. There is an
ancient bridge over the Anio and part of a road up to Tivoli in
wonderful preservation. Our party pleased their imaginations

[1] I believe it to be the Sibyl's Temple. There is a frightful square
building close to it they call the Sibyl's Temple, but I do not see by what
authority. Nibby says it is Vesta, but everybody else says the Sibyl.—
FORSYTH, CRAMER, &c.

by thinking that Augustus and Mæcenas had probably gone
cheek by jowl over the road and bridge, but Stupendous told
me it was built by Valerian, A.D. 253, though he had no
notion who Valerian was, except that he was an Emperor.
There are some curious remains of Mæcenas's Villa, particularly the places (if they are really so) where the slaves
were kept, which are just like cellars. I cannot remember
seeing any apartments destined for slaves at Pompeii, but
from all one sees and hears and reads of the Roman slaves,
they must have been treated in a manner that it is inconceivable they should have endured, considering their
numbers, and of what they were generally composed—bar-
barian prisoners or free citizens reduced to servitude. We
ended the *giro* at the Villa d'Este, and breakfasted on the
terrace; the rest of the party then retired to sleep and play
at cards at the inn, and I started with Stupendous to see
the remains of an ancient city, and some specimens of Cyclopean walls, about four or five miles off. The first place
is called Ventidius Bassus', because that gentleman had a
villa there built on the ruins of a little Cyclopean town,
where there are still some walls standing. From thence to
Mitriano, which must have been a large town, the vestiges
still covering several hills, and the remains of walls being
very large; there is nothing left but a few broken fluted
columns, and one flat marble stone perfect, with an inscription. This jaunt was hardly worth the trouble.

When I came back from Mitriano, I went down to the
Grotto of the Syrens, from whence the view of the cascade
s much finer than from the other grotto, and really grand;
but the path is very slippery from the clouds of spray constantly falling over it. I did not go quite to the grotto, for
Stupendous told me he had nearly slipped down the rock and
cracked his crown; so I declined running that risk, but saw
just as well, for I went nearly to the bottom.

At half-past four we went to Adrian's Villa, with which
I was as much delighted as I was disappointed with Tivoli.
Nothing can be more picturesque than the ruins, and nothing
gives such an idea of the grandeur of the ancient masters of

the world.   They are six miles in circumference, and the
remains are considerable, though not very distinct, but it is
very easy to perceive that they are the ruins of a villa, or a
collection of ornamental and luxurious buildings, and not of
a town, which from their size they might be.   Almost all
the ruins of antiquity that adorn Rome were found here,
or in Caracalla's Baths, which latter were supplied from this
stock—all the Albani collection, most of the Museo Bor-
bonico at Naples, and half the Vatican.   The Albani collection was made by a nephew of Clement XI., the Albani
Pope.   They say only one-fourth has been excavated.   The
ruins are overgrown with ivy and all sorts of creepers.   The
grounds are full of pines and cypresses of great size, and it
is altogether one of the most interesting and beautiful spots
I have seen in Italy.   The Villa Adriani now belongs to
Duke Braschi, nephew of Pius VI.   He has not excavated,
but the truth is that there is little temptation to individuals
to do so.   The Government have taken all the ruins under
their protection, and no proprietor is allowed to destroy any
part of them.   So far so good, but if he digs and finds anything, he may not sell it; the Government reserves to itself
a right of pre-emption, and should he be offered a large
sum by any foreigner for any object he may find, he is not
allowed to take it, although the Government may not choose
to buy it at the same price.   They will fix a fair, but not
a fancy price, but the vendor is often obliged, when they do
buy it, to wait many years for his money.   Albani employed
1,000 men to excavate.

We came back in a deliciously cool evening.   The Duchess
wanted us to keep with her carriage (she had a pair and
we had four horses), for fear she should be robbed—for she
had heard that somebody had been robbed somewhere a
little while ago—which we promised; but our postilions
set off in a gallop, we fell asleep, and they were left to their
fate.

At night.—This morning as I was sitting at Torlonia's
reading the newspapers, a woman came in, whom Luigi
Chiaveri soon after begged to introduce to me.   She was a

Mrs. Kelly, of whose history I had already heard, and I told Chiaveri I would assist her if I could. She told me her case in detail. The short of it is this:—She and her daughter (who is very pretty) got acquainted at Florence with a family of Swifts. Young Swift seeing the girl was good-looking, and hearing she was rich, made up to her, gained her affections (as they call it), and proposed to marry her. She agreed, provided her mother did. They came to Rome. Swift followed, established himself at the same inn, and wrote to the mother to propose himself. The mother declined. He wrote a second letter—same reply. He then prevailed on the girl to promise not to give him up, but failed in persuading her to elope with him. She said she would marry him when she was of age. He pressed her to give him a written promise to this effect before witnesses. After some hesitation she agreed, and one evening (having been previously appointed by him) she met him in another room, where she found a priest and two men. She signed two papers without reading them, heard a short form muttered over, which she did not understand, and then was told to run downstairs again. A few days after she got uneasy as to what had happened, and confessed it all to her mother, who immediately conceived that this was a marriage ceremony into which she had been inveigled. She told her lover what she had done, who asked her what her mother had said. She told him that her mother fancied that it was a marriage, but that she had told her it was not, when he informed her it was, and this was the first intimation he gave her of the sort, and the first time he had given her to understand that he regarded her as his wife. She reproached him with his duplicity and the imposition he had practised on her, and told him she would have no more to say to him. This took place in St. Peter's one Friday at vespers. Soon after they went to Naples, where Swift followed, and wrote to her mother saying he had married her daughter, and asking her forgiveness; that she might fancy the marriage was not valid, but she would find it was, having been celebrated by an abbé, witnessed by the nephew of a cardinal, and the

certificate signed by a cardinal, with the knowledge of the
Pope. She sent no answer, when he begged an interview,
which she granted, and then he told her that he was a
Catholic, and that her daughter had become so too, and had
signed an act of abjuration of the Protestant religion. The
mother and daughter, however, declined having anything to
do with him, and the latter declared that she had never
changed her religion at all. He then claimed her as his
wife, and tried to prevail on Hill and Lushington (Sir Henry
Lushington, Consul—the present Lord Berwick, Minister)
to prevent their leaving Naples. They declined to interfere,
and advised the mother to go home, and let the matter be
settled between them in England. She took the hint and
set off. He followed, and overtook them at Rome, and there
by representations to the civil and religious authorities that
they were taking away his wife to prevent her being a
Catholic, and make her relapse to the Protestant faith, he
got them to interfere, and their passports were refused.
Such is their story. They have nobody to advise, assist, or
protect them.

I went to La Ferronnays, who was all good-nature, and
said he would go with me to Cardinal Albani; but I went
first to the hotel and saw the girl alone, who corroborated
all her mother had said. I wrote down her evidence, and
made her sign it, and then went with the Ambassador to
the Cardinal in the Quirinal Palace. The door of his cabinet
was locked, but after a sort of *abbé suisse* had knocked a
little he came and opened it, and in we went. He did not
recollect my name the last time I saw him, nor my person
this. La Ferronnays explained the business, with which he
was already acquainted, partly through Kestner (the Hanoverian Minister) and partly through the Roman authorities,
who had given him the case of the adventurer, for such he
seems to be.[1] The Cardinal seemed disposed to do nothing

---

[1] [It will be seen from the foregoing narrative that Mr. Greville was
appealed to by Mrs. Kelly to assist her at a very critical moment, and that
he chivalrously attempted to rescue the young lady from what he was led to
believe was a forced and invalid marriage. But he was entirely mistaken

(Bunsen assures me he is a very sensible man, and right-headed and well disposed), and said she was married. We said, not at all. Then he hummed and hawed, and stammered and slobbered, and talked of the ' case being in the hands of the Saint Office [the Inquisition!!] under the eyes of his Holiness. What could he do?' We fired off a tirade against the infamy of the action, said that the English tribunals ought to decide upon the validity of the marriage, that all they wanted was to go home, that the man might follow and make his claim good if he could, and that the story (if they were detained here) would make a noise in England, and would be echoed back to France by the press of both countries, and that it was very desirable to avoid such a scandal. He seemed struck with this, and said it would be best to send them off to settle their disputes at home, but that they must have patience, that time was necessary and the case must be examined. We were obliged to be contented with this, and saying we were sure the case was in good hands (which I doubt, for he would leave it there if he dared), with many scrapes and compliments we took our leave. The girl has never dared to show her face, for fear of being carried off by the lover or shut up in a convent by the Grand Inquisitor, so I tranquillised their minds and sent them out an airing. In the evening I spoke to Monsignore Spada, who has promised to help to get up a case in Italian, if it should be wanted.

Dined with M. de la Ferronnays, and went to his villa (Mattei) afterwards. He has been perfect in this affair, full of prompt kindness; but what a Government! how imbecile, how superannuated! a Minister of ninety almost, a sovereign of whom all that can be said is that he is a great canonist, and all that little bubbling and boiling of priestery and monkery, which is at once odious, mischievous, and contemptible, a sort of extinct volcano, all the stink of the sulphur

in supposing that Mr. Swift was an adventurer. Mr. Swift was a gentleman of good family and some landed property in the county Dublin, on which he still resides. Travelling in Italy, in 1830, with his mother and sisters, he saw, and fell in love with, Miss Kelly: but he certainly resorted to very extraordinary practices to gain her hand.]

without any of the splendour of the eruption. They want the French again sadly. English subjects detained by the Inquisition in 1830 ! ! La Ferronnays advised me to ask the Pope for a moment of audience, and to request him to see the girl himself, and interrogate her, and learn the truth of the case.

I had just done writing the above when a note came from La Ferronnays with the passports for the Kellys, which Albani had sent him, so I had only to thank the Cardinal instead of mentioning it to the Pope. I did not think he would have been so quick. How enchanted they will be to-morrow morning !

May 29th.—At ten Kestner called for Lovaine and me, and we went to the Pope.[1] His Court is by no means despicable. A splendid suite of apartments at the Quirinal with a very decent attendance of Swiss Guards, Guardie Nobili, Chamberlains—generally ecclesiastics—dressed in purple, valets in red from top to toe, of Spanish cut, and in the midst of all a barefooted Capuchin. After waiting a few minutes, we were introduced to the presence of the Pope by the Chamberlain, who knelt as he showed us in. The Pope was alone at the end of a very long and handsome apartment, sitting under a canopy of state in an arm-chair, with a table before him covered with books and papers, a crucifix, and a snuff-box. He received us most graciously, half rising and extending his hand, which we all kissed. His dress was white silk, and very dirty, a white silk skullcap, red silk shoes with an embroidered cross, which the faithful kiss. He is a very nice, squinting old twaddle, and we liked him. He asked us if we spoke Italian, and when we modestly answered, a little, he began in the most desperately unintelligible French I ever heard; so that, though no doubt he said many excellent things, it was nearly impossible to comprehend any of them ; but he talked with interest of our King's health, of the antiquities, and Vescovali, of Lucien Buonaparte and his extortion (for his curiosities), said when he was Cardinal he used to go often to

---

[1] [The Pope was Pius VIII. (Francisco Xaverio Castiglioni), whose reign was a very short one, for he succeeded Leo XII. in March 1829, and was succeeded by Gregory XVI. in December 1830.]

Vescovali. He is, in fact, a connoisseur. Talked of quieting religious dissensions in England and the Catholic question; and when I said, 'Très-Saint Père, le Roi mon maître n'a pas de meilleurs sujets que ses sujets catholiques,' his eyes whirled round in their sockets like teetotums, and he grinned from ear to ear. After about a quarter of an hour he bade us farewell: we kissed his hand and backed out again. We then went to the Cardinal, whom I thanked warmly for his prompt attention to my request in having given the passports to my *protégées*. It is the etiquette in the Court of the Quirinal for the servants to descend from behind the carriage, and the horses to go a foot pace.

After this audience I took the passport to the Kellys. The mother was in bed, but the girl came to me in a transport of gratitude and joy. They went off in the evening to Florence. La Ferronnays advised me to send them off directly, for fear the priests should begin to stir in the matter and raise fresh obstacles.

In the afternoon went to Gibson's, the sculptor. He is very simple and intelligent, and appears to be devoted to his art. There is a magnificent Venus, composed from various models, like Zeuxis's statue of Juno at Crotona.

> Quando Zeusi l'immagine far volse
> Che par dovea nel tempio di Giunone,
> E tante belle nude insieme accolse,
> E per una farne in perfezione,
> Da chi, una parte, e da chi, un' altra tolse.

May 31*st*.—Yesterday the advocate to whom I had advised Mrs. Kelly to go came to me, and said he could not understand what she said, and she had desired him to call on me. I told him the story, and he said he would look into it and see what was to be done. I had advised her before she went to consult an Italian lawyer as to the necessary steps to be taken here in order to prove the invalidity of the marriage in England. This man, whose name is Dottore Belli, was recommended to me by Monsignore Spada as a clever lawyer, and particularly good for the case,

because brother of one of the judges (or other officer) in the
Vicar-General's court.   But I suppose he has less influence
over the brother than the brother over him, for this morning
he sent me a very civil but formal letter, saying 'the
parties were married, and had abjured after instruction received'—evidently a letter dictated by the court or by his
brother, or at all events by some ecclesiastical interest.
They evidently want to make the marriage good to save
their own credit, but there is a great mystery in the whole
affair.   Cardinal Weld told La Ferronnays that they had
not yet found the priest who had performed the ceremony.
Bunsen at my request undertook to enquire into the affair,
but up to the present moment (June 13th) he has only made
the case more confused and inexplicable.[1]

To-day there was a grand ceremony of the transportation
of the standard of a new saint (that is, one made about fifty
years ago) from St. Peter's to San Lorenzo in Lucina, his
own church.   This saint is San Francisco Carraccioli, a
Neapolitan.   All the peasantry came in, covered with
religious gewgaws, and the streets were crowded.   There
was a balcony at the Cardinal's as for the Girandola, but the
Duc de Dalberg and I went to the Piazza di San Pietro,
and saw it there; it was curious.   First came the guards;
then the footmen of the cardinals in State liveries, four for
each, carrying torches; the clergy of various orders with

---

[1] The conclusion of this affair is not less curious than its commencement.   The parties returned to this country.   Swift sued Miss Kelly in the
Ecclesiastical Court for the restitution of conjugal rights.   After much delay
the case was elaborately argued before Sir John Nicholl, who at very great
length pronounced judgment against the validity of the marriage.   Swift
appealed to the Judicial Committee of the Privy Council, when the sentence
of the Court below was reversed, and the ceremony at Rome decided to
be a good and binding marriage.   The parties were thus irrevocably made
man and wife, and after some time had elapsed their mutual friends and
relations set on foot a negotiation for a reconciliation, and eventually Miss
Kelly agreed to live with Mr. Swift, on condition that the marriage ceremony
should be regularly performed, which was accordingly done: certain settle-
ments were made, and they are now (for all I know to the contrary) living
happily and harmoniously together.   [The further proceedings in this cause
are described in the second volume of this Journal, when they came before
the Privy Council.]

chandeliers, crucifixes, immense crosses, standards, and all
with torches; a long file of Jesuits, whose appearance was
remarkable, so humble and absorbed did they look; bands
of music and soldiers, the whole reaching from the door of
St. Peter's to the other side of the Castle of St. Angelo.
This procession made the *giro* of the city, for we fell in with
it again in the Piazza della Colonna two hours afterwards.
The Church of San Lorenzo and the adjoining houses were
illuminated, and there was a picture, inscription, &c., stuck
up over the door.   The Cardinal Galetti, who is the patron
of this order, asked the General of the Jesuits to send some
of his flock to swell the procession, which he was desirous of
making as brilliant as possible.   The General excused himself on the ground that the Jesuits were not in the habit of
attending processions. The Cardinal complained to the Pope
of the General's refusal.   The next time the Pope saw him
(he goes once a week to the Quirinal to make his report),
after discussing all their matters of business and giving him
the benediction, just as he was leaving the room, the Pope
called after him, ' O reverend Father, I hope you will not
send less than a hundred of your Jesuits to the procession
to-morrow.'   The General was thunderstruck, but obliged to
obey.   This ecclesiastical anecdote makes a noise here. The
present General is a Belgian, and a man of great ability.
The Jesuits have a college here, and a seminary; a hundred
in the one, and three hundred in the other.

The process of saint-making is extremely curious.   There
are three grades of saintship; the first, for which I forget
the name, requires irreproachable moral conduct; the second
(beatification), two well-proved miracles; the third (sanctifi-
cation), three.   It costs an immense sum of money to effect
the whole, in some cases as much as 100,000 piastres.   The
process begins by an application to the Pope, on the part of
the relatives of the candidate, or on that of the confraternity
if they belong to a religious order.   The Pope refers the
question to a tribunal, and the claimants are obliged to
appear with their proofs, which are severely scrutinised, and

the miracles are only admitted upon the production of the most satisfactory evidence. Individuals continually subscribe for this purpose, particularly for members of religious orders, in order to increase the honour or glory of the society. These trials last many years, sometimes for centuries. There is a Princess of Sardinia, sister of the late King, who died lately, and they want to make a saint of her. The money (estimated at 100,000 piastres) is ready, but they cannot rout out a miracle by any means, so that they are at a dead stand-still before the second step. Nobody can be sanctified till two hundred years after their death, but they may arrive at the previous grades before that, and the proofs may be adduced and registered.

June 1st.—Yesterday news came of the change in the French Ministry,[1] of which La Ferronnays knew nothing the night before, and from which Dalberg anticipates an increase of desperate measures on the part of the Court. Went in the morning to Gibson's; in the evening to the Orti Sallustiani, one of the many objects here not worth seeing, though they show two great holes in a wall, which they call the Campo Scelerato, and they say it is the place where the frail vestals were buried. Coming back we met the Pope taking a drive—two coaches-and-four, with guards and outriders. We got out of the carriage and took off our hats, and our *laquais de place* dropped on his knees. The Pope was in white, two people sitting opposite to him, and as he passed he scattered a blessing. All persons kneel when he appears—that is, all Catholics. The equipage was not brilliant. To the Corsini Villa, the gardens of which are some of the shadiest and most agreeable in Rome, but nobody inhabits the palace. The Corsinis live at Florence, and when they come here they lodge elsewhere, for the malaria, they say, occupies their domain. Thus it is that between poverty and

---

[1] [Charles X. had signed the decree for the dissolution of the existing Chamber of Deputies on the 16th of May: on the 19th of May another ordinance appointed M. de Chantelauze to the Ministry of Justice, M. de Peyronnet to the Interior, M. de Montbel to the Finances, and M. Capelle to the Department of Public Works. These appointments, more especially that of M. de Peyronnet, were deemed in the highest degree hostile to the Liberal party.]

malaria Rome is deserted by its great men. But the population ought to be increasing, for almost every woman one meets is with child. Gell denies the malaria, says he should not mind living where they say it is dangerous to live; but can this be matter of opinion?

In the evening looked into the Church and Piazza of San Lorenzo in Lucina. The church is hung with drapery, adorned with statues, and illuminated by innumerable wax candles. The piazza is illuminated too, and drapery hung out from the windows. There were crowds of people, lines of chairs, and boys bawling to the people to come and sit upon them; others selling lemonade, others the life and exploits of the saint on penny papers; a band of military music on a scaffolding, and guards patrolling about. Between the intervals of the band the bells, in discordant chorus, regaled ' the ears of the groundlings.' This strange, discordant scene, the foundation of which is religious, but which has but little of the appearance of religion in it, lasts eight successive days, and costs a vast sum of money—they say 9,000 scudi—the greatest part of which is furnished by the Government. It probably answers some end, for it is difficult to conceive that any Government, even this, should spend money, of which they have so little to spare, on these fooleries while poverty overspreads the land. This ceremony has not taken place before for a hundred years. The sight is certainly very gay. Close by, in the Palazzo Fiani, is a theatre of marionettes, who play a comedy of Goldoni's. The Duke Fiano lets part of his palace for this purpose. What an exhibition of wretchedness! He reserves a box which his servants let to anybody, whether on his account or their own I don't know.

Evening.—Went before dinner to the Villa Madama, a ruined villa belonging to the royal house of Naples, with fine paintings still on the walls and ceilings, the vestiges of former luxury, and a capital view of Rome, the Tiber, the Milvian Bridge, and the mountains. After dinner to the San Gregorio to see the frescoes, the ' Martyrdom of St. Andrew,' the rival frescoes of Guido and Domenichino, and afterwards drove about till dark, when we went to a most

extraordinary performance—that of the Flagellants. I had
heard of it, and had long been curious to assist at it. The
church was dimly lit by a few candles on the altar, the congregation not numerous. There was a service, the people
making the responses, after which a priest, or one of the
attendants of the church, went round with a bundle of whips
of knotted cord, and gave one to each person who chose to
take it. I took mine, but my companion laughed so at seeing
me gravely accept the whip, that he was obliged to hide his
face in his hands, and was passed over. In a few minutes
the candles were extinguished, and we were left in total
darkness. Then an invisible preacher began exhorting his
hearers to whip themselves severely, and as he went on his
vehemence and passion increased. Presently a loud smacking
was heard all round the church, which continued a few
minutes; then the preacher urged us to fresh exertions, and
crack went the whips again louder and faster than before
as he exhorted. The faithful flogged till a bell rang; the
whips stopped, in a few minutes the candles were lit again,
and the priest came round and collected his cords. I had
squeezed mine in my hands, so that he did not see it, and I
brought it away with me. As soon as the candles were extinguished the doors were locked, so that nobody could go
out or come in till the discipline was over. I was rather
nervous when we were locked up in total darkness, but nobody
whipped me, and I certainly did not whip myself. A more
extraordinary thing (for sight it can't be called) I never witnessed. I don't think the people stripped, nor, if they did,
that the cords could have hurt them much. From thence to
St. Peter's, where we found the *quarant' ore* and the high
altar illuminated with heaps of candles. Only a few lights
scattered at a great distance through the rest of the church,
very few people there; but the dim light, the deep shades,
the vast space, and the profound stillness were sublime.
Certainly nothing in the world can approach St. Peter's, and
it always presents something new to admire.

From St. Peter's to the Vatican, to see the statues by
torchlight. The effect is wonderful, and totally unlike that
which is produced by day. The finest statues unquestion-

ably gain the most, and it is easy, after seeing this, to understand why most of the best are found in the baths; a better notion, too, may be formed of their magnificence. It would seem as if some statues had been formed expressly to be thus exhibited. There is a mutilated statue they call a Niobe (God knows why), with drapery blown back by the wind and appearing quite transparent. This effect cannot be produced by daylight.

June 2nd.—Called on Bunsen, who has not yet got an answer from the agent he sent to the office of the Grand Vicar. I had a long conversation with him about the expediency of appointing an English Minister or agent of some sort at Rome, which he thinks very desirable and very feasible, upon the same plan on which the diplomatic relations of Prussia with Rome are conducted, and which he says go on very smoothly, and without embarrassment or inconvenience. There is good faith on both sides. The Catholic bishops do not attempt to deceive the Government, and he thinks that the Court of Rome does not attempt to hold any clandestine intercourse with the Prussian States. He says Albani is a sensible man; that the cardinals are bigoted and prejudiced, hostile to England, and most of them forgetful of all the See of Rome owes to our country ; but they are still aware that, in the hour of danger, it is to England and the Protestant countries they must look for protection, as they found it when Austria wanted to strip them of the March of Ancona. He thinks there is much superstition among the lower classes, little religion among any, great immorality in all; the same desire of intriguing and extending its influence which the Romish Church has always had, but with very diminished means and resources. The Inquisition is still active in repressing heresy among Roman subjects, but not venturing to meddle with the opinions of foreigners. Its principles and its forms are the same as in former times. He says we have an inefficient Consul at Ancona, who was put in by Canning on account of his Liverpool connections. It would be very desirable to establish a regular Protestant church in Rome, with an able and permanent minister ; but there is only an occasional church, with anybody who will serve in it, and who is paid by the congregation; but such a man is totally unable to cope with the Catholic preachers, and consequently many converts are made to the Catholic religion. A Consul-General at Rome might answer the purpose of an agent, and, without being an accredited Minister, perform all the functions of one. This was the pith of what he said, besides a great deal about the Catholic religion itself, its inferiority to the Reformed, its incompatibility with free institutions, and a good deal more, not much to the purpose. Bunsen is a man of very considerable information, learned, very obliging, and communicative, sensible, moderate, but rather prejudiced. At this moment he is full of the French expedition [to Algiers], and their colonising projects, of which he is thoroughly persuaded and not a little afraid.

The Duc de Dalberg told me that at the Congress of Vienna he was deputed to speak to Consalvi about ceding the March of Ancona to the Austrians. He answered, ' My dear Duke, the Congress can treat us as it pleases. If we are pressed, we must retreat to the walls; further we cannot go, and we are there already.' The Cardinal afterwards spoke to the Emperor, and the next day Metternich said he had orders from the Emperor to declare that he would take nothing from the Pontifical States without the free concurrence of the Pope; so there ended that question.

At night.—Just returned from Frascati with Henry de Ros—a very agreeable expedition. We went to the inn, a most execrable hotel, but dined very well on a repast we had the foresight to take with us. Before dinner went to the Villa Conti, which has a delicious garden, with fine trees and ample shade, and one of the prettiest falls of water I have seen. The house we did not enter, but it appeared small. To the Villa Marconi, without any garden, but a capital house, and the only one which looks well kept and inhabited. The Marconi house in the Conti garden would be perfect. After dinner to Tusculum, a beautiful walk under shade, with magnificent views over the Campagna on one side and Monte Cavo, Rocca di Papa, and the Prati d'Annibale on the other. The remains at Tusculum are next to nothing, part of a theatre, of an aqueduct, and of the walls. I believe the town was destroyed by Pope Celestine III. (1191), in order to extirpate a band of robbers which had long infested the country and made Tusculum their stronghold. All the country hereabout is beautiful, and the air excellent, so that a more perfect residence cannot be imagined. To the Villa Belvidere, belonging to Prince Aldobrandini, deserted and neglected, but very enjoyable, full of childish waterworks, but a good house, which is to be hired for 150*l.* a year, and might be made very comfortable. Here is Mount Parnassus, and the water turns an organ, and so makes Apollo and the Muses utter horrid sounds, and a Triton has a horn which he is made to blow, producing a very discordant noise. I fell in with Lady Sandwich, and went back to tea with her at a villa which belonged to the Cardinal York. There are the royal arms of England, a bust of the Cardinal, and a picture of his father or brother. We also went to the Rufinella, whence the view is extremely fine: this was Lucien Buonaparte's villa, and the scene of the capture of a painter and a steward by the banditti, who carried them off from the door of the villa and took them into the Abruzzi, which may be descried from the terrace. The cicerone who went with us (a tiresome and chattering fellow) told us that he had attended Queen Caroline, that they had come to him for evidence against her, and he had declared he knew nothing; but he said he could have deposed to some things unfavourable to her, having seen her and Bergami together and witnessed their familiarity.

June 4th.—Yesterday rode round the walls. In the evening to the Vatican, and afterwards to Bunsen's. He gave me his memorandum to read, which is contained in a letter to Wilmot Horton of the 28th of December, 1828, upon the settlement of the Catholic question, and his view of the mode in which it might be done. He approves of Wilmot's plan, not knowing at that time that the Duke had resolved to grant unqualified emancipation. In this paper he describes the existing arrangements between the other Protestant Powers and the Court of Rome, and states in what manner he thinks we might pursue a similar course. It is well done,

and his ideas appear to me very clear and sound.   It is pretty
evident that we should meet with no difficulties here, and
that they would practically agree to everything we should require, provided we did not insist upon their doing so in specific
terms.   Our difficulties would arise from the extreme parties
at home—the ultra-Catholics and the ultra-Protestants—
but a steady hand might steer betwixt them both.   Bunsen
describes what has been done in Prussia, Hanover, Netherlands, and the minor German States; the Prussian arrangements appear to be the wisest.   When the King of Prussia
began to negotiate, he did not allow his Ministers to enter
upon any discussion of principles, nor to ask for any express
sanction of the *status quo*.   On the other hand he did not
prescribe to the Church of Rome the canonical form in which
an express or tacit acknowledgment of the claims and rights
of the Crown was to be made as to the secularisation of Church
property.   The Netherlands went on a different plan, and
framed a constitution of the Roman Catholic Church in their
dominions, called a Pragmatic Sanction, which they wanted
the Pope to acknowledge.   The Hanoverian Government
also wished to conclude a formal treaty, and oblige the Pope
to sanction certain civil regulations concerning Church government.   He observes that the Court of Rome will appear
ignorant of, and thus tacitly acknowledge, many things which
it never will nor can expressly sanction and approve.

Throughout Germany, both Catholic and Protestant, all
correspondence between the clergy and the Pope goes
through the Government by the law of the country—all
matters public and private—the Pope's bulls and briefs are
returned in the same way; and whenever any of these
contain expressions which run against the national laws,
the *placet regium* is only given with clauses reserving the
rights of the Crown, and annulling what is irreconcilable
with the civil law.   The Court of Rome is quite aware of
this practice, and the legations of Bavaria and Austria, as
well as those of Prussia and Hanover, present the respective
petitions of their clergy through their Roman agents.
Bunsen says nothing can be practically more established,

but that no consideration would induce the Pope formally to sanction the practice in a treaty.

In the arrangements respecting the appointment of bishops and dignitaries, Prussia proposed the establishment of chapters, with the same right of election which had existed before the French Revolution. The smaller States of Germany followed a similar plan. Hanover proposed and obtained a veto. The chapter presents a list; the Government strikes out any name, but must leave two, out of which the chapter may elect, but in case of irregularity or inconvenience the chapter may make a second list. The Netherlands have the same system of limited veto and second list, and the confidential brief in addition.[1] The chapters have the right of election, the Pope of confirmation, by canonical institution as the necessary condition of the bishop's consecration; but besides a confidential brief was agreed on desiring the chapter not to elect as bishop a person 'minus gratam serenissimo regi;' this ensures respect to the royal recommendation.

June 5th.—Yesterday morning called on M. de la Ferronnays, but only saw him for a minute, for the Austrian Ambassador arrived, and I was obliged to go. He is in great alarm as well as sorrow at the appointment of M. de Peyronnet[2] and the aspect of affairs in France. He told me that he had so little idea of this appointment that he would have guessed anybody rather than that man, who was so odious that he had been rejected for three successive places, for the representation of which he had stood when he was Minister; that Villèle, with all his influence, could not get him elected; and that in the Chamber of Peers he had been so intemperate that he had been repeatedly called to order, a thing which hardly ever occurred; that the Government had evidently

---

[1] [These facts, originally suggested by Bunsen at Rome to Mr. Greville, were afterwards used by him as the basis of his argument for the establishment of diplomatic relations with the Court of Rome in his book on the 'Policy of England to Ireland,' published in 1845.]

[2] [M. de Peyronnet was the Garde des Sceaux in the Polignac Cabinet; he was considered one of the most reactionary members of that ill-fated Administration.]

thrown away the scabbard by naming him on the eve of a general election, and thus offering a sort of insult to the whole nation; that it rendered his own position here very disagreeable, although his was an ecclesiastical and not a political mission, and that he in fact considered it only as an honourable retreat; yet he had written to Polignac the moment the news reached him, saying that if he considered him as in the least degree implicated politically with his Government he should immediately resign, and that if he found by his answer that he looked upon him as in the remotest degree connected with their measures he should instantly retire. I saw Dalberg afterwards, who appears to me deeply alarmed. He looks with anxiety to the Duke of Wellington as the only man whose authority or interference can arrest the French Ministry in the career which must plunge France into a civil war, if not create a general war in Europe. He believes that Metternich and the Austrians are backing up Charles X., and that, in case of any troubles, they will, in virtue of the Treaty of Chaumont, pour troops into France. His hope, then, is that the Duke will interpose and prevent this Austrian interference.

When La Ferronnays told Polignac his opinion of the course he was beginning, the other only said, ' Mon cher, tu ne connais pas le pays.' The King told Dalberg himself that he would rather labour for his bread than be King of England; that it was not being a king. In his presence, too, he asked General ——, the Governor of Paris, what was the disposition of the troops, and he answered, ' Excellent, sir; I have been in all the *casernes*, and they desire nothing so much as to fight for your Majesty;' and such words as these the King swallows and acts upon. Their confidence, audacity, and presumption are certainly admirable, disdaining any art and management, and apparently anxious to bring about a crisis with the least possible delay.

June 7th.—Drove about yesterday taking leave of people and places, the former of which I probably shall, and the latter shall not, see again. I have seen almost everything, but leave Rome with great regret, principally because I am afraid I shall never come again. If I was sure of returning I should not mind it.

Three o'clock.—Have determined to stay till after the Corpus Domini. Called on the Cardinal, who received me *à bras ouverts*, was full of civilities, and reconducted me to the outward room ; talked of the Catholics and of the anxiety of his Government to see relations established with ours. I was obliged to go and take leave of him, for Bruti brought me a message full of politeness and a letter to convey to the Nuncio at Paris. Then to La Ferronnays, who says, as does Dalberg, that he is persuaded it will end by the recall of Villèle to the Ministry, a compromise that all parties will be glad to make—that he has had the prudence to decline being a party to Polignac's Administration, and when he is called to form one he will have nothing to say to Polignac.[1] It certainly will be curious if Villèle, after being driven from the Government with universal execration, and almost proscribed, should in two years be recalled by the general voice as the only man who can save France from anarchy and civil war. La Ferronnays says that Villèle is not a great Minister, but a clever man, with great ingenuity and the art of management. He wishes to be thought like Pitt, who was also obliged to quit the Ministry, and afterwards resumed it ; and he considers Polignac as his Addington, not that the resemblance holds good in any of the particulars, either of the men, or the times, or the circumstances.

June 8th.—Last night to the La Ferronnays', when the Princess Aldobrandini was so delighted with the anecdote of my horse-shoe that she has gone off to the Pantheon to look at it. It was a full moon and a clear night, so I went to the Coliseum, and passed an hour there. I never saw it so

---

[1] [M. de Villèle had come to Paris from his country seat in April, and a secret attempt had been made to bring him back to power. Prince Polignac offered him a seat in the Cabinet, but showed no disposition to make way for him. The King feared Villèle and preferred Polignac. Yet if M. de Villèle had then returned to power, he would probably have saved the monarchy and changed the course of events in Europe. (See Duvergier de Hauranne, 'Histoire du Gouvernement parlementaire en France,' tome x. p. 468, for a narrative of these transactions.)]

well; the moon rode above without a cloud, but with a
brilliant planet close to her; there was not a breath of air,
not a human being near but the soldiers at the gates below,
and the monk above with me; not a sound was heard but
those occasional noises of the night, the bark of a dog, the
chimes from churches and convents, the chirp of a bird,
which only served to make silence audible. Though I have
seen the Coliseum a dozen times before, I never was so
delighted with its beauty and grandeur as to-night. No
description in poetry or painting can do it justice; it is a
'wreck of ruinous perfection,' whose charm must be felt,
and on such a night as this. The measures which the
Government have taken to save the Coliseum from destruction will certainly accomplish that end, but its picturesque
appearance will be greatly damaged. There is no part of
the ruin which is not already supported by some modern
brickwork, and they are building a wall which will nearly
surround it. If they had been more selfish they would
have left it to moulder away, and posterity to grumble over
their stinginess or indifference. I am always tossed backwards and forwards between admiration of the Coliseum and
St. Peter's, and admire most that which I see last. They
are certainly 'magis pares quam similes,' but worth everything else in Italy put together, except Pæstum.

To-day the spiritual arms of the Church are to be fulmi-
nated against a sinner in a case which is rather curious.
There are two brothers who live at a place called Genazzano,
in two adjoining houses, which formerly formed but one,
belonging to the Colonna family, of whom the progenitors
of these men bought it. A short time ago a man came to
the brothers and told them that in a particular spot on the
premises there was a treasure concealed, the particulars of
which he had learned from a memorandum in the papers of
the Colonna family, to which he had got access, and he
proposed to discover the same to them, if they would give
him a part of it. They agreed, when he told them that
under a little column built against a wall they would find a
flat brick, covering a hole, in which was an earthen pot

containing 2,000 ducats in gold. The column was there, so at night the brothers set to work to take it down, and beneath it they found the flat stone as described. When one of them (an apothecary) said to the other that, after all, it was probably an invention, that they should be laughed at for their pains, and he thought they had better give up the search, the other (who must be a great flat) said, 'Very well,' and they retired to bed. In the morning the apothecary told the other that in the night he could not help thinking of this business, and that his curiosity had induced him to get up and dig on, and that he had actually found the pot, but nothing in it. The other, flat as he was, could not stand this, and, on examining the pot, he found marks which, on further investigation, turned out to be indications of coin having been in it. The thief stuck to his story, so the dupe complained, and, as the presumption is considered to be strongly against him, they are going to try what excommunication will do. It is remarkable that they asked this man if he would swear upon the Host that he had not found any money, and this he refused to do, though he continued to deny it and to decline restitution. He was accounted a very religious man, and these were religious scruples, which, however, were not incompatible with robbery and fraud. His refusal to swear was taken as a moral evidence of guilt, and he was to be excommunicated to-day.

June 9th.—Saw Torlonia's house ; very fine, and the only one in Rome which is comfortably furnished, and looks as if it was inhabited. A great many good pictures, and Canova's 'Hercules' and 'Lycus,' which I do not admire. In the evening to the convent of SS. Giovanni e Paolo, which is remarkably clean and well kept. There are forty-five friars (Passionisti), whose vows were not irrevocable, and though the cases do not often occur, they can lay aside the habit if they please. They live on charity. In their garden is a beautiful palm, one of three which grow in Rome. They have several apartments for strangers who may like to retire to the convent for a few days, which are very decently furnished, clean, and not uncomfortable. They were at

supper when I got there, so I went to look at them.   They
eat in silence at two long tables like those in our college
halls, and instead of conversation they were entertained by
some passages of the life of St. Ignatius, which a friar was
reading from a pulpit.   Their supper seemed by no means
despicable, for I met a smoking *frittura* which looked and
smelt very good, and the table was covered with bread, fruit,
vegetables, and wine.   But they fast absolutely three times
a week, and whip themselves (*la disciplina*) three others.
They teach theology and *la dogmatica*, and there is a
library containing (they told me) books of all sorts, though
their binding (for I only saw them through a trellis) looked
desperately theological.   At night to a very fine *feu d'artifice*
in the Piazza San Lorenzo, which ended the festivities in
honour of San Francesco Caraccioli, whose name appeared
emblazoned amidst rockets and squibs and crackers, and the
uproarious delight of the mob.   Afterwards to the Pantheon
to see it by moonlight, but the moon was not exactly over
the roof, so it failed, but the effect of the partial light and
the stars above was fine with the torches below half hid behind the columns.

June 10th.—I thought I had seen everything here worth
seeing, yet, though I have been several times to the Capitol,
I have somehow missed seeing the Palazzo dei Conservatori,
containing the famous wolf that suckled Romulus and Remus,
in bronze, said to have been struck by lightning (of which
it bears all the marks) the day Julius Cæsar was killed ; the
boy picking the thorn from his foot ; the statue of the first
Brutus ; the geese of the Capitol (which are more like ducks) ;
and the Fasti Consulares.   It just occurred to me in time,
and I went there yesterday morning.   After dinner to the
Villa Ludovisi with the Dalbergs and Aldobrandinis, which
must owe its celebrity principally to the difficulty of getting
access to it.   I was extremely disappointed ; Guercino's
' Aurora ' is not to be compared to Guido's ; his ' Day ' and
' Night ' are very fine, and the ' Fame ' magnificent, but the
ladies bustled through so rapidly that it was not possible to
examine anything.   The gardens are large, but all straight

walks and clipped hedges. The gallery of statues contains three or four fine things, but they are huddled together and their effect spoilt.

June 11th.—Whilst the carriage is getting ready I may as well scribble the last day at Rome. And this morning went at eight to the Palazzo Accoramboni, to see the procession of the Corpus Domini, and was disappointed. This Palazzo Accoramboni, in which we were accommodated, belonged to a very rich old man, who was married to a young and pretty wife. He died and left her all his fortune, but, suspecting that she was attached to a young man who used to frequent the house, he made the bequest conditional upon her not marrying again, and if she did the whole property was to go to some religious order. She was fool enough (and the man too) to marry, but clandestinely. She had two children, and this brought the marriage to light. They therefore lost the property amounting to 10,000*l*. or 12,000*l*. a year; but the Pope, in his vast generosity, allows her out of it 300 piastres (about 65*l*.) a year, and gives a portion of 1,000 piastres (200*l*.) to each of the little girls. It is supposed that she consulted some priest, who urged her to marry secretly, and then revealed the fact to the order interested. Otherwise it is difficult to account for their folly.

The magnificence of ceremonies and processions here depends upon the locality, and the awnings and flowers round the piazza spoilt it all. It was long and rather tiresome — all the monks and religious orders in Rome, the cardinals and the Pope, plenty of wax-lights, banners, and crosses, the crosses of Constantine and Charlemagne. The former is not genuine; that of Charlemagne is really the one he gave to the See. The Pope looks as if he was huddled into a short bed, and his throne, or whatever it is called, is ill managed. He is supposed to be in the act of adoration of the Host, which is raised before him, but as he cannot kneel for such a length of time, he sits covered with drapery, and with a pair of false legs stuck out behind to give his figure the appearance of kneeling. Before him are borne the triple crown and other Pontifical ornaments. The Guardia Nobile,

commanded by Prince Barberini, looked very handsome, and
all the troops *en très-belle tenue.* All the Ambassadors
and foreigners were in this palace, and from it we flocked
to St. Peter's, which is always a curious sight on these occasions from the multitudes in it and the variety of their appearance and occupation—cardinals, princes, princesses,
mixed up with footmen, pilgrims, and peasants. Here, Mass
going on at an altar, and crowds kneeling round it; there,
the Host deposited amidst a peal of music at another; in
several corners, cardinals dressing or undressing, for they all
take off the costume they wore in the procession and resume
their scarlet robes in the church; men hurrying about with
feathers, banners, and other paraphernalia of the day, the
peasantry in their holiday attire, and crowds of curious
idlers staring about. All this is wonderfully amusing, and
is a scene which presents itself in continual variety. Went
afterwards and took leave of all my friends—La Ferronnays,
Dalbergs, Bunsens, Lovaines, &c.—and at seven, to my great
sorrow, left Rome. But as I do all that superstition dictates,
I drank in the morning a glass of water at the Fountain of
Trevi, for they say that nobody ever drinks of the Fountain
of Trevi without returning to Rome.

The road about Narni and Augustus's Bridge is beautifully
picturesque. I set off directly to the cascade, with which I
was as much delighted as I was disappointed with that of
Tivoli. It is difficult to conceive anything more magnificent
than the whole of this scenery.

Florence, June 10*th.*—The horses were announced, and I
was obliged to break off my account of Terni and resume it
here, where I arrived after a tedious journey of forty hours
from Rome.

Most people are dragged up the mountain by *bovi,* see the
upper part of the fall, and walk down. But as the *bovi* were
not at hand, I reversed the usual order, walked to the bottom,
and then toiled to the top. The walk, which is lovely, lies
through the grounds of a count, who has a house close to
the Nera (the Nera (Nar) is the river into which the Velino
runs, and in which there is very good trout fishing), where

the Queen of England once lived for a month. At the different points of view are little cabins (which would be very picturesque if they were less rudely constructed) for the accommodation of artists and other travellers. This gentleman has got a house which he reserves for the use of artists, of which there are always several on the spot during the summer. They pay nothing for the accommodation, but each is obliged to leave a drawing when he goes away; and by this means he has got an interesting collection of the scenery of Terni. Nothing can be more accurate, as well as beautiful, than Byron's description of the cascade, and it is wonderful in his magnificent poetry, how he has kept his imagination within the bounds of truth, and neither added a circumstance nor lavished an epithet to which it is not entitled.

> Horribly beautiful! but on the verge
> From side to side, beneath the glittering morn,
> An Iris sits amidst the infernal surge,
> Like Hope upon a death-bed, and, unworn
> Its steady dyes, while all around is torn
> By the distracted waters, bears serene
> Its brilliant hues with all their beams unshorn :
> Resembling, 'mid the torture of the scene,
> Love watching Madness with unalterable mien.

The rainbows are very various, seen from different points: from the middle, where the river rushes from the vortex of the great fall to plunge into another, the stream appears to be painted with a broad layer of divers colours, never broken or mixed till they are tossed up in the cloud of spray, and mingled with it in a thousand variegated sparkles. Above, an iris bestrides the moist green hill which rises by the side of the fall; and, as the spray is whirled up in greater or less abundance, it perpetually and rapidly changes its colours, now disappearing altogether, and now beaming with the utmost vividness. The man told me that at night the moon forms a white rainbow on the hill. There is a delicious but dangerous coolness all about the cascade. All the scenery about is as beautiful as possible. Just above the great fall is the Velinus tearing along in the same channel, which was first made for him by the Roman Consul 2,200 years ago—

> Velino cleaves the wave-worn precipice—

and there, the guide told me, some years ago a man threw in a young and beautiful wife of whom he was jealous. He took her to see the cascade, and when he got to this part (which is at the end of a narrow path overhung with brush-wood) he got rid of the boys who always follow visitors, and after some delay returned alone, and said the woman had fallen in. One scream had been heard, but there was no-body to witness the truth. The mangled body was found in the stream below. Jealousy is probably common here. As I was walking a man passed me, going in great haste to the mountain, but I paid no attention to him. When I got back I heard that he was escaping from justice (into the Abruzzi, which are in the Neapolitan dominions), having stabbed his brother-in-law a few moments before out of jealousy of his wife. The wounded man was still alive, but badly hurt. The murderer was *un bravo meccanico*.

The mountain and the river have undergone many revolutions. The rock through which the present path is cut has been formed entirely by petrified deposits, and there are marks in various parts of former cascades, from which the water has been turned away. Clement VIII. (Aldobrandini) turned the water into its present course. At the bottom the old outlet of the Romans is dry, but is marked with that solidity which defies time, like all their works of this kind. Great part of the road from Terni is beautiful, and the Papal towns and villages appear to be in much better condition than on the other road. Some of them perched on the mountains are remarkably picturesque.

Bologna, June 14th.—I went yesterday morning to Pratolino to see the statue of the genius of the Apennines, by John of Bologna, six miles from Florence. Pratolino was the favourite residence of the famous Bianca Capello. The house has been pulled down. It is in a very pretty English garden belonging to the Grand Duke, and, I think, amazingly

grand, but disgraced by presiding over a duck pond. They
told me that if he stood up (and he looks as if he could if
he would) he would be thirty *braccia* in height. I went
into his head, and surveyed him on all sides. He ought to
be placed over some torrent, or on the side of a mountain;
but as he is, from a little distance (whence the ducks and
their pond are not visible) he is sublime. Myriads of
fire-flies sparkled in every bush; they are beautiful in a
night journey, flitting about like meteors and glittering like
shooting stars.

Dined with Lady Normanby at Sesto, set off at half-past
eight, and arrived here at nine this morning. The first thing
I did was to present my letter to Madame de Marescalchi
from her sister, the Duchesse de Dalberg, who received me
graciously and asked me to dinner; the next to call on
Mezzofanti at the public library, whom I found at his desk
in the great room, surrounded by a great many people reading. He received me very civilly, and almost immediately
took me into another room, where I had a long conversation
with him. He seems to be between fifty and sixty years of
age, short, pale, and thin, and not at all remarkable in
countenance or manner. He spoke English with extraordinary fluency and correctness, and with a very slight accent.
I endeavoured to detect some inaccuracy of expression, but
could not, though perhaps his phraseology was occasionally
more stiff than that of an Englishman would be. He gave
me an account of his beginning to study languages, which
he did not do till he was of a mature age. The first he
mastered were the Greek and Hebrew, the latter on account
of divinity, and afterwards he began the modern languages,
acquiring the idioms of each as he became acquainted with
the parent tongue. He said that he had no particular disposition that way when a child, and I was surprised when
he said that the knowledge of several languages was of no
assistance to him in mastering others; on the contrary,
that when he set to work at a fresh language he tried to
put out of his head all others. I asked him of all modern
languages which he preferred, and which he considered the

richest in literature. He said, ' Without doubt the Italian.'
He then discussed the genius of the English language, and
the merits of our poets and historians, read, and made me
read, a passage of an English book, and then examined the
etymology and pronunciation of several words. He has never
been out of Italy, or further in it than Leghorn, talks of
going to Rome, but says it is so difficult to leave his library.
He is very pleasing, simple, and communicative, and it is
extraordinary, with his wonderful knowledge, that he should
never have written and published any work upon languages.
He asked me to return if I stayed at Bologna. The library
has a tolerable suite of apartments, and the books, amounting to about 80,000 volumes, are in excellent order. One
thousand crowns a year are allowed for the purchase of new
books.

The Bolognese jargon is unintelligible. A man came
and asked him some questions while I was there in a
language that was quite strange to me, and when I asked
Mezzofanti what it was, he said Bolognese, and that, though
not harmonious, it was forcible and expressive. Afterwards to the gallery, which contains the finest pictures in
Italy, though only a few: the Guidos and Domenichinos are
splendid. I think Domenichino the finest painter that ever
existed.

June 15th.—Dined yesterday with Madame de Marescalchi,
who lives in a great palace, looking dirty and uncomfortable,
except one or two rooms which they occupy. There is a
gallery of pictures, all of which are for sale. Seven or eight
Italians came to dinner, whose names I never discovered.
After dinner she took me to the Certosa, to see the Campo
Santo, which is a remarkably pretty spot, and the dead appear
to be more agreeably lodged at Bologna than the living. I
had much rather die here than live here. It is very unlike
the Campo Santo at Pisa, entirely modern, and looks exceedingly cheerful. Guido's skull is kept here.

Went again to the gallery, and the Zambeccari Palace,
where there are a few good pictures, but not many. All the
pictures in all the palaces are for sale.

In the ferry, crossing the Po (i.e. written in the ferry).

Called on Madame de Marescalchi to take leave. Set off at half-past one, and in clouds of dust arrived at Ferrara. It is curious to see this town, so large, deserted, and melancholy. A pestilence might have swept over it, for there seems no life in it, and hardly a soul is to be seen in the streets. It is eight and a half miles round, and contains 24,000 inhabitants, of which 3,000 are Jews, and their quarter is the only part of the town which seems alive. They are, as usual, crammed into a corner, five streets being allotted to them, at each end of which is a gate that is closed at nine o'clock, when the Jews are shut in for the night. The houses are filthy, stinking, and out of repair. The Corso is like a street in an English town, broad, long, the houses low, and with a *trottoir* on both sides. The Castle, surrounded by a moat, stands in the middle of the town, a gloomy place. In it lives the Cardinal Legate. I went to see the dungeon in which Tasso was confined; and the library, where they show Ariosto's chair and inkstand, a medal found upon his body when his tomb was opened, two books of his manuscript poetry; also the manuscript of the 'Gerusalemme,' with the alterations which Tasso made in it while in prison, and the original manuscript of Guarini's 'Pastor Fido.' The *custode* told me that in the morning the library was full of readers, which I did not believe. There are some illuminated Missals, said to be the finest in Italy. Though the idea of gaiety seems inconsistent with Ferrara, they have an opera, corso, and the same round of festivals and merriment as other Italian towns, but I never saw so dismal a place.

Venice, June 16*th.*—We crossed the Po, and afterwards the Adige, in boats. The country is flat, and reminded me of the Netherlands. I was asleep all night, but awoke in time to see some of the villas on the banks of the Brenta. Of Padua I was unconscious. Embarked in a gondola at Fusina, and arrived at this remarkable city under the bad auspices of a dark, gloomy, and very cold day. It is Venice, but living Venice no more. In my progress to the inn I

saw nothing but signs of ruin and blasted grandeur, palaces
half decayed, and the windows boarded up.   The approach
to the city is certainly as curious as possible, so totally unlike everything else, and on entering the Great Canal, and
finding

> The death-like silence and the dread repose

of a place which was once the gayest and most brilliant in the
world, a little pang shoots across the imagination, recollecting
its strange and romantic history and its poetical associations.

Two o'clock.—I am just driven in by a regular rainy day,
and have the prospect of shivering through the rest of it in
a room with marble floor and hardly any furniture.   However, it is the only bad day there has been since the beginning
of my expedition.   The most striking thing in Venice (at
least in such weather as this) is the unbroken silence.   The
gondolas glide along without noise or motion, and, except
other gondolas, one may traverse the city without per-
ceiving a sign of life.   I went first to the Church of Santa
Maria dei Frati, which is fine, old, and adorned with painting
and sculpture.   At Santa Maria dei Frati Titian was buried.
Canova intended a monument for him, but after his death his
design was executed and put up in this church, but for him,
and not for Titian, the reverse of ' sic vos non vobis.'   Here
are tombs of several Doges, of Francis Foscari, with a pompous
inscription.   The body of Carmagnola lies here in a wooden
coffin ; his head is under the stone on which it was cut off
in the Piazza di San Marco.   He was beheaded by one of
those pieces of iniquity and treachery which the Venetian
Government never scrupled to use when it suited them.
Then to the Scuola di San Rocco, containing a splendid
apartment and staircase, all richly gilded, painted by Tintoret,
and with bronze doors.   To the Church of Santa Maria della
Salute, containing a very rich altar-piece of precious stones,
which is locked up, and produced on great occasions ; and in
the sacristy three fine pictures by Titian.   To the Church
of St. Mark and the Doge's Palace—all very interesting,
antique, and splendid.   But the Austrians have modernised
some of the rooms, and consequently spoilt them.   They

have also blocked up the Bridge of Sighs, and the reason (they told me) is that all the foreigners who come here are so curious to walk over it, which seems an odd one for shutting it up. The halls of audience and of the different councils are magnificently gilded, and contain some very fine pictures.·

The Hall of the Council of Ten (the most powerful and the most abominable tribunal that ever existed) has been partly modernised. In the Chamber of the Inquisitors of State is still the hole in the wall which was called the ' Lion's Mouth,' through which written communications were made ; and the box into which they fell, which the Inquisitors alone could open. There were ' Bocche di Lioni ' in several places at the head of the Giant's Staircase, and in others. The mouths are gone, but the holes remain. Though the interior of the Ponte di Sospiri is no longer visible, the prisons are horrible places, twenty-four in number, besides three others under water which the French had closed up. They are about fourteen feet long, seven wide, and seven high, with one hole to admit air, a wooden bed, which was covered with straw, and a shelf. In one of the prisons are several inscriptions, scrawled on the wall and ceiling.

> Di chi mi fido, mi guardi Iddio,
> Di chi non mi fido, mi guardo io.
>
> Un parlar pocho, un negar pronto,
> Un pensar in fine può dar la vita
> A noi altri meschini.
>
> Non fida d'alcuno, pensi e tacci
> Se fuggir vuoi di spioni, insidie e lacci.
> Il pentirti, il pentirti, nulla giova
> Ma ben del valor tuo far vera prova.

There are two places in which criminals, or prisoners, were secretly executed; they were strangled, and without seeing their executioner, for a cord was passed through an opening, which he twisted till the victim was dead. This was the mode pursued with the prisoners of the Inquisitors; those of the Council were often placed in a cell to which

there was a thickly grated window, through which the
executioner did his office, and if they resisted he stabbed
them in the throat. The wall is still covered with the blood
of those who have thus suffered. From the time of their erec-
tion, 800 years ago, to the destruction of the Republic nobody
was ever allowed to see these prisons, till the French came
and threw them open, when the people set fire to them
and burnt all the woodwork; the stone was too solid to
be destroyed. One or two escaped, and they remain as
memorials of the horrors that were perpetrated in them.

June 17th.—This morning was fine again, and everything
looks gayer than yesterday. From the Rialto to the Piazza
di San Marco there is plenty of life and movement, and it
is exactly like Cranbourne Alley and the other alleys out of
Leicester Square. While Venice was prosperous St. Mark's
must have been very brilliant, but everything is decayed.
All round the piazza are coffee houses, which used to be open
and crowded all night, and some of them are still open, but
never crowded. They used to be illuminated with lamps all
round, but most of these are gone. One sees a few Turks
smoking and drinking their coffee here, but they are all
obliged to dine and sleep in one house, which is on the
Grand Canal, and called the Casa dei Turchi. I went this
morning to the Chiesa Scalzi, San Georgio Meggiore, Re-
dentore, SS. Giovanni e Paolo, and the Gesuiti. The
latter is the most beautiful church I ever saw, the whole of
it adorned with white marble inlaid with verd antique in a
regular pattern. SS. Giovanni e Paolo has no marble or
gilding, but is full of monuments of Doges and generals.
To the Manfrini Palace for the pictures. The finest picture
in the palace is Titian's ' Deposition from the Cross,' for which
the Marchese Manfrini refused 10,000 ducats. A Guido
(Lucretia) and some others. Tintoret was no doubt a great
genius, but his large pictures I cannot admire, and Bassano's
still less. Titian's portrait of Ariosto is the most interesting
in the collection. To the Arsenal, which is three miles in
circumference, and a prodigious establishment. In the time
of the Republic there were nearly 6,000 men employed in it,

in that of the French 4,000, now 800. The old armoury is very curious, full of ancient weapons, the armour of Henry IV. of France, and of several Doges, Turkish spoils, and instruments of torture. The Austrians have made the French much regretted here. It is since the last peace that the population of Venice has diminished a fourth, and the palaces of the nobles have been abandoned. There is no commerce; the Government spend no money, and do nothing to enliven or benefit the town (there has not yet been time to see the effect of making it a free port). The French employed the people, and spent money and embellished the place. They covered over a wide canal and turned it into a fine street, and adjoining it they formed a large public garden, which is a delightful addition to the town. Till the French came the bridges were dangerous; there was no balustrade on either side, and people often fell into the water. They built side walls to all of them, which was the most useful gift they could bestow upon the Venetians.

This morning I asked for the newspapers which came by the post yesterday, and found that they had not yet returned from the police, and would not be till to-morrow. Before anybody is allowed to read their newspapers they must undergo examination, and if they contain anything which the censor deems objectionable they detain them altogether. After dinner I went to the public gardens, and into a theatre which is in them; there is no roof to it, and the acting is all by daylight, and in the open air. I only arrived at the end, just in time to see the deliverance of a Christian heroine and a very truculent-looking Turk crammed down a trap-door, but I could not understand the dialogue. Nothing certainly can be more extraordinary or more beautiful than Venice with her adjacent islands, and nothing more luxurious than throwing oneself into a gondola and smoothly gliding about the whole day, without noise, motion, or dust. At night I went to a dirty, ill-lit theatre, to see the ' Barbiere di Seviglia,' which was very ill performed. There was a ballet, but I did not stay for it.

June 18th.—To the Church of St. Mark, and examined

it. It is not large, but very curious, so loaded with ornament within and without, and so unlike any other church.
The pavement, instead of being flat, is made to undulate
like the waves of the sea. All the sides are marble, all the
top mosaic, all the pavement coloured marble in exquisite
patterns. There is not a single tomb in it, but it wants no
ornament that the wealth and skill of ages could supply.
Climbed up the tower to see Venice and the islands; a
man is posted here day and night to strike the hours and
quarters on a great bell, to ring the alarm in case of fire in
any part of the city. It is a very curious panorama, and
the only spot from which this strange place can be completely seen. In the Grimani Palace there are some Titians
(not very good) of Grimani Doges, and others of the family;
the famous statue of Agrippa, which Cardinal Grimani
brought from Rome, and a ceiling by Salviati of Neptune
and Minerva contending to give a name to Athens. In the
Pisani Palace, a fine picture of P. Veronese, ' Darius's Family
at the Feet of Alexander.'[1] The Barbarigo Palace has never
been modernised, has kept all its original form and decorations. It is full of Titians, all very dirty and spoiling. The
finest is the ' Magdalen,' which is famous. The Royal
Academy, called the Scuola della Carità, contains a magnificent collection of the Venetian school.

In I forget which church is the ' Martyrdom of St. Peter '
by Titian, so like in composition the same subject by
Domenichino at Bologna that the one is certainly an imitation of the other (Titian died in 1576; Domenichino was
born in 1581). There is the same sort of landscape, same
number of figures, and in the same respective attitudes
and actions, and even the same dress to each. In the hall
of the Academy are preserved Canova's right hand in an
urn, and underneath it his chisel, with these words inscribed : ' Quod amoris monumentum idem gloriæ instru-
mentum fuit.' There is also a collection of drawings and
sketches by various masters; some by M. Angelo and some
by Raphael.

[1] [This fine work is now in the National Gallery, London.]

Vicenza, June 19*th.*—This morning went again to St. Mark's to examine the library and the palace, which I could hardly see the other day, it was such gloomy weather. The library is open to everybody, but with a long list of rules, among which silence is particularly enjoined. The *custos librorum* is a thorough Venetian; talked with fond regret of the splendour of the Republic, and is very angry with Daru for his history. The Hall of the Great Council, containing the portraits of the Doges (and Marino Faliero's black curtain), is splendid, and adorned with paintings of Paul Veronese, Bassano, Tintoret, and Palma Giovane. At twelve o'clock I got into the gondola and left Venice without the least regret or desire to return there. The banks of the Brenta would be very gay if the villas were inhabited, but most of them are shut up, like the palaces at Venice. There is one magnificent building, formerly a Pisani palace, which belongs to the Viceroy, the Archduke Rainer.

Padua is a large and rather gloomy town. They say it is beginning to flourish, having been ruined by the French, and that, since their downfall, the population has increased immensely. The University contains 1,400 scholars. It contained 52,500 in the time of the French, and in the great days of Padua 18,000. I went to look at the outside of the building, which is not large, but handsome. The old palace of the Carraras is half ruined, and what remains is tenanted by the commandant of the place. The old Sala di Giustizia, which is very ancient, is now a lumber room, and they were painting scenes in it. Still it is undamaged, and they call it the finest room in Europe, and perhaps it is. It is 300 feet long, 100 wide, and 100 high. At one end of it is the monument and bust of Livy, the latter of which they pretend to have found here; they also talk of his house and the marbles, &c., that have been dug up in it, which they may believe who can. The Cathedral has nothing to boast of, except that Petrarch was one of its canons, and in it is his bust, put up by a brother canon. I had not time to go to the churches.

The whole road from Fusina to this place is as flat as

the paper on which I am writing. I really don't believe
there is a molehill, but it is extremely gay from the variety
of habitations and the prodigious cultivation of all sorts.
Vicenza is one of the most agreeable towns I ever saw, and
I would rather live in it than in any place I have seen since
Rome. It is spacious and clean, full of Palladio's architecture; besides the Palazzo della Ragione, a very fine
building, there are twenty-two palaces built by him in
various parts of the town. They show the house in which
he lived. From the Church of Santa Maria del Monte, a
mile from the town, there is a magnificent view, and the
town itself, under the mountains of the Tyrol, and the end
of a vast cultivated plain, looks very inviting and gay. There
is a Campo di Marte, a public walk and drive, and from it a
covered walk (colonnade) half a mile long up to the church
on the hill. One of the most remarkable things here is the
Olympic Theatre, which was begun by Palladio and finished
by his son. It is a small Grecian theatre, exactly as he
supposes those ancient theatres to have been, with the same
proscenium, scenes, decorations, and seats for the audience.
There appeared to me to be some material variations from
the theatre at Pompeii. In the latter the seats go down to
the level of the orchestra, which they do not here, and at
Pompeii there is no depth behind the proscenium, whereas
here there is very considerable. It is, however, a beautiful
model. The air and the water are good, and there is shooting, so that I really think it would be possible to live here.
They talk with horror of the French, and of the two seem to
prefer the Austrians, but peace is better than war, *cæteris
varibus.*

Brescia, June 21*st.*—This is a particularly nice town,
airy, spacious, and clean, and in my life I never saw so
many good-looking women. There is a drive and walk on
the ramparts, where I found all the beauty and fashion of
Brescia, a string of carriages not quite so numerous as in
Hyde Park, but a very decent display. The women are excessively dressed, and almost all wear black lace veils, thrown
over the back of the head, which are very becoming. The

walks on the ramparts are shaded by double rows of trees, and command a very pretty view of the mountains and country round. This inn is execrable. I stopped at Verona to see the Amphitheatre, which is only perfect in the inside, and has been kept so by repeated repairs. It is hardly worth seeing after the Flavian and the Pompeiian. There is a wooden theatre in it, where they act, and the spectators occupy the ancient seats. The tombs of the Scaligeri are admirable, the most beautiful and graceful Gothic; their castle (now the Castle Vecchio) a gloomy old building in a moat, but with a very curious bridge over the Po. The Church of St. Zeno is remarkable from its Gothic antiquity and the profusion of ornament about it of a strange sort. Here is the tomb of Pepin, erected by Charlemagne, but empty; for the French, in one of their invasions, carried the body to France. In the Cathedral is a fine picture of the ' Assumption of the Virgin' by Titian. I saw many Veronese beauties in their balconies, but none quite like Juliet. Her tomb (or, as they would say at Rome, ' sepolcro detto di Giulietta ') I did not see, for it was too far off. I was in a hurry to be off, and there was nobody to detain me with a tender ' Wilt thou be gone? It is not yet near' *night*. The road, which is excellent, runs in sight of the Alps all the way, and the Lago di Garda is excessively pretty.

Milan, June 23rd.—Milan is a very fine town, without much to see in it. The Duomo, Amphitheatre, Arch of the Simplon, Brera (pictures). There are a few fine pictures in the Brera; among others Guido's famous ' St. Peter and St. Paul,' Guercino's ' Hagar and Abraham ; ' a row of old columns which were broken and lying about till the French set them upon their legs; Leonardo da Vinci's fresco, which is entirely spoilt. The view from the top of the Duomo is superb, over the boundless plain of Lombardy with the range of the Alps, and the Apennines in the distance. I like the Duomo, but I know my taste is execrable in architecture. I don't, however, like the mixture of Italian with the Gothic —balustrades over the door, for instance—but I admire its tracery and laborious magnificence. Buonaparte went on with it (for it was never finished), and this Government are completing it by degrees; there will be 7,000 statues on different parts of the outside, and there are already 4,500. St. Charles Borromeo's tomb is very splendid, and for five francs they offered to uncover the glass case in which his much esteemed carcase reposes, and show me the venerable mummy, but I could not afford it. The entrance to Milan from Venice, and the Corso, are as handsome as can be. The Opera is very bad, but the Scala is not open, and none of the good singers are here.

Varese, June 26th.—Left Milan at six o'clock on the 24th, and got to Como after dark. Embarked in the steam boat at eight yesterday morning, went as far as Cadenebbia, where I got out, saw the Villa Sommariva, then crossed over and went round the point of Bellagio to see the opening of the Lake of Lecco, turned back to the Villa Melzi, saw the house and gardens, and then went back to dine at Cadenabbia, and waited for the steam boat, which returned at four, and got back to Como at half-past six. Nothing can surpass the beauty of all this scenery, or the luxury of the villas, particularly Melzi, which is the best house, and contains abundance of shade, flowers, statues, and shrubberies. The owners live very little there, and principally in winter, when, they say, it is seldom cold in this sheltered spot. The late Count Melzi was Governor of Milan under Napoleon, and used to feast the Viceroy here. He once gave him a *fête*, and had all the mountain tops illuminated, of which the effect must have been superb.

Evening. Top of the Simplon.—Set off at five from Varese, travelled very slowly through a very pretty road to Navero, where I crossed the Lago Maggiore in a boat, and landed at the Isola Bella, which is very fine in its way, though rather flattered in its pictures. The house is large and handsome, and there is a curious suite of apartments fitted up with pebbles, spars, and marble, a suite of habitable grottoes. The garden and terraces are good specimens of formal grandeur, and as the Count Borromeo's son is a botanist, they are full of flowers and shrubs of all sorts and climates.

Whatever fruits in different climes are found,
That proudly rise or humbly court the ground;
Whatever sweets salute the northern sky
With vernal flowers, that blossom but to die;
These, here disporting, own the kindred soil,
Nor ask luxuriance from the planter's toil.

The expense of keeping this place up is immense, but the owner is very rich. He lives there during August and September, and has fifteen other country houses. All the island belongs to him, and is occupied by the palace and gardens, except some fishermen's huts, which are held by a sort of feudal tenure. They live there as his vassals, fishing for him, rowing him about the lake, and their children and wives alone are employed in the gardens. It was built about 150 years ago by a younger son (a nephew of San Carlo), who was richer than his elder brother. He was his own architect, and planned both house and garden, but never completed his designs. The cost was enormous, but if he had lived and finished it all, he would have spent four millions more. There is a laurel in the garden, the largest in Europe, two trees growing from one stem, one nine and the other ten feet round and eighty high; under this tree Buonaparte dined, as he came into Italy, before the battle of Marengo, and with a knife he cut the word 'Battaglia' on the bark, which has since been stripped off, or has grown out—so the gardeners said at least. Breakfasted at Baveno, which is the best inn I have seen in Italy. The road from Baveno is exceedingly beautiful, but on the whole I am rather disappointed with the Simplon, though it is very wild and grand; but I am no longer struck with the same admiration at the sight of mountains that I was when I entered Savoy and saw them for the first time. I walked the last thirteen miles of the ascent to this place, and found one of the best dinners I ever tasted, or one which my hunger made appear such.

Geneva, June 29th.—Got here last night, and found twenty letters at least. I only think of getting home as fast as I can. Left the Simplon in torrents of rain, which lasted the whole day. The descent is uncommonly grand,

wild, savage, and picturesque, the Swiss side the finest. All
along the valley of the Rhone fine scenery; and yesterday,
in the most delightful weather I ever saw, the drive from
Martigny, along the lake and under the mountains, was
as beautiful as possible. The approach to Geneva is gay,
but Mont Blanc looks only very white, and not very tall,
which is owing to the level from which he is seen. They
tell me it has never ceased raining here, while on the other
side of the Alps hardly a drop has fallen. Only three rainy
days while I was in Italy—one at Venice, one at Rome, and
a couple of halves elsewhere.

Evening.—Passed the whole day driving about Geneva, in
Bautt's shop, and at the Panorama of Switzerland. Dined
with Newton, drove round the environs by Sécheron; a
great appearance of wealth and comfort, much cultivation,
no beggars, and none of the houses tumbling down and
deserted. Altogether I like the appearance of the place,
though in a great hurry to get away from it. We had a
storm of thunder and lightning in the evening, which was
neither violent nor long, but I had the pleasure of
hearing

> Jura answer from her misty shroud
> Back to the joyous Alps, that call on her aloud.

Mont Blanc was hid in clouds all day, but the mountains
owe me some grudge. Mont Blanc won't show his snows,
nor would Vesuvius his fires. It was dark when I crossed
the Cenis, and raining when I descended the Simplon.

Paris, July 3rd.—Got here last night, after a fierce
journey of sixty-three hours from Geneva, only stopping
two hours for breakfast; but by never touching anything
but bread and coffee I was neither heated nor tired. The
Jura Mountains, which they say are so tedious, were the
pleasantest part of the way, for the road is beautiful all
through them, not like the Alps, but like a hilly, wooded
park. It rained torrents when I set out, but soon cleared
up, and when I got to the top of the first mountain, I saw a
mass of clouds rise like a curtain and unveil the whole land-

scape of Geneva, lake, mountains, and country—very fine sight. We heard of the King's death in the middle of the night.

Calais, July 6th.—Voilà qui est fini. Got here last night, and found the Government packet only goes out five days a week, and not to-day. I am very sorry my journey is all over, but glad to find myself in England again—that is, when I get there. I saw Lord Stuart at Paris, just breaking up his establishment and sending his wife off to the Pyrenees. Heard all the news of London and Paris, such as it was. Not a soul left in Paris, which was like a dead city. I only heard that, notwithstanding the way the elections are going against the Government, Polignac is in high spirits. The King of France was very civil about the death of our King,[1] and, without waiting, as is usual, for the announcement of the event by the English Ambassador, he ordered the Court into mourning upon the telegraphic account reaching Paris.

Here is the end of my brief but most agreeable expedition, probably the only one I shall ever make. However this may be, I have gained thus much at least—

> A consciousness remains that it has left,
> Deposited upon the silent shore
> Of memory, images, and precious thoughts,
> That shall not die, and cannot be destroyed.

---

[1] [George IV. died at Windsor on the 26th of June, 1830.]

NOTE.

FREQUENT REFERENCES will be remarked in these volumes to the con-
nexion of their author with the Turf, which was his favourite
amusement, and to his position as an influential member of the
Jockey Club. It may, therefore, be worth while to record in this
place the principal incidents in his racing career; and we are tempted,
in spite of the strange and incorrect phraseology of the writer, to
borrow the following notice of them from the pages of 'Bailey's
Magazine,' published soon after Mr. Greville's death :—

' Though the Warwick family have long been identified with the
sports of the field, it is fair to assume that Mr. Greville's love for
the turf came from his mother's side, as the Portlands, especially
the late Duke, have always been amongst the strongest supporters
of the national sport, and raced, as became their position in society.
That Mr. Greville took to racing early may be imagined when we
state he saw his first Derby in 1809, when the Duke of Grafton's Pope
won it, beating five others. At that period he was barely fifteen years
of age, and the impression the sight of the race made upon him at the
time was very great, and it was rekindled more strongly when, in 1816,
travelling with his father and mother to Ickworth, the seat of the
Marquis of Bristol, he stopped at Newmarket and saw Invalid and
Deceiver run a match on the heath ; and subsequently he saw a
great sweepstakes come off between Spaniard, Britannia, and Pope,
which the latter won. Four years elapse, and, as a proof that the
lad we have described had kept pace with the times, we find him
selected to manage the racing establishment of the late Duke of
York, on the death of Mr. Warwick Lake. The first step taken by
Mr. Greville on being installed in office was to weed the useless ones
and the ragged lot; and with the aid of Butler (father of the late
Frank and the present William Butler) he managed so well that in

his second year he won the Derby for him with Moses. As the Duke's affairs at that time were in anything but a flourishing condition, Mr. Greville did not persuade him to back his horse for much money; still his Royal Highness won a fair stake, and was not a little pleased at the result. He likewise carried off the Claret with him the following year. With Banker, who was a very useful horse at all distances, he won for him many good races; and, by a reference to the " Calendars " of the day, it will be seen the Duke won in his turn, if he did not carry all before him. To reproduce the names of his horses now would not be worth while, as from the effluxion of time the interest in them has ceased. The first animal in the shape of a race-horse that Mr. Greville ever possessed was a filly by Sir Harry Dimsdale, which he trained in the Duke's stable with a few others of no great standing.

' Circumstances with which the world are familiar rendering the retirement of the Duke of York requisite, his stud came to the hammer, and Mr. Greville came to the assistance of his uncle, the Duke of Portland, who trained with Prince. With the Duke Mr. Greville remained some little time, and afterwards became confederate with Lord Chesterfield, who was at that time coming out, and was in great force with his Zinganee, Priam, Carew, Glaucus, and other crack horses. During this time he had few horses of any great account of his own, although his confederate had nothing to complain of in the shape of luck. At the termination of this confederacy Mr. Greville entered upon another with his cousin, Lord George Bentinck, who, from his father's hostility to his racing, was unable to run horses in his own name. The extent of this stud was so great that we are unable to deal with it at the same time with the horses of the subject of our memoir, who can scarcely be said to have come across a really smashing good mare until he met with Preserve, with whom, in 1834, he won the Clearwell and Criterion, and in the following year the One Thousand Guineas, besides running second for the Oaks to Queen of Trumps. A difference of opinion as to the propriety of starting Preserve for the Goodwood Stakes led to their separation, and for a time they were on very bad terms, but by the aid of mutual friends a reconciliation was effected. From what Preserve did for him, Mr. Greville was induced to dip more freely into the blood, or, as old John Day would have said, to take to the family, and accordingly he bought Mango, her own brother, of Mr. Thornhill, who bred him. Mango only ran once as a two-year-old, when, being a big, raw colt, he was not quick enough on his legs for the speedy Garcia filly of Col. Peel and John Day's Chapeau d'Espagne, and was easily beaten. In the spring Mango made so much improvement that Mr. Greville backed him for the Derby for a good stake; and had he been able to have continued his preparation at Newmarket, and been vanned to Epsom, as is the custom in the present day, there is little doubt he would have won; but having to walk all the way from Newmarket, he could not afford to lose the days that were thus consumed, and although he ran forward he did not get a place. That this view of the case is not a sanguine one is proved by his beating Chapeau d'Espagne, the second for the Oaks, for the Ascot Derby, and within an hour afterwards bowling over Velure, the third in that race, for William the Fourth's Plate. On the Cup Day he likewise beat the Derby favourite, Rat-Trap, over the Old Mile. At Stockbridge, in a sweepstakes of 100 sovs. each, with thirteen subscribers, he frightened all the field away with the exception of Wisdom, whom he beat cleverly, and then he remained at Dilly's, at Littleton, to be prepared for the St. Leger. Having stood his work well, John Day brought over The Drummer and Chapeau d'Espagne from Stockbridge to try him on Winchester race-course. Both Mr. Greville and Lord George Bentinck had reason to be satisfied with what Mango did in his gallop on that morning, and the latter backed him very heavily for the race—much more so, indeed, than his owner. Mr. Greville was anxious to have put up John Day, but the Duke of Cleveland having claimed him for Henriade, he was obliged to substitute his son Sam, a very rising lad, with nerves of iron and the coolest of heads. The race was a memorable one, inasmuch as William Scott, who was on Epirus, the first favourite, fell into the ditch soon after starting, and Prince Warden running over him and striking him with his hind leg, he sustained a severe fracture of the collar-bone. Henriade also came down about a distance from home from a dog crossing the course. John Day, however, soon righted him, but the *contretemps* spoilt his chance. At the stand there were but three in the struggle—The Doctor, Abraham Newland, and Mango. The two former seemed to be making a match of it, and it looked impossible for Mango to get up; but a slight opening presenting itself, which was not visible to the spectators, Sam Day, with a degree of resolution which justifies the attributes we have before ascribed to him, sent his horse through with such a terrific rush that his breeches were nearly torn off his boots, and won by a neck.

'After the race Lord George, who was a very heavy winner, gave Honest John 500*l.* for his trial with the Drummer; the like sum to Sam Day for having ridden him better than he was ridden in the Derby, and an equivalent proportion to

Montgomery Dilly for preparing him better than Prince for the same race. Mango was afterwards sent to Newmarket for the St. Leger, and " Craven," who then edited the " Sporting Magazine," having asserted that Mr. Greville had caused it to be reported that Mango was lame to get him back in the markets for that race, he called on him to apologise for the statement, which proving, by the volunteered testimony of Lord George Bentinck, Colonel Anson, and Admiral Rous, to be wholly without foundation, the writer in question made Mr. Greville the fullest *amende honorable*. Mango only won once again as a four-year-old, when he carried off a sweepstakes of 300 sovereigns at Newmarket, beating Chapeau d'Espagne and Adrian. Having thus established himself with Dilly, owing to Mr. Payne, with whom he had become confederate, training at Littleton, Mr. Greville made no change until Dilly gave up, when he continued his confidence to his brother William Dilly, who succeeded him on his retirement from Lord Glasgow.

'It was some few years before Mr. Greville had another good horse, at least one that is worth dwelling upon, and Alarm must be considered the legitimate successor to Mango. This colt Mr. Greville purchased of his breeder, Captain George Delmé, and tried him good enough to win the Derby in 1845 in a canter, even in the face of such animals as Idas and The Libel. But just prior to starting an accident occurred by which all Mr. Greville's hopes were destroyed; for The Libel flying at Alarm very savagely, he jumped the chains, threw Nat, who lay for a time insensible on the ground, and ran away. He was, however, soon caught and remounted, and although much cut about ran forward enough to justify the idea that but for his accident he must have won, as no other animal could have got through the Cambridgeshire with 7st. 10lb. on him so easily as he did in a field of such quality as he met. In the following year Alarm made some amends for his Epsom failure, by winning the Ascot Cup, as well as the Orange Cup at Goodwood, the latter after a terrific race with Jericho. He also, at Newmarket in the autumn, won three great matches in succession, viz. with Oakley, the Bishop of Romford's cob, and Sorella. Going through the " Calendar," Cariboo is the next most noteworthy animal we come across, for it will be recollected he ran second to Canezou for the Goodwood Cup, having been lent to make running for her. But it is almost needless to add that, had Mr. Greville known him to be as good as he was, he would have been started on his own account, in which case the cup in all probability would have gone to Bruton Street instead of to Knowsley. Continuing our track through the " Calendar," we light on a better year for Mr. Greville, in 1852, when he had really two good animals in Adine and Frantic. With the former, at York, he had perhaps the best week he ever had in his life, having won both the Yorkshire Oaks and Ebor Handicap with her, besides beating Daniel O'Rourke with Frantic, who two months before had carried off the Union Cup for him at Manchester. The following year Adine did a good thing for him by winning the Goodwood Stakes, and two years afterwards he again won that race with Quince.

'Between Adine and Quince's years came Mr. Greville's last good horse, Muscovite, whom he thought impossible to lose the Metropolitan, and backed him accordingly. He was much put out, however, by old John Day telling him he had no chance with his mare Virago. At first Mr. Greville was incredulous at what John told him, and made him acquainted with the form of Muscovite. This made not the slightest impression on the old man, who merely went on repeating Mr. Greville must back Virago for 500l., and the value of the advice was proved by the mare beating the horse very easily. Muscovite's career for a time was a very unfortunate one, for when in Dockeray's stable he was so " shinned " that his chance for the Goodwood Stakes was completely out, and his trainer, who could not discover the offender, and who was terribly annoyed at the circumstance, begged he might be transferred to William Dilly's, at Littleton. While there he was betted against for the Cæsarewitch in the same determined manner as he had been for his other races, and when he arrived at Newmarket, and stood in Nat's stables, which were perfectly impregnable, there was no cessation in the opposition to him, although his trainer told everybody that unless he was shot on the Heath, which he could not prevent, he would walk in. This he did, and the crash he produced is still fresh in the public recollection; but it is creditable to the bookmaker who laid the most money against him to state that out of 23,000l. which he lost, he paid 16,000l. down on the spot, an act which procured him time for the remainder.

'Since Muscovite, who is now at the stud at Newmarket, Mr Greville has had no animal that has done a really good thing for him, though Anfield made another determined attempt at the Goodwood Stakes this year; and having, at Lord Ribblesdale's sale of General Peel's horses, purchased Orlando, and added him to his establishment at Hampton Court, he has turned his attention perhaps more to breeding than racing. For some time his returns were very large, but of late, from the age of Orlando, and from getting some of his stock so small, they have diminished in amount, although the old horse looks as fresh as a four-year-old, and preserves all that fine symmetry for which he was remarkable both in and out of training. Latterly

Mr. Greville, from being the confederate of Mr. Payne, has trained with Alec Taylor at Fyfield; but with Godding he has generally two or three at Newmarket.

'In turning to Mr. Greville in his private capacity we hardly know how to treat him, for his is a nature that shrinks from having his good deeds brought before the glare of the public eye. No man, ever so high or low, we believe, ever sought his advice and assistance in vain; and to no one individual, probably, have so many and such various difficulties been submitted. Neither can we remember a new trial or even an appeal demanded by those who had sought his counsel. Beloved by his friends, and feared by his opponents, Mr. Greville will ever be considered one of the most remarkable men that have lent lustre to the English turf.'

END OF THE FIRST VOLUME.

LONDON : PRINTED BY
SPOTTISWOODE AND CO., NEW-STREET SQUARE
AND PARLIAMENT STREET

1306357R0

Printed in Great Britain by
Amazon.co.uk, Ltd.,
Marston Gate.